The Complete Idiot's Reference Card

10 Steps to Adoption

1. Forget everything you've heard about how impossible or hard it is to adopt. Today adoption is an option for people of all backgrounds and lifestyles.

2. Decide whether you want to adopt a baby, an older child, a child with special needs, or a child of another race. There are all kinds of children out there who need families.

3. If you want to adopt your child from the U.S., read Chapter 10 and make sure you understand the adoption laws in your state.

4. Consider international adoption. Thousands of children worldwide need parents. If you'd like to pursue international adoption, there are specialized adoption agencies that can help you.

5. Do your homework. Find agencies and adoption experts in your area. Ask for brochures or handouts. Attend seminars. Join local adoptive parent groups.

6. Tell friends, family, colleagues, physicians, and everyone else that you want to adopt. Ask them to think of you if they hear of anyone who may want a child adopted.

7. Screen any adoption agency or attorney that you are thinking about using. Ask for references and check if any complaints have been made. Maintain a healthy skepticism.

8. Keep your cool during the home study investigation. Remember that no parents are perfect. Use the experience as an exercise in self-exploration.

9. When you hear about a child you might adopt, ask questions about the child's health and early life experiences. Learn as much as you can about the birthparents.

10. Your child arrives! Congratulations. Enjoy parenting and your new life together.

D1304041

cut here

10 Hints for Adoptive Parents

1. It is possible for many people to adopt children, babies, and older kids from the U.S. and other countries. Find out what resources are available in your community and state, and network your way to adoption success.

2. Learn as much as you can about a child you are thinking about adopting but remember that sometimes information is just not available. At some point, a leap of faith is required to adopt.

3. Avoid telling your extended family everything you know about your child's background, especially anything that might be negative. It should be private and for him to share if he wishes.

4. Don't keep the adoption secret from your child. Tell her she was adopted, and share information as the child is ready to understand it. Say that her birthparents weren't ready or able to care for her—but you were.

5. Most adopted kids grow up to be successful, happy adults. Some grow up to be Presidents, Olympic athletes, or successful entrepreneurs. Others are simply everyday nice people.

6. Being adopted can sometimes affect children, but remember, adopted kids are still just kids. Give them lots of love and help them achieve their potential.

7. Don't expect yourself to be perfect. It's too much work trying to achieve the impossible. Don't expect your child to be perfect either.

8. Try to teach people to use positive adoption language, such as "birthmother" instead of "real mother." But realize it takes time to change attitudes.

9. If your adult child decides to search for a birthparent, it doesn't mean you failed as a parent. He needs your support.

10. Ignore anyone who tells you adoption isn't as good as biological parenting. If they haven't adopted, how would they know?

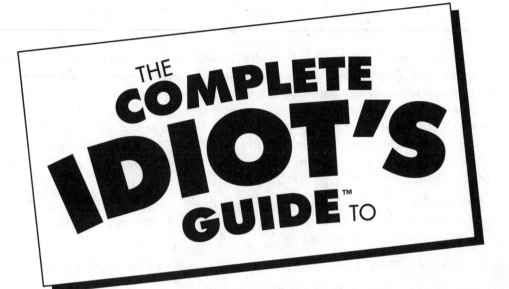

THE COMPLETE IDIOT'S GUIDE™ TO

Adoption

by Chris Adamec

alpha
books

A Division of Macmillan Reference USA

A Simon & Schuster Macmillan Company

1633 Broadway, New York, NY 10019

Copyright © 1998 by Chris Adamec

All rights reserved. No part of this book shall be reproduced, stored in a retrieval system, or transmitted by any means, electronic, mechanical, photocopying, recording, or otherwise, without written permission from the publisher. No patent liability is assumed with respect to the use of the information contained herein. Although every precaution has been taken in the preparation of this book, the publisher and author assume no responsibility for errors or omissions. Neither is any liability assumed for damages resulting from the use of information contained herein. For information, address Alpha Books, 1633 Broadway, 7th Floor, New York, NY 10019-6785.

Macmillan Publishing books may be used for business or sales promotional use. For information please write: Special Markets Department, Macmillan Publishing USA, 1633 Broadway, New York, NY 10019-6785.

The COMPLETE IDIOT'S GUIDE TO name and design is a trademark of Macmillan, Inc.

International Standard Book Number: 0-02-862108-5
Library of Congress Catalog Card Number: 97-80971

00 99 98   4 3 2 1

Interpretation of the printing code: The rightmost number of the first series of numbers is the year of the book's printing; the rightmost number of the second series of numbers is the number of the book's printing. For example, a printing code of 98-1 shows that the first printing occurred in 1998.

Printed in the United States of America

Alpha Development Team

Brand Manager
Kathy Nebenhaus

Executive Editor
Gary M. Krebs

Managing Editor
Bob Shuman

Senior Editor
Nancy Mikhail

Development Editors
Jennifer Perillo
Amy Zavatto

Editorial Assistant
Maureen Horn

Production Team

Production Editor
Kristi Hart

Copy Editor
Damon Jordan

Cover Designer
Kevin Spear

Cartoonist
Judd Winick

Designer
Glenn Larsen

Indexer
Chris Barrick

Production Team
Mike Henry
Linda Knose
Tim Osborn
Staci Somers
Mark Walchle

Contents at a Glance

Contents

Part 3: Finding Your Child   141

12 Getting to Know You: The Home Study   143

13 Special Interests: The Non-Traditional Parent   157

Foreword

After nearly 30 years in the child welfare field, I've seen adoption become a more and more acceptable option for people who want to start or add to their families. These days, many people are adopting or talking about adopting; open a newspaper or magazine, or turn on a TV talk show, and chances are you'll come across some story related to adoption.

While adoption has become more widespread, the adoption process has grown more difficult. Chris Adamec's book does a very good job of providing a beacon through the often tangled and varied paths to parenting through adoption. (I should mention here that Chris and I co-authored a reference book and have been colleagues on a number of projects.)

As you read *The Complete Idiot's Guide to Adoption,* it will become clear that there are at least two (sometimes more) differing opinions about nearly every subject related to adoption. Because adoption is so intensely personal and so directly linked to many of the controversial topics of our day, this diversity of opinion is inevitable. In this book, Chris does a good job of reflecting that diversity in a fair and even-handed manner.

There are two suggestions I'd like to make as you think about, or prepare for, an adoption. First, you need to take responsibility for your own actions. Second, you need to listen to sound advice.

On the first point, always use your common sense. Be cautious if an expert says something that strikes you as dubious. Use your instincts. Ask questions. Be skeptical, especially of those who come across as slick or facile or who may have no solid basis for their claims (in my opinion, that includes much of what is on the Internet). Only do what you're comfortable with.

On the other hand, as you read this book (and after), check out the resources that Chris has listed for you. Many thoughtful, careful, and astute observers of the adoption scene have summarized decades of experience for your critical consideration. You can especially benefit by taking heed of their cautionary notes.

The adoption process will require a great deal of time, thought, and careful research. Remember, adoption will not just require a substantial investment of money. It will change your life.

—William Pierce
President, National Council for Adoption

Introduction

I'm assuming you've picked up this book because you'd like to become an adoptive parent. What a great idea! I'm an adoptive parent myself, and I wrote this book to help steer you through the rough spots and move you onward to smooth sailing—with some extra guidance for a few unexpected rocky moments that may occur as your child grows into adulthood.

Why do you need this book? Because to succeed at adoption and adoptive parenting, you need to understand how it is like and unlike biological parenting. Many people who are trying to adopt don't realize that adoption is a system with its own special rules and terminology. You don't have to master it all (few people do!). But if you want to "win" at adoption, you first have to learn the basics.

If your goal and dream is to parent an adopted child, I hope you find that the information here steers you toward a very happy and successful adoptive parenthood. And that you'll enjoy some of the silly stories as well as the heart-tuggers within these pages.

One thought I must share with you, as a kind of mantra for you to adopt: Never give up! Whether you're in the process of adopting or you're trying to cope with issues as an adoptive parent—the answers are out there. Good luck!

How the Book Is Organized

This book is organized to make it easy for you to find what you need when you need it.

Part 1: Adoption: A Wonderful Option! Why do people adopt? How do you know if you're ready to adopt? Why do birthparents place children for adoption? And who are the children who need families? This part provides you with an overview.

Part 2: What Are Your Options? This valuable part will help you discover which kind of "adoption arranger" is right for you. I've also included valuable information on how to avoid adoption scams. It's crucially important to realize that adoption laws vary radically from state to state, which is explained and also illustrated with a state-by-state adoption law chart and an "adoption friendly" state-by-state evaluation. Finally, I devote an entire chapter to international adoption, an increasingly popular option.

Part 3: Finding Your Child. You've decided to adopt, found your adoption arranger, and launched yourself on the path to adoption. This part walks you through the process. You'll learn how to survive a "home study" background investigation. You'll also learn how to apply if you are a "non-traditional parent"—that is, if you are single, gay or lesbian, disabled, or older. This part also shows you what you need to know about birthparents and about a child you may adopt.

Part 4: Raising Your Adopted Child. Congratulations! There's a child for you! From the day you first hear the news, to the day you bring your new child home, and beyond, this part covers key issues involved with parenting an adopted child. I'll show you how to introduce your child to the family, explain adoption to the child at different ages, and deal with problems that may come up.

Part 5: If Your Adult Child Searches. Plenty of material has been written for adopted adults searching for birthparents. But how do adoptive parents feel about this and what should they do? If your adopted child searches, does that mean you've failed as a parent? Will your child abandon you? This part explains why adult children search, how they search, and what happens when adoptees and birthparents meet.

Extras

In addition to the main narrative of *The Complete Idiot's Guide to Adoption*, you'll find other types of useful information in sidebars throughout the book.

Adopterms
Definitions of adoption words and phrases that are used frequently by experts in the field. Get a heads-up and learn the jargon! It'll help.

Adoptinfo
Adoption research or newsworthy topics that can help or interest you.

Real Life Snapshots

Anecdotes about real adoptive parents or adoptees. Sometimes heartwarming and other times startling, these stories should make you stop and think.

Familybuilding Tips
Tips on how to deal with common problems and issues.

Adoption Alert
Situations to watch out for. The information in these boxes may save you from minor (and sometimes major) problems.

Acknowledgments

To research and write a book covering many aspects of adoption, you can't do it alone! You need the emotional support of someone close to you, and I have always had that in my husband of 25 years, John Adamec. Thanks, John!

You also need assistance with information gathering and advice. In particular, I would like to single out Jerri Ann Jenista, M.D., a pediatrician from Ann Arbor, Michigan, who has generously reviewed medical passages. I would also like to thank Daphne Kent, Media Relations Specialist for CompuServe, Inc. in Columbus, Ohio for the valuable research help that she has provided. It's also a certainty that I could never have succeeded without the help of the wonderful reference librarians at the DeGroodt Library in Palm Bay, Florida: Mary Scholtz, Chief Reference Librarian, and reference librarians Marie Faure and Pam Hobson. They truly are "goddesses of knowledge."

Special thanks to my editor, Jennifer Perillo. An adoptee herself, Jennifer has provided highly insightful advice on many key issues.

I am most grateful to the following attorneys (and one judge!) who provided me with information on state adoption laws throughout the country and enabled me to prepare my adoption law chart. Of course I am responsible for the interpretation of the data provided to me.

Thanks to: Carolyn Arnett, Louisville, Kentucky; Barbara Bado, Edmond, Oklahoma; David Allen Barnette, Charleston, West Virginia; Alfred E. Barrus, Burley, Idaho; W. Thomas Beltz, Colorado Springs, Colorado; Shelley Ballard Bostick, Chicago, Illinois; Lawrence I. Batt, Omaha, Nebraska; Richard Bell, Charleston, South Carolina; Judith M. Berry, Gorham, Maine; Jill Bremyer–Archer, McPherson, Kansas; S. Dawn Coppock, Strawberry Plains, Tennessee; Heidi Bruegel Cox, Fort Worth, Texas; Susan Crockin, Newton, Massachusetts; Catherine Dexter, Portland, Oregon; The Honorable Susan L. Fowler, Burlington, Vermont; Debra M. Fox, Haverford, Pennsylvania; Gregory A. Franklin, Rochester, New York; Peter J. Feeney, Casper, Wyoming; Rhonda Fishbein, Atlanta, Georgia; Steven L. Gawron, Bloomington, Minnesota; Sharon L. Gleason, Anchorage, Alaska; Margaret Cunniff Holm, Olympia, Washington; Larry Ivers, Eagle Grove, Iowa; Eugene Kelley, Rogers, Arkansas; Steven M. Kirsh, Indianapolis, Indiana; Doris Licht, Providence, Rhode Island; Monica Farris Linkner, Berkley, Michigan; Linda W. McIntyre, Coral Springs, Florida; Ellen S. Meyer, Wilmington, Delaware; Diane Michelsen, Lafayette, California; James Miskowski, Ridgewood, New Jersey; Edith Morris, New Orleans, Louisiana; Scott E. Myers, Tucson, Arizona; Susan I. Paquet, Weatherford, Texas; Nancy D. Poster, Great Falls, Virginia; Leslie Scherr, Washington, DC; Victoria Schroeder, Delafield, Wisconsin; Mary Smith, Toledo, Ohio; Toby Solomon, Livingston, New Jersey; Janet Stulting, West Hartford, Connecticut; W. David Thurman, Charlotte, North Carolina and Bryant Whitmire, Birmingham, Alabama. I hope that I have not inadvertently left anyone's name out.

Individuals at state department of social services offices nationwide assisted me with information for the book and for the law chart. I would especially like to thank: Robert Gioffre, Director, Adoption and Residential Service Unit for the Department of Public Welfare in Harrisburg, Pennsylvania; Lynda Hart, Adoption Program Officer for the Child and Family Services Division in the Department of Public Health & Human Services, Helena, Montana; Patricia T. Ossorio, Adoption Program Manager for the Department of Social and Health Services in Olympia, Washington; Allen Pittinger, Adoption Services Unit, Division of Children & Family Services, Department of Human Services in Little Rock, Arkansas; Bill Rankin, Wyoming Department of Family Services Adoption Liaison in Cheyenne, Wyoming; Kelly Shannon, Permanency and Adoptions Program Manager for the Oregon State Offices for Services to Families and Children in Salem, Oregon; and Jan P. Stanley, Supervisor, Central Adoptions in the Protective Services Division of the Children, Youth & Families Department for New Mexico. Other state officials also provided assistance but did not wish to be listed.

Special Thanks to the Technical Reviewers

The Complete Idiot's Guide to Adoption was reviewed by two experts who not only checked the technical accuracy of what you'll learn in this book, but also provided valuable insight to help ensure that this book tells you everything you need to know about adoption. Our special thanks are extended to Nancy Poster and Mary Beth Style.

Nancy Poster is an attorney who specializes in adoption and adoption-related matters. She is a member of the Virginia State Bar, the Maryland State Bar, and the District of Columbia Bar Association. Ms. Poster has been active in numerous adoption-related organizations, including Families for Private Adoption and Parents for Private Adoption. She is also a member of the American Academy of Adoption Attorneys.

Mary Beth Style was the vice president for the National Council for Adoption, a voluntary, non-profit education and advocacy organization. She has lobbied for improved federal and state adoption legislation and has authored numerous articles on adoption and pregnancy counseling. Prior to joining the National Council, Style worked for Catholic Charities USA, where she was involved in a wide range of social work issues related to adoption. Style received her Masters in Social Work from Fordham University in New York City.

Part 1
Adoption: A Wonderful Option!

This part gives you the who, what, when, where, and why of adoption: who needs to be adopted and why, where they are, and more. The chapters in this part give you essential information on adoption, whether you're a "wannabe" adopter or someone who has already succeeded at adoption.

This part will also help bust some common myths about adoption. So forget everything you've read or heard before, and read on to gain important core knowledge to build from.

Chapter 1

All About Adoption

In This Chapter
➤ How many people are adopted?
➤ How adoption affects adopted children
➤ Who adopts and why
➤ What the adoption process is like

Steve and Lori wanted a baby, but they could not have a biological child. They considered their options and chose to adopt. Friends of theirs had recently adopted a baby through an attorney, Ms. Nize, so they made an appointment with her. After an hour-long interview, Ms. Nize said she'd put them on her list and let them know if a "situation" came up. A few months later, Ms. Nize called to tell them about a pregnant woman who wanted a family for her baby. Were they interested? Yes! They asked about a million questions; later, a social worker asked *them* what seemed like a million questions. Three months after Ms. Nize's call, Lori and Steve took home their newborn girl.

Tim and Amy were thrilled about adopting a baby from Russia. They'd paid an adoption agency more than $17,000, and eagerly awaited their healthy infant. Six months later, the agency called about a child selected for them. The agency sent a videotape, and Tim and Amy saw that the child, nearly a year old, moved very little and couldn't walk or

Adopterms

Adoption refers to the complete transfer of parental rights and obligations from one family to another family. The adoptive family assumes all the legal obligations and responsibilities of raising the adopted child, and the adoption ends the rights and responsibilities of the biological family to the child.

In many cases, the transfer of rights and responsibilities is not direct from biological parents to adoptive parents; for example, the responsibility for the child may be initially transferred from the birthparents to an agency. Ultimately, however, the adoptive parents become the parents by law, and the biological parents have no further legal rights.

crawl. A pediatrician who watched the tape said that the child had severe problems. The agency director refused to give Amy and Tim any more information—unless they were willing to pay more money. She also said they could either take the child or not take him: The agency would keep the money no matter what. Tim and Amy didn't know what to do.

Dan and Lucy were in their late forties and had talked about adopting older kids. They had seen a TV show about three brothers who needed a family, with a number for interested viewers to call. Dan and Lucy phoned, asked for information, and began adoption classes. Several months later, their new sons came home.

What do all these people have in common? They all attempted to build their families through adoption. Adoption is a successful familybuilding institution that has created millions of very happy families nationwide. It's also a pervasive family choice. Most of the time, adoptions work out well. But sometimes, they don't. This book will show you how to create your own successful adoption and how to sidestep any problems that may occur if you attempt to adopt.

In this chapter, I'll describe the prevalence of adoption and offer some basic information that you need to know if you are considering it. I'll also cover why people want to adopt and what they are like. In addition, I'll try to explain the most common fears people have about adoption.

How Many People Choose Adoption?

No one knows for sure how many people adopt in any given year. However, an estimate of adoptions made in 1993 by the National Center for State Courts suggests that 118,779 people were adopted that year. About half of these children are adopted by nonrelatives, and half are adopted by relatives such as grandparents or stepparents. (It's safe to assume that these statistics are about the same this year.) In addition, about 10,000–11,000 children from other countries are adopted by Americans each year.

But many, many more people are affected by adoption. There are at least 6 million adopted men, women, and children in the U.S. They all have biological parents, many still alive (let's estimate 10 million people). And many have adoptive parents who are still living. (Let's estimate 9 million adoptive parents, since they're generally older than birthparents.) Many adopted children and adults also have siblings by birth or adoption: add another half million or so. Not counting grandparents, aunts, uncles and cousins, adoption directly affects 25.5 million people. That's about 1 in 8 Americans.

Table 1.1, provided by the National Center for State Courts, shows the total number of adoption filings in 29 states.

You may not think you know many adopted people or adoptive parents because many people affected by adoption don't talk about it all the time. But if you bring up the subject, you may be very surprised to find Aunt Mary telling you that your cousin Billy was adopted. Or she may confide in you about the child she placed for adoption 40 years ago. I have found that when I mention I'm an adoptive parent, people very often share these kind of stories with me.

Real Life Snapshots

At a school outing a few years ago, another mother and I sat on a park bench watching our children. After I made a positive comment about adoption in passing, she told me about the baby that she had placed for adoption years ago. She also told me that she herself was adopted and was very happy with her own adoptive parents. I said to her, "So you knew that adoption would be a good choice for your child, too." She responded with one of the most radiant smiles I've ever received. It said to me, "You understand me."

If you are considering adoption, try an experiment: Mention the subject to a few close friends or relatives. Then sit back and see what kind of response you get.

Table 1.1 Total Adoption Filings Per Year in 29 States, 1985–95

STATE NAME	1985	1986	1987	1988	1989	1990	1991	1992	1993	1994	1995
Alaska	720	627	594	671	639	611	625	633	590	571	517
Arizona	1,944	1,708	1,702	1,574	1,675	1,773	1,605	1,548	1,734	1,456	1,536
Arkansas	1,705	1,637	1,551	1,628	1,647	1,641	1,716	1,697	1,792	1,792	1,750
Colorado	1,896	1,921	1,985	1,794	1,890	1,894	1,981	1,989	1,737	1,706	2,039
Connecticut	981	1,109	1,080	1,266	1,254	1,186	1,260	1,124	1,009	875	847
Delaware	210	213	211	198	217	211	190	211	176	193	197
District of Columbia	316	290	287	309	269	297	205	334	353	475	247
Hawaii	770	677	690	717	724	822	620	687	567	458	438
Idaho	1,008	947	1,014	929	897	909	898	972	937	912	948
Kansas	1,951	1,745	1,811	1,833	1,765	1,810	1,730	1,838	1,785	1,715	1,815
Kentucky	2,238	2,185	1,827	2,186	2,120	2,213	2,099	1,982	2,139	1,924	1,951
Maryland	2,446	2,708	2,585	3,169	3,128	2,986	2,995	3,120	3,369	3,067	3,023
Massachusetts	2,428	2,334	2,371	2,630	2,809	2,986	2,736	2,946	2,773	3,037	3,273
Michigan	3,901	4,115	4,426	5,304	5,181	5,294	5,408	6,092	5,679	5,069	5,761
Montana	668	684	673	696	693	691	729	739	712	734	712
Nebraska	1,027	981	1,022	998	1,032	976	973	991	977	962	960
New Hampshire	670	727	677	743	726	701	562	551	546	534	529
New Jersey	2,204	2,477	2,265	2,538	2,613	2,544	2,400	2,410	2,274	2,158	2,047
New York	6,724	6,366	6,244	6,404	6,787	7,231	7,263	8,170	7,587	7,911	9,650
North Dakota	402	323	400	388	369	331	313	313	301	327	291
Ohio	5,715	5,449	5,426	5,410	5,340	5,045	5,498	5,247	4,895	4,797	4,677
Oregon	1,703	1,834	1,751	1,893	1,929	1,828	2,065	2,022	1,816	1,786	1,752
Pennsylvania	4,690	4,850	4,905	4,782	4,712	4,597	4,362	4,421	3,760	3,737	3,737
South Dakota	419	419	398	418	398	433	378	462	432	360	360
Tennessee	2,294	2,228	2,407	2,480	2,480	2,515	2,585	2,764	2,678	2,691	2,668
Vermont	510	508	521	499	546	484	502	509	466	401	446
Washington	2,714	2,792	2,698	2,723	2,843	2,889	2,944	2,611	2,364	2,419	2,352
West Virginia	968	903	898	970	942	816	941	869	788	763	758
Wisconsin	2,290	2,370	2,328	2,140	2,079	2,071	1,994	1,871	1,710	1,938	1,931
Grand Total	**55,512**	**55,127**	**54,747**	**57,290**	**57,704**	**57,785**	**57,577**	**59,123**	**55,946**	**54,768**	**57,212**

Reprinted with permission, National Center for State Courts, Court Statistics Project, 1994

Adoption Is Forever

Adoption is a *permanent* option. An adopted child has the same legal rights and privileges as a biological child. Adoption is not the same as *foster care* or *guardianship*, both of which are usually temporary (or are supposed to be). Instead, adoption is forever. In fact, many adoptive families refer to themselves as "forever families."

When you adopt, the child becomes your "real" child and you're regarded (or should be) as "real" parents. I place real in quotation marks because this word is a sore point to many adoptive parents and adopted children. (And if you adopt a child, you may be surprised at how heated the issue becomes in your own mind.)

What's the big deal? Well, if you're not the "real" parent, the implication to some is that you're a "fake" parent. The term "natural parent" is also quite unpopular with adoptive parents and many adopted people. If you're not natural, then you must be . . . unnatural. That has a very negative connotation.

Adopterms

A *foster child* is a child who is placed with another family for days, months, or even years.

The government or private adoption agency that arranges foster care retains primary legal custody of the child while in care. A foster child cannot be adopted except by consent of a parent or by order of the court.

A *legal guardian* of a child is a person who can make legal (and often parental) decisions for the minor child. But the legal guardians cannot adopt the child and become full parents unless the biological parents (or whomever has custody) agrees.

How Happy Are Adopted Children?

Many media stories and made-for-TV movies present adopted children as alienated, unhappy, or even criminal. But the truth is, most adopted children grow up to be normal adults who blend in with everyone else.

In 1994, the Search Institute in Minneapolis released the results of "Growing Up Adopted," a four-year study of 881 adopted adolescents, 1,262 adoptive parents, and 78 nonadopted siblings. The study found that the majority of the adopted teens were strongly attached to their families and psychologically healthy. (And if they're doing well in adolescence—a tough time for most of us—imagine what they might achieve as adults!)

In fact, the adopted teens in the study scored *better* than their nonadopted siblings or a sample of their peers in:

➤ Connectedness—having three or more friends and having access to two or more non-parent adults for advice.

➤ Caring—placing a high value on helping other people.

➤ Social competency—friendship-making and assertiveness skills.

Adopted teens also scored higher than nonadopted adolescents in:

➤ School achievement—having a B average or better and aspiring to higher education.

➤ Optimism—expecting to be happy in 10 years and expecting to be successful as an adult.

➤ Support—having a high level of support from parents and from school.

Most people don't realize that many adopted adults are quite successful and famous. This doesn't mean that an adopted child should be expected to be some kind of super achiever. But you never know what might happen!

Real Life Snapshots

Here are some famous adoptees:

Halle Berry (actress)

Robert Byrd (U.S. Senator)

Nat King Cole (singer)

Eric Dickerson (football player)

Former President Gerald Ford

Melissa Gilbert (actress)

Scott Hamilton (Olympic Gold Medalist skater)

Debbie Harry (singer: Blondie)

Steve Jobs (co-founder of Apple Computers)

Jim Lightfoot (Congressman)

Jim Palmer (professional baseball player)

Nancy Reagan (Former First Lady)

Dave Thomas (founder of Wendy's International Restaurants)

Successful Adoptions: A Well-Kept Secret?

These positive findings seem to contradict those of some older studies on adoption, which indicated that adopted people had a higher rate of problems than nonadopted people. Why the discrepancy? Here's the primary reason.

Older studies on adoption almost invariably lumped together kids who were adopted as infants with kids who lived in troubled situations (sometimes for years) before they were adopted. These included kids who were abused, for example, or kids who were shuffled from foster home to foster home until they were finally adopted when they were 10 or 11 years old or older.

Children who were adopted as foster children are usually children with heavy emotional baggage. They are very different from kids who were adopted as infants! But too many researchers group all adopted children or adults together.

Another problem is that many other older studies contain subtle biases against adoptive parents or adoptees.

For example, in 1960, psychiatrist Marshall Schecter conducted a study that remains frequently cited. In a population of 120 child mental patients, Dr. Schecter noted that 16 had been adopted, or 13%. This 13% statistic was mistakenly interpreted by later researchers to mean that 13% of *all* adopted people are mentally ill, an error Dr. Schecter himself tried to correct. (Other studies have found few differences between adoptees and nonadoptees—even those studies which examine only psychiatric patients. For more information on troubled adoptees, read Chapter 21.)

Another complicating factor in the Schecter study and others is that researchers did not differentiate between problems that children had which may have been related to adoption vs. problems related to non-adoption issues.

Some of the adoptive parents in the Schecter study were given bad advice that contributed to (if not caused) problems the children were experiencing; for example, a pediatrician told one family adopting a 14-month-old child to force toilet training immediately. (Most experts today don't push potty training at such a young age.) It's not surprising the child had trouble with potty training and with adjustment into her family. Had she been born to the family and had they pursued potty training with the same zealotry, it's likely she would have also experienced problems.

What I'm trying to say here is that many of the myths surrounding adoption—that adopted children do not thrive, or that all adopted families are unhappy—can be traced back to flawed research or unfounded generalizations. Adoption isn't perfect. But millions of Americans have used adoption to create happy, successful, and loving families.

Media Bias

Some suggest that another reason adopted children may get a bad rap is because the media has a bias against adoption. They're backed up by researchers such as Dr. George Gerbner of the Annenberg School of Communications at the University of Pennsylvania in Philadelphia. In 1988, Dr. Gerbner found evidence of negative bias against adopted children in many movies and TV shows, which often portrayed them as "problem children"—drug addicts, victims, and so on.

Unfortunately, many people get their ideas of adoption from these shows. But do you *really* think that life is like a soap opera? If you do, then maybe you have been married eight times, have suffered amnesia or a multiple personality disorder, have had dozens of affairs, and have forgotten the co-creators of your biological children. If you're like most of the rest of us, this does not describe you.

Adoption Alert

You've just watched "A New Day Dawning," your favorite soap, and Felicity Ferule has suddenly changed her mind—she wants her adopted son back! (He was placed with the Halfmain family six years ago.)

Can that happen in real life? No way! Most states have a time period during which a birthparent can challenge an adoption; depending on the state, that time period can be hours, days, or even months. But once an adoption is finalized, it can rarely be overturned.

There's also a bias in news reports of actual events. For example, if an adopted person commits a crime, the adoptive status is often accentuated. (In one case, a reporter wrote that an adopted man had committed a crime because he had been torn from his "roots" as a baby. This was news to the criminal. He stated frankly that he thought it was because he'd been high on crack cocaine and alcohol. Silly him.)

The fact is that most adopted people are not more criminally inclined, nor more violent, than nonadopted people. When we're talking about millions of people who were adopted, from those who are infants to those who are elderly, it's impossible to generalize. Some are very talented or brilliant, some are less capable. Most are within the normal range, just like most nonadopted people of the world.

The media also tends to pounce on adoption horror stories. Sensation sells. For example, you may have heard about the "Baby Richard" case. Baby Richard was placed with an adoptive family in Illinois in the early 1990s. Three years later, after a long court battle, he was placed with his biological father.

In this case, after placing the baby with the adoptive couple, the birthmother told the birthfather that the baby had died. When she reconciled with him, she told him the child had been adopted, and he sought and subsequently won custody. It has been reported since then that the biological father has left his wife and the child. Interestingly, the wife has no parental rights, and her husband has sole legal custody. Some have suggested that she should adopt her child.

What you probably do not know is that people in Illinois were so distressed by this case (as was the state governor) that the state legislature tightened up adoption laws so that this kind of situation could not happen again. In the wake of the Baby Richard case, many other states changed their adoption laws as well.

Adopters—A Club You'd Want to Join?

Adoptive parents come from all walks of life. Most are middle class people; they're not especially rich or famous. (Tom Cruise and Nicole Kidman are adoptive parents, but you don't have to be gorgeous to adopt!)

Age-wise, new adoptive parents generally range from their early 30s to mid-40s; however, some are younger and some are older. Many are married—most adoption agencies and attorneys like to place children with couples who have been married at least three years—but it's also true that single people adopt kids. (For more information on adopting as a single parent, read Chapter 13.) Adopters are both religious and indifferent to religion. They are extroverted and introverted, short and tall, chubby and thin. Their common denominator is that they want to be parents.

Adoptinfo

Roughly 30,000 infant adoptions take place in America each year. Counting international adoption, the number is at least 40,000 per year.)

Very few challenges are made to most of these adoptions, particularly after the babies are placed with adoptive families. But successful adoptions are usually not considered newsworthy or interesting by the media. This is why most media stories about adoptions focus on those few in which the adoption process does *not* work.

Real Life Snapshots

Here are some famous adoptive parents:

Mona Charen (columnist and TV commentator)

Jamie Lee Curtis (actress)

Helen Hayes (actress)

Mary Landrieux (U.S. congressperson)

Rosie O'Donnell (talk show host and actress)

Sally Jessy Raphael (talk show host)

Former President Ronald Reagan

Roy Rogers and Dale Evans (movie and TV stars of the past)

Gail Sheehy (author)

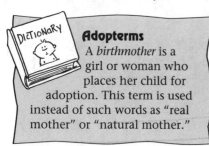

Familybuilding Tips
It's a well-kept secret, but there are agencies and attorneys who *need* adoptive parents. For one thing, there are untold numbers of infants and children in foreign orphanages who need families. In other cases, sometimes birthmothers seek a particular kind of adoptive parent. Bottom line, no matter what your profile, *do not* assume adoption is impossible for you. It isn't.

There are some categories, however, that adoptive parents generally *do not* fall into. They are not criminals or drug addicts or child abusers; social workers check out the backgrounds of adopting parents to make sure that irresponsible or unsuitable people are not allowed to adopt. However, the adoption system and the people who work in it are not infallible. On rare occasions, unsuitable parents are allowed to adopt.

Adoptions Inside and Outside the Family

When most people think of adoption, they envision a set of parents adopting a child who is a complete stranger to them. Yet this is often not the case. *Relative adoptions*—in which the adopted child is related to the adoptive parents—are almost as prevalent as *nonrelative adoptions*. I'll explain both kinds in more detail.

All in the Family

Of the roughly 119,000 American children who are adopted by Americans each year, probably half are adopted by relatives. For example, actor Jack Nicholson was adopted by his grandparents. (But he didn't learn this until adulthood—not a good idea. I'll talk more about discussing adoption in Chapter 20.)

In a relative adoption, grandparents can become the legal parents of their grandchildren, aunts or uncles can adopt their nieces and nephews, and so on. Some children will refer to their adoptive relative as "Grandma" or "Uncle Bob"; others consider the adoptive relative to be "Mommy" or "Daddy."

Why do people adopt children from within their biological family? There are many reasons; here are just a few:

Adopterms
A *birthmother* is a girl or woman who places her child for adoption. This term is used instead of such words as "real mother" or "natural mother."

➤ The birthmother is too young to be a parent, and her own parents decide to adopt the child (grandparent adoption).

➤ The birthparent is ill.

➤ The birthparent has abandoned the child.

➤ The birthparent is considering adoption, and the adopting relative disapproves of nonrelative adoption.

➤ The adopter thinks relative adoption is easier than nonrelative adoption.

➤ The birthparent wishes to remain in touch with the child.

Grafting onto Your Family Tree

About 70,000 children, including about 10,000–11,000 children from other countries, are adopted by American families who are not related to them biologically.

There are many reasons why people adopt children who are not in their biological family. Probably 95% or more of these adopters are infertile, but some of them could have a child if they wished to. Some adopters are single and don't know if pregnancy would be possible—they never tried to achieve one!

Here are a few reasons people adopt children not related to them:

> ➤ They want a family, but they cannot have a biological child.

> ➤ They want to help a child.

> ➤ They feel "called" to adopt.

> ➤ They already have a child of one gender and want a child of another gender.

> ➤ They want a sibling for another child.

Adopterms

A *relative adoption* refers to an adoption in which the adopter is biologically related to the adopted child or is married to the child's parent. A stepparent adoption is also usually considered a relative adoption.

In a *nonrelative adoption*, the adoptive parent is a biological stranger to the child, with no common genetic bonds, and is not a stepparent.

Most adoption professionals agree that the best reasons to adopt, whether inside or outside the family, are because the adopter wants a child to love and wants to provide a good family for that child.

The Adoption Process: What's It Like?

A lot of people—and you may be one of them—are interested in adoption, but they're not so sure they want to go through the adoption process. If you think you'd like to become a parent by adoption but you're afraid, join the crowd. Here are some reasons why people are afraid to adopt a child:

> ➤ Fear that the adoption process will take too long—at least five years.

> ➤ Fear they will be rejected as potential parents by either birthparents or the adoption arranger.

> ➤ Fear that they won't be able to find an adoption agency.

> ➤ Fear that once they find a potential adoptive child, the birthparents will suddenly change their minds.

> ➤ Fear that it's impossible to afford adoption fees.

➤ Fear that the child could have medical or genetic issues/problems.

➤ Fear that they might not be able to love a child unrelated to them.

Most of these fears aren't justified, as I'll explain in the following sections and in other chapters of the book.

How Long Does It Take?

Some people succeed in adopting a child within a few months or a year; for others, it can take several years or more. There are numerous factors involved in the time frame needed to adopt. Here are a few:

➤ The age of the child you want to adopt. You may have to wait an extended period to adopt a toddler. Why? Because most birthmothers choose adoption when their children are babies. After that, they become too attached to them.

➤ The amount of information you demand about the child. With international adoptions, for example, often very little is known about the child's history before he or she arrived in the orphanage.

➤ Your own willingness to contact a variety of agencies and attorneys.

➤ Your own circumstances: age, health history, marital status, financial stability, and so on.

➤ Your level of perfectionism (how flexible you are willing to be in terms of the type of child you will adopt).

The above factors are all major contributors to the amount of time that you will wait before adopting. But be sure to read Chapter 6 for the inside scoop on the adoption arrangers—agencies, attorneys, and others. They will have a great effect on how quickly you are able to adopt.

Will You Look Good on Paper?

Your individual circumstances affect the adoption process, and healthy married people between the ages of 30 and 40 are generally considered the most desirable by agencies, attorneys, and birthparents who place children for adoption. But you are *not* automatically shut out if you are single, disabled, gay or lesbian, or over 40! Contrary to popular belief, it is very possible for most people to adopt a child. I'll talk more about how nontraditional applicants can successfully adopt in Chapter 13.

Life (and Adoption) Are Not Perfect

As for your "level of perfectionism," it's okay to want a healthy child. Most people do, whether they have children biologically or through adoption. But if you want an absolutely risk-free adoption, with the perfect child and the perfect birthparents, you may have a long wait. (Maybe forever.)

The Least You Need to Know

➤ Adoption is a permanent way to build your family.

➤ Most adopted children grow up healthy and well-adjusted.

➤ Adoptive parents come from many walks of life. There is no single profile of a "successful" adoptive parent.

➤ Adoptions do not necessarily take a long time; nor will you be rejected if you are not a perfect potential parent.

➤ Despite the negative myths and stories emphasized in the media, most real-life adoptions are positive.

Chapter 2

Is Adoption Right for You?

In This Chapter

➤ What are your reasons for choosing adoption?

➤ How will adoption affect your life?

➤ Figuring out if your partner wants to adopt

➤ Can you handle the screening process?

➤ The financial costs of adoption

➤ Discussing adoption with family and friends

"I'm sick of these treatments!" said Amy about the various methods she used in order to get pregnant. So far she'd been trying for four years and nothing had worked. And everyone had a different idea of what Amy and her husband Bob should do. Her mom urged them to "keep trying just a little longer." Bob's brother Bill asked why they didn't just adopt. Amy's best friend Sue, mother of three kids, wondered why they didn't give up on having children and enjoy their freedom instead.

Carol and Bill are having a very rocky time in their marriage. Bill says maybe what they need is a child to focus on. It would probably save their marriage if they adopted, give them a fresh start. Carol isn't so sure, but she does want her marriage to work . . .

Many of us are raised to think of a family as a biological unit: Mom, Dad, and the 2.3 kids born to them. Nobody talks much about infertility or adoption. So it's one thing to think that, in general, adoption is a good thing. It's a whole other ball game to think about adopting a child yourself.

For example, how you feel about infertility—if you are infertile—is one major issue. Then there's how your extended family might react to a new person joining the family through adoption. You also have to think about the day-to-day constraints that would be placed upon you as a parent. These are just a few issues that need to be "processed" before you adopt. And this chapter will help you do that.

I'll show you how to look at adoption as a possible choice for you, while at the same time balancing the various influences that push and pull you toward and away from adoption.

Fiction Is Stranger Than Truth: Realities of Adoption

In the first chapter, I talked about outlandish adoption stories on soap operas and also about rare but highly publicized adoption scandals that make the news. Here's the "boring" process that an actual adoption takes for most adopters:

1. They decide to adopt.
2. They apply to an agency or attorney.
3. They are investigated by a social worker.
4. They are approved.
5. A child is placed with them.

Of course, between the starting point and the finish line, there can be some heart-thumping scares about the adoption—such as, is it a good idea? And yet, for many people, most fears and problems come from within, rather than from anything that actually happens during the process. Throughout the rest of this chapter, I'll help you examine some of the common fears and issues you need to face before you begin.

Why Adopt?

If you've been going through infertility treatments for any length of time, your goal has been to create a biological child. So if pregnancy is not happening, you may feel a variety of emotions:

➤ Angry. It isn't fair that other parents can push out kid after kid! Why can't you have one?

➤ Cheated. It's part of your dream to grow up, get a job, and have children. So how come it hasn't happened for you?

➤ Guilty. There must be some bad thing you did that is causing this infertility.

➤ Inferior. Other people can have babies but you can't, so that must mean that you (or your partner) are inadequate and defective.

➤ Resigned or hopeless. Pregnancy isn't going to happen. You've tried and tried, and nothing works.

Not everyone feels all of these emotions, but most people who are infertile experience at least some of them. If you feel them too, you are normal. Even if you adopt a child, you may feel some sadness over infertility. But you should be well beyond constantly obsessing over the unfairness of it all.

Other people are not infertile, but they choose to adopt anyway. (Some call such people *preferential adopters*.) Here are some reasons why fertile people opt for adoption:

➤ They think it makes more sense to adopt a child "already here" than to bring another child into the world.

➤ They don't want the hassles of caring for a baby and would rather adopt an older child.

➤ They have a genetic problem that they don't want to pass on to biological children.

➤ The wife has a medical problem that would make pregnancy difficult.

➤ The person is single but does not wish to create a pregnancy outside of marriage.

Adopterms
Some people have had one or more children and then can't have any more. They have what is called *secondary infertility*. These couples often want to adopt for the same reasons as infertile couples: they don't have as many children as they would like. (I am one of these people, because I had two "biological" children before becoming infertile and adopting.)

Many adoption agencies in the U.S. will turn down couples who are fertile. How do they know? They may require a statement from your physician describing an infertility problem. Preferential adopters generally adopt a child from another country, or they have to find agencies or attorneys willing to work with them.

Is Adoption Good Enough For You?

Here's another tough issue that most people don't like to think about. Is adoption good enough for you?

You may have wanted a biological child but couldn't have one, so you decide to adopt. It's important that the adopted child be perceived as the child that you really want. If you have never had a child, how do you know your love will be strong?

Consider the fact that you are able to love lots of people who aren't related to you—your spouse and your close friends, for example. Also, consider the true importance of biological relationships to you. If you feel that what is most important is to have a child who resembles you or carries forth your genes, then adoption wouldn't be right for you. If you feel that the primary reason to adopt is to become a parent, a role you strongly want, then adoption might be right for you.

In addition, know that nearly all adoptive parents believe their children are the right ones for them, the ones they were meant to parent.

Are You Ready for Adoption?

The readiness to adopt is based on rational as well as completely emotional issues, fears, concerns, and constraints. You need to achieve a state of *adoption readiness*, which enables you to then become very proactive and directed—what I call an *adoption mindset*. Here are just a few of the issues you must confront first—many of which are the same or similar to issues people face (or should face) if they are thinking about biological parenthood:

➤ Marital issues. If you are married, is your marriage stable?

➤ Lifestyle issues. Can you change your life to accommodate a child?

➤ Your health. You don't have to be an Olympic athlete, but can you manage the hard work involved in parenting? Also, is your health good enough that you can reasonably expect to be able to parent a child for the next 18 years or until the child's adulthood?

➤ Financial issues. Can you afford the expenses of clothes, toys, furniture, child care, and other hidden expenses?

➤ Your job. How does a child fit into your career?

Let's explore some of these issues in more detail.

Marital Bliss

Adopting a child primarily because you are unhappy with a spouse is a bad idea for a lot of reasons. Here are just a few of the problems that can occur if you adopt to "save your marriage":

➤ The child knows that he's supposed to hold you together, and feels a strain no child should feel.

➤ If your marriage does fail, the child will feel he failed you. (Children think a lot of bad things are their fault.)

➤ Parenting is hard work. If your marriage is under strain already, adopting a child could break fragile ties.

➤ Children need a stable environment where they feel emotionally safe.

Adopterms

Adoption-readiness refers to your state of mind when you feel ready to explore adoption. The *adoption mindset* is an attitude in which you not only *want* to adopt a child, but you *need* to adopt a child and you plan to act on this need.

A person who feels *adoption-ready* may not move into the *adoption mindset*. This can happen for a variety of reasons: a spouse doesn't want to adopt; they think they can't afford the fees; and so on. Conversely, some people jump into the adoption mindset without ever going through the adoption readiness phase. These people may not be ready to adopt.

Real Life Snapshots

In 1994, Pat Williams, manager of the Orlando Magic basketball team, and his wife Jill told *Good Housekeeping* magazine they adopted 14 children because they wanted to save their marriage. Jill had suffered a severe depression. According to Pat, he thought, "If that is what will pull Jill from her depression, and possibly save our marriage, then I will do it. Whether I like the idea or not."

Said Jill, "Initially, Pat adopted for me, but ultimately, it changed him as much as it changed our marriage." Jill was afraid to adopt because Pat had opposed the idea. "But I felt that even if adopting didn't help our marriage, I would have 5 rather than 3 children to love, and the little girls would have a good home." They ultimately adopted 14 children, in addition to their 4 biological children.

In 1997, Pat and Jill Williams divorced, and he obtained custody of all the children. Shortly thereafter, he remarried.

Does this mean that if sometimes you get annoyed with your spouse for snoring or for forgetting to pick up bread and milk on the way home from work, your marriage isn't good enough? Of course not. All marriages have ups and downs. What matters is if you and your spouse feel a strong, positive, lifelong bond to each other.

Lifestyle Changes

Whether you adopt an infant or an older child, you can be sure that your life and your lifestyle will change. Does that sound all right to you?

For example, what if you are very outgoing and carefree, and the child you adopt is shy and clingy? Scientists say that children are born with temperaments—outgoing, shy, and so forth. And a good parent must adjust to the child's personality. (If you think this is only a problem for adoptive parents, think again! Many biological parents are baffled by their children's personalities, which are radically different from their own.)

Whether your child was born to you or adopted by you, he or she may have a very different temperament from your own. You will need to make adjustments to the child's needs.

You should also ask yourself if you are ready to devote yourself to your child. When you become a parent—whether through birth or through adoption—there's this other person who needs constant attention. So take that into account.

Is Your Partner Adoption-Ready?

You may feel very confident that you are ready to adopt—and you may be right! If you have a partner, how does he or she feel? Of course, you can (and should) ask. But sometimes people, especially those we love, don't want to hurt our feelings or make us angry with them.

Both you and your partner should take the Adoption Readiness Quiz on page 23 to see how much you agree on adoption. These questions are not meant to trap your partner in any way. Instead they are designed to elicit true feelings, as well as to encourage your partner to actually think about adopting. It's good to try to imagine your life as an adoptive parent. Do you like your partner's description? Does it parallel your own? Only you can be the judge.

When your partner describes the child he or she envisions adopting, you may be surprised to learn that your partner really wants an infant. Or an older child. You may find your partner receptive to adopting a child with special needs or a child of another country. You may also find that your partner doesn't want to think about this imaginary child at all. This is valuable information, too. Maybe your partner is not ready to make a decision about adoption yet. Or maybe your partner is dead set against the idea.

I included one question each on both the pros and cons of adopting and the pros and cons of parenting. Does your partner think it's silly to ask both questions? This may mean that he or she sees adoption as equal to biological parenting. Does your partner see them as radically different? If so, he or she may not be receptive to adoption.

I included the question about what you would do as a family during your spare time because this question can give you a good idea of how your partner envisions parenting. If your partner thinks nothing will be different, he or she is being unrealistic. If your partner talks about family trips, picnics, and other outings, then he or she is probably at least willing to consider adoption.

The questions I've included on what a biological child and an adopted child would be like can give you important information about how your partner views adoption. If the biological child and adopted child are both depicted in favorable terms, then your partner is probably at least considering the adoption option. If the biological child is described in glowing terms, and the adopted child is seen more negatively, this may indicate a problem. Of course, if the adopted child is described in idealistic terms, that isn't good either. What you're looking for is realism and balance.

Adoption Readiness Quiz

Imagine that we *do* adopt a child. What is our life like?

_____

_____

_____

What do you think are the main pros and cons of adopting?

Pros: _____

_____

Cons: _____

_____

What do you think are the main pros and cons of parenting?

Pros: _____

_____

Cons: _____

_____

What would we do as a family in our spare time and on vacations?

_____

_____

_____

What would our biological child be like if we had one? (Even if there is no chance that you could have one.)

_____

_____

_____

What would our adopted child be like?

_____

_____

_____

Getting Screened

Figuring out whether you are adoption-ready takes some serious thinking and a clear-eyed look at yourself, at your spouse (if you are married), and also at your individual life situation. This kind of thinking is rarely, if ever, required of people who have biological children. (Although it certainly would be nice if more people did think harder about this issue!)

But when you adopt a child, social workers expect you to undergo some serious introspection, as well as to share information about yourself. You may feel like you're under a microscope, an interesting specimen for the social worker to analyze, catalog, and ultimately approve or not (no matter how nice the social worker is). Maybe you're successful in the business world, academia, or elsewhere. It doesn't matter. When you enter the adoption system, you go in at "Start," along with everyone else.

In most cases, adopters are screened. In fact, they are screened quite a lot. I talk about the screening process in Chapter 12, so I'm not going to delve deeply into it here. Rather, I want to talk about the anger and irritation that many people have about the "unfairness" of being asked what seem to be multi-gazillion questions when they want to adopt.

Adoption Alert
Occasionally, even with screening, potential adoptive parents fail to seriously evaluate themselves. They make it through the adoption process on automatic pilot, without ever considering various issues. They think that chanting the party line on adoption is the right thing to do.

The problem with spouting the "party line" is that people who somehow manage to jump into adoption without much thinking never attain that "state of grace" that I call adoption-readiness. This is not good. Adoption should be preceded by both adoption-readiness and the adoption mindset.

Some people believe it should be much easier to adopt than it is, and they think that going through background investigations, physical examinations, reams of paperwork, and talks with social workers is just too much trouble and shouldn't be so hard.

I understand their frustration and can empathize with how they feel. But I simply do not agree with people who think it should be easy to adopt. I think that adoptive parents should be evaluated for three basic reasons:

➤ A screening can help avoid abuses of the system, such as baby selling to the highest bidder or putting undue pressure on a birthmother.

➤ A screening can help adoptive parents think about whether adoption is truly right for their family and to prepare for the adoption if they decide that it is.

➤ Screening can usually protect the child from very inappropriate adopters.

Sure, it's no fun to be evaluated, and some people—maybe most people—feel very insecure when they are being judged as potential parents. They fear they won't make the grade.

And yet, I still think it's important for adoptive parents to be screened. Children deserve the best chance they can get. With adoption, this can and should be the goal. And the evaluation process is a big part of all that.

The Financial Costs of Adoption

Is it fair to charge fees to adopt a child? Many people don't think so. Although I'll talk more about adoption fees in Chapter 8, let's look at the financial issue, which is another blocking point for many potential adoptive parents.

Here are some reasons why people think adoption should be free or at least very inexpensive.

➤ Because they don't want to pay a five-figure sum to adopt a child.

➤ Because adoption is a positive social goal.

➤ Because they think paying fees to adopt is like buying a child.

➤ Because they think if they had a biological child, it would be free—because they have insurance.

Let me address the last one first. It's not "free" to bear a child. There are prenatal fees and fees incurred at the hospital, when the child is actually born.

When you adopt a child, you may be the one to pay the birthmother's doctor and hospital bills because often birthmothers have no health insurance. In addition, adoption agencies and adoption attorneys have expenses. It may not seem romantic or idyllic to think about this, but adoption is a business and adoption providers have business expenses. It's not evil—it's life.

> **Adoption Alert**
> Some adoption arrangers charge much higher fees than everyone else. I wouldn't go to such people, and before you do, read Chapter 6.

Let's look at the other reasons for not wanting to pay to adopt. Okay, so you don't want to expend your life savings or borrow money. Who does? You must operate in the reality that the rest of us live in.

What about adoption as a benefit to society? I agree that adoption *is* a social good. But do you think that social goods are free? Think again. Without getting too political here, think about public assistance and other programs to help those in need. Think about the arts. Think about your favorite charity. None of these are free.

Is paying to adopt equal to buying a child? Not unless you're doing something illegal. What you're paying for are the services of the attorney or agency. Sometimes you may be paying for the birthmother's living expenses or her medical expenses, too. But you are *not* paying for your child.

As for the argument that the child won't have to go into foster care because you are benevolently adopting him or her, think again. If the child is not already in the foster care system and if you don't adopt this child, then in most cases someone else will. Most birthmothers will seek other adoptive parents if you don't work out.

Family Values

You can be sure that if you're thinking about adoption, just about everyone you know will have an opinion about whether you should (or shouldn't) adopt. But the problem with listening to everyone else is that you will receive conflicting advice from your friends and family. Also, they probably don't know squat about adoption. They all want what they think is best for you—but how can they know what truly is the right choice for your situation? Answer: It must be your decision.

Only you (and your partner, if you have one) can make such an important and life-changing decision as to whether or not you are ready to adopt a child. After all, no matter how much you love your family and friends, who's going to stagger out of bed at 2 a.m. to feed the baby? It's *you*, babe, who will take the responsibility for your child, and no one else.

If you decide to adopt a child who is of a different race or from another country, you may get additional flak from your family. You may also receive family disapproval if you are a single person wishing to adopt. Explain to them what you want to do. If their objections seem unreasonable to you, and they are unswayable, you must decide if and how their feelings will affect your decision to adopt and your future relationship.

Breaking the News

If you decide to tell your family that you plan to adopt, here's what you should do:

➤ Listen to what is said and screen out reality from fears. If Aunt Louise says her friend Sarah adopted a child and he turned out "just awful," ask her what she means. As you ask questions, it will frequently become clear that Aunt Louise really has no idea what happened.

➤ Listen for the underlying emotions and try to restate them. "Mom, it sounds like you are saying that you're worried the birthmother will change her mind and we'll be brokenhearted."

➤ Tell your family that you are learning about adoption and adopted kids and soon you'll be able to share information.

➤ Try to find out what the underlying fear *really* is. My mother seemed to have doubts about adoption, but I couldn't figure out why. She finally told me she thought it would be hard for me to parent a disabled child. But I had no plan to adopt a child with special needs. Problem solved.

Opinions After Adoption

Even before you adopt a child, you need to know that others will ask aggravating questions and sometimes will make stupid comments. What's more, these questions and concerns will continue long after you've adopted a child. So, can you take it? Most adoptive parents answer with a resounding "Yes!" But I suggest that all potential adoptive parents imagine ahead of time how they might feel.

For example, would it bother you if people challenged your "realness," your entitlement to be a parent when you adopt? Or if they make wrongheaded comments based on silly ideas? If you aren't confident that you could tolerate such remarks, well, fasten your seat belt. You may be in for a rocky ride.

Am I trying to talk you *out* of adoption? No way! But to my mind, the most successful adoptions occur when families are prepared for situations that commonly occur.

Selflessness and Selfishness

Despite how many times you hear about adoptive parents who are "saints" because they "took in" the poor little darlings—and, incidentally, this imagery makes most adoptive parents nearly retch—adoption is in many ways a selfish action. If a parent believes that adoption is totally selfless, it can be very problematic for the child.

Many people who have adopted children did seek to have a biological child first, which is okay. But it's important that people who do adopt accept their children as the first-class beings that they are. If you think you "should" adopt so you can help a poor little orphan somewhere, even though you know in your heart you could never love her the same as "your own," my advice is: Don't adopt.

Adoption Alert
Adoptive families are the recipients of some uniquely strange comments. Think about how you'd feel if your family was discussed this way:

"Isn't it wonderful that they gave that little orphan a home?"

"She is so cute! Good thing her real mother can't see her, she'd snatch her right away from you."

"I bet he is hyperactive because all those adopted kids have that attention deficit disorder thing."

"You are such a good mother. It's almost like he was really your own."

"You're so lucky you didn't have to go through labor to have her. You did it the easy way."

The best reason to adopt a child is because you want to become a good parent to a child who needs a family. You want to adopt because you want to give your love to a child and provide as happy a life as you can. But you are also selfish in that you want to receive love from the child as well and to enjoy watching your child grow up. The trick is finding the balance.

Here's another important point, one worth ending this chapter with. Adopt the kind of child you want, not the child that is pressed upon you by social workers or others. If you want to adopt a healthy infant of the same race as you, fine. If you want to adopt a child from another country, also fine. And if your goal is to adopt an older child—from the U.S. or abroad—that's okay too. More information on this topic is included in the next chapter.

The Least You Need to Know

➤ As a potential adoptive parent, you need to assess your "adoption readiness."

➤ Talk to your partner to find out how he or she really feels about adoption.

➤ Understand the financial costs of adoption.

➤ Realize that your family and friends may offer unsolicited advice about your adoption.

➤ Make sure you are adopting for the right reasons.

Chapter 3

Children Who Need Families

In This Chapter

➤ Adopting an infant

➤ Who are children with "special needs?"

➤ Understanding the foster care system

➤ Adopting the older child

➤ Adopting the disabled child

➤ Adopting a child of a different race

Marie is single, pregnant, and thinking about adoption. She wants a good family for her baby, preferably a couple of the same religion with strong values. The Adorable Babies Adoption Agency has given Marie five "resumes" of approved couples to consider. She wants to select a family now so that everything will be all settled when it's time to deliver.

Tommy, 8, and Timmy, 10, have been in foster care most of their lives, sometimes living together, sometimes living apart. The rights of their parents have been terminated by the court, and the boys need a family who can love two active children.

Natasha is a Russian child who is nine months old and has lived in an orphanage since just after birth. She seems active and healthy, but she hasn't been adopted because she is a little small for her age.

These are just a few of the scenarios describing children (and children-to-be!) who need families all around the globe. Some of these children will be adopted quickly. For others, it will take much longer. This chapter will show you the different kinds of children who need permanent, loving families.

Where the Babies Are

Many people want to adopt an infant, preferably a healthy baby and preferably tomorrow—if not today. But the adoption process contains rules and regulations and an entire system to deal with. Learn the ins and outs of the adoption system, and you will succeed much faster and with less emotional and financial pain than the people who rush in to accept any offer.

At least 30,000 babies are adopted from the U.S. each year, and another 10,000 children, mostly babies, are adopted from other countries. This is not an "upper limit"—more babies could be adopted if more birthparents chose adoption over struggling to raise children they are unready to parent.

Infants who need adoptive families come in all colors: White, brown, black, and other various shadings. They come from the U.S. (some call this *domestic adoption* as opposed to *international adoption*) and other countries. They are healthy or may have correctable health problems. Some are very ill. It may be a little easier and faster to adopt a child who is of mixed race or is black, but whites who wish to adopt white children certainly can succeed, as can families of other races or ethnicities also adopt inracially, if they wish.

If you want to adopt an infant, there are many possible choices for you to make. Here are the major options available:

➤ You can adopt an American infant through an adoption agency in your state or another state.

➤ You can adopt an American baby independently, with the assistance of an attorney.

➤ You can adopt a child from another country, through an adoption agency in your state or another state.

➤ You can find your own child in another country and ask an adoption agency to manage the paperwork for you.

In many cases of infant adoption, the child is not yet born when the adoption arrangements are made. The reason for this is simple: The birthmother wants to know that her child will be placed with an adoptive family immediately—straight from the hospital. Some birthmothers are very adamant about this.

Why Adopt an Infant?

It's self-evident to many people why adopters want infants, but the question is a valid one. After all, say some people, there are many older kids and abused kids who need families. So why don't most people want to adopt an older child?

Here are some reasons why people want to adopt infants rather than older children:

➤ They want to provide a continuously positive environment beginning when the child is young, believing that they will have a greater influence that way.

➤ They like babies.

➤ They don't want to deal with the after-effects of abuse and neglect that older children may have suffered.

➤ They want to watch the child grow from a tiny infant.

Adoption Alert

Should people adopt only children with "special needs"? Because such children urgently need a family and there are lots of them?

My position is that a family should adopt the type of child they want to adopt. If they want to adopt a healthy same-race infant, I believe it is wrong to attempt to coerce them into adopting a child of another race, or with medical problems, or an older child. However, if the family does wish to adopt a child with a special need and they under-stand the pros and cons of whatever the problem is, I think they should not be dissuaded.

How to Adopt an Infant

There are three primary ways to adopt an infant or child: through the state social services agency, which manages the foster care program; through a private adoption agency in your state or another state; and independently, either through an adoption that you arrange or one that is arranged for you by a third party.

Few infant adoptions occur through state government agencies, although some babies with serious medical problems are adopted this way. Instead, most infant adoptions are arranged either by adoption agencies, by the adopters and birthparents themselves, or by adoption attorneys. An estimated one-half to two-thirds of all infant adoptions are "independent," non-agency adoptions.

Adopterms

An *agency adoption* is arranged by workers at a licensed adoption agency. This term usually refers to private adoption agencies, rather than state or county government (public) agencies. In an agency adoption, the agency is the primary facilitator of the adoption.

An *independent adoption* is a non-agency adoption. Often, however, adoption agencies are involved, in that they will do home study investigations of the adopters, and they may also provide counseling services to the birthparents.

Adopterms

Agencies designate children who they believe are hard to place as children with *special needs*. How a special need is defined depends entirely on the agency. And, what some agencies regard as special needs are not viewed that way by other agencies—and often not by hopeful adoptive parents.

State agencies may have a legal definition of the term "special needs." Some states may include the definition in their state law.

Kids with Special Needs

Many people adopt children with *special needs*, including older kids, children with medical problems, siblings, multiracial kids, and others. Some children with special needs are right here in the U.S.; others languish in foreign orphanages. All urgently need parents. Now.

Children who fit the categories defined by law as "special needs" may qualify for state and/or federal benefits, such as Medicaid and monthly payments.

Here is a summary of children who are often defined as having "special needs" (keep in mind that children may have more than one special need):

➤ Children with a minor or serious medical problem—everything from a correctable birthmark to being HIV-positive

➤ Children who were abused, neglected, or abandoned

➤ Children over the age of six or seven

➤ Children who have siblings (and whom the agency hopes to place together)

➤ Children who are African-American or biracial

➤ Children with serious psychological or psychiatric problems

Advertisements from adoption agencies sometimes offer descriptions of their special-needs kids. For example, an ad in *Adoptive Families* magazine last year described a five-year-old Asian child: "She speaks in sentences, can count to ten, and recognizes colors, shapes, and sizes. She is independent in self-help skills and is reported to interact well with both peers and adults." The child was also said to have been "diagnosed with a moderate to severe hearing loss. Reports indicate that this has not inhibited her ability to communicate."

Infants with Special Needs

Some babies are said to have special needs; for example, infants with serious medical problems. Not only agencies, but also families vary a lot in what they think is a special need or not even a problem at all.

International Babies with Special Needs

An infant born in another country may have a problem like a cleft palate or some other medical condition that would be considered easily correctable in the U.S. but is a major problem that won't be corrected in the child's country. As a result, some families decide to adopt a child from overseas with a special need.

Children born overseas may also suffer from malnutrition, rickets, or other illnesses, and often many of the effects can be overcome by good nutrition and lots of TLC. However, this is *not* always true—it should never be assumed that "love conquers all." Don't forget about consulting with your pediatrician *before* you adopt a child with special needs—in or outside the U.S. (And be sure to read Chapter 15 on health issues in adoption.)

"Waiting Children" in Foster Care

Thousands of kids in foster care need adoptive families. State agencies generally refer to them as "waiting children," and you may see their photos in local newspapers or even on television programs. (Some Web sites on the Internet offer photos of children who need families.)

Table 3.1 shows the median length of stay in the foster care system for some states broken down by state. ("Median" means that for half the children, the stay fell below this figure, and for half, it was above it.)

Familybuilding Tips
Often (but not always), private agencies charge lower fees to families planning to adopt children with special needs. State government social service agencies (formerly called the "welfare department") don't charge fees, but most of the children they place have special needs, by virtually anyone's definition. Attorneys who place children with special needs generally do not lower their fees. This may be because they place few children with special needs.

Adoptinfo
According to the U.S. Department of Health and Human Services, only 20,000 of 470,000 foster children were adopted in 1995. The numbers probably were about the same in 1996 and 1997. According to the department's statistics, adoption is the "case plan goal" for about 16% of the children in the 21 states that reported statistics for 1996. For over half the children, the goal was to place the child back with the biological family.

Other "goals" for foster children are: subsidized guardianship, kinship care (care by relatives), long-term foster care, and emancipation (to be regarded as an adult).

Table 3.1 Median Length of Stay of Children in Foster Care as of December 31, 1994 (21 States Reported)

State	Median Length of Stay (in Months)	Number of Children
Alaska*	9.33	1,105
Arizona	18.04	3,997
Arkansas	16.59	2,049
California	25.99	87,382
District of Columbia	24.30	2,380
Florida**	22.54	12,587
Georgia	18.04	12,631
Idaho	10.94	1,032
Illinois	25.69	45,657
Kansas	16.89	5,911
Kentucky	21.29	3,949
Massachusetts	20.04	14,667
New Jersey	19.81	6,920
New Mexico	19.53	1,506
New York	38.54	60,216
Ohio	14.59	14,531
Oregon	13.96	5,439
Rhode Island	15.05	3,074
South Carolina	20.07	4,482
Texas	19.25	16,415
Utah	10.68	1,415
Totals	24.48	307,345
National Estimate of children in foster care		**469,073**

* *Data were extracted from an Information System under development.*
** *Does not include relative placements.*

U.S. Department of Health and Human Services; Administration for Children and Families; Administration on Children, Youth, and Families; Children's Bureau; and the Adoption and Foster Care Analysis and Reporting System (AFCARS).

How Do Kids Enter Foster Care?

When a child is abused, neglected, or abandoned and the protective services division of the state or county learns of the problem, the parents or primary caregivers are investigated. The child may also be removed from the family while the investigation occurs, especially if severe physical abuse or sexual abuse is suspected. Sometimes the child is placed in an emergency shelter or group home while it is determined by social workers if the child needs longer term care or not. If the child appears to need longer term care because it would be unsafe to return her to the biological family, she may then be placed with a foster family.

If the state or county finds that no abuse or other serious problems have occurred, the child is returned to the family (although sometimes red tape delays the return).

Adopterms
Waiting children refers to kids in foster care who need adoptive families.

The abusive or neglectful family is given a *performance agreement* or a "goal," which is a plan to change their behavior so they will be able to be reunited with the child. They may be given a time limit or target date to complete these goals. But often, a sympathetic judge will extend the time period.

Many abusive parents may have problems with drug or alcohol abuse or have difficulty holding a job. In addition, they may have criminal records and jail time on their dossier. A performance agreement could include such stipulations as staying off drugs or alcohol, getting a job, and staying out of trouble. Taking parenting classes is a frequently imposed requirement, too.

If all attempts to preserve the biological family fail, the biological parents may consent to an adoption or, as more commonly happens, the parents' rights are involuntarily terminated. Termination of parental rights (TPR) is *not* taken lightly by the courts, and in most cases, courts bend over backwards to give biological parents chance after chance to overcome whatever problem caused their children to be placed in foster care.

If and when a foster child *is* released for adoption, the child may be emotionally distressed by years in and out of foster care. Consequently, adoptive parents must prepare for the probability that the child will need therapy and extra support as he or she learns to trust in the permanency of the adoptive family.

Real Life Snapshots

I asked a group of state adoption specialists, "What is the biggest mistake or misunderstanding people have about children placed for adoption through the state?" Here are a few of the responses I received.

"Not all older children considered special needs are 'problem' children. Though they may have suffered abuse or have multiple needs, most respond *very* well to a loving, structured home." (New York)

"They think that 'Love cures everything' and expect some level of gratitude for having 'rescued' a child from foster care." (Washington)

I also asked what was the most important thing to know about the children their agencies had placed for adoption.

"Most have experienced serious abuse and/or neglect with lifelong consequences. Nevertheless, most show dramatic improvement with stability and committed adoptive parents." (Washington)

"These are children who have been *victims* of neglect, abuse, and other circumstances beyond their control, and who need and deserve a safe and loving family in which to grow and thrive. They bring great joy and sometimes great challenges to families waiting to share their lives with a child." (Florida)

Familybuilding Tips

Social workers say that many prospective adoptive families make mistakes at two extremes when it comes to adopting foster kids: They either assume that foster children have no problems that can't be cured by lots of love *or* that they are children who cannot recover from the abuse and neglect. In most cases, neither is true.

Foster kids who need families are often photographed in special photolisting books that state agencies maintain for prospective parents. The books may include short descriptions of the child. Sometimes, videotapes of children in the U.S. (and overseas) are also available, and these can be very informative.

Legal Risk Adoptions

Some states offer *legal risk* (also called *fost/adopt*) programs. This means that you may become a foster parent to a child who the state or county agency believes will soon become available for adoption.

The intent is that the agency will seek to terminate the biological parents' rights to the child. *Legal risk* is also a term sometimes used by some attorneys to denote the time frame during which a child could be legally reclaimed by a birthparent; for example, during the days allowed by a state (if any) to revoke consent.

The reason why this program is called a "risk" is that the biological parent may fight the loss of parental rights. Another risk is that social workers change, and a new social worker may decide to try to reunite the child with the biological family—no matter how many workers in the past have tried and failed. So it's possible that you may be unable to adopt the child.

Adopterms
Legal risk refers to a program in which parents may become foster parents to children who may become available for adoption. Some states also use the term "fost/adopt" to describe the same program.

Adopting the Older Child

Usually the public agencies (state and county government services) consider an older child to be over six or seven, but sometimes they raise the bar higher to age eleven or twelve. So it's important to ask for a definition of what is an older child from every agency that you contact. It's difficult to know exactly *how many* older children may be adopted in the U.S. because less than half the states have reported full data to the federal government. It is also true that the average ages of foster children vary from state to state. It is probably safe to say that at least 20 percent of the foster children could be adopted—about 100,000 children of all ages nationwide. And probably more.

Adoptinfo
Political leaders have recently begun to take action to change the foster care system. In 1996, President Clinton announced "Adoption Initiative 2002" in which he directed federal leaders to increase the number of adoptions of foster children. By raising public awareness and eliminating barriers to permanent placements, Clinton suggested that the number of children who are adopted or permanently placed could double by the year 2002.

Older Children Overseas

Some international agencies also place older kids, usually kids who've been living in orphanages for years. They, too, may have been abused, but the physical, emotional, or sexual abuse could have occurred at the orphanage rather than at the hands of their birthparents. Some families think that orphanages overseas are "better" than foster homes in the U.S. The fact is that some overseas orphanages are well-run and staffed by caring people—others are not. One overall truth, however, is that no orphanage is as good as a family.

Real Life Snapshots

In a very unusual case several years ago, "Gregory K," a 12-year old boy, sought to have his mother's parental rights terminated against her wishes. (The father willingly consented to end his parental rights.) Gregory had been in foster care most of his life, and while in a group home he had met the Russ family, whom he wanted to be adopted by.

George Russ was an attorney himself, and the case did make it to the courtroom (it was even featured on Court TV). The biological mother argued that she should be given another chance. Her attorney said if children could decide when parental rights should be ended, they'd all be flocking to be adopted by rich people. Jerri Hall, Gregory K's attorney, argued that the child deserved a chance himself. Gregory (who subsequently changed his name to Sean) prevailed in the case.

Older Children in Non-Agency Adoptions

Very occasionally, adoption attorneys place older children in families. In these unusual cases, the biological parents find themselves unable to parent and often they don't trust the state social services division. They want to feel they have some control over the adoption process. It's also true that in many cases, the state agency will refuse involvement unless the child is abused or neglected. As a result, a private agency or attorney is the only way to go for a non-abusive but overburdened biological parent.

In most cases, however, it's preferable for an agency to be involved in the placement of older children to ensure that counseling is provided. With an older child adoption, the birthparents and adoptive parents are not the only ones who need counseling—the children, if they are old enough, will need counseling as well. They need counseling to learn to understand that it's not their fault that their birthparents could not care for them. Counseling also can help children deal with the loss of their biological parents while at the same time enabling them to learn to trust in the permanency of their new family.

Real Life Snapshots

Several years ago, I learned about a mother who discovered she had terminal cancer. She had three young children, no living relatives, and the children's father had died. So the mother concluded the only answer for her children was adoption, and she began to look for a family.

She contacted a local adoption agency, but the agency didn't understand or accept that she wanted to choose the family herself. Her reasoning was this: Who knew her children better than she did? So she resolved to locate the right family. She found several possible families and personally interviewed them all.

One of the families had older children and seemed kind, friendly, and upbeat. They contacted an attorney who handled all the details for them, and they found an agency to do the home study. The mother prepared her children as best she could, and the family sought the help of a counselor to help the children and the mother. The mother and the family decided they'd finalize the adoptions before the mother died, so she would know the kids were safe. But the family swore that the mother could see her kids until the end of her life. They kept their promise.

Adopting Disabled Children

Some children who are adopted have medical problems, ranging from relatively minor and temporary conditions all the way up to terminal illnesses. In fact, parents sometimes adopt children from foreign countries who they know must receive surgery as soon as they arrive in the U.S. to correct life-threatening conditions. (Be sure to also read Chapter 15 on health issues and adopted children.)

The checklist on page 40 shows some of the issues you should consider if you are thinking about adopting a disabled or special needs child.

Some people adopt children with medical problems because they (a) love children and (b) have medical expertise to care for such children.

Special Needs Checklist for Prospective Parents

Some children have physical, mental, or emotional conditions which require special attention. Please indicate the type(s) of child(ren) you would consider:

	Yes	No
1. A child who is mentally retarded but may be capable of living independently and holding a job as an adult.		X
2. A child who is mentally retarded and may require supervision as an adult in his or her living and working environment.		X
3. A child who is mentally retarded and may require total supervision and care as an adult.		X
4. A child who has a physical condition which can be managed on a long-term basis with treatment, medication, or orthopedic braces.	X	
5. A child with an illness that may be terminal.		X
6. A physically disabled child who, as an adult, may not be able to provide for his or her own self-care needs and whose physical activity may be significantly restricted.		X
7. A physically disabled child who as an adult may need help in performing some self-care functions and have some restrictions on physical activity.		X
8. A child with learning disabilities.	X	
9. A child who is experiencing emotional problems that slightly affect his or her socialization with others.	X	
10. A child who is experiencing considerable difficulty in relationships with others and exhibits inappropriate behavior.		X
11. A child whose ability to socialize is extremely impaired (for example, severely withdrawn or aggressive).		X
12. Would you accept a legal risk placement where the parental rights of one or both parents have not yet been terminated?		X
13. Would you accept a foster care placement?		X
14. Are you currently a member of an adoptive parent group?		X

Add any comments here including other conditions and/or physical characteristics you will consider or will not accept:

_____

_____

Reprinted with the permission of Lorraine Boisselle, Executive Director of The Adoption Centre, Inc., Winter Park, Florida.

Of course, not all medical problems are life-threatening, and some problems may even seem silly to some people. If you wanted to adopt an older child, would you turn down a child who had mild attention deficit disorder? Or a mild speech impediment? Or a cleft palate? These conditions would be minor to some people, but beyond toleration for others. Luckily, there are wonderful adoption social workers who can figure out which kids fit with which parents.

Real Life Snapshots

About 10 years ago, I led a small adoptive parent support group and published a monthly newsletter. An agency contacted me about a baby girl who had a correctable hernia problem—they didn't have a family who wanted to adopt her. I published the information in my newsletter, and a family contacted the agency. They adopted her! Luckily, they did not consider the girl's problem as a reason to not adopt her.

Why Adopt Special-Needs Kids?

There are many reasons why people adopt children with medical, psychological, or other problems or kids who are older. Here are a few reasons:

➤ Their biological children are grown, and they feel they have more love to give a child.

➤ They feel they can empathize with the child's problems.

➤ They believe they are "called" to adopt the child(ren), by a higher power or by their own conscience (or both).

➤ They have expertise in teaching, social work, or another field with which they feel can help the child.

As discussed earlier, some special-needs children have survived physical, emotional, or sexual abuse (and often all of these). These problems are not automatically wiped out the day they are adopted, no matter how loving and helpful the adopters are.

Some adopters want to ignore the past and pretend the child was born the day he entered their family. This is a bad idea, and adoptive parents should work to maintain realistic expectations of themselves and their children. I bring this up now because it's important to think of such issues even before you adopt a child. (For more information on parenting older adopted children, read Chapter 21.)

On the other hand, with love, attention, and sometimes counseling, many special-needs children can and do turn their lives around.

Real Life Snapshots

In an unpublished article written in 1996, psychiatrist Aaron Lazare described the arrival of his adopted daughter, Hien, age 4½, in 1973. She was a mixed race child born to a Vietnamese mother and an African-American soldier.

When the prospective parents were told about this child, a volunteer wrote, "I hope you like strong-willed children."

When Hien arrived, she was "frightened and angry. She was homely and appeared malnourished with a protruding stomach. She made funny sounds that made me think she was mentally retarded. All of her teeth were decayed, and she occasionally held her jaw as if to soothe the pain. She then became mute for several weeks." Although she did have a learning disability, Hien later graduated from college with a 3.5 average.

Said her father, "Hien is no longer the homely child I described earlier. She is the attractive, strong willed, determined survivor as forecast in the letter we had received earlier."

(Reprinted with permission of Aaron Lazare, M.D., Chancellor, University of Massachusetts Medical Center.)

Adopterms

Transracial adoption refers to the situation in which a family adopts a child of another race. Generally, transracial adoption specifically alludes to whites adopting African-American children.

A *biracial* child is a child who has parents of different races.

A *multiracial* child has a heritage of more than two races in her background.

Are We There Yet—Racially Speaking?

Many people seek to adopt children who are the same race as they are. But it's also a fact that there are children of all races in foster care who need adoptive families.

Whether biracial or African-American children should be adopted by whites has been a subject of intense debate. In 1994 and again in 1996, the federal government passed laws that forbade racial consideration as the sole reason to deny a prospective adopter a chance to adopt a child of another race. It will probably take time for state bureaucracies to "catch up" to the law and rescind old policies that decreed race was a primary consideration in adoption.

Families who wish to adopt children of another race or children who are biracial usually must adopt through a private adoption agency, rather than through the state social services department. Although this should be changing with the passage of federal laws that now forbid race as the primary consideration in adoption. Sometimes families adopt a child of another race through an adoption attorney. Agencies (but not attorneys, usually) may charge lower fees for children who are non-white because it is harder to find adoptive families.

Here are a few issues to consider if you are thinking about adopting a child of another race from your own, regardless of your race or the child's race:

➤ Your child will probably face some racial slurs, as may you and other family members.

➤ People will ask you intrusive questions.

➤ Some people will be very positive toward you and others very negative.

People who support *transracial adoption* say that what children need is a loving family and that too many African-American children remain in foster care while African-American adoptive families are sought. Some people (like me) believe that if people of a certain race are "good enough" to be long-term, stable foster parents, then they are also good enough to become adoptive parents. But unfortunately, many foster children who are placed with families of a different race have been eventually removed to a same-race placement, purely for racial reasons. Of course, this does *not* mean that children should always be placed outside their race. Whenever possible, foster children should be placed with appropriate foster/adoptive families of their own race. However, race should not be the reason to prevent a child from having a family at all.

Those who oppose transracial adoption believe that it's important for a child to be parented by people of the same race. They think the child would be racially and culturally deprived—some call it racial genocide—if the child were adopted by parents not of the same race. They also believe that the parents could not understand how to deal with racial insults and slurs and that such insults would be more prevalent in a child adopted transracially than in a child adopted in-racially.

Real Life Snapshots

Comedian Tommy Davidson (formerly of the TV program "In Living Color") is a black man who was adopted by a white family. In a 1996 interview with *Jet* magazine, he talked frankly about the pros and cons of his own experience. His mom had two biological children, and Tommy said that he was often questioned about why he and his siblings were different skin colors and he often had to face racism. But there were also some advantages.

Said Davidson, "When I hear blacks talking about white people, saying, 'white people are this and white people are that,' I say to myself, 'that is not true.' . . . And when I hear white people saying, 'Black people are this or that,' I'll say, 'I know that is not true because I'm black.' That's what makes me me. It's a very cool thing."

Multiracial Children

A logical problem arises when a child is of mixed racial heritage—what then? Some people, like professional golfer Tiger Woods, who is part Asian, part African-American, and part Native American, don't like to be identified with any particular race. Nor is he alone. As a result, a new category, *multiracial*, has been created.

Tiger Woods wasn't adopted. But when multiracial people like him are adopted, the opponents of transracial adoption like to insist that they be placed in a non-white home. Their position is that when a child is multiracial, then you should default to the minority race that seems physically most obvious. (Not always an easy call!)

Thus, by this reasoning, a child born to a white parent and an African-American parent should be adopted by only African-American parents. In fact, this has been the generally accepted practice in public agencies for years—although enforcement of new laws may eventually change these policies. As a result, in most cases if white parents wish to adopt a child of mixed race, they may find it easier to adopt through a private adoption agency, no matter how many mixed-race children wait in foster care for families.

Longitudinal (long-term) studies of children adopted transracially indicate that most of the children adopted as infants do well in their adoptive families. As with other children not adopted transracially, the children at most risk for future problems are those who are adopted over the age of two or three—although many older adopted children adjust well to their new families.

Two other at-risk groups are children abused at any age and those who lived with many families before their adoption occurred.

The Least You Need to Know

➤ Babies and older children in the U.S. and overseas need families.

➤ Agencies and attorneys are the primary adoption arrangers.

➤ Some children with "special needs" need families—but the definition of special needs can vary a great deal.

➤ Children in foster care can be adopted once the rights of their biological parents have been terminated.

➤ Adopting a child of another race is an option, but one that is opposed by some people.

Birthparents Who Choose Adoption

Mary Ann and Brian loved each other, but both agreed that in no way were they ready to get married and raise a child. She was 18, and he was 19 and a college freshman. Old enough to parent a baby, but they just weren't ready, in their own minds. The pregnancy was accidental, and they didn't think abortion was a good choice. But they couldn't "give up their own flesh and blood" to strangers—could they? Despite the intense pressure to parent, the two decided on adoption.

Tom and Elizabeth were shocked to learn she was pregnant. Again. They already had four kids and they had used precautions! And yet here it was, another baby on the way. They'd seen an ad in a newspaper about couples who couldn't have children and who wanted to adopt. Maybe they'd call the phone number in the ad and learn some more.

But what would people think? After all, they were married people, not some 14-year -old kids who didn't know what was what.

These cases illustrate just a few of the many scenarios faced by birthparents when they consider the adoption option for their babies. In this chapter, I'll discuss the issues birthparents face when they choose adoption.

Who Chooses Adoption?

Today, abortion or single parenting are the approved choices for many people with unplanned pregnancies. High school girls who "keep" their babies are admired. In fact, among some groups of teenage girls, having a baby is considered a rite of passage.

Still, despite the fact that adoption is a less common choice for pregnant women, it's also true that some birthparents in the U.S. *are* still deciding on adoption. Adoption also now appears to be gaining more attention from pregnancy counselors, as both they and the general public have become aware of the enormous difficulties that teenage parents face in caring for infants.

Who are these people? Here is a profile of birthparents who choose adoption:

➤ Most are unmarried, but some are married or divorced. (Some married birthmothers choose adoption as a solution to an unplanned pregnancy, because they cannot cope with another child. Or, they feel they aren't ready to be parents. In some cases, the child may have a disability that they find too difficult to handle.)

➤ Most are not 14-year-old unwed teens; instead, they are usually women over age 17 or 18. (Most very young pregnant women decide to parent their babies instead of placing them for adoption.)

➤ There are also birthparents of children adopted from other countries—a category I'll also cover in this chapter.

Why Choose Adoption?

Some of the reasons birthparents are placing their children for adoption are:

➤ They feel they are unready to be parents.

➤ They don't plan to marry but want the child to be raised by two parents, as they were.

➤ They don't want to go on welfare but can't think of another way to support the child adequately.

➤ They want to continue or launch a career and want the child to have the attention they won't be able to provide.

➤ They have other children and feel they cannot support any more.

➤ The relationship has broken up, and they want the child to be raised by two parents.

Women and men who choose to place their children for adoption are different people with different reasons for making the adoption decision. But most of them want adoptive parents who will be loving and kind and who will help the child achieve his or her potential. They want financially secure adoptive parents, and sometimes they want adoptive parents who are deeply religious—if the birthparents are also strongly religious. In other cases, religious orientation is not a major consideration to the birthparents.

Real Life Snapshots

What do birthmothers want? They want their children to be happy and loved. Here are some comments written by a birthmother:

"That day she was asleep when I told her goodbye. And that was also the day I had to sign the adoption papers. It was the hardest thing I have ever had to do. I had to remind myself that I was doing this for her, but I cried for days afterward.

"I had told my social worker that if my child wasn't adopted by my next birthday, I would take her back. But 10 days before my birthday she was placed in a home. I took that as God's sign that I had made the right choice. Six months later I received pictures and a 10-page typed letter from the adoptive parents, who agreed to send pictures of her every year.

"When people see a picture of my daughter, I get different reactions when I tell them I put her up for adoption. Most want to know more about the adoption process and I gladly share what I know. But some try to condemn me for my decision, saying I ran away from the problem. According to them, I'm cruel and don't deserve ever to have another child.

"But I made my choice. It was the one that I thought would be best for my baby and for me."

(*Written by Christa Jones, excerpted from the June 1995 issue of* Essence.)

The Difficulties of Choosing Adoption

If you think it's easy to be a pregnant woman choosing adoption today, you are very wrong. Birthparents who choose adoption often have to endure many offensive comments from people who should know better. Here are some of the most common:

➤ How can you do that? That's your own flesh and blood!

➤ Why didn't you get an abortion?

➤ I could never give my baby to strangers!

➤ What if you can't ever have another child?

➤ Are you doing it for money? Selling your baby? That's disgusting!

➤ Why don't you at least *try* raising it? You could always have the kid adopted later.

➤ Why? Don't you care at all about your baby?

➤ You made your bed, now you should lie in it.

Birthparents deal with these comments in different ways. Some hide their adoption plan, while others don't talk about it much. Some argue with the people who make such comments, by asking if *they* are willing to support the baby.

Birthparents who are married (or even divorced) who choose adoption face even more vitriol.

What about *after* the baby is placed with the adopters? How does the birthmother feel then?

Most experts agree that birthmothers do grieve this loss. Although counseling can help them deal with the issues involved, it cannot make the grief disappear. Feelings of grief usually abate as time passes; however, birthmothers often feel sad on the child's birthday, just as many people feel sad when they think about someone important but unavailable on that person's birthday. The grief and sadness is mitigated by the birthmother's belief that adoption was the right choice for the child. Studies indicate that birthmothers who are the most satisfied with the adoption decision are those who did not feel that they were pressured into it but made the choice for adoption voluntarily themselves.

Real Life Snapshots

Diane, a woman in her late twenties, learned she was pregnant even though she had used birth control. Since she decided against abortion, her coworkers assumed she'd become a single mom. But Diane assured them that adoption was her plan.

They didn't believe her. Diane was nice, smart, and had a great job! Of course she would raise the baby. Her coworkers threw a surprise baby shower and gave her many beautiful gifts for the child. They meant well, but they broke her heart. Diane went through with her adoption plan and gave the gifts to the adoptive parents.

Adoption Slanguage

Aside from direct criticism and questioning, birthparents who consider adoption often have to face implicit, unconscious put-downs in some of the terms used to describe adoption. You should avoid words that offend or annoy birthparents who are considering adoption. Consult the following for examples:

No	Yes
Gave up a baby	Placed a baby
Gave away a baby	Made an adoption plan
Put up for adoption	Chose adoption
Real parent	Birthparent
Real mother	Birthmother
Real father	Birthfather
Relinquished for adoption	Consented to adoption

It's His Baby, Too: The Birthfather's Role

In the fairly recent past, people didn't think much (if at all) about what a biological father thought when his unmarried girlfriend decided on adoption for their child. It was assumed that he didn't care or he was glad someone else would take care of "the problem." But this was not and is not now always the case, particularly as the stigma of nonmarital childbearing has plummeted. More and more birthfathers are getting involved in the decisions that affect their children.

However, there is still a clash between the widespread belief in the value of "blood" relatives and the contempt in which most people still hold unwed fathers. (Some people call unwed fathers "sperm fathers" or "sperm donors" in an attempt to belittle the biological connection.) As a result of this confusion, laws on birthfathers' rights vary drastically from one state to the next:

Adopterms

A *birthfather* is a man who, with a woman, conceives a child who is later adopted or for whom an adoption is planned. He may also be called the *biological father*.

A *putative father* is a man who is alleged to be the birthfather, usually by the birthmother. He may or may not verify that he is in fact the father.

➤ Some states have *adoption registries*, where the birthfather must register his desire to parent the child if he wishes to assert his paternal rights.

Adopterms

A *legal father* is a man who is married to the birthmother at the time of conception or birth and who must consent to the adoption even if he is not the biological father. If another man is the biological father, the agency will usually provide notice to him as well about the adoption (although his consent may not be necessary, depending on state laws).

➤ In other states, the burden of responsibility for resolving the birthfather consent issue lies with the adoption agency or attorney.

➤ In some states, birthfathers must take immediate and decisive action to claim paternity rights and block an adoption.

➤ In other states, the burden is laid on the agency or attorney to locate the birthfather and determine if he will consent to the adoption.

➤ Some states have birthfather registries, where the birthfather must register his paternity if he wishes information on the adoption. (Some states require that he be notified whether he registers or not.)

➤ If the birthmother is married, most states assume that the biological father is her husband, even if that is not true. Thus, his consent to the adoption is nearly always necessary. (Some exceptions might be if he was in prison at the time of conception or out of the country. In such cases, the birthmother might be able to convince a judge to terminate the legal father's rights without his consent. But this varies greatly from state to state.) Some adoption arrangers, if they believe the biological father is another person, will obtain the consent of the husband *and* the alleged father.

Confusing, isn't it? Read Chapter 10 for more information on state adoption laws and for a guide to the laws in your state.

Real Life Snapshots

In nearly all cases of adoption disputes, the highest court in each state is the court of last resort. However, the U.S. Supreme Court has stepped in to set some parameters on birthfather rights because constitutional issues of due process were involved.

In the case of *Stanley v. Illinois* (1972), for example, an unmarried father had lived with a woman for many years, and together they had parented their three children. After her death, the state removed the children from his custody solely because he had not been married to the mother. Stanley won custody of the children.

Several stepparent adoption cases have also made it to the Supreme Court. For example in *Quillon v. Walcott* (1978), Quillon, who was not married to his partner at any time, attempted to block the adoption of their child by the man she later married. He had never supported the child in any way, and he lost the case.

Finding the Birthfather

State laws vary a great deal on the responsibility of a *putative* (alleged) father in asserting his paternity. A few states rely on what some call the "pants-on" law: The assumption is that if a man has intercourse with a woman, he should assume that he may have made her pregnant. If he wants to know if he is to be a father, under this viewpoint, it's his responsibility to find out.

In many states, the adoption agency or attorney has an obligation to seek out the alleged father, either through phone calls, letters, or other means. If the father is unknown, the agency or attorney may publish a notice in the legal section of the newspaper (for example: "The child of Cheryl X, born on May 7, 1997, is to be adopted. If you think you may be the father of Cheryl X's child, then you must come forward within some timeframe.")

The birthmother may be uncomfortable with such advertising, but if it is required by state law, she must agree if she wants the adoption to go forth.

In some states, such as Illinois and Utah, if the birthmother says she does not know who the birthfather is, she must provide a statement explaining why she cannot identify him.

As a result, how a birthfather is regarded and treated in one state may be (and often is) very different from how he would be treated in another state. Until and unless some uniformity is created in birthfather adoption laws, this situation will continue.

About half the states have a *putative father registry*, where men who think they have fathered children can register to assert their paternity and their desire to parent the child. (See Chapter 10 for more information.) They may be notified of a pending adoption by this registration and, if they are opposed to the adoption, can take legal steps to attempt to block it.

Prebirth Consent

About a third of the states allow unwed birthfathers to consent to an adoption before the baby is born. (See Chapter 10 for more information.) If the father has signed the pre-birth consent, generally, after the child is born, the consent to the adoption is needed only from the birthmother.

Real Life Snapshots

In a very few isolated cases, birthfathers who have conceived children through rape are given control over the birthmother's adoption decision. In Wisconsin in 1992, a convicted rapist prevented a 14-year-old girl he had impregnated from placing her baby for adoption. He didn't want to give up his paternal rights. Outraged Wisconsin legislators subsequently changed the law so that the parental rights of rapists would be involuntarily terminated and birthmothers would not need the consent of the birthfather to place a child of rape for adoption.

Consent to an adoption is not required in Virginia if the child is the result of a rape *and* the rapist was convicted of the crime. Other states are attempting to pass such laws. It seems only fair, though, that in these cases the adoption decision should be the birthmother's alone.

It's important to note here that the consent of the biological father is not always necessary, although notice to him is usually required. If the man who has been named by the birthmother signs a document denying paternity, the consent of the birthmother alone may be sufficient. Again, it's very important to remember that state laws vary drastically on this and other adoption matters.

It's important that the agency or attorney and prospective adoptive parents feel confident that the alleged father *is* the father (whether he admits to paternity or not) to avoid the problem of some other man stepping forward and attempting to assert paternal rights.

For this reason, many adoption social workers or attorneys seek either consent to an adoption or a denial of paternity from any man who might be the father of the child, including any men with whom the birthmother had sexual intercourse during the timeframe that she may have become pregnant.

Proclaiming Paternity

Despite the heavy media coverage of birthfathers upsetting adoptions, most biological fathers do not protest or try to stop them. Here are a few reasons why a birthfather might assert his paternal rights:

➤ He wants to raise the child himself.

➤ He has parented the child in the past and wants a continuing relationship with the child.

➤ His parents want to raise the child and have convinced him to help them.

➤ He is angry with the birthmother and wants to exert power over her. He thinks this will force her to return to him.

➤ He wants to force the birthmother to raise the child. He assumes if he fights the adoption, she'll agree to parent.

➤ It's a macho thing—no one else should parent *his* child.

Of course, birthfathers are not always opposed to adoption, and in some cases, they may help the birthmother to locate adoptive parents, attend counseling sessions, and participate fully in the process.

International Birthparents

Many people don't think about it much, but children who are adopted from other countries did get conceived and born, in the usual way. This may sound facetious, but you'd be amazed at how many people tell me they want to adopt a child from another country so they don't have that "birthmother problem."

I know that what they mean is they don't want to fear that the birthmother might change her mind about adoption. But sometimes I wonder if they realize that there *is* a mother in this equation and that at some point she will need to be acknowledged.

Birthmothers from other countries choose adoption for their children for many of the same reasons as do birthmothers in the U.S.: they aren't ready to be parents, they don't have the financial means to raise a child, and so on. Additionally, many countries still retain strong cultural biases against nonmarital births; some birthmothers believe (rightly) that they and their children would be stigmatized if they became single parents.

For more information about adopting children of other countries, see Chapter 11.

Adoptinfo

OH.

If a pregnant woman and a man both agree that he is the father of her child, this is usually assumed to be true; however, the only definitive proof is DNA paternity testing. The problem with paternity testing is timing: Testing cannot be performed safely until the baby is born, and then it takes six days to six weeks or more before results are received. Most birthmothers do not want to delay placement of the baby while waiting for paternity tests.

Testing delays and hassles also mean that many adoptive families do not request paternity testing at all. As a result, paternity testing is usually done only if there is a challenge to paternity or there is some other legal reason for the test.

The Least You Need to Know

➤ Society makes it hard for most birthparents to choose adoption for their babies.

➤ Most birthmothers who choose adoption are over 17 and unmarried, but some are older, younger, married, or divorced.

➤ Most birthmothers who choose adoption are looking for safe, stable, happy homes for their children.

➤ Birthfather rights vary from state to state.

➤ Birthmothers from other countries choose adoption for many of the same reasons as birthmothers in the U.S.

Gathering Information

Diane and Jim wanted to adopt, but they had no idea where to begin. Then they read in the newspaper that a local adoptive parent group would be holding an information session. They called and were urged to attend—and they did. Speaking at this meeting were social workers from three different agencies, an adoption attorney, and also several parents who talked about adopting babies and older children. A birthmother talked about her decision to place her child for adoption. Even an adopted adult talked about growing up adopted! There was plenty to absorb and think about.

Louisa had many questions about adoption, but she didn't feel comfortable bringing them up in a group session. She found a "warmline" phone number sponsored by a parent group. The "warmline lady" was really helpful and nice. She couldn't answer a few questions but did direct Louisa to someone who could.

Tom wanted some information about adoption agencies, so he decided to search the Internet. He found five agencies that sounded like possible "candidates" for him and his wife, and he sent the agencies e-mail requests for more information.

Information sources, whether they are parent groups, specialized experts, or online sources, can all provide you with the most current adoption and parenting information. In this chapter, I'll show you the best local, regional, and national information sources available.

Been There, Done That: Adoptive Parent Groups

> **Familybuilding Tips**
> Many people join more than one adoptive parent group. They may decide to become members of one group because of the great newsletter it produces—but they live too far away to attend meetings regularly. So they then join a local group to fulfill the need for face to face interaction. You, too, may decide that more than one group in your area can meet your needs.

There are hundreds of active adoptive parent groups nationwide; some are new and some are well-established. Some are very large and well-organized, such as Adoptive Families of America in St. Paul (the largest group in the U.S.) or the Adoptive Parents Committee in New York, which has many chapters throughout the state. Another major group is the North American Council on Adoptable Children (NACAC), which specializes in the adoption of children with special needs. Others are tiny groups comprised of as few as 20 or 30 people who enjoy getting together and sharing information.

Some adoptive parent groups cater to specific interests. Some concentrate on U.S. (also called *domestic*) adoption; others center on intercountry adoption. Some cater to families of specific ethnic or religious groups. Some concentrate on infant adoption, while others focus on older child adoptions. Other groups—particularly the large ones—provide information on all adoption options. Some groups are politically active and lobby for changes to state and federal adoption laws, while others don't see that as part of their mission.

For more information about adoptive parent groups, see Appendix E.

Join the Group

Why re-invent the wheel? Believe it or not, almost any kind of adoption problem that you encounter has been faced by someone else. And almost any fear that looms paramount in your mind has been previously vanquished by another person. By joining an adoptive parent group, you stand to gain from the experience of others.

Here are just a few of the advantages of joining a group:

➤ A chance to learn the latest information

➤ An opportunity to meet people who have adopted—and to see their children

➤ A chance to meet social workers or attorneys and ask questions

➤ A feeling of camaraderie and support that you can't duplicate elsewhere

➤ Empathy and understanding for what you need

Of course, it's important to connect with a group that meets your needs—or is as close to what you need as possible. So, for example, if you want to adopt a child from China and a nearby parent group is made up solely of people who have adopted children in the U.S., this group won't really be able to help you much. (They *can* empathize with your desire to adopt, the aggravation of waiting for your child, and so forth, so don't necessarily rule them out.) What you really need is to associate with others adopting children from other countries, especially from China.

> **Adopterms**
> An *adoptive parent group* (sometimes called an *adoptive parent support group*) is a group of people who meet to discuss issues related to adoption. Often these groups can be very helpful to people who are trying to adopt a child.

On the other hand, if you want to adopt an infant through an attorney in the U.S. and have no interest in intercountry adoption, a group focusing on adopting Chinese children would not be what you really need.

Finding a Group That's Right for You

So how do you find an adoptive parent group anyway? And, once you've found one, how do you know if it's right for you?

Here are some ways that others have located parent groups:

➤ Call Adoptive Families of America (AFA) at 800-372-3300 or write to them at: AFA, 2309 Como Ave., St. Paul, MN 55108. They can put you in touch with groups near you. They can also answer many general questions about adoption.

➤ Ask the National Council For Adoption (NCFA) if they can recommend a group in your area. Call them at 202-328-1200, or write to them at: 1930 Seventeenth St. NW, Washington, DC 20009.

> **Familybuilding Tips**
> Both the National Council For Adoption (NCFA) and the Adoptive Families of America (AFA) offer informational packets for wannabe adopters. The NCFA hotline package is free; call them at 202-328-1200 to order. The AFA information package is $4.95; call them at 800-372-3300 to order.

➤ Ask your local RESOLVE group for recommendations. RESOLVE is a national group for people seeking help with infertility and also provides information on adoption. If you don't know of a local group, call RESOLVE at their main office, 617-623-0744, or write to them at RESOLVE, Inc., 1310 Broadway, Somerville, MA 02144-1731.

Adoption Alert
The downside of joining an adoptive parent group is that you may not always agree with other members' opinions. For example, one person may tell you that a particular adoption attorney should be avoided; others may like this attorney. It's also true that some groups are managed by an adoption agency or attorney, so their views prevail. So as you gather information, don't be overly reliant on what any one person (or couple) says, and don't assume that what another person thinks or feels is how you would or should think or feel.

➤ Ask your clergyperson.

➤ Ask your doctor.

➤ Call the nearest state adoption office and ask the state or county social workers if they know of a group.

➤ Look in the Yellow Pages of your phone book under "Adoption." Some larger groups advertise there.

➤ Ask local adoption agencies for recommendations. (Note, however, that some agencies run their own parent groups for parents who have adopted through their agency. I recommend you start with a group of members who have adopted through a variety of sources instead.)

➤ Check the newspaper for listings of groups that meet regularly. (If you can't find such a list, call the newspaper and ask if and when they include this information.)

➤ Ask hospital social workers at local hospitals (or within a 50-mile radius) if they know of any parent groups. (Hospital social workers often become involved, if only peripherally, in infant adoptions.)

➤ Check Appendix E in this book.

Networking Works

As you learn more about adoption, you may be very surprised to learn that there are people in your own backyard who are knowledgeable about adoption. Some of your own friends may have very helpful hints on how to handle the adoption process.

Some local sources you could contact are your own physicians (and nurses) and social workers who work at local agencies or for the state or county public agency. Do keep in mind, however, that most government (public) social workers who work in the field of adoption concentrate on the placement of older children or children with special needs. So if you want to adopt a healthy infant, they may or may not be aware of the latest information on healthy infants. By the same token, social workers and attorneys who concentrate on infant and international adoptions may be unable to advise you about adopting an older child from the foster care system.

Keep in mind, however, that if you want to talk to a person about very basic "how-to-adopt" information, it's often best to ask parent groups or adoption agencies rather than national experts. Part of the reason is that state laws differ so radically (and change so frequently) that it's very hard for any national group to advise you on the situation in your state.

Another reason is that it's a time-waster for experts within national groups to provide very basic information that you could obtain locally. But if you have a specific question or problem—for example, related to a specific health problem or some other unique issue—then national experts are often a good resource. Just don't assume that someone who is an expert on one aspect of adoption (say, health or legal issues) also knows everything there is to know about other adoption topics.

Hot Type

If you want to learn even more about adoption, then read, read, read! There are many good (and some mediocre) books on adoption. There are also magazines and newsletters that can help. But as with parent groups, you may disagree or feel unsure about some of the things you read. Opinions in adoption vary and are sometimes controversial. Read carefully and skeptically, and discard positions that conflict with your values or do not pass the common sense test.

Many adoption books are available in the stacks of your local library. But the bad news is that many libraries keep books just about forever. And a book that purports to tell you the latest about adoption—and was published in 1976—is not going to help you. Stick with books published at least in this decade, if not this year or last year. For the absolutely newest books on adoption, check your bookstore.

Another good idea is to peruse the catalog offered by Tapestry Books. This mail-order company specializes in adoption books and sells virtually every adoption book you could ever want. Call Tapestry for a free catalog at 1-800-765-2367.

> **Familybuilding Tips**
>
> Let's say you've identified four or five books you need, but you can't afford them all or you aren't really sure you want them all. If the books are a year old or more, ask your reference librarian to order them through Interlibrary Loan. Through this system, your librarian can obtain books from libraries in other towns (or even other cities or states).
>
> One additional hint: Since you're talking to the reference librarian anyway, ask if there's any information on adoption in the vertical files. These are folders on a variety of topics, and they often contain pamphlets, newspaper clippings, and other information.

You can also order books online through Amazon Books. Check out their Web site at http://www.amazon.com. Barnes & Noble bookstores also offer an online store on America Online. Both sites say that they offer virtually any book in print.

There are also a few books and newsletters that, while not available in stores or libraries, may be well worth a special order. See Appendix H for a listing of adoption publications.

Periodically, popular general and women's magazines publish articles on adoption that may be helpful to you—although you should watch out for the adoption horror stories that continue to predominate in much of the media.

Most parent groups produce some sort of newsletter, whether it's a 2-pager with a lot of typos or a slick 8–10-page production. There are also specialty newsletters, on intercountry adoption, transracial adoption, and others.

Don't forget that many adoption agencies and some attorneys publish their own brochures and booklets on adoption. Each time you contact an adoption professional, ask if he or she has any written material to send you.

Conference Calls

Some of the larger adoption support groups offer annual conferences, where you have the opportunity to listen to speakers, peruse the latest adoption books, and meet other people seeking to adopt. These are usually very uplifting and positive experiences. And, if a group in your area—or even in your state—offers an annual conference, I recommend that you attend.

Occasionally, hospitals or other organizations offer seminars on how to adopt a child. I attended such a seminar in my area several years ago and found it very well organized and informative. You might try contacting the major hospitals in your area and asking the public relations director if they plan to offer any seminars on adopting a child. Who knows? You might inspire them to create such a program!

Familybuilding Tips
Organize the material you amass. It's far too easy to misplace something important. Put all your brochures, pamphlets, and so on in one or two big boxes so you know where they are when you need them. You might also consider arranging them in legal-sized folders.

Buy a notebook to keep track of information you obtain during phone calls. When you connect with an adoption professional, write down the date, who you talked to, and a summary of what was said. Make notes during the phone conversation, and afterwards jot down any questions you may have or opinions you may have formed about the agency.

Cyberadoption: The Internet and Online Sources

As you can probably guess, adoption is a hot topic online. Here are a few of the services you can find when you search the Internet and the World Wide Web:

➤ Web sites maintained by individuals or organizations (adoption agencies or attorneys; new adoptive parents that want to share what they know; organizations that want to change state adoption laws; people who are trying to search for their birthparents)

➤ Newsgroups maintained by special-interest groups (on topics related to adoption, infertility, and parenting/family issues)

➤ Experts or organizations whose Web sites enable you to e-mail them with questions or comments

➤ Subscription list services maintained by special-interest groups

➤ Chat groups or special conferences on adoption

➤ Actual photos of children who need families

➤ Advertisements from lawyers and other adoption groups

➤ Editorials and news articles related to adoption

➤ Self-help information for adoptive parents, adoptees, or birthparents

Familybuilding Tips

My favorite private service is the Adoption Forum on America Online (AOL). It includes information from adoptive parents and adopted adults, sections where people may leave messages, regularly scheduled live "chats," and a comprehensive software library.

If you are an AOL subscriber, you can type the keyword "adoption" to be connected to the Forum.

Cyberadopting on the Internet

There are various ways you can find adoption-related material on the Internet. One way is to use a search engine (a program that browses for Web sites) and try the keyword "adoption." Often, this will find you hundreds of possible Web sites to wade through (including scads of sites related to the "adoption" of an interesting array of animals—dogs, cats, lemurs, and so forth. The animal sites are readily identifiable and can be easily ignored—unless you also want a pet!).

There are also several specific Web sites you may wish to check out:

➤ The National Adoption Information Clearinghouse (NAIC) at http://www.calib.com/naic/ maintains a site that offers some full-text articles.

➤ One new entry is adoption.com, a site that concentrates rather heavily on the needs and interests of adoptive parents and prospective adoptive parents. Its address is http://www.adoption.com. This site covers both international and U.S. adoption.

➤ Two other sites that impressed me with the depth and breadth of information were these: http://www.adopting.org and http://wwwiNet.net/adopt/. Both sites have many links to a broad array of other sites. (You could spend hours surfing through this information and completely lose track of time. I know. I have.) The State Department also has Web sites for countries from where children are adopted.

There is also a great deal of information out there in cyberspace for adoptees who are searching for birthparents. (For more information on adults searching for birthparents, read Part 5.)

There are also several newsgroups on the Internet that concentrate on adoption and adoption issues; as of this writing, the primary ones are alt.adoption and alt.agency. You can read the messages and post your own, if you like.

One amazing and exciting aspect of the Internet is that some sites actually post photographs of waiting children in the U.S. and other countries. So your computer can "show" you who your future child might be! Very heady stuff.

There are a variety of adoption e-mail lists you can subscribe to, merely by sending the message "subscribe" to the appropriate address. For example, aft-list@mlists.nombas.com is a list for people interested in special-needs children (such as those with ADHD, fetal alcohol syndrome, cerebral palsy, and other problems).

Some lists generate hundreds of messages in days and are unwieldy for most of us, but you can't really tell until you try a list out. If you find you don't like a list, you can "unsubscribe."

Evaluating Sites

As you surf the Net, remember that all Web sites present a particular agenda or point of view, whether they are run by individuals, agencies, or organizations. Many people use the Net to promote their own ideas about how adoption should be.

You won't always agree with everything that is said on many of the sites you find. Sometimes people can become heated in their differences, and sometimes people state their own opinions as if they were facts. Here are a few questions to ask yourself as you cruise through Web sites or user newsgroups:

➤ What does the purpose of this site seem to be? To arouse viewers to action, to provide information, to sell you a product, to do something else?

➤ Can you determine how current the information is? It's a normal tendency to assume that anything posted on the Internet is current. This may not be true.

➤ Who appear to be the target viewers? Adoptees, adoptive parents, birthparents, all of the above?

➤ Who is providing this information? An agency, an attorney, an organization, an individual? The harder this is to determine, the more wary of the information you should be.

➤ If this site is linked to others, what are the other sites like? Remember "birds of a feather flock together." Good guys usually hang out with other good guys. And vice versa.

➤ Don't believe everything you read on the Internet. Keep your watchful eye and skeptical mind in high gear.

As long as you maintain some healthy skepticism about the material you come across on the Internet, you will probably be quite dazzled by the wealth of information you find.

There's a great deal of information available out there for people who want to adopt and who are willing to do their homework. Information from people you know; magazines, newsletters and books; adoption agency and attorney experts; and, of course, the ubiquitous cyberspace community is all available to you. You'll have to do some weeding and your own independent thinking, but there has never been a better time for gathering the information you need to adopt a child.

Adoption Alert
If you do decide to post questions and opinions online, always remember that what you write can be read by whomever "logs on." Nor does it "scroll off": Material is often saved for years.

Also, be careful when sending electronic mail. You don't have control over to whom your mail is forwarded or shown. So even with e-mail, be careful what you say about your family or private life.

The Least You Need to Know

➤ Adoptive parent groups can offer information as well as support.

➤ Look for expert sources in your own "back yard."

➤ Many books, magazines, and newsletters specialize in adoption issues.

➤ Cyberspace is an exciting new adoption resource.

Part 2
What Are Your Options?

This part tells you about the "adoption arrangers"—the agencies and lawyers who can help you adopt a child. It explains the rules of U.S. and international adoptions, and what you can do to afford an adoption. There's also an important chapter on screening out incompetent or unethical adoption arrangers. They're few and far between, but they're out there.

Don't be like some people and spend years "flying blind," wasting time and a lot of money. When it comes to adoption, knowledge is most definitely power.

The Adoption Arrangers

Some people think the only acceptable way to adopt a child is to go through a traditional adoption agency. That's what Tom and Lisa did: They applied to a local agency that had been in business for a hundred years. The agency said the wait would be three years, but Tom and Lisa felt that was reasonable.

Sarah and Bill decided to adopt through an agency, too, but they felt that the New Age Agency, which just opened six months ago and promised very short waits, would be the right answer for them. They applied and were quickly accepted.

Lori wanted to adopt, but because she was single, several agencies turned her down. She'd heard about private adoption and decided to hire a lawyer who handled adoptions instead.

This chapter is about the "adoption arrangers": the agencies and attorneys who make adoptions a reality.

The Facts on Adoption Agencies

As I've mentioned earlier, there are public and private adoption agencies. The public agencies are those that are run by state or county governments; these agencies usually deal with foster children who were removed from the homes of their biological parents or who were abandoned by their birthparents. Most public agencies call themselves the Department of Social Services or something similar.

In contrast, private agencies are licensed by the state to arrange adoptions. They are usually run by someone with an advanced degree in social work or psychology. Once adoption agencies are licensed, they manage their own organizations. If a complaint is made, however, and the state licensing officials determine the agency has behaved improperly, the state may choose to take away the agency's license.

State government social service agencies don't charge adoption fees because they are funded from federal and state tax dollars. Private agencies do charge fees, and sometimes these fees can be quite substantial—over $20,000 or more. However, there are enormous differences among agencies in fees they charge, the children they place, and other issues.

Adopterms

Public agencies are run by state or county governments; these agencies usually deal with foster children. *Private agencies* are licensed by the state to arrange adoptions and are usually run by someone with an advanced degree in social work or psychology.

Some agencies place children only within their county or state, while others actively engage in placing children in many areas of the country or even outside the U.S. Some adoption arrangers place U.S.–born children, while others concentrate on placing children from other countries. Sometimes agencies handle both U.S. and intercountry adoption, although they usually specialize in one or the other.

If you're thinking about adopting a child from the U.S., there are hundreds of agencies to choose from. If you are interested in international adoption, many agencies concentrate on one country or one area; for example, as of this writing, adoptions from China and Russia are very popular, and some agencies are centering on orphans from these countries. However, the laws surrounding international adoption are very changeable, so if you are interested in an international adoption, be sure to read Chapter 11.

There are religious-based (*sectarian*) agencies, such as Catholic Social Services, Jewish Social Services, LDS Social Services, and so on. There are also *non-sectarian* agencies for whom religion is not a pivotal matter.

Some agencies specialize in placing children with special needs, while others concentrate on placing mostly infants who are healthy. (If an infant is born not healthy, these agencies may give the child to a state agency or another agency, unless one of their approved families will adopt the child.)

> **Adopterms**
> *Sectarian* agencies specialize in helping families with particular religious interests although they may also work with families of other religions. *Non-sectarian* agencies do not have a particular religious orientation.

Why Use an Agency?

Many people believe that the right path to adoption starts when you walk through the door of an adoption agency. Here are some reasons why many people choose to adopt through agencies:

> ➤ They think agency adoptions are safer.
> ➤ They believe the only valid adoptions are performed by agencies. (In reality this is not true.)
> ➤ Their friends have adopted through agencies.
> ➤ They're worried that in a non-agency adoption, the birthmother might change her mind and they'll lose all fees paid.
> ➤ They like the idea of the birthmother receiving counseling through the agency.

Finding an Agency

How do you locate a reputable and competent adoption agency? Many people merely pick up the Yellow Pages and start dialing every number listed under "Adoption." Not a good idea. The agency with the splashiest advertisement isn't necessarily the best one. (Although it might be.)

> **Adoption Alert**
> In the past, agency adoptions were generally safer because agencies did not place children with families until and unless the birthparent rights were terminated and the agency had taken custody. Today, however, some agencies are involved in *direct placement* adoptions, in which a birthmother chooses the adoptive family. In these adoptions, if the birthmother changes her mind about adoption, the adoptive parents lose the child and might also lose some of the fees they've already paid.
>
> For this reason, it's important to ask the agency *what* happens if an adoption falls through.

Adoption Alert

Snob appeal works in many places, even sometimes in adoption. Some people believe that if they pay very high fees, they'll have a fast, problem-free adoption. Affluent people may pay fees of $35,000 and more due to these beliefs.

But here's the thing: You don't get a better baby from the expensive agency. In fact, media reports over the past few years have documented that some very high-priced agencies skimped on many services.

This does not, of course, mean that the expensive agency is a bad guy. But you have to ask yourself what you're really getting for your money.

So how do you find a good adoption agency? That depends on what you're looking for. If you want to adopt a child from another country, the agency that mostly handles U.S. adoptions may not be good for you. And vice versa. It's also true that if you want to adopt a toddler or an older child, the agency that specializes in newborns is the wrong one for you.

You need to research what agencies are available in and out of your state and narrow them down to the organizations that you feel best suit your needs.

Here's how to track down reputable agencies:

1. Ask your local adoptive parent group (see Chapter 5 and Appendix E) for names of reputable agencies that specialize in U.S. or international adoptions.

2. Ask your friends and relatives for names of good agencies.

3. Call up the state social services department and ask if they have had any complaints about any agencies. Ask for names.

4. Ask your doctor for names of experienced agencies.

5. Call a social worker at the agency and ask brief questions about the agency. Are they accepting applications? Do they place mostly infants or older children? From the U.S. or other countries? Do not expect her to be instantly available or responsive: She could be in the midst of a crisis when you call. Be sure to ask if now (when you call) is a convenient time to ask a few quick questions.

6. Ask the agency for references of families they have worked with. Understand that only names of happy adopters will be provided, but at least you can obtain some inside information from such references.

Scoping Out an Agency

Once you've located a list of potential agencies, you should screen each one. Here are the questions you should ask:

1. Ask the agency if it offers a free orientation you can attend. Go and ask questions.

2. Ask for brochures and literature.

3. Ask how long the agency has been in business. It need not be 50+ years, but if it opened last week be careful. New agencies may need applicants; they also don't have track records and often charge higher fees. On the other hand, old agencies may be more stodgy and may have longer waits. But, old agencies are also more likely to still be in business if you encounter a problem later on.

4. Ask the agency director if he or she started the agency. If so, why? Many agencies were launched by adoptive parents and some by adopted adults. Understanding the motivation for creating the agency may help you choose which agency (if any) to sign up with.

5. Ask the agency how many children it placed last year and the year before. Ask if the number of placements this year will be roughly the same.

6. Ask how long most potential adoptive parents have to wait before their home study (screening) is done.

Familybuilding Tips
One question to ask when choosing an adoption agency is whether or not the agency is affiliated with a larger "parent" organization, preferably one with a track record. Many newer, smaller adoption agencies have sprung up in the past three to five years, and some are essentially "kitchen tabletop" operations.

There's no inherent protection in dealing with a large agency, nor are you invariably at risk by dealing with a stand-alone adoption agency. Still, always find out what kind of organization you are dealing with before you sign up.

7. Find out if the agency has any limiting criteria for adopters: upper age limits, marital status, and so on.

8. Ask about the average wait for a placement. It is often possible to find an agency that will work with you and place a child with you in a time frame that *you* think is reasonable. (Unless you want the baby tomorrow. In that case, forget it.) Note: Most agencies fudge on this one, adding an extra six months to a year (at least) to the time it normally takes to arrange a placement.

9. Find out if the agency has a program to let birthmothers choose parents. This may work to your advantage.

10. Ask if the agency provides counseling for birthmothers. What does the agency do if the birthmother refuses counseling?

11. Ask if the agency provides funds for food or shelter for the birthmother. If so, will these costs or other expenses be passed on to you in addition to the fees charged by the agency? Or are these expenses included in the basic fees you will pay? Find out.

Familybuilding Tips
How can you estimate how long the wait will be at any given agency? One way is to ask the agency when it could do your home study, assuming you applied today. Add about a year to the time frame you get. For example, if the agency can do your home study in six months, then it could probably place a child with you in about a year and a half. Why? Because most agencies don't want to place a child with someone whose home study is over a year old.

Adopterms
An *open adoption* is an adoption in which there is an exchange of identities between the adopting parents and the birthparents. They may or may not decide to have a continuing relationship. Often the agency or attorney creates a contract that spells out what is expected of each side. Note: Ask the agency how they define open adoption.

12. Ask if the agency involves the birthmother's parents in the planning. Studies have revealed that if the birthmother's parents are supportive, the outcome is better for all concerned. For example, they will not be shocked to learn that the newborn baby is to be adopted and make last-minute attempts to dissuade the birthmother from adoption. In addition, the birthparents' parents can provide medical information about themselves regarding possible inherited conditions.

13. Find out how the agency obtains medical information on the children.

14. Ask how the agency defines "special needs" in a child. (Refer to Chapter 3.)

15. If the agency specializes in U.S. adoptions, find out its policy on working with birthfathers.

16. Ask if the agency arranges *open adoptions*, and how it defines open adoptions. Do birthmothers get to choose adoptive parents? If so, how? Do birthmothers usually meet prospective adoptive parents? What do they think are the main benefits and disadvantages to open adoption? (See Chapter 16 for more information on open adoptions.)

17. If the agency arranges intercountry adoptions, has anyone on the staff traveled to the other country and visited the orphanages there?

18. Find out what fees the agency charges and when they are payable. Is there one fee, or are there separate fees for different services? If there are separate fees, at what points are they due? Try to determine at least a range of the total fees you might expect to pay.

19. Ask what they think is the most important thing to know about the agency. The answer to this question can sometimes be very revealing.

20. Ask if there is anything that you haven't asked that is important to know. Wait for the person to think and respond. Listen.

Real Life Snapshots

I knew a woman who had extremely good intentions in her desire to open an adoption agency. She wanted all adoptions to be nearly free and she had recruited social workers and others to work at very low fees.

But she hit a snag when she tried to create a business plan required by the state before she could obtain a license. She came up with a board of directors and met most of the requirements. However, she just couldn't put together a workable annual budget. She couldn't figure out how to do adoptions for free—and still pay the phone, electric, and other bills. Her plan fell through, but sometimes marginal agencies do obtain licenses and they cannot handle the business side of the equation. This is why it's important for you and also the agency to realize: Adoption is a business.

Screening an Agency

Finally, make sure you screen the agency carefully. No matter what good things you may have heard about an agency, people change and policies change, and the agency that was aboveboard last year may now have problems from taking on too many adoption applicants, problems that it's now trying to bury with cash flow. Protect yourself.

This does not mean that I think most agencies are "bad." In my view, only a very small number of agencies will knowingly rip you off. There is a slightly greater number of agencies that are incompetent at either adoption practice or at dealing in the business world. Since adoption represents a considerable investment of your time and money, it's well worth it to be careful.

Here are some effective screening questions to ask the adoption agency:

1. Does it have a board of directors? Ask for a list of board members.

2. Is it non-profit? This is no guarantee of "purity," but in adoption, a non-profit adoption agency is preferable. Ask if it is a 501(c)(3) corporation. This means it is registered with the state and also the IRS as a non-profit organization.

3. Does it produce an annual report? Ask to see the last one.

4. Does its staff have child welfare training—degrees in social work, psychology, or counseling?

5. Does it provide a contract to its adoptive family applicants? Ask to see a standard contract.

6. How large is the staff? If there are only one or two people in the agency, this could mean that it is understaffed or that it is a startup agency. Find out.

7. What will the agency do if a family adopts a child and the child turns out to have unexpected problems? If the answer is "None of our children ever have problems," or "God helps all our families cope with any problem," they are probably in denial. Problems occasionally happen, and the agency should be willing to assist you within a reasonable time after the adoption. (If you adopt a baby and he then becomes a problem as a 16-year-old adolescent, the agency probably couldn't predict this!)

8. Does the agency have a business manager or accountant who handles its financial affairs? Remember, *adoption is a business*.

9. Call the local Better Business Bureau and find out if anyone has complained about the agency. Also call the state adoption office, usually located in the capital of your state. (See Appendix D for listings of public social services offices in each state.)

10. Don't be afraid to ask these questions and others that you may think of! You could save yourself thousands of dollars and untold heartache by just being a little careful.

Signs of an A+ Agency

Although it's certainly not foolproof, there are some indications that an agency may be "good," meaning that it behaves ethically and honorably to both adopters and birthparents. Here are a few signs that an agency may be one you should consider:

➤ The agency brings previous adopters and birthparents to a meeting where you can ask questions.

➤ Social workers and staff seem to know and understand their roles.

➤ No complaints have been made to the state or Better Business Bureaus against the agency. Keep in mind, however, that even a good agency may have been complained about for causes that the average person might find silly or unreasonable. So find out the nature of the complaint.

➤ The agency hasn't been sued more than once or twice. (Even a good agency can be sued. These are litigious times. Find out the reason for the lawsuit.)

➤ The agency provides an explanation of its fees.

➤ The agency doesn't demand five figures ($10,000) or more right away.

Of course, there are also indications that an agency should not be trusted. I'll cover adoption scams in Chapter 9.

State Government Agencies

As mentioned earlier, state agencies primarily place foster children for adoption when their biological parents' rights are terminated (or willingly given up). The children may have been physically or sexually abused, neglected, or abandoned. Their biological parents may have had problems with drug or alcohol abuse or mental illness.

As with private agencies, there are advantages and disadvantages to adopting through a government (public) agency. Here are some key advantages:

➤ The adoption should be free of charge or nearly free because it is supported by tax dollars.

➤ The biological parental rights are clearly terminated.

➤ The child may be able to retain public medical insurance, even after adoption. (Medicaid)

➤ The child may be eligible for a monthly subsidy. (A money payment. Don't factor that out. It might help a lot.)

The primary disadvantages are:

➤ The wait may be very long.

➤ There may be extensive parental classes that are required.

➤ The child may need therapy to deal with the aftereffects of abuse.

➤ The child may need treatment for a medical condition.

➤ It may be difficult to obtain the adoption subsidy.

➤ You may need to apply a lot of pressure to workers to give you referrals to children. The reason for this is that government social workers work in a bureaucracy and sometimes are overburdened with details and paperwork. They need to know that you are very eager to adopt.

What You Need to Know

When a social worker is considering you for a particular child, she should give you general information about the child's background and problems. Most social workers are very forthcoming with this information, although it is illegal for them violate the confidentiality of the biological family.

If you are considering adopting a child through the state or county agency, you should know the following:

➤ Many foster children have received very poor (or no) medical care.

➤ Foster children often have an intense desire for a family of their own. Possibly yours!

➤ Some foster children are very resilient.

Adoption Alert
Studies have documented that many foster children receive abysmal medical care or no medical care at all. This may be because they get moved around a lot or because their medical records don't follow them.

Thus the medical information on a child may be outdated or non-existent. Find out when the child's last complete medical examination was, and have the child checked before you adopt.

Confidentiality is not an excuse to prevent you from seeing state case files. Insist on seeing the child's records. Names of birthparents or other identifying data can be blanked out. Ask about any discrepancies, omissions, or problems that you see.

➤ Abuse is not always documented, so some past incidents may not be in the child's record.

➤ It will take time for the child to adjust to a new family—the older the child, the longer the time needed.

➤ You can turn a child's life around. And change your own life, too.

➤ The child may begin to act up when he or she starts to feel comfortable with you. (It's a test, only a test.)

Also, know that if you have an approved home study, you may be able to adopt a child from another state government agency. It certainly is no easy process, but it can and has been done. A New Hampshire woman, Carole Huxel, and her husband are adopting several children from the foster care system in California. You can't get much further away from New Hampshire than California!

"Make sure you mention that they have *no* attachment disorders or mental instability or any irregular or deviant behavior at all," said Huxel of her children. "Other than one child's minor cerebral palsy and developmental delay, the kids are perfectly normal and delightful. They're glad to be here, happy in school, and in day to day life, [and there were] no sobbing hysterics over leaving the foster home."

Inside Info on Lawyers

Adopterms
An *independent, private,* or *direct placement adoption* refers to an adoption that is arranged through private individuals, attorneys, or adoption facilitators, rather than adoption agencies.

When you arrange an adoption yourself or through an attorney (or an adoption "facilitator" in some states), this is called *independent adoption* or *private adoption*. Some people also call it *direct placement* adoption.

There are good lawyers and bad lawyers, just as there are good agencies and bad agencies. But for some reason, many people associate lawyers with the bad guys, and there are some who still think that attorney-arranged adoptions are "black market adoptions." If the attorney is following the state law, an adoption is thoroughly legal.

Here are some reasons why some people adopt privately:

➤ They think they can adopt faster.

➤ They want more control over the process than they think an agency will give.

➤ The adoption agencies won't accept them—or they think that they won't.

➤ Their friends have adopted privately.

➤ They want first-hand contact with birthparents (although adoptions through attorneys may be confidential-in some states).

➤ There are no agencies in their area, and they don't wish to deal with an arranger not in their area.

Adoption, Esq.

As with adoption agencies, many people seek adoption lawyers by looking in the Yellow Pages. Bad idea. Why? Because some attorneys advertise under "Adoption," but they have little experience in this field. Or, they handle mostly stepparent adoptions, which are very different (and much easier) than nonrelative adoptions. Some good adoption attorneys don't even believe in advertising at all, so you'll miss them if you dedicate yourself solely to a phonebook search.

So how do you find a good lawyer? I'm glad you asked . . .

1. Ask your local adoptive parent group for names.

2. Get a list of adoption attorneys from the American Academy of Adoption Attorneys.

3. Find out which judges finalize adoptions. Ask them (or their staff) for names of reputable adoption attorneys.

4. Ask your family and friends for names of adoption attorneys. Make it clear that you want experienced adoption lawyers.

Adopterms

A *black market adoption* refers to an adoption that is arranged outside the law, and usually involves very large sums of money paid to an attorney, agency worker, or other individual.

A *gray market adoption* is a term that some people use to connote an adoption that is not quite "on the level," and again is often used in association with non-agency adoptions. But the reality is that an adoption is either legal or it is illegal.

Familybuilding Tips

Can you adopt faster through a lawyer? You can. If you are very active in identifying a birthmother or if your attorney may arrange matches in your state. The reason is that pregnant women who seek adopting parents for their children are usually in their second or even third trimester. So the wait may be just a few months.

There is no guarantee that non-agency adoption is faster, however. A lot depends on you and how picky you are.

5. Ask your physician (or a local gynecologist or pediatrician) for the names of adoption lawyers.

6. Ask your friends to ask their doctors for names of adoption lawyers.

7. Call all the possible candidates and find out how many adoptions each has handled. fewer than 10 per year is not enough.

8. Zero in on attorneys who specialize in adoption or who primarily work on adoptions.

Ask Questions!

Just as I urged you to check out adoption agencies, you should also check on adoption attorneys. You need an attorney who is experienced, ethical, and competent. You also need someone you can get along with. Follow your instincts and work with a lawyer whom you feel comfortable with.

Adoption Alert

What an attorney can do for wannabe adopters varies from state to state. In some states, people who wish to adopt must "find" the birthmother. They then notify the attorney and she starts the adoption process. In other states, birthmothers go directly to lawyers and are matched with prospective parents.

Some people live in one state and adopt a child from another state. In such cases, the Interstate Compact on the Placement of Children (a sort of treaty between states) is followed, and the social services department in each state signs off that their state laws have been complied with.

Here are some questions to ask an attorney whom you are thinking of working with:

1. Do you specialize in adoptions or concentrate heavily on adoptions? What percentage of your business is adoptions?

2. Are you a member of any professional organizations related to adoption? (Such as the American Academy of Adoption Attorneys in Washington, DC? Or a state adoption attorney organization or local adoptive parent groups?)

3. Have you participated in any state legislation on adoption? (Many times, experienced attorneys involve themselves in adoption law.)

4. When you receive adoption fees, do you place them in escrow in the bank until a birthmother match has been made? (The wrong answer would be that the money is put in a Swiss bank account!)

5. If paying birthmother expenses is lawful in your state, do you receive receipts from the birthmother for expenses she incurs, such as rent, electricity, doctor bills, and so on?

6. Have you ever been sued by an adoptive parent or birthparent? If so, what happened?

7. Have any of your adoptions been overturned? If so, what happened?

8. Why do you do adoptions?

9. What is the most important thing to know about you in relation to adoption?

10. What services do you provide to birthparents?

11. What services do you provide to adoptive parents?

12. What are your fees? What does that include?

13. What do you expect from us?

14. What happens if an adoption has been arranged but the birthparents change their minds?

15. What do you think of *adoption cancellation insurance*, to protect us if the birthmother changes her mind about adoption?

Checking Behind the Scenes

Here are some further screening actions that you should take. (For more information on adopting through attorneys, see Chapter 9.)

➤ Check with the local Better Business Bureau and see if they have had any complaints about the attorney.

➤ Check with the state Bar Association, usually located in the capital city of the state.

➤ Check with the adoption unit at the state social services department.

➤ Check with adoptive parent groups in the area.

➤ If possible, ask other attorneys this question: If they wanted to adopt, would they hire this person? (They may not wish to give you details, but a "no" or silence is revealing.)

Adopterms

One relatively new invention that has made non-agency adoption seem a whole lot safer is *adoption cancellation insurance*, a new form of insurance whose intent is to protect your money if the adoption falls through.

Some attorneys disapprove of adoption cancellation insurance, while others think it's a good idea. Before rushing out to sign on the dotted line, ask your lawyer what she thinks.

For further information, call 800-833-7337.

The Least You Need to Know

➤ Agencies and attorneys should be screened before you sign on the dotted line.

➤ Don't assume a more expensive adoption arranger is good or bad. Get more info.

➤ Adoption is a business for adoption arrangers. Agencies and attorneys should be kindhearted, but they should also be able to manage a business.

➤ When screening agencies or lawyers, if you have a question, ask it! Don't be afraid.

Going Your Own Way

Passivity is no virtue when it comes to adoption, especially if you want to adopt an infant. (Not that it works well with adopting an older child, either!) It can often be tremendously helpful to mobilize your very own "people assets"—your circle of friends and relatives. And, in turn, you could also ask them to get the word out to *their* friends and relatives. This tactic can help you amass a great deal of information, as well as possible leads on a birthmother interested in adoption. In this chapter, I'll show you how you can arrange an adoption on your own.

Networking

Not everyone among your family and friends will think that adopting a child is the greatest idea they've ever heard (as discussed in Chapter 1). So you will need to learn to deflect criticism and intrusive questions in order to gain their information and moral support. You'll also need to expand your informational search outwards, to parent support groups and local experts (see Chapter 5). Increasing numbers of wannabe adopters are also using the Internet's vast capabilities, which I discuss later in this chapter.

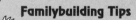

Real Life Snapshots

Several years ago, I led an adoptive parent group which included a couple in their 50s. They had learned that their son and daughter-in-law (who lived in another state) wanted to adopt a child, and they decided they were going to help.

They asked me what books to read and how to obtain information on agencies and attorneys, and they came to our meetings and asked lots of questions. Did their son adopt? He sure did! And it's safe to say he succeeded a lot faster than he would have on his own, aided by his parents' tremendous informational and moral support.

Warning: If you're in the "I don't know whether I want to adopt yet" stage—or even in the "I guess I sorta/kinda/maybe want to adopt" stage, I recommend you consider holding off telling your friends and relatives. But if you've made up your mind that you do want to adopt a child, networking can pay off in informational dividends.

There are many ways that people let their friends and relatives know they're interested in adopting:

➤ They send notes in Christmas and birthday cards.

➤ They call them up.

➤ They e-mail them.

➤ They write letters. (Yes, some people actually still do that.)

➤ They hand out little business-sized cards, which explain their interest in adoption.

➤ One couple rented a billboard, although I don't recommend such a radical and expensive tactic. (I don't know if it worked for them.)

Familybuilding Tips
Although many people interested in adopting a baby from the U.S. actively seek to locate a pregnant woman who is considering adoption, others don't want to search for birthmothers. Is networking a waste of time for them?

No! Even if you don't want to find your "own" birthmother, spreading the word about your interest in adoption can gain you information about agencies and attorneys—who's good, who's not so good, and so forth.

What Do You Say?

If you plan to network with your family and friends, you need to keep your message clear and short to everyone you tell. And send it in writing, whenever possible, so they have something to refer to. It's easy to forget when it's not *you* who wants to adopt.

Here are the basics your friends and family need to know—and remember to keep it simple! Tell them:

➤ Whether you want to adopt an infant, toddler, or older child.

➤ Whether you want to adopt in the U.S. or another country. (If another country, which one?)

Real Life Snapshots

Here's an anecdote provided to me by Los Angeles attorney David J. Radis:

"I was contacted by a birthmother living in Ireland who was an American citizen. She asked my office to put her in touch with prospective adopting families and indicated that she wanted to come to California to deliver and place the baby. I had a family I felt would be a perfect match for her and tried to contact them. I was advised that they were out of the country—in Ireland. I was put in touch with them in Ireland the day before they were scheduled to return to the U.S. and discovered that they were a few miles from the birthmother's home and, in fact, knew her father. They met, agreed to the terms of the placement, and the birthmother placed her baby with them. In fact, she later placed another child—a biological sibling—with the same family."

—*Printed with permission of David J. Radis, Attorney, Los Angeles, California.*

➤ How they can contact you. Well, there's your phone numbers at home and at work. Or your e-mail address. And your fax line, if you want to release that information. You could also give them your parents' name and phone numbers, if that might work. Keep in mind that your friends and relatives need a way to contact you within a reasonably quick period in case they hear of a lead.

What about deflecting annoying questions about *why you can't have children* (which, at a family gathering, probably sounds to you as if it were being announced at earshattering levels with a bullhorn to the world at large)? If pressed for details, say that it's just not possible. You do *not* owe everyone the innermost details of what works and doesn't work, plumbing-wise. If people continue to press you, you can smile mysteriously, play deaf, and change the subject or wander off.

What if others question whether you should adopt a child who falls into a certain category, say a Romanian child or a foster child? Assure the questioner that you're thoroughly researching the issues (you can tell them that you've read this book!) and thank them for their concern. Then if they persist, use the same tactics I recommended for intrusive questions about your infertility.

Real Life Snapshots

Sometimes the people doing your networking can surprise you. In one case, it was a six-year-old boy!

The Gladney Center, an adoption agency in Fort Worth, Texas, reprinted an article by an adoptive mother in their newsletter, *Bright Futures*. The mom had been shopping in the supermarket with her little boy, who was wearing his "I'm a big brother" tee shirt. When a lady in the vegetable aisle commented on his shirt, he told her all about his adopted baby sister. The mom walked away thinking how the poor lady had been bored silly by her enthusiastic little son.

But she was wrong. Several weeks later, the lady saw them again and thanked the child. Why? Because a woman in her family was agonizing over what to do about an unplanned pregnancy. The lady was so impressed with this little boy's explanation about adoption and his positive attitude that she conveyed the information to the niece, who decided to place her baby for adoption.

Said the mother, "Who would have ever guessed that in the vegetable aisle at a grocery store, a six-year-old could make such an impact!"

And what if they *do* find a potential lead for you?

Let's say your networking pays off, and Auntie Em and Uncle Henry call you excitedly. They've heard of a young woman, age 19, who belongs to a neighboring church and who wants her baby adopted! She's due in about a month. She wants her baby adopted by a childless couple in another state, someone of her religion. And you fit! Is this a done deal or what?

Before you decide to rush your relatives into getting all the info on this young woman and then seeing if they can sign her up for you, step back a moment and think about this. It's far better for you to enlist the aid of an adoption agency or an adoption attorney, who can kindly but detachedly work on obtaining the information on the young woman. And if you haven't had a home study (required in most states) but think this adoption might occur, now is a very good time to find out how to obtain one.

I also recommend that you take an additional action, and this can be very hard: Very sweetly ask your relatives to step back and let the adoption experts (and you) make the next moves. The young woman should not be pressured in any way. It's probably okay for others to tell her how wonderful you are—once. It's natural for your relatives to want to follow this thing through. But it's better if they do not.

Also, be sure to read Chapter 12, "Getting to Know You," for more information on the home study and what social workers do during the course of the home study.

Taking Out a Classified Ad

Another route to get the word out is advertising in the classified ads section of the newspaper. In the classifieds, people advertise if they want to hire workers, if they want to sell a car, if they want to know if someone found their dog—and if they want to adopt a baby.

You'll see these ads in *some* national and *some* local newspapers (that is, if adoption ads are legal in your state). "Happy loving couple longs to adopt a child. Please call us at..." They may give first names. They may mention that they are a Christian couple, or vegetarians, or even talk briefly about their pets. Whatever they think might work to attract someone who'll consider adoption is what they put in their ad.

Does It Pay to Advertise?

Do classified ads work? Yes, they do, although not for everyone.

Here are the major benefits to advertising in classified ads:

➤ You spread the word that you want to adopt far beyond your own neighborhood or even your own city.

➤ The probability of an interested person reading your ad is greater.

➤ If your ad gets responses, you can screen the calls yourself or have them referred to your attorney or agency. (Some states don't allow attorneys to screen such calls.)

➤ Your waiting period to adopt may be cut down considerably.

But there are also disadvantages to advertising in the classifieds:

➤ People who want to scam you may see you as an easy mark.

➤ Annoying people may call you.

➤ You may have trouble knowing what to say—and not say—when someone calls.

➤ If you take the calls yourself, you may decide to get an extra phone line—which increases your costs.

➤ Classifieds can be expensive, depending on how many places and where you advertise. Some people choose to put in an 800 line or a separate "adoption" phone line.

Adoption Alert
Advertising your desire to adopt in the classified ads is not legal in every state: California, Florida, and other states ban all advertising by people seeking to adopt. And even if states do allow adoption ads, some newspapers refuse to accept them.

So what if you live in a state that bans advertising? You can buy ads in states where advertising is legal. You can read the classifieds to find adoption agencies and attorneys, who may be allowed to advertise. See Chapter 10 to find out more about which states allow advertising by prospective adoptive parents.

Taking Out an Ad

If you do opt to advertise, plan it ahead of time. Read the ads written by others. Consider paying extra for a box around your ad or stars or some other attention-getting device. Try to make your ad stand out. Here are some items to mention:

➤ If your religious orientation is important to you, then list it.

➤ If you love pets, say so. (If you have a dog, state what breed it is. Birthmothers might be afraid it's a dangerous breed. So if you have a friendly collie or beagle, say so.)

➤ If you love sports, say so.

➤ Think about what is appealing about your environment: safe neighborhood, good schools, and so on.

➤ If you're married, stress your joint commitment. One birthmother told me that it was the husband and adoptive father-to-be who was important to her. He was the element she could not provide.

➤ If your entire family is excited about your adopting, this is a plus to mention.

➤ It's also a good idea to make some reference to your intense desire/longing to adopt a child as well as your eagerness and excitement.

Do *not* however, state your gross or net income. Do not state your profession if you could be easily identified in your area; for example, you're a neurosurgeon. For other dos and don'ts of advertising, contact your adoption agency or attorney.

Familybuilding Tips
Should you include an 800 number in your ad? Some prospective parents pay extra for an 800 number, while others say that birthmothers believe all 800 numbers are really numbers for agencies or attorneys. Some parents give a toll-call number in their ad and tell birthparents to call collect. However, some birthmothers may feel funny about leaving their name when they call collect. So weigh the advantages and disadvantages.

I read a note on America Online from someone who recommended saying in your ad that you're looking forward to 2 a.m. wakeups and changing diapers. That's good advice; when writing your ad, think about what might appeal to a pregnant woman who is considering adoption.

For more help writing an ad, ask the classified salesperson for suggestions. Alternately, some adoption agencies urge their applicants to advertise and bring birthmothers to the agency; they may provide helpful hints on how and where to advertise. Attorneys, too, may instruct prospective adopters on how, where, and when to place ads.

Taking Calls

How do you handle a call from a birthparent who answers your ad? I'll cover what you need to know about birthparents in Chapter 16. For now, though, I want to show you how to set up your phone service so you are fully prepared to act on any calls that come in.

When you're in the process of adopting, your primary link to a possible birthmother or to the agency itself is often your telephone. Your phone may well become your most important device, even surpassing your microwave, VCR, and computer. But what normally works with your home and work phone might need to be re-evaluated during the pre-adopt stages. Here are a few tips:

➤ If you are having your phone calls forwarded to your cellular phone, make sure that you have it turned on and fully charged at all times!

➤ If you are having calls forwarded to a work phone, tell your assistant or anyone who shares your line what you are doing, if you feel comfortable with that. If not, alert them you might be receiving an important but private phone call and that the caller might not want to leave a message. You don't have to elaborate. Either way, you want to make sure that your co-workers will rush to find you if a call comes through.

➤ Should you get two phone lines? Opinion is mixed on this one. Consider your own situation. If someone in your family (maybe you!) is a phone-aholic, then you probably should get two phones. Also, if you have two lines, you can make one the "Adoption Phone," dedicated only to adoption calls.

➤ Should you get a toll-free (800 or 888) number? Again, opinion is mixed. If you get an 800 phone line, then birthmothers not in your local dialing area can call you at no charge. On the other hand, you will have to pay an extra fee. And some birthmothers assume that only attorneys and agencies have toll-free phone numbers.

➤ Caller ID can be an asset if you worry about annoying calls. If you place an ad about adopting a child, for example, you might receive calls from people who want to tell you just how you and they can make a baby together (in rather blunt terms). If you tell the caller you have Caller ID and can trace the call, he might be persuaded to hang up. (Of course, you can say you have Caller ID even if you don't.)

Adoptinfo

Are there any times during the year that are better to advertise than other times? Experts say yes; pregnancies among young women are especially likely after social occasions, such as spring break, summer vacation, and the winter holidays. Remember, most pregnant women don't seriously consider adoption until their second or third trimester.

Familybuilding Tips

One way to get around missing calls with one line is to find out if your phone company has a special messaging option, whereby the phone company itself will take messages for you even if you are on the line when someone calls.

You record your message, choose a code, and then, when you receive messages (you'll know by a special sound of your dial tone), you dial a specific number, give your code, and retrieve them. This service usually only costs a few dollars a month.

➤ If annoying calls become a problem, you can contact your phone company about a "call blocking" option, which allows you to block either a specific number or the number of the last person who called you. (You can get full details from a telephone company representative.)

Real Life Snapshots

One woman who has successfully adopted several children always asks the birthparents who call for their phone number and address. She then asks permission to send them a brief list of questions. She says her questions are not what's really important—what's more important is that only people seriously considering adoption are willing to give their name and address and to return her questionnaire.

If you want to use this tactic, but not give your own address, you might think about getting a post office box in your city or a nearby city.

➤ Do you rely mostly on your portable phone at home? Keep in mind that it's very easy (although illegal) for your neighbors and anyone nearby to tune in. And what could be more fascinating than someone talking about adopting a baby! Few people could resist eavesdropping on that conversation. As a result, it's probably better if you stick with your main phone(s)—those directly connected to the wall.

Creative Advertising

Some wannabe adopters create business card–sized ads that say things like "Please help us adopt" and include a phone number. They staple them to bulletin boards, hand them out to people, and send them in holiday greeting or birthday cards. The same risks apply here as in the classifieds: Be careful and screen anyone who calls you. Alternatively, include the name of your attorney or adoption agency on the card.

Advertising on the Internet

There are also some Web sites that will let you advertise yourself as prospective parents, either for free or for a fee. For example, adoption.com (http://www.adoption.com) has photos and information on people wanting to adopt.

If you do choose to advertise on the Internet, read the ads written by others to see what's been done. Think carefully and don't submit your material in a rush or a panic.

What if a birthmother contacts you, probably by e-mail? She's fallen in love with your Internet photo, and you seem like you might be perfect. She's in New Mexico and you're in New York. Are you on the next flight out there? I don't recommend this. Instead, get basic information, such as when she is due, how old she is, how long she's been thinking about adoption, and if she's working with a particular agency or attorney. If this is her first adoption contact, it's a good idea to refer her to your adoption agency or attorney. Or tell her you'd like to give her e-mail address to your adoption arranger. Then the arranger can work on obtaining details, making contacts with an arranger in the other state, and so forth.

Do You Have to Advertise?

Let's say advertising is legal in your state. But you don't feel comfortable about doing it. Does this mean you should abandon all hope for adopting your child? Not at all! Instead, use the networking tips described at the beginning of this chapter to work on identifying a birthmother.

And finally, there are still adoption arrangers who will identify birthmothers and make matches between them and you—basically handling the adoption in the traditional and confidential manner. If this is what you truly want, then locate an agency with this service (see Chapter 6).

Straight Talk About Adoption Facilitators

Some states, including California, allow people who are not agency social workers or attorneys to help people find birthmothers (for a fee). These people are called *adoption facilitators* or *adoption consultants*.

Adoption Alert

If you decide that you want to advertise yourself on a Web site as someone who wants to adopt, think carefully. Obtain information on the Web site, including who owns it, what organization sponsors it, and what its primary goals are.

In addition, keep in mind that any information you provide can be read by people worldwide. Be careful about offering information about your personal income or other data that could leave you open to scammers.

Adoption Alert

Incidentally, when you are in the process of adopting, it's also a very good idea to muzzle yourself with regard to telling your friends and relatives everything you know about the birthmother and the child. Much information should be kept private, but as a newbie adopter, you probably want to blurt it all out to the world at large. Resist this tendency. Sadly, people tend to remember the negative, and it's really not necessary for everyone to know that the birthmother's uncle was an alcoholic. If you tell them this, they will remember it. Forever.

> **Adoption Alert**
> If you identify a birthmother through advertising, often you will find that she confides many of her problems to you. Experts say it's common to feel you should give her advice or counseling. But even if you are a trained and very skilled counselor, you should *not* counsel the birthmother, because of your very personal interest in this case and your lack of professional detachment. Instead, let the agency, attorney, or other adoption arranger help the birthmother with her personal problems.

They may coach people seeking to adopt, assist them with writing or placing ads or adoption resumes (see Chapter 12), tell them what to say when a call comes in, and so forth. They are usually not licensed (although some facilitators may be licensed social workers) and thus may not be policed by any governmental authority.

Then, if a birthmother does say she wants to place her child, the adoption must be followed through by an adoption agency or an attorney.

As with just about everything else, there are good and bad facilitators. My own personal preference is to go with an agency or an attorney, but if you believe a facilitator is the right path to your child, (and if using such a middleman is legal in your state), then be sure to ask plenty of questions. Here are just a few questions you might ask:

➤ Do you have one fee or several fees? What are they and how much are they? Some consultants charge a flat rate; others charge by the hour, or charge different fees for different services. Also, find out if you will be billed for miscellaneous expenses like phone calls.

➤ What services are included in your fee?

➤ What are your credentials? (Some adoption consultants are social workers; some are not licensed in any capacity. Be sure to ask.)

➤ How many adoptions have you helped arrange?

➤ How many adoptions that you helped arrange fell through? If the number is more than 20 or 30 percent, the facilitator may not be a very effective screener of birthmothers. But neither is it normal for a facilitator to claim that none of her adoptions have fallen through. If the facilitator says that she has arranged 500 adoptions and not one has "gone south," she's probably lying. Go to someone else.

➤ How do birthparents find you, and what services do you provide them?

➤ Can you give me some references? Although it's true that many adoptive parents do *not* want their names released to anyone, it's also true that some people are willing to talk to hopeful adopters. The facilitator should be able to provide the names of some people who are willing to talk to you about their adoption.

She may even bring them to a seminar or other group meeting. That's okay, but you should also try to talk to the people privately, either in person or for just a brief chat on the phone. Why? Because if you're at a seminar where the facilitator is present, she can see and hear them. If you talk to them by yourself, she can't. Thus, you may get more candid responses to your questions.

➤ Do you have a contract? May I see a sample? A contract should spell out what the facilitator is expected to do, how much you will pay, and other conditions of the service to be rendered. A contract isn't an assurance that you will adopt a baby or that you'll be happy with the service, but at least it will give you an idea of who is supposed to do what, for how much, and when.

Adopterms

In certain states, *adoption facilitators* or *adoption consultants* help people identify birthmothers, write adoption resumes, deal with birth-mother meetings, and so forth.

Note: Some people use the term "facilitator" to refer to anyone who is a non-social worker engaged in arranging adoptions. Thus, they would include adoption attorneys in this definition. However, I do not include lawyers in my own definition.

In addition to talking to the facilitator, checking references, and reviewing a contract, you should also contact outside organizations. Do local adoptive parent groups know about this individual, and if so, what do they think? Does the state social service office have any experience with this person?

You can also ask local adoption agencies and attorneys their opinion; however, expect that many will be disdainful and negative. After all, the facilitator is doing something which they believe is really *their* job, and there's bound to be some professional jealousy. Keep in mind that in some states, it is unlawful to pay anyone other than a licensed agency or an attorney to assist with a child placement.

The Least You Need to Know

➤ With some guidance, your family and friends can help you adopt a child.

➤ Advertising works for many people, as long as you know the pitfalls.

➤ The Internet is an amazing informational source that can facilitate your adoption.

➤ Adoption facilitators may be another route to your child. Make sure you screen a facilitator carefully before hiring him or her.

Chapter 8

Affording Adoption

In This Chapter

➤ Adoption costs vary considerably—but are workable for most people!

➤ How to make an adoption financial plan

➤ Investigating state and federal options

➤ Considering benefits your employer may offer

In an earlier chapter, I talked about whether it was "fair" that adoption is usually not free—not even close to being free. So I won't beat that drum again. (Read Chapter 2 if you missed it.)

Adopting a child who is not a foster child affiliated with the public social services system will cost you. In this chapter, I'll show you how you can afford adoption.

How Much Does It Cost?

An adoption of a healthy infant could cost $8,000 or $9,000. It could cost over $25,000 or more, depending on the situation. It's very difficult to give flat figures or averages because of variations in state laws, differences in agency and attorney policies, and a myriad of other factors.

To try to determine an "average" cost of adoption is comparable to asking what is the average cost of a book in the U.S., including hardcovers, paperbacks, and expensive reference books. Or the average fees to incorporate your business or the average fees of a wedding.

Having said that, however, if I were pressed up against a wall and compelled by a manic adopter wannabe to state an average fee to adopt a child not in the state social services system—stand and deliver—I'd reluctantly say that average fees could run about $18,000, whether U.S. or international.

In the case of an adoption through the state or county, there should be either no fees or minimal fees. (And the adoption is usually an older child adoption.) The costs to a public adoption are borne by the taxpayers.

Familybuilding Tips

If you are matched to a particular birth-mother, some agencies (and most attorneys) may be willing to reduce their fees if the birthmother is on Medicaid or a private insurance plan—because that insurance will cover the prenatal care and the delivery of the child. This could lower your costs by at least $5,000–$7,000 or more.

Ask the agency or attorney if fees are changed in any way if the birthmother has private insurance—either on her own or on a relative's insurance—or Medicaid.

Also, keep in mind that sometimes birthmothers choose to place their babies for adoption after the birth, when the child is a few months old or older. In that case, there should be no medical fees. Ask the agency or attorney what the fees are when that happens.

If an adoption arranger gives you a flat fee, ask what it includes! The fee could (but might not) include the following:

➤ Lawyer's fees and court costs

➤ Travel expenses, in the case of international adoption or the adoption of a child from another state

➤ Home study fee (this could run up to several thousand dollars)

➤ Living expenses for the birthmother, if legal in that state

➤ Medical expenses of the birthmother, if legal in that state

➤ Placement fee of adoption agency (fee paid upon placement of the child. Could be $5,000 or more.)

A good agency or attorney will give you a breakdown of approximate costs. Of course, expenses may change. For example, if the birthmother must have a C-section instead of a vaginal delivery, the surgery and hospital bills will be greater. Attorneys and agencies should give you a range of high to low, when birthmother expenses are involved, and that includes most contingencies. (Experienced adoption arrangers can't predict everything that might happen, but they can give you a very good idea of most cases.)

Some agencies charge adopters flat rates, regardless of whether or not the birthmother has her own insurance.

How is money paid to the adoption arranger? If there is no birthmother or child who is immediately matched to you, usually you will pay an application fee (if an agency) or a retainer (if an attorney). The amount of this fee varies. Usually next is the home study fee, paid to an adoption agency, and this involves several thousand dollars or more, depending on the agency.

When a particular birthmother or child is identified, if living or medical expenses are involved, you will pay estimated expenses to the arranger. You may also need to pay court costs and other fees in advance. The time of placement, or just before the child is placed, is usually when the largest sums are due to the agency or attorney, and these can involve sums of $10,000 or more.

Of course if you travel, you will have to pay the airlines for your tickets and bring money with you to pay for hotel, meals, and so on. Of course if travel costs go up, you will have to pay more. Some agencies also encourage you to bring gifts and toys to the orphanage.

Birthmother expenses should not increase drastically, and if they do, you should demand an explanation of what has happened.

Payments to adoption arrangers are usually made in installments unless a particular child will be placed immediately. Even in such a case, you should pay an agency and application fee and home study fee and possibly birthmother expense fees, if applicable. The bulk of the payment is at the time of placement. In the case of adopting through an attorney, if the lawyer and you are working with a particular birthmother, then the lawyer may wish to place a substantial sum—most or all of the expected payment—in a special bank account.

Making a Financial Plan

Once you've got an estimate of about how much you'll need, either from your agency or attorney, then you can start to make a financial plan. You'll need one—that is, unless you have 20 grand in the bank. Most of us don't—but I hope that you do!

Familybuilding Tips
Some agencies charge on a sliding scale. That means that they tag the fees to your income, with a minimum and maximum fee. Thus, affluent people are charged at the uppermost levels, and those less affluent pay fees on the lower end of the scale. Be sure to ask the agency if they use the sliding-scale system.

Familybuilding Tips
If you're new to the adoption system, and Agency A tells you that adoption expenses are about $10,000, and Agency B says fees are about $18,000, then the smart thing is to go with Agency A, right? Not so fast! First, you need to find out what Agency A is including in their fees.

In our example, let's say Agency A was not including living expenses for the birthmother (estimated at about $2,000) or lawyer fees. You might find out that the total fees for Agency A are equal to (or even more than) what Agency B is charging. Get the information on total costs, and then you can make a valid financial comparison.

Adoption Alert

Most of us groan over having to pay thousands of dollars to adopt. Although adoption arrangers may sympathize, I advise you to *not* groan endlessly about your financial agony. They've heard it before and they don't need to hear it again. And if you continue to make a big deal about it, they may wonder if you can truly afford the adoption and/or if you really want to adopt.

This does *not* mean, however, that you should never question where your money is going. Au contraire! Find out when payments will be due and what they are for; and if there are any changes, ask why they've occurred. But zip your lip on the general complaints. If arrangers think you've taken a vow of poverty, they may see others as more suitable parents.

If not, how the heck do you come up with the money? Here are some ways you may be able to afford adoption fees:

➤ Ask family members for a loan. (They may even offer you money as a gift.) Sure, it can be a little embarrassing to be 35 or 40 years old and asking your parents for money. But the truth is, the adoption fees may be beyond your current means, even though you do have the financial ability to support a child.

The "up" side of asking your parents or relatives for a loan is that you just might get it. The downside is that they might not ever let you forget it. You know your own family. Take into account the pros and cons.

➤ Ask someone in your family to co-sign for you on a loan application.

➤ If you have a 401(k) plan with your employer, find out if you can borrow on it.

➤ Find out if your employer has an adoption plan. Increasing numbers of employers are offering adoption benefits of up to $2,000. They see this as a way of granting adoptive parents similar benefits as biological parents, who often receive benefits for prenatal care and childbirth. Others offer paid or unpaid leave beyond what is required by the Family Medical and Leave Act.

Real Life Snapshots

When my son was a newborn, I took him to the pediatrician, and the nurse casually asked me if I had received insurance coverage. "No, he's adopted," I told her. She said, "I know. Your husband's company covers adopted newborns for after they're born." I checked with the company, and she was right. We provided the bills for the hospital pediatrician and other items related to my son and were reimbursed.

So don't forget to find out what your company offers in terms of grants, loans, and insurance coverage.

➤ Find out if your employer or your spouse's employer offers low-interest loans.

➤ Check with your credit union, if you belong to one. You may be able to borrow a considerable sum and have it slowly deducted from your paycheck until it's paid off.

➤ Find out if you can borrow on your insurance policy.

➤ You may be able to charge some fees on your credit card. (Although remember, this is *not* Monopoly money you're using! Keep in mind that you'll have to pay back everything you borrow, with interest.)

➤ You may be able to get a bank loan at your bank or another bank.

Adoptinfo
The Family Medical and Leave Act (FMLA) of 1993 is a federal law that requires employers of more than 50 workers to give full-time employees up to 12 weeks of *unpaid* leave for the birth or adoption of a child. (Adopted children are specifically included in the law.) Check with your Human Resources supervisor for more details.

Government Funding

Luckily, the federal and many state governments now offer a number of benefits or reimbursements for some adoption costs.

Thanks, Uncle Sam!

The federal government gives adopters a break in the form of an income tax credit of $5,000 for adoption expenses. If you adopt a special-needs child in the U.S. (see Chapter 3), that credit increases to $6,000. (Children with special needs from other countries are eligible for the $5,000 tax credit max.)

The exciting news is that you can *also* exclude up to $5,000 of income that your employer pays you for adoption expenses. (Increasing numbers of employers are offering adoption benefits.) This is a very good deal!

The adoption tax credit can be applied to all allowable expenses, which include agency fees, attorney fees, court costs, travel (including meals and lodging), medical expenses for the birthmother, and other fees related to the adoption. Expenses that are *not* allowed under this law are expenses for stepparent adoptions or surrogate parent arrangements. The adoption must also comply with federal and state laws.

Adoption Alert
What if an adoption falls through? If it's an agency adoption, the agency should be willing to work with you and not charge full fees for every adoption attempt. The most you should lose is money directly associated with the birthmother's expenses: medical, living, and so on. Many attorneys will also be willing to work with you if an adoption falls through—but assume nothing. Ask up front what would happen if an adoption doesn't work out and if you would like to "try again." You should also ask about *adoption termination insurance*, discussed in Chapter 6.

Familybuilding Tips
Ask the social worker if she knows how others have afforded adoption fees. She may be able to direct you to a state or local source of information. Of course, it's important to make it clear that you can afford to adopt a child. Still, for the average person, it's hard to quickly come up with $10,000 or more, and that's understandable.

Don't forget to ask local adoptive parent groups, too. They may have devised good ways to finance adoptions. In addition, they are probably aware of state adoption benefits as well as benefits offered by many employers in the area.

Adoptinfo
New York was the first state to pass a subsidy for adopted children with special needs through the state, in 1977. Since then, all states have passed subsidy programs. Don't assume, however, that any foster child you adopt will automatically be eligible. The definition of "special needs" varies from state to state.

The income of adoptive parents is irrelevant in determining eligibility for a subsidy, but may be considered in determining the amount.

Of course, there are income limitations; more affluent people are not eligible for this credit. For example, if you earn over $75,000 in modified adjusted gross income, the amount of the credit declines; it disappears altogether if your earnings exceed $115,000. Use IRS Form 8839 to take the credit and/or income exclusions. For more information, ask the IRS for Publication 968, "Tax Benefits for Adoption," published in March 1997.

The credit is taken in the year the adoption becomes final. In the case of an international adoption that is finalized abroad, the U.S. readoption of the child in your home state is apparently what the IRS would consider as "final." (Some countries finalize the adoption in their country. Many adopters choose to readopt the child in their own state so they can obtain a U.S. adoption decree, rather than relying solely on the foreign birth certificate and/or adoption documentation.)

To apply for an income tax credit, be sure to keep records for all your adoption expenses so that you can document them. You may have to give the IRS information such as the name of the adoption arranger and other details.

State of Adoption

Be sure to check if your own state offers adoption deductions. For example, in 1996 Oklahoma passed legislation to offer a deduction of up to $10,000 from state income taxes for nonrecurring adoption expenses. Maybe your state has such a deduction! If your state has an income tax, check out whether they offer any adoption credits or deductions. Ask adoptive parent groups in your area or the state social services department. The state office of taxes should also be aware of this provision.

Additionally, if you adopt a child from the state or county public social services department, the child may be eligible for Medicaid (free medical care). The child may also be eligible for a monthly payment from the state social services department (for which you would be the payee), particularly if the child has very serious health or psychiatric problems. This money is assumed to be used for the child.

It would be great if adoption were free, but it's not. But do not abandon hope, all ye who wish to enter Adoption World! There is most definitely hope if you explore the various alternatives available.

The Least You Need to Know

➤ Most people can afford to adopt, but it takes good financial planning.

➤ Your employer may have an adoption benefit— the average is about $2,000. Don't assume it can't be there or you'd know about it. Ask.

➤ Some birthmothers may have private insurance or Medicaid, and this might reduce your expenses.

➤ Some insurance policies (and some state laws require this) will pay for hospital expenses of a child to be adopted—after he or she is born.

➤ Some states have adoption income tax credits. The federal government now has an adoption income tax credit.

Adoptinfo

What if you receive adoption monetary benefits from your employers? Does that affect the federal income tax credit? Keep in mind that you can only credit expenses that were actually incurred. And if your employer gives you adoption money, you must subtract that before taking the tax credit. Here are two simple examples. (Based on information provided in *Adoptive Families* magazine, March/ April 1997.)

Let's say your expenses were an incredibly low $3,000 and your employer gave you $2,000. You could only count an additional $1,000 tax credit because you only incurred $3,000 in total expenses.

In another example, your expenses were $15,000. Your employer gave you $5,000. You exclude that $5,000 from tax and deduct it from your expenses. Now you have $10,000 in expenses left. You take the $5,000 federal income tax credit.

WANNA BUY A BABY?

Chapter 9

Who Can You Really Trust?

In This Chapter

➤ Signs of an unethical adoption agency

➤ Common adoption scams

➤ What to do if you get ripped off

This may sound cruel, but it seems to me that sometimes very intelligent people seem to lose at least 20 IQ points when they enter the adoption arena. They are bedazzled by the dream of a child to love, and they will agree to anything, anyhow, any way.

Just remember this: If you listen to promises that would sound ridiculous to you under normal circumstances but you turn your radar off because you are seeking to adopt, you are being very foolish. Don't let your brains fall out because you want to adopt! This chapter will show you how to avoid common adoption scams.

Adoption Scammers

Most of the people involved in arranging adoptions are good, honest, sincere, hard-working people whose primary goal is to help children be placed with good families. But there are others whose goals are not so honorable and still others who are well intentioned but not competent. And you can't always tell them by how they look or how they sound. (After all, if they looked evil and scary, or inept, they wouldn't be very effective at ripping people off, right?)

Scammers can be attorneys, agencies, or anyone else even peripherally involved in adoption. Do not presume that an agency license or Bar membership infuses its holder with goodness—would that it did!

You learned how to evaluate a quality adoption agency back in Chapter 6. Here are some indications an agency may be a problem:

➤ The agency asks for the entire fee up front, before a birthmother has been matched with you or has chosen you.

➤ The agency keeps asking you for money for "special funds," implying that if you don't pay you may wait longer for a child.

➤ The agency promises you a child within three to six months. No one should make promises unless or until you've at least been interviewed in person. (Not even then, really. They should wait until your home study is completed before talking about particular children or birthmothers.)

➤ The agency seems to be withholding information.

➤ The agency resists answering your questions or is evasive.

➤ The agency tells you that they've never had a child with a serious medical problem. If they've been in business more than a few years, they probably have seen at least one problem.

Common Adoption Scams

What kinds of bad things do scammers do to people who want to adopt? You want specifics? Okay. In this section, I'll warn you about major scams to avoid.

Money Manipulators

Beware of any agency that asks for a *lot* of money up front, even though there is no birthmother or child matched to you. (By "a lot," I mean $25,000 or more). Often, fraudulent agencies will spend your money, rather than putting it in an escrow account. They'll use any excuse to ask for more money—"birthmother funds" or special fees or anything else they can think of.

Moral: Don't pay more than a few thousand dollars up front unless there is a specific birthmother or a specific child that the agency can tell you about, in detail. Also, make sure you have a contract in writing (see Chapter 6). A contract doesn't ensure you won't get ripped off. But it does spell out terms and conditions and what you should be able to expect. Be sure to also check with state licensing authorities to find out if the agency is in good standing and if any complaints have been made against them.

International adopters are especially vulnerable to financial scams. I've heard of agencies charging up to $30,000 (not including airfare!) to adopt children from Russian orphanages. The child is already born, there are no prenatal care or hospital costs that need to be paid, there is no birthmother who needs support money, and the child is living in a state institution. There's no reason why the agency should be charging so much money!

Moral: Remember to deal with only reputable adoption agencies that have been in business for at least three or four years *and* that have a track record in the country where you want to adopt from. Newer is not better when it comes to international adoption agencies. Sometimes a new country begins to allow adoption, and no one has a track record there yet. In such cases, stick with well-established international adoption agencies, who can anticipate potential problems.

Another scam I've witnessed (infrequently) goes like this: The adoption arranger offers Family Number One a child but warns them it will be a very expensive adoption. Family Number One thinks about it for a few days. In the meantime, the arranger finds Family Number Two, who is willing to pay the fee and a little extra. The arranger gives the child to the second family before Family Number One has a chance to give an answer. The arranger makes up a story to pacify Family Number One. But he also keeps their fee.

Moral: If an arranger tells you that an adoption is going to cost "more than usual," find out why. If it's high medical bills because the birthmother or child was ill, or for some other rational reason, that may be okay. Ask to see the bills. If the reasons for the high fees don't make sense, don't agree. Don't even think about it.

Another major point to be made here is that if an adoption falls through, and the reasons why the child suddenly is not available don't ring true, they probably aren't. Run, don't walk, away from this arranger. But be sure to alert the state licensing bureau or Bar association and the State Attorney or District Attorney's office.

Guilt Trips

Guilt is a very effective way to scam people. "If you don't adopt this poor little sick infant," some adoption arrangers might say, "she'll have to go to foster care!" Or, if she's a foreign child, she'll go to the orphanage!

> **Adoption Alert**
> Experienced agencies who handle international or U.S. adoptions usually charge fees from about $20,000-$25,000 and sometimes a few thousand more. Be wary if an inexperienced agency asks for a lot more. Anyone who asks you for over $50,000 should be immediately suspect.

> **Adoption Alert**
> One adoption applicant I know cried bitterly when her very high-priced adoption agency went under. She and her husband had given them their life savings. The agency had repeatedly asked for more money—once, supposedly, to help the birthmother—and had implied that if she gave money faster, they would find a child for her faster. But the agency didn't find her a child. They went out of business instead.

Adoption Alert

Be skeptical if an international adoption arranger assures you that a foreign child is completely healthy; these people are not doctors, and by giving you a medical opinion, they are setting themselves up for a possible lawsuit if you adopt the child and later find out that the child is very ill.

By the same token, adoption arrangers cannot and should not guarantee lifelong physical and psychiatric health for every child they place. Instead, they should provide you with all the medical and psychiatric information they have. Then you should ask a physician to evaluate it and also to advise you if the information provided may not be reliable.

She might die! Scammers who work these angles know that most prospective adoptive parents are very soft-hearted. (Look at the huge surge of Americans who adopted Romanian children back in 1990–91, after the news media documented the horrible conditions in Romanian orphanages.) Compassion is good but should always be tempered with old-fashioned common sense.

The guilt tactic can be combined with the expensive-adoption tactic. For example, this poor little sick child may have incurred horrendous medical bills that the arranger wants you to pay.

First of all, you should require medical information for any child you are thinking about adopting (see Chapter 15). If the child is indeed sick, make sure the agency can document any and all medical expenses that the child has incurred. Check on the extent of the hospital bill. Is it really that high? And does a doctor really need $1,500 to do a physical examination?

Another aspect of the international adoption scam is that, all too frequently, inadequate medical information is provided, and the agency refuses to try to obtain any, saying they can't (which usually means they won't). Although they may not be able to provide information about prenatal conditions and what kind of shape the child was in at birth, they should be able to provide a health status of the child since he arrived in the orphanage. If you are thinking about adopting a four-year-old child, and all you are given is a paragraph or two, this isn't enough. (See Chapter 15 for more on medical information.)

Birthmother Scams

Most women who say they're considering adoption really *are* considering adoption. Sometimes they change their minds after the baby is born, but it's usually a sincere change of heart.

Very infrequently, though, a pregnant woman or her friends will scam one or more couples, by convincing each couple that they want the couple to adopt the child. The reason? Simple. As with all these scams, the underlying cause is dollars. If they can get several thousand dollars from one family, then they may be able to get even more from another family, and another and another. Sometimes the woman involved in this scam is not even pregnant. In some cases, the woman is prosecuted, but often nothing happens because charges aren't pressed.

Real Life Snapshots

A 1997 *Washington Post* article chronicled the story of a Barbara and Andrew Ship, a doctor and her graduate-student husband who lost nearly $28,000 in an adoption that went sour.

First, the couple found out that the attorney for their adoption agency had been suspended from practicing law for three years in another state. Then the agency apparently failed to find information on the birthfather. Next, the couple learned that the birthmother was not receiving support money they had paid to the agency. Finally, they read a scathing article about their agency in a national magazine. But still the couple convinced themselves that everything would be all right.

It wasn't. Just before the baby was born, the birthmother contacted the birthfather to tell him about the adoption. He subsequently hired an attorney to fight for custody. The agency told the couple not to worry. They took the baby home.

They should have worried. They contacted a reputable attorney, who told them they could fight for custody in court but they would probably lose. When the child was one month old, the birthmother revoked her consent to the adoption.

The good news is that the couple *did* subsequently adopt a baby through another adoption agency.

Keep in mind that thousands of adoptions sail through the courts every year. Luckily, stories like these are the exception, not the rule.

Moral: Don't let your intense desire to adopt allow your brains to fall out. Don't give any money to any pregnant woman directly. And don't give any money to an intermediary until it has been verified that the woman is actually pregnant. If you talk to the woman directly and she's far more interested in your bottom line than your parenting capabilities, that's a bad sign. (For more information on birthmothers, see Chapter 16.)

Instead, make sure all financial arrangements are handled by a professional, either an agency worker or an attorney. It's very difficult for most adopting parents to say no to the birthmother of their child—but some financial requests may be inappropriate or even illegal.

The Wrong Child for You

In some cases, the arranger may not have the kind of child you want to adopt—but they don't tell you this. One family stayed with an agency for an astounding 10 years. They told the agency they wanted to adopt a healthy infant, but the agency offered them one child after another with severe disabilities. The agency actively urged them to stay on, because "their child" would surely appear at any time. And, after all, they had so much time invested . . . When someone outside this private adoption agency suggested that they should apply elsewhere, that they weren't going to adopt a child with that agency, they finally decided to leave.

Moral: Find out what kind of children (age, race, and so on) the adoption arranger places. If they never (or almost never) place the type of child you want, don't sign up. If you have already signed up and you have any qualms about it, bail out. Now.

A few arrangers will try to insist that you adopt a child they do have, whether or not the child is right for you. In this scam, the adoption arranger may tell you that there are *no* children available like the kind you want to adopt. Instead, you should adopt a child from the group that they have.

Moral: Adoption arrangers want to place the children they have experience with placing. But it is immoral and unethical for them to tell you that you can't adopt a child merely because they do not place the sort of child you wish to adopt. Maybe it would be harder to adopt the child you seek. But if you have your heart set on adopting a particular child, don't go for what would be "second best" in your mind and heart—unless you have a change of mind and heart. You are not doing the child any favors if you really cannot handle his special needs. Seek out other adoption arrangers.

False Promises

If an adoption arranger promises to give you a baby within six months or a year, watch out! No reputable arranger would make such a promise, even if they think they could probably fulfill it. They certainly wouldn't make such a promise before you have completed the home study process. If it sounds too good to be true, it probably is.

Adoption Alert
If something about your adoption seems wrong, and alarm bells are clanging in your head, don't ignore them. Many victims of adoption scams later said they felt that something was wrong at the time but that they ignored their gut feelings.

Think about why those alarms are ringing. Talk to others about your fears, such as people in adoptive parent groups or even other agencies or attorneys.

Moral: Many arrangers may be able to place children within a relatively short time. But they usually warn you that situations can change and they cannot make guarantees. If they don't give you this kind of caveat, don't deal with them.

How Do They Get Away with It?

How can adoption arrangers get away with such abuses? Here are some reasons:

➤ Prospective adopters think they're stupid, and they're embarrassed to complain to anyone.

➤ They think maybe the arranger doesn't really mean to scam them. (But even if it's incompetence and not malevolence, the person should be stopped.)

➤ They think there's no way to get their money back, so why bother doing anything.

➤ They feel too emotionally upset to pursue any remedies.

➤ They think that this kind of thing never happened to anyone else, ever. (They're wrong.)

A failed adoption can be an emotionally and financially draining event. But just because you are upset and disappointed doesn't mean that you shouldn't seek recourse if you are the victim of a scam. In the next section, I'll show you how.

If You Get Ripped Off

I hope you digest this information in time to avoid any adoption scammers. But what if you've already been trapped and squeezed by one? Here are your options:

➤ If it's an adoption agency who ripped you off, report the problem to the state licensing bureau, the state adoption coordinator's office, the Attorney General's office, the Better Business Bureau, local adoptive parent groups, and any other group that might be able to take action against the offending agency.

➤ If it's an attorney, contact the Bar Association, the Attorney General's office, the Better Business Bureau, local adoptive parent groups, and any county or other attorney groups. You can also contact the American Academy of Adoption Attorneys in Washington, DC.

➤ If it's a private social worker or adoption facilitator, inform the state adoption coordinator, the National Association of Social Workers (if a social worker), the Attorney General, the Better Business Bureau, and local adoptive parent groups.

➤ If it's a birthmother, contact the Attorney General's office and any other organizations your attorney or agency recommend. If she gets away with it once, she may try it again. Try to stop her from inflicting this financial and emotional pain on others. You could also consider alerting the media.

➤ Some people choose the courts and file lawsuits against the attorney, agency, or even the birthmother.

Keep in mind that you may not have enough proof that a scam occurred, or you might even be dead wrong. It could be an adoption that just went wrong and it was nobody's fault. But you want to blame somebody. Don't be bitter. If people in authority who should know tell you that things were on the level, they probably were.

Adoption Alert

I've said this before (in Chapter 6) but I'll say it again: Don't trust an arranger just because you like him or her. Get references, talk to people who have used the arranger before, talk to licensing boards, and follow all of the screening tactics I laid out for you. Don't fool yourself that this background work isn't important or that it's too hard.

The Least You Need to Know

➤ Most adoption arrangers are ethical and efficient. But you should be aware of possible adoption scams.

➤ Carefully screen any adoption arranger you are thinking about dealing with.

➤ Never release a large amount of money to an adoption arranger without knowing that they have a birthparent or child for you.

➤ If you are scammed, contact the Better Business Bureau, state Bar Association, and local adoptive parent groups.

Chapter 10

State to State

In This Chapter

➤ Are adoption laws different from state to state?

➤ What are the rights and responsibilities of birthparents?

➤ What are the rights and responsibilities of adoptive parents?

➤ Which states have the most favorable adoption laws?

Remember that old television show "L.A. Law?" Maybe you saw the storyline when Ann and her husband Stuart adopted a baby in a private adoption. Several months later, the birthmother showed up and demanded her baby back. A courtroom battle ensued and the birthmother won. After that, many people nationwide worried about adopting a baby because the birthmother would "change her mind."

What many people didn't know then (and still don't know now) is that adoption is governed by state law, and the law in California was (and is) very different from laws in other states.

In this chapter, I will show you how state laws affect the adoption of children from the U.S.

Birthparent Rights

The laws governing birthparents' rights and responsibilities differ widely from state to state. Birthfather rights, in particular, are a hot legal issue.

Here is a small sampling of birthparent issues that different states handle differently:

➤ Whether a birthmother or birthfather may revoke consent (change their minds) or whether consent is irrevocable

➤ Whether the state has a putative father registry for alleged unmarried fathers to assert paternity

➤ Whether a state allows pre-birth consent by the birthfather

➤ What happens if the birthmother doesn't know (or refuses to name) the birthfather

I'll look at each of these in turn over the next few pages.

Revoking Consent

In Chapter 16, I'll talk about certain signs which may indicate whether birthmothers are more or less likely to change their mind about adoption. But to adoptive parents, another factor is very important: how *long* do they have to change their minds? A few hours, a day, a week, months? Or no time at all?

Well, it depends. Most people assume that birthparents automatically have until the day the adoption is finalized to take back (revoke) their consent to the adoption. But in most cases, this is not true. Unless a fraud has been committed, many states allow no time after signing consent to change one's mind. (Some states only allow a matter of hours—say, 72 hours, although a few allow for much longer periods.) It's also true that some states impose a waiting period before birthparents may sign. See the adoption law chart at the end of this chapter for specific timeframe information in each state.

So, you might say, how come we had that Baby Richard case in Illinois, where the three-year-old boy was given to his birthparents? That highly unusual case, discussed in Chapter 1, occurred because the birthfather claimed his rights had been violated, and the court agreed since the birthmother had lied to the birthfather about what happened to the child. The ruling caused a furor, however, and because of it, Illinois adoption laws were changed.

Getting Registered

Many states have *putative father registries* where unmarried men who believe they have fathered a child can register their paternity. (Check the adoption law chart at the end of this chapter to see which states have such registries.)

In some states, if the birthfather fails to register, then the birthmother may place the child for adoption without taking any further action with regard to the birthfather. In other states, additional efforts must be made to serve notice about the child's birth to the birthfather. A birthfather can usually block (or at least delay) an attempt by the birthmother to place the child for adoption.

Whether it's fair or unfair to require an unmarried father to register his paternity can be debated endlessly. Supporters say that it is a man's responsibility to find out whether or not a woman he has had sex with has become pregnant and whether or not he wishes to assert paternal rights. The registry protects the birthfather by notifying the court of his paternity in cases where the birthmother chooses to withhold the information.

Opponents say that fathers should not have to guess if a pregnancy has occurred, and that a man should not be separated from his genetic child without his knowledge or permission. Some say the birthfather's right to his child should be equal to the birthmother's right. It's likely this debate will continue.

Adopterms

Consent to an adoption means the birthmother (and, hopefully, the birthfather) voluntarily agree that their child may be adopted. To *revoke consent* means that they take back consent.

If consent is *irrevocable*, it may not be taken back. Even in states where consent is irrevocable, however, there is usually some provision for cases of fraud or duress (if the birthparents were deceived by the adoptive parents or the adoption arranger, for example).

In some states, consent can be revoked for any reason. In others, a birthparent who wishes to revoke consent must request a hearing so a judge can decide if consent may be revoked. Usually if any significant amount of time has passed, the court will be asked to consider the "best interests of the child."

Pre-birth Consent

A new "animal" for many states, *pre-birth consent*, means that a birthfather who is not married to the birthmother can agree to an adoption while a woman is pregnant and does not have to wait until the child is born.

DICTIONARY

Adopterms

In many states, unmarried men who believe that they have fathered children may register their alleged paternity in a *putative father registry*. This registry provides protection by ensuring fathers are notified in a timely manner if an adoption is planned. If the birthfather has not registered, in some states he will not be able to claim rights at a future date when his rights are terminated.

OH.

Adoptinfo

Putative father registries are very much in the news: in June of 1997, Governor George Bush of Texas signed a bill creating a putative father registry in that state, with the provision that men would have 30 days from a child's birth to establish their paternity. After that, their rights could be terminated.

Alabama, Arkansas, Delaware, Illinois, Indiana, Louisiana, Michigan, North Carolina, Nevada, New Mexico, New York, North Carolina, North Dakota, Oklahoma, Oregon, Pennsylvania, South Dakota, Tennessee, and Texas all have pre-birth consent laws. Usually the consent is irrevocable after the birth, although it may be, depending on the state.

Birthmothers, however, almost always sign consent after the child is born, usually within a specified timeframe of hours or days.

Pre-birth consent is a hotly contested issue. Is it fair? If the birthmother can't sign until the child is born, why can the birthfather sign beforehand? One response is that the birthmother who is considering adoption must take action soon after the child is born. Most birthmothers don't want the child placed in foster care while a birthfather is sought or while he makes up his mind. Remember that pre-birth consents are allowed in some states, and they are not required. They are generally used for birthfathers who want to end their involvement prior to the child's birth.

Birthfather Unknown

State laws vary in cases where the birthmother does not know who the biological father is (or refuses to name him). In some states, she must swear before a judge that she doesn't know who the birthfather is, or she must provide a reason why she can't (or won't) name him. In other states, the responsibility lies with the birthfather—he's expected to come forward if he wants to assert his paternal rights.

It's a good idea, however, for the adoption arranger to try to determine who the biological father is before birth whenever possible. The arranger can then try to legally terminate his paternal rights and also obtain genetic and medical background information from him.

Adoptive Parent Rights

There are also many other adoption issues that affect adoptive parents which are handled differently by different states. Here are a few of them:

➤ When an adoption can be finalized in court

➤ What medical and genetic information should be provided to the adopting parents

➤ Whether a home study is required, and if so, when it must be done

➤ Whether prospective adopters may advertise for birthparents

Again, I'll explain each issue in more detail on the following pages.

Are We There Yet? Finalizing Adoption

When an adoption is finalized, the child is recognized as the adoptive parents' legal child. I'll explain the process of finalization more in Chapter 18. For now, you should know that finalization times vary from state to state. In some states, it takes just a few months; in others, it takes nine months or more. But most states set finalization at around six months after placement.

I can't emphasize enough that in most states this does *not* mean the birthparents can claim the child anytime up until finalization in every state. Not at all. As explained earlier, many states make the consent to an adoption irrevocable upon signing, although others allow certain time periods during which consent can be revoked. (One exception is if the birthmother has been defrauded—in that case, she may be allowed to revoke consent, within a reasonable period of time from placement.) Very few states allow the birthmother to revoke consent until finalization.

Medical History

Many states also require that the agency or attorney collect medical or genetic information, although most states do not specify exactly what information should be gathered. There are several reasons for collecting this data. One is that such information is valuable to the adoptive parent and later will be valuable to the adopted child.

Another is that in some rare cases, medical or psychiatric information that was known by an adoption arranger was withheld. A new tort called *wrongful adoption* has sprung up in the past decade as a result. (A tort is a civil action for damages resulting from wrongdoing.)

Adopterms

To *finalize* an adoption means to go to court before a judge to receive legal permission and recognition that the child is yours.

Adopterms

Wrongful adoption refers to an adoption that would;wrongful not have taken place had the adopters been given information that was known to the adoption arranger. The information was purposely withheld or misrepresented.

Wrongful adoption claims may not be upheld if the agency did not have access to information or could not have known information because the birthparents or others did not provide it or if the contract between the agency and the adopters limited their liability. Adoption arrangers should not be expected to be guarantors that the child is perfectly healthy, now and forever. They should, however, provide the information that they do have.

The first such case was *Burr vs. Board of County Commissioners of Stark County* in Ohio, in 1986. In 1964, the Burrs adopted a child. They were told his birthmother was a healthy young woman. In fact, she was a psychiatric inpatient, and other important information about the child himself had been withheld. After years of difficulty with the child, the information came to light when the Burrs obtained permission to open sealed adoption records.

Real Life Snapshots

Gibbs v. Ernst was a recent wrongful adoption case that occurred in Pennsylvania. After the Gibb family adopted a five-year-old boy in 1985, they began having serious problems: The child was extremely violent and dangerous. In 1989, they were told that the child had experienced severe physical and sexual abuse before he was adopted. This information was in the record but had never been disclosed, despite the family's requests for complete information.

The adopters sued and won their case. The court said, "Providing full and complete information is crucial because the consequences of non-disclosure can be catastrophic, ignorance of medical or psychological history can prevent the adopting parents and their doctors from providing effective treatment, or any treatment at all. Moreover, full and accurate disclosure ensures that the adopting parents are emotionally and financially equipped to raise a child with special needs. Failure to provide adequate background information can result in the placement of children with families unable or unwilling to cope with physical or mental problems, leading to failed adoptions."

It's important to note that wrongful adoption cases are rare, and the overwhelming majority of adoption arrangers provide prospective parents with all the non-identifying information they have access to. Still, there may well be a few misguided arrangers who fail to provide information, believing it will not matter to the child and will only upset the parents.

Home Study

While it has long been standard practice in agency adoptions, most state laws now require *preplacement home studies*. This means the child cannot be placed until the family has been deemed suitable. In my opinion, this is a good idea for the adopters and the child. (See Chapter 12 for detailed information on what is involved in the home study.)

OK to Advertise?

State adoption laws differ on whether or not people who wish to adopt may advertise for birthparents in newspapers or other media. Some states ban such advertisements outright; others allow it. In a few states, the hopeful adopters must first have an approved home study.

As discussed in Chapter 7, advertising works well for some people and not for others. Many adopters believe that they should have the right to advertise for birthparents. They argue that there are advertisements for strip clubs and all sorts of unsavory activities—how could advertising the desire to adopt be any worse?

Others believe that advertising reduces adoption and even children to the level of a commodity. The National Council For Adoption, for example, is opposed to advertising by prospective parents. This debate is likely to continue.

Changing Laws

It's important to understand is that states are constantly changing their adoption laws (which is quite frustrating for an adoption writer!). As I write this, for example, I've just been notified that Montana and Oklahoma have significantly rewritten their state adoption laws.

Why can't they just get it right and leave it alone? Because states are constantly reacting to new situations, to pressures from constituents, and many other factors. The aforementioned Baby Richard case, for example, caused many states to change their laws regarding the rights of biological fathers. Other cases and situations are also likely to inspire legislators to try to fine-tune the law more—or radically revise it, in some cases.

Adoption Alert

Adopting parents should always insist that they obtain all medical and psychiatric information available to the arranger. I suggest that adoptive parents send a letter to the arranger stating that they assume they have received all medical, psychiatric, and social information and that if that is not true, they need to know right away. When adopting an older child, parents should find out the child's abuse and placement history.

Remember, if the agency does not have access to information, then they can't give it to you. Nor should you expect your child to be perfect because the agency didn't find any serious medical or psychiatric problems in the information provided.

Adopterms

A *preplacement home study* is a background investigation and interview of the adopting parents, accomplished before a child is placed with the family.

A postplacement home study is a background investigation and interview of the adopting parents after the child has already been placed with the family.

Familybuilding Tips If you aren't happy with the adoption laws in your state—for example, if you think your state *should* have a birthfather registry—then you should contact your state legislators and let them know.

Laws are also subject to the interpretation of judges, and even judges within the same state or county may differ in their interpretation.

States legislatures are also constantly looking at the laws of other states. If one state enacts a law that appears reasonable and effective, other states may enact it.

Cross-Country: Interstate Adoption

Although many people adopt children from the state where they reside, it's also possible to adopt children from other states. The Interstate Compact on the Placement of Children (ICPC) is a sort of treaty that governs how interstate adoptions are managed. There is a "sending" state and a "receiving" state and it's up to the Compact Administrators to ensure that laws of both states are complied with. If those laws conflict, the Administrators, who are based at the state social services office headquarters, work it out.

Interstate adoptions are not always smooth sailing. Potential adopters who don't know anything about interstate adoption may arrange their own adoption with a birthmother from another state but fail to contact an adoption agency or attorney in either state. This is a mistake.

Familybuilding Tips I advise most people to try to adopt a child in their home state first. It can be more complicated when you are involved with the laws of several states, although good attorneys should be able to smooth over any rough edges.

Sometimes people adopt a child from another state because they don't want the birthmother to live nearby, whether it's an open adoption or a confidential one. But there is no guarantee that she will always live in that faraway state.

To arrange an interstate adoption correctly and lawfully, you will probably have to hire an agency or attorney in both states to ensure that the laws are complied with. This adds to your financial costs.

Do You Need a Law Degree?

If you're not an attorney—and even if you are—you shouldn't expect to handle all or even most of the details of your child's adoption. Still, you should obtain some basic adoption law education. Here's how:

1. Check with local adoptive parent groups. They may have summarized the basics of adoption law in your state.

2. Your attorney may have encapsulated key adoption issues in a pamphlet or handout.

3. You can read the law yourself. Contact the reference librarian in your public library and ask to see a copy of the state laws (specifically, the adoption statutes). Some state adoption statutes are well-written and easy to understand; unfortunately, in others, they may be tough to get a handle on.

4. If your public library doesn't have a copy, contact the nearest law library. (Law libraries are usually located at the courthouse.) Ask the law librarian where the state adoption statutes can be found.

Do keep in mind that you will not become an instant expert after reading the adoption law. There are limits as to what you can expect to understand and achieve on your own, especially since case law affects interpretation. Consequently, my opinion is that, with the possible exception of a stepparent adoption, it's a bad idea to try to manage the legal paperwork yourself.

The best "defense" is to hire the best attorney you can find to handle all the legal details surrounding the adoption of your child. And make sure the attorney is an adoption attorney—not your mother's cousin Fred, who is a great tax attorney but knows nothing about adoption.

State Adoption Law Chart

I decided to create a state-by-state adoption law chart so you can compare and contrast laws in your state with the laws in other states.

To obtain the data for the chart, I recruited prominent adoption attorneys throughout the country and requested that they respond to my questionnaire. In addition, I also sent questionnaires to every state department of social services agency headquarters responsible for adoption. (Yup—All fifty of them.)

While this chart reflects the most recent information I could find, remember that adoption laws are subject to change. Consult with an attorney in your own state (or the state from which you wish to adopt a child). The chart should be used as a general guide only.

I scored each state based on its policies. Those scores are explained in more detail in the next section of this chapter.

Table 10.1. State Adoption Laws

State	When May Consent Be Signed?	Time to Revoke Consent?	#	BDad Registry?	#	Ads OK?	#	Pre-Birth Consent of Un-married BDad?	#
Alabama	Any time before or after birth	5 days after birth	1	Yes	1	Yes	1	Yes	1
Alaska	Any time after birth	10 days	1	No	0	Yes	1	No	0
Arizona	72 hours after birth	Not revokable	2	Yes	1	Yes	1	No	0
Arkansas	Any time after birth	10 days	1	Yes	1	Yes	1	Yes	1
California	Upon placement	90 days	0	No	0	No	0	No	0
Colorado	After birth: court term. to agency	Not revokable	2	No	0	Yes	1	No	0
Connecticut	48 hrs. after birth	Up to court hearing, about 30 days	1	No	0	Yes	1	No	0
Delaware	Any time after birth	Until hearing or termination filed	1	No	0	No	0	Yes	1
DC	Any time after birth	Agency: 10 days	1	No	0	Yes	1	No	0
Florida	Any time after birth	Not revokable	2	No	0	No	0	No	0
Georgia	Private: After birth, Agency: 24 hrs	10 days	1	Yes	1	No	0	No	0
Hawaii	Any time after birth	Until placement	1	No	0	Yes	1	No	0
Idaho	Any time after birth	Not revokable	2	Yes	1	No	0	No	0
Illinois	72 hours after birth	Up to 72 hours from birth	1	Yes	1	Yes	1	Yes	1
Indiana	Any time after birth	Not revokable	2	Yes	1	Yes	1	Yes	1
Iowa	72 hours after birth	Up to 96 hours from signing	1	Yes	1	Yes	1	No	0
Kansas	12 hours after birth	Not revokable	2	No	0	No	0	No	0
Kentucky	72 hours after birth	20 days	1	No	0	No	0	No	0
Louisiana	5 days after birth	Not revokable	2	Yes	1	Yes	1	Yes	1
Maine	Any time after birth	3 days	1	No	0	No	0	No	0
Maryland	Any time after birth	30 days	1	No	0	Yes	1	No	0
Massachusetts	4 days after birth	Not revokable	2	Yes	1	No	0	No	0
Michigan	In court, after birth	Not revokable	2	Yes	1	Yes	1	Yes	1
Minnesota	72 hours after birth	10 working days from execution of consent	1	Yes	1	Yes	1	No	0
Mississippi	72 hours after birth	Not revokable	2	No	0	Yes	1	No	0
Missouri	48 hours after birth	Until judge acts on	1	Yes	1	Yes	1	No	0
Montana	72 hours after birth	Not revokable	2	Yes	1	No	0	No	0

Time to Finalize?	#	Med Expenses of BMom May Be Paid?	#	Living Expenses of BMom May Be Paid?	#	BParents' Med. Info Req?	#	Home Study Required? (Preplacement study includes followup)	#	Total score
3 months	2	Yes	1	Yes	1	Yes	1	Yes, preplacement	2	11
20 days	2	Yes	1	Yes	1	No	0	Yes, preplacement	2	8
6 months	1	Yes	1	Yes	1	Yes	1	Yes, preplacement	2	10
11 days	2	Yes	1	Yes	1	Yes	1	Yes, preplacement	2	11
6 months	1	Yes	1	Yes	1	Yes	1	Yes, postplacement	1	5
6 months	1	Yes	1	Yes	1	Yes	1	Yes, preplacement	2	9
No minimum	2	Yes	1	Yes: $1500 w/o court approval	1	Yes	1	Yes, preplacement	2	9
6 months	1	If agency, yes	1	If paid through agency	1	Yes	1	Yes, preplacement	2	8
6 months	1	Yes	1	Yes	1	Yes	1	Yes, postplacement	1	7
Ninety days	2	Yes	1	Yes	1	No	0	Yes, preplacement	2	8
4-5 months	2	Yes	1	Yes, through agency	1	Yes	1	Private: postplacement Agency: preplacement	1	8
No specific time	2	Yes	1	Yes	1	Yes	1	If court-ordered	0	7
No minimum	2	No	0	Yes	1	Yes	1	Yes, preplacement	2	9
6 months	1	Yes	1	Yes	1	Yes	1	Yes, postplacement	1	9
At least 31 days	2	Yes	1	Yes	1	Yes	1	Yes, postplacement	1	11
6 months	1	Yes	1	Yes	1	Yes	1	Yes, preplacement	2	9
30-60 days	2	Yes	1	Yes	1	Yes	1	Yes, preplacement	2	9
Upon placement	2	Yes	1	Yes	1	Yes	1	Yes, preplacement	2	8
One year	0	Yes	1	Yes	1	Yes	1	Yes, preplacement	2	10
6 months	1	Yes	1	Yes	1	Yes	1	No, unless court orders	0	5
6 months	1	No	0	No	0	Yes	1	No	0	4
6 months	1	If agency, yes	1	Yes, through agency	1	Yes	1	Yes, preplacement	2	9
6 months	1	Yes	1	Yes	1	Yes	1	Yes, preplacement	2	11
90 days	2	Yes	1	Yes	1	Yes	1	Yes, preplacement	2	10
6 months	1	If agency, yes	1	Yes, through agency	1	Yes	1	Yes, postplacement	1	8
6-9 months	0	Yes	1	Yes	1	No	0	Yes, preplacement	2	7
6 months	1	Yes	1	Yes	1	Yes	1	Yes, preplacement	2	9

continues

Table 10.1. Continued

State	When May Consent Be Signed?	Time to Revoke Consent?	#	BDad Registry?	#	Ads OK?	#	Pre-Birth Consent of Un-married BDad?	#
Nebraska	Any time after birth	Not revokable	2	Yes	1	Yes	1	No	0
Nevada	72 hours after birth	Not revokable	2	No	0	No	0	Yes	1
New Hampshire	72 hours after birth	Not revokable	2	Yes	1	Yes	1	No	0
New Jersey	72 hours after birth	Not revokable	2	No	0	Yes	1	No	0
New Mexico	48 hours after birth	Not revokable	2	Yes	1	Yes	1	Yes	
New York	Any time after birth	45 days	0	Yes	1	Yes	1	Yes	1
North Carolina	Any time after birth	Child < 3 mos: 21 days Child > 3 mos: 7 days	1	No	0	No	0	Yes	1
North Dakota	Before or after birth	Until hearing, 1-6 wks	0	No	0	Yes	1	Yes	1
Ohio	72 hours after birth	6 mos—court hearing decides	0	Yes	1	No	0	No	0
Oklahoma	Any time after birth	Not revokable	2	Yes	1	Yes	1	Yes	1
Oregon	1 day after birth	Not revokable	2	No	0	Yes, if have home study	1	Yes	1
Pennsylvania	72 hours from birth	Until hearing: 2-4 mos.	0	Yes	1	Yes	1	Yes	1
Rhode Island	15 days after birth	Agency: if court approves, 15 days after birth Private: until final	0	No	0	Yes	1	No	0
South Carolina	Any time after birth	Not revokable	2	No	0	Yes	1	No	0
South Dakota	After birth, in court	Until finalization	0	No	0			Yes	1
Tennessee	4 days after birth	10 days	1	Yes	1	Yes	1	Yes	1
Texas	48 hours after birth	If private: 10 days if relinquishment affidavit.	0	Yes	1	No	0	Yes	1
Utah	24 hours after birth	Not revokable	2	Yes	1	Yes	1	No	0
Vermont	72 hours from birth	21 days	1	Yes	1	Yes	1	No	0
Virginia	Private: 10 days from birth Agency: any time	15-25 days	1	No	0	Yes	1	No	0
Washington	Before or after birth	48 hours	1	No	0	Yes, if have home study	1	No	0
West Virginia	72 hours from birth	Not revokable	2	No	0	Yes	1	No	0
Wisconsin	When court action occurs	Not revokable	2	Yes	1	Yes	1	No	0
Wyoming	Any time after birth	Not revokable	2	Yes	1	Yes	1	No	0

Time to Finalize?	#	Med Expenses of BMom May Be Paid?	#	Living Expenses of BMom May Be Paid?	#	BParents' Med. Info Req?	#	Home Study Required? (Preplacement study includes followup)	#	Total score
6 months	1	Yes	1	Yes	1	Yes	1	Yes, preplacement	2	10
6 months	1	Yes	1	Yes	1	Yes	1	Yes, preplacement	2	9
6 months	1	Yes	1	Yes	1	Yes	1	Yes, preplacement	2	10
9 months	0	Yes	1	Yes	1	Yes	1	Yes, preplacement	2	8
6 months	1	Yes	1	Yes	1	Yes	1	Yes, preplacement	2	10
Private: 6 months Agency: 3 months	1	Yes	1	Yes	1	No	0	Yes, preplacement	2	8
6months	1	Yes	1	No	0	Yes	1	Yes, preplacement	2	7
6 months	1	Yes	1	Yes	1	Yes	1	Yes, preplacement	2	8
6 months	1	Yes	1	No	0	Yes	1	Yes, preplacement	2	6
6 months	1	Yes	1	Yes	1	Yes	1	Yes, preplacement	2	11
2-6 months	1	Yes	1	Yes	1	Yes	1	Yes, preplacement	2	10
6-12 months		Yes	1	No	0	Yes	1	Yes, preplacement	2	7
6 months	1	Yes	1	Yes	1	No	0	Agency: preplacement, Private: postplacement	1	5
3-6 months	1	Yes	1	Yes	1	No	0	Yes, preplacement	2	8
6 months	1	Yes	1	Yes	1	Yes	1	Yes, preplacement	2	7
6 months	1	Yes	1	Yes	1	Yes	1	Yes, preplacement	2	10
6 months	1	Yes	1	No	0	Yes	1	Yes, preplacement	2	7
6 months	1	Yes	1	Yes	1	Yes	1	Yes, preplacement	2	10
6 months	1	Yes	1	Yes	1	Yes	1	Yes, preplacement	2	9
6 months	1	Yes	1	Yes	1	Yes	1	Yes, preplacement	2	8
6 months	1	Yes	1	Yes	1	Yes	1	Yes, preplacement	2	8
6 months	1	Yes	1	No, unless court approves	0	Yes	1	Yes, preplacement	2	8
6 months	1	Yes	1	No	0	Yes	1	Yes, preplacement	2	9
6 months	1	Yes	1	Yes	1	Yes	1	No, unless court orders	0	8

Note: The State-By-State Adoption Law Chart is based on information I compiled from both attorneys and state adoption law specialists. I am not an attorney myself, thus there could be some errors of interpretation. It's also true that state laws change, so do not assume the laws described on this chart are etched in granite for all time. They aren't. Instead, use the chart as a guide only, and consult with your adoption arranger on the current laws as of the time that you adopt.

Is Your State Adoption Friendly?

Using the scores in the adoption law chart, I tried to derive a measure of "adoption friendliness" of each state. I set my own criteria, based on my own biases about what is "good" for adoptive parents. Here is how I scored each category:

➤ *Revocation of consent.* Many adopters fear that birthparents can "change their mind" about adoption. If a state did not allow revocation, I gave it a "2." If the state allowed 30 days or less to revoke consent, I gave it a "1." If the state allowed more than 30 days to revoke consent, I gave it a "0."

➤ *Birthfather (Putative Father) registries.* I support birthfather registries because I believe they represent a positive step toward acknowledging birthfathers. As a result, if a state had a birthfather registry, I gave it a "1." If it didn't have a registry, I gave it a "0."

➤ *Allowing advertising.* There are mixed views on whether advertising for birthparents is good or not. However, I decided that most adoptive parents would like to have the option available. As a result, if a state allowed prospective adoptive parents to advertise for birthparents, I gave it a "1." If it did not, I gave it a "0."

➤ *Pre-birth consent.* As I discussed earlier in the chapter, pre-birth consent is one way to ease the mind of a birthmother considering adoption. As a result, states that offered pre-birth consent were given a "1." States which did not have such an option were given a "0."

➤ *How long?* How long it takes to finalize the adoption of a child is very important to adoptive parents. If the state allowed finalization at less than six months, I gave that state a "2." If the adoption was finalized at or around six months, I scored the state with a "1." And if the finalization generally took longer than six months, I scored the state with "0."

➤ *Medical or financial assistance for birthmothers.* Many birthmothers in their last trimester of pregnancy find it difficult or impossible to work. As a result, many states allow prospective adoptive parents to pay the birthmother's medical and living expenses. Since some states allowed one but not the other, I divided this issue into two columns. If the state allowed the expense, I gave it a "1." If it did not, I gave it a "0."

➤ *Health history.* Many adoptive parents want all the health and genetic information they can get. I gave a state a "1" if the information was required and a "0" if it was not required.

➤ *Home study.* Many adopters see the home study as an ordeal. My personal bias is that a home study is an important tool. I gave a state a "2" if it required a preplacement home study. If a state required a postplacement home study only, I scored it with a "1." And if no home study was required, I scored it with a "0."

Note that in some categories, some states had one policy for private (independent) adoptions and another for agency adoptions. For example, if a state required one length of time to finalize an agency adoption and a different length of time for a private adoption, I would have had to deal with two scores. To simplify my task, I defaulted to the lower score.

I'd also like to strongly emphasize that these scores do not mean some states are "good" while others are "bad." I am not saying that it is easy to adopt in the high-scoring states and impossible to adopt in the lower-scoring states.

If all this scoring information confuses you, then ignore the scores. It is probably far more important for you to look at the laws in your state. Table 10.2 classifies each state by its "adoption friendliness."

Table 10.2 Adoption Friendliness of States

Most Adoption-Friendly States (Scores 10–12)

Alabama	Nebraska
Arizona	New Hampshire
Arkansas	New Mexico
Indiana	Oklahoma
Louisiana	Oregon
Michigan	Tennessee
Minnesota	Utah

continues

Table 10.2   Continued

Adoption Friendly (scores 7–9)

Alaska	Montana
Colorado	Nevada
Connecticut	New Jersey
Delaware	New York
D.C.	North Carolina
Florida	North Dakota
Georgia	Pennsylvania
Hawaii	South Carolina
Idaho	South Dakota
Illinois	Texas
Iowa	Vermont
Kansas	Virginia
Kentucky	Washington
Massachusetts	West Virginia
Mississippi	Wisconsin
Missouri	Wyoming

Least Adoption Friendly (scores 4–6)

California	Ohio
Maine	Rhode Island
Maryland	

The Least You Need to Know

➤ State laws affect the rights and responsibilities of both birthparents and adoptive parents.

➤ State adoption laws are subject to change.

➤ Adopters who wish to arrange interstate adoption must comply with the laws of both states.

➤ While it's important to educate yourself about state adoption law, you must leave the legal work to an attorney.

Chapter 11

Going International

In This Chapter

➤ Trends in international adoption

➤ Pros and cons of international adoption

➤ How to arrange an international adoption

➤ Bringing your child home

Single mom Donna Sanford spent about 18 months preparing herself to adopt a child from China. She read everything she could and learned as much as possible. When she was matched with her daughter, she felt very ready and was tremendously excited. In fact, Sanford, the publisher of the trade magazine *EXPO, The Magazine for Exposition Management*, wrote about her adoption in her publisher's column! Here's a brief excerpt:

"The two-week trip to pick up my daughter was exhilarating, exhausting, awe-inspiring and humbling—much like labor and delivery has been described to me. There were about 10 families traveling together, and the first three days were spent sight-seeing at such wonders as the Forbidden City and the Great Wall. On the fourth day we received our babies from the orphanage, and Nia took one look at me and literally screamed for five solid hours. After crying herself to sleep, she awoke the next morning happy to see me and we've been best friends ever since. The next nine days were a mixture of official business—notarizations, registrations, medical exams, visa photos, embassy interviews—sight-seeing and bonding time."

Sanford says one thing she was *not* prepared for was the five-hour-straight crying jag, and she cautions people about it. She believes that Nia had probably never seen a blue-eyed blonde-haired woman before and it scared her! But Donna Sanford is definitely "Mom" now.

It's tough enough to actually decide that you want to adopt a child—but, as Donna Sanford's story shows, it can be even tougher if you want to adopt a child from overseas—especially if you aren't as prepared for most contingencies as Sanford was. This chapter discusses the issues you need to know about how to prepare yourself for an international adoption.

Adopting Abroad

International adoption has become a very popular option in the United States. Americans adopted more than 11,000 children from other countries in 1996, and this number will probably continue to grow as we move closer to the millennium.

OH. **Adoptinfo**
The Hague Conference on Private International Law is an organization of countries that are trying to set rules and standards for how international adoption should be handled. The participants have worked out a document that has been signed by the U.S. several years ago; however, ratification and implementation is not expected until the turn of the century at the earliest.

Orphanages worldwide are filled with children who need parents. Dr. Nina Scribanu, an associate professor of pediatrics and gynecology at Georgetown University and an expert on health conditions in foreign orphanages, estimates that there are at least 100,000 children in Romanian orphanages and 700,000 in orphanages in former Communist countries who need adoptive families. These figures do not include the enormous numbers of children in Asian or Latin American orphanages.

Trends in international adoption are strongly affected by changes in the adoption laws of foreign countries. For example, with the "opening" of Eastern European countries to legalizing intercountry adoption in 1991, thousands of children were adopted from Romanian orphanages.

Within the past several years, China has also "opened" as a country from which Americans adopt children. Due to a national policy allowing only one child per family, and a cultural preference for male children, many Chinese parents send their female children to orphanages so that they have another chance at having a male child. Thus, there are many Chinese girls available for adoption.

As of this writing, the largest regions from which children are adopted by Americans are China and the former Communist countries of eastern and central Europe. Countries "close" and "open" periodically, but international adoptions as a whole continue.

How do families choose the country from where they adopt their child? Often they choose a particular country because a friend or relative successfully adopted from that country. They may choose a country based on what an adoption agency advises.

Sometimes they select a particular country because they have relatives there or because they have lived in or visited the country and had a positive experience. In some cases, a country is chosen because the family believes they can adopt quickly and without much difficulty. These are only a few of the reasons—which range from emotional to carefully reasoned—why families choose particular countries to adopt from.

Countries "open" and "close" their doors to adoption for many reasons, including economic, political, social, and others. For example, the country may wish for its citizens only to adopt their children needing families, rather than for people in other countries to adopt them—a reason for closing the door. Or it may be facing serious economic problems that have created a situation in which there are many orphans—a reason for opening the door. Sometimes the reasons for openings and closings are not apparent.

Should You Adopt Internationally?

As mentioned earlier, international adoption is not easy. But it is also not impossible, and some families consider it more "do-able" because of the vast numbers of children in foreign orphanages who need families. Yet because you are dealing with two countries in an international adoption, it is also more complicated than a U.S. adoption. I'd like to examine some of the common fears about international adoption. Many people are concerned about international adoptions because:

➤ They think U.S. adoptions are easier.

➤ They are concerned about the health of a child raised in an orphanage.

➤ They are worried about the high cost of many international adoptions.

➤ They don't like the idea of traveling to a foreign country and staying for days or weeks in another culture while waiting for the paperwork to be processed. In addition, foreign travel can be costly.

Other adopters have equally strong views about why international adoptions are preferable:

➤ They believe their waiting time will be very short.

➤ They feel they can't adopt a same-race child in the U.S. but can from another country.

➤ They are opposed to open adoptions involving contact with birthparents (most intercountry adoptions are not open).

➤ They think birthparents changing their minds is not an issue in intercountry adoptions.

➤ They think children in orphanages are better adjusted than foster children.

I'll examine many of these opinions over the next few pages.

Table 8.1 International Adoptions, 1986–1996

	1986	1987	1988	1989	1990	1991	1992	1993	1994	1995	1996
All Countries (Total)	9,945	10,097	9,120	7,948	7,093	9,008	6,536	7,348	8,195	9,679	11,340
Europe	103	122	99	120	262	2,761	874	1,521	2,406	2,711	3,664
Romania	—	—	—	—	121	2,552	145	88	199	275	555
Russian Federation	—	—	—	—	—	—	432	1,107	1,530	1,896	2,454
Other Frmr. USSR	—	—	—	—	—	12	297	326	268	341	342
Other Europe	103	122	99	120	141	197			409	199	313
Asia	7,679	7,614	6,484	5,112	3,779	3,194	3,032	3,163	3,641	5,040	6,055
China, Total	140	137	157	142	95	157	263	388	856	2,193	3,388
China-Mainland	10	15	52	81	29	62	201	330	787	2,130	3,333
China-Taiwan	90	66	56	14	66	55	35	31	35	23	19
Hong Kong	40	56	49	47	—	40	27	27	34	40	36
India	588	807	698	677	348	448	348	342	406	371	380
Japan	46	64	69	74	57	83	71	59	49	63	36
Korea	6,188	5,910	4,942	3,552	2,620	1,817	1,787	1,765	1,795	1,666	1,516
Lebanon	19	21	23	21	17	17	16	24	16	20	15
Pakistan	12	9	10	14	14	9	15	12	17	6	17
Philippines	634	593	476	481	421	417	353	358	314	298	229
Thailand	27	31	75	99	100	127	90	65	47	53	55
Vietnam	—	—	—	—	—	—	23	105	88	318	354
Other Asia	25	42	34	52	108	119	66	45	53	52	65
Africa	22	22	28	36	52	41	63	59	91	101	96
Oceania	21	3	15	13	10	16	13	1	7	8	3
North America	885	973	844	910	959	1,047	1,136	1,133	846	771	725
Canada	13	17	12	5	8	12	6	7	1	3	2
Mexico	143	178	123	107	112	106	104	97	85	83	76
Caribbean	102	124	140	202	156	159	134	150	132	124	124
Dominican Rep.	31	52	54	69	58	50	41	39	17	15	13
Haiti	19	25	41	80	64	52	49	49	61	49	68
Jamaica	38	37	38	43	28	39	29	48	35	45	34
Other Caribbean	14	10	7	10	6	18	15	14	19	15	9
Central America	626	654	568	595	683	770	892	878	628	561	523
Belize	5	12	6	7	10	4	8	5	3	1	7
Costa Rica	72	72	73	78	105	55	65	48	29	19	20
El Salvador	147	135	88	92	103	122	115	97	38	30	17
Guatemala	228	291	209	208	257	324	428	512	436	449	427
Honduras	135	114	161	191	197	244	253	183	77	28	28
Nicaragua	14	5	8	9	7	11	8	9	18	10	14
Panama	25	25	23	10	4	10	15	24	27	24	10
Other N. America	1	0	1	1	0	0	0	1	0	0	0
South America	1,235	1,363	1,650	1,757	1,995	1,949	1,418	1,471	1,204	1,048	797
Bolivia	25	25	21	28	30	51	74	123	37	21	33
Brazil	193	148	164	180	228	178	139	178	149	146	103
Chile	317	238	252	254	302	263	176	61	79	90	63
Columbia	550	724	699	735	631	527	403	416	351	350	255
Ecuador	25	31	41	19	59	11	36	9	48	67	51
Paraguay	32	90	300	254	282	177	244	405	483	351	258
Peru	71	84	142	269	440	722	324	230	37	15	17
Other S. America	22	23	31	18	23	20	22	10	20	8	17

Copyright © by the National Council For Adoption, Washington, D.C., and reprinted with permission. Originally published in National Adoption Reports.

Are International Adoptions More Difficult?

Is it easier to adopt a child in the U.S. than in another country? With a few exceptions, I don't think adoption is easy no matter what, whether your child comes from the U.S. or anywhere else. Children don't drop into your lap from the sky (which is good—it would be pretty painful if they did!).

In some ways, U.S. adoptions are easier. For example, there's no language barrier with most U.S. adoptions. (You are not allowed to consider a Southern drawl or New England accent as "another language!") But language barriers are frequent with international adoptions, in which you must rely on your agency and their interpreters for a lot of information.

U.S. adoptions also seem easier to people who want to avoid the expense and difficulties of foreign travel, which is mandatory in most cases. In some countries, you actually adopt the child in the country itself; thus, your presence is required. In the case of a married couple, sometimes one person can travel; however, it's probably best if both go and provide moral support to each other.

> **Adoption Alert**
> In many countries, the adoption is considered final in the country the child is from; and, as a result, if there are any problems after you leave the country, such as undetected medical problems or other issues, the child is still your legal responsibility.

> **Adoption Alert**
> If you are considering an international adoption agency, find out if the director or any of the staff has ever traveled to the countries with which they arrange adoptions. It's not a good sign if no one in the agency has ever traveled to the country from which they make placements. How do you find out? You ask!

Are International Adoptions Faster?

The time it takes to successfully adopt a child in the U.S. can be measured in months or years, depending on the speed of your adoption agency, attorney, or your own efforts.

Whether the wait to adopt a child from another country is shorter than adopting a child in the U.S. depends on a lot of variables: which country you choose to adopt from, the age of the child you want, how fast you can put together your application, and other factors. It might be six months, several years, or longer (which is also true with U.S. adoptions). Or, you might apply for a child from a particular country, such as Romania or a Latin American country, and the country closes. All adoptions are "on hold." You have to wait until your agency gets the word that adoptions may resume.

Getting Medical Information

The medical and genetic information that you receive on a U.S.–born child will usually be more comprehensive than the medical information you can obtain on many orphans from other countries.

Often there is very little health information available on children living in overseas orphanages, particularly health data about their lives before they entered the orphanage. To complicate matters further, if a child does have medical records, the records may be in a foreign language and may use medical terminology not familiar to U.S. physicians.

As a result, children may have undisclosed illnesses or infections—sometimes serious ones—when they are adopted. With good medical care, many of the children thrive; however, some do not. Still, the overwhelming majority of intercountry adopters report that they are happy with their children and glad they adopted.

For those reasons, experts strongly recommend that you find a pediatrician or nurse practitioner who will advise you on the health of any child you may adopt. The person you choose should be able to diagnose unidentified medical problems (such as intestinal parasites, hepatitis B, HIV, and rickets) and be willing to work with a child who may have illnesses that are not common in the U.S. (Appendix G lists medical experts who specialize in international adoption.)

Adopt International is an agency that has developed forms for "Medical Risks in International Adoption" and "Child Acceptance and Medical Release" to emphasize possible health problems that a child adopted from another country may have. I've reprinted those forms here so you can see the health issues involved. See the figures on the following two pages.

Racial Issues Play a Role

It's very clear that many Americans adopting children from Eastern and Central Europe are choosing kids there because they are white. Many Caucasian people in the U.S. state quite openly that they want to adopt a white child and they don't want to wait years to adopt—so they'll adopt a child from a European orphanage or hospital. What they may not realize is that the wait is *not* always years and years for healthy white infants in the U.S. It's also true that thousands of Americans are adopting children of other races—that for them, race is not an issue.

Intercountry Adoptions Are Usually Not Open Adoptions

Another reason why people adopt from other countries is they hate the idea of an open adoption (in which the adoptive parents and birthparents are in contact). In an international adoption, the child has usually been relinquished to the orphanage and the birthmother will *not* be met. Nor will she have any choice in the selection of the parents of her child.

Most foreign birthmothers don't change their minds about adoption because their rights have been terminated already by the time the child is adopted. However, it does happen occasionally, even in intercountry adoptions, that a birthmother has a change of heart and struggles to gain her child back.

Lynne Jacobs, Executive Director
A Non-Profit Agency
Licensed by the State of California and Hawaii

Medical Risks in International Adoption

I/We_____and_____,
have been given information about various medical conditions and about the medical risks in foreign
adoptions, including but not limited to the following conditions:

Salmonella	Tuberculosis	Hepatitis A, B, C, and D
Milk Intolerance	Scabies/Lice	Parasites
Pneumonia	Chronic infections	Depression
Developmental delays	Vision problems	Hearing problems
Decayed teeth	Learning disabilities	Malnutrition
HIV positive	Physical Abuse	Sexual Abuse
Undiagnosed Genetic Problems	Retardation	Chronic ear/sinus infection
Fetal Alcohol Syndrome or Effects	Mental Deficiency	Premature Birth
Complications of Prematurely	Attachment Disorder	Hernias
Post Traumatic Stress Disorder	Post Institutional Care Symptoms	

I/We have been fully informed about the risks inherent in international adoption due to unknown birth
parents, lack of information, and/or unreliable testing. I/We understand that I/we will receive all
information and medical diagnosis that has been provided by the foreign country for the child/ren referred to
me/us. I/We have the opportunity to discuss medical, emotional and psychological risks with a physician of
our choice and have the right to have the child/ren examined and tested by a physician of our choice should
I/we choose to do so. I/We acknowledge, understand and accept the medical policy of Adopt International
and hold them harmless for diseases and conditions that cannot be diagnosed with reliability.

_____   _____   _____
Signature   Signature   Date

STATE OF _____
COUNTY OF _____

On this _____ day of _____ in the year of 19__, before me, the undersigned, a Notary
Public in and for said State, personally appeared_____, personally
known to me (or proved on the basis of satisfactory evidence) to be the person(s) whose name(s) is/are
subscribed to the within instrument and acknowledged to me that he/she/they executed the same in
his/her/their authorized capacity(ies), and that by his/her/their signature(s) on the instrument the person(s),
or the entity upon behalf of which the person(s) acted, executed the instrument.
WITNESS my hand and official seal.

_____
Signature of Notary

MEDICAL RISK 4/24/97

121 Springdale Way, Redwood City, California 94062
Fax: (415) 369-7400   Tel: (415) 369-7300

900 Fort Street Mall, Pioneer Plaza, Suite 1700, Honolulu, Hawaii 96813
(808) 523-1400   (800) 969-6665

Internet: 74734.3044@COMPUSERVE.COM

Medical Risks in International Adoption. [Reprinted with permission of Adopt International, Redwood City, California. The agency is waived from any liability from the use of information in this form. Each agency must seek legal counsel in its own state to determine specifics to be included or excluded in their own forms.]

Child Acceptance and Medical Release. [Reprinted with permission of Adopt International, Redwood City, California. The agency is waived from any liability from the use of information in this form. Each agency must seek legal counsel in its own state to determine specifics to be included or excluded in their own forms.]

Lynne Jacobs, Executive Director
A Non-Profit Agency
Licensed by the State of California and Hawaii

CHILD ACCEPTANCE AND MEDICAL RELEASE

I/We, acknowledge that I/we accept the following named child for adoption placement:

_____   _____
Child's Name   Date of Birth

The attached medical diagnosis has been made in the child's country of origin:

I/We, acknowledge that I/we have received from Adopt International all information made available to them about the medical, emotional, and psychological status of this child. I/We also understand that every attempt has been made, by Adopt International, to gather complete medical information regarding this child.

I/We have fully read and confirm our understanding of the "Risks Which May Occur in International Adoptions."

I/We understand that the above named child may arrive in the United States with previously undiagnosed medical, physiological, emotional, or psychological problems.

I/We understand that accurate testing procedures for Hepatitis B and HIV may not be possible. I/We accept the risks that this child may test positive after entry into the U.S.

Further, I/We voluntarily release Adopt International and its staff of any liability for any such problems.

_____   _____
Adoptive Mother   Adoptive Father

STATE OF CALIFORNIA
COUNTY OF _____

On this_____day of _____in the year of 19__, before me, the undersigned, a Notary Public in and for said State, personally appeared_____, personally known to me (or proved on the basis of satisfactory evidence) to be the person(s) whose name(s) is/are subscribed to the within instrument and acknowledged to me that he/she/they executed the same in his/her/their authorized capacity(ies), and that by his/her/their signature(s) on the instrument the person(s), or the entity upon behalf of which the person(s) acted, executed the instrument.

WITNESS my hand and official seal.

_____
Signature of Notary

121 Springdale Way, Redwood City, California 94062
Fax: (415) 369-7400   Tel: (415) 369-7300

900 Fort Street Mall, Pioneer Plaza, Suite 1700, Honolulu, Hawaii 96813
(808) 523-1400   (800) 969-6665
Internet: 74734.3044@COMPUSERVE.COM

Life in an Orphanage

Some Americans seem to believe that children don't get abused or neglected in overseas orphanages. Actually, some are. The deprivation inherent in orphanage life is enough to be harmful to children.

The effects of orphanage life can be seen as long as three years after adoption. Experts such as Dr. Dana Johnson of the International Adoption Clinic at the University of Minnesota consider institutionalized children to be a "high-risk" group. According to Johnson, "over 50% of institutionalized children in Eastern Europe are low birth weight infants, many were born prematurely, and some have been exposed to alcohol *in utero*."

It's also true that the longer the child lives in an orphanage, the higher the probability that the child will experience health or psychological problems later on.

> **Adoptinfo**
> According to Nina Scribanu, M.D., a Romanian physician and professor at Georgetown University, infants in orphanages lose one month of development for every three months in the institution.

> **Real Life Snapshots**
>
> Back in 1990–91, when the media broke the story of thousands of Romanian children languishing in orphanages, many Americans rushed to Romania to adopt. Roughly 3,500 Romanian children were adopted by Americans. Many adopters assumed that with enough love and care, the children would recover.
>
> How are they doing now? Canadian physicians found that three to four years after the adoption, the children adopted after the age of two were at least two and a half years behind in development, and none had achieved an average intelligence level.
>
> In another study of Romanian adoptees who were taken to the U.S., approximately 20 percent of the parents said the experience was harder than they anticipated; however, only 7 percent said they had considered disrupting the adoption, and 91 percent felt positive about the adoption.

Arranging an International Adoption

Americans wanting to adopt children from other countries must comply with the requirements of the U.S. Immigration and Naturalization Service (INS). The INS has requirements for adopting parents and also for the children they adopt.

135

Adopterms

A *dossier* is a collection of legal documents that you must compile to adopt a child from another country.

The *Immigration and Naturalization Service (INS)* is one federal agency that oversees international adoption.

An *orphan visa* is permission granted to a child from another country to be admitted to the U.S. for purposes of adoption.

In international adoption, an *orphan* is a child who has no parents or who has only one parent who can care for him or her. Many orphans have been abandoned because this is the only way the child can be adopted under the laws of the country.

If you want to adopt a child from another country, the INS requires the following:

➤ A preplacement *home study* (somewhat comparable to a background investigation) to be done by a licensed adoption agency (whether your state law requires one or not).

➤ Your *dossier* (a set of documents, including your birth certificate, marriage certificate, and other documents).

➤ Your fingerprints.

➤ Proof of citizenship. (If you're married, either you or your spouse must be a U.S. citizen in order to adopt a child from another country. If you're not married, then you must be a U.S. citizen to adopt.)

➤ Copies of your last three income tax statements (this is a new requirement, instituted in 1997).

➤ Your signature on a statement of financial responsibility, stating that should the child have to enter the foster care system, you will reimburse the state or county.

➤ You will also complete an application for an orphan visa, the document that will enable your child to enter the U.S.

Finding Your Child

When you decide to adopt internationally, you also need to decide whether you should leave most of the details to an adoption agency or whether you'd prefer to manage virtually everything yourself. If I knew nothing about international adoption (and even if I did!), I'd go the safer route, which is through a reputable agency. Why take a chance that you might make an unrecoverable legal, financial, diplomatic, or other sort of error? And if you find yourself dealing with unscrupulous people, who will protect you? Don't think it's easy to sue a foreign doctor or lawyer in their country. It isn't.

But although a home study by an adoption agency is mandatory, it is possible for you to do much of the legwork yourself on finding a child, if you wish. For example, if you or your spouse is originally from the country, you may decide this is a good choice for you.

When you obtain a "referral" on a child, whether through your agency, a foreign attorney, or another source, be sure to find out everything you can about the child. What was the birth date, and how do they know it? When was the child's last physical examination? Is there a videotape of the child you can view before deciding? Does she have any allergies or medical problems? Does she have any emotional or psychiatric problems? Ask for any medical records on the child. (You will probably need to get these translated.)

Sometimes, everything can happen very quickly. For example, you might apply to an agency, the agency needs families (as many international adoption agencies do), and you're able to pull all your paperwork together in record time. The agency submits your paperwork, a child is identified for you, you receive the information and decide you want the child, and then you're approved to travel.

When an agency does find a potential child for you, obtain as much background information as you can. Here are some questions to ask:

> ➤ How much time has the child spent in the orphanage? (The longer, the worse.)

> ➤ How does the child compare to other children of the same age?

> ➤ Does the child have any medical problems or allergies?

> ➤ Is a videotape of the child available? Can you receive this tape along with medical records?

> ➤ Does the child have any siblings? If so, where are they?

When a child is assigned to you, contact the State Department and you'll receive a visa for the child. Of course, you should have your own passport ready as well.

Whenever possible, travel with other couples or singles who are also adopting. You may find each other's help invaluable! Also, contact other couples who have traveled recently. Find out if there are any travel services they used that were particularly helpful—or should be avoided. Get the latest information you can find.

Adoptinfo

If you are interested in adopting internationally, gain as much information as you can before you travel to another country. If possible, plan to travel with other adopters. Take a phone calling card so you won't have to pay hotel fees for international calls. Also bring your credit cards. (However, check with agency staff or parents who've recently traveled. In some countries, cash is the only acceptable currency.)

Be sure to bring extra supplies, in case your stay is longer than intended. (Particularly any medicines you need—it may be difficult to obtain them in another country.) If you're adopting a baby, bring diapers. Bring clothes for the child you adopt (find out the child's weight and height ahead of time).

Finally, don't forget your shots! Your physician can tell you which immunizations you will need based on the country you are traveling to.

Before you leave, be sure to find out if any shots are a good idea. Often you may need injections for tetanus and hepatitis B. You might also need shots for cholera or other diseases. Anyone who accompanies you should be injected as well; for example, excited grandparents should definitely get their shots, too. Bring any medications you need, and bring at least an extra week's supply in case you get held up. Be sure to bring clothes for the child, and if she's an infant or toddler, bring diapers!

Making Your Child Comfortable

What can you do to help your child make the transition to your culture and your life easier? Here are a few suggestions:

Adoption Alert

If you adopt a child from another country, be sure to obtain your child's U.S. citizenship within a year of the adoption. He is not automatically a U.S. citizen just because you are.

The risks of not applying for citizenship? Later on, if your child wants to obtain a passport, special security clearances, a federally funded scholarship, and other benefits to citizens, he would be denied as a non-citizen. In addition, if he should get into even minor trouble, he runs the risk of being deported to the country of his birth.

Call the U.S. Immigration and Naturalization Service (800-870-3676) and ask for Form N-643, "Application for Citizenship in Behalf of an Adopted Child."

➤ If the child is an infant on formula, buy a few cans or a case of formula in the other country. Gradually switch over to U.S. formula by mixing the foreign formula and U.S. formula ½ and ½ for a few weeks, as an addition to other foods you provide.

➤ If she's an older child, try to get a few recipes from the child's culture, understanding you'll never get it just right. But do *not* continue an inadequate diet! Just don't rush the child off to the nearest fast food place when you get off the plane. She'll have time for that later. Instead, keep it simple at first: rice, bread, noodles, cereal, and fruit are good choices.

➤ Don't swamp the child with toys and gifts. He's not used to it, and it could cause a "systems overload." Start with one or two toys, and introduce more toys gradually. Even if it's Christmas!

➤ Give the child a chance to get used to your family and maybe the grandparents, too. Wait a few weeks before throwing a party.

➤ Find out what fabrics the child is used to wearing. If cotton, buy some cotton clothes. Ask the agency to ask the orphanage for this information.

➤ Learn some words from the other country, such as "Hello" and "I like you." You don't have to become an expert overnight. Children pick up language rapidly. But knowing some basic words in the beginning can help.

➤ Don't force eye contact. Look at your child, but don't move the baby or child's head to look directly at you. That can be very stressful. Give him a chance to get used to you.

Getting Physical

Within about two to four weeks of arrival, your child should be given a comprehensive physical examination. Be sure to let your pediatrician know that *The Red Book*, a source available to all pediatricians from the American Academy of Pediatrics, lists the medical tests that should be performed on children adopted from other countries. Contact the AAP at 800-433-9016. For very specific medical problems, you may wish to consult with one of the international adoption medical experts listed in Appendix G.

For More Information

It's impossible to encapsulate everything you need to know about international adoption in one chapter. For a comprehensive step-by-step guide, read *How to Adopt Internationally: A Guide for Agency-Directed and Independent Adoptions* by Jean Nelson-Erichsen and Heino R. Erichsen (Fort Worth, Texas: Mesa House Publishing, 1997).

Another extremely useful resource is *Report on Intercountry Adoption* (International Concerns for Children 911 Cypress Drive, Boulder, CO 80303-2821. Fee is $20.). This report is updated annually and includes essays on international adoption as well as listings of virtually every adoption agency in the U.S. that handles international adoption.

The Least You Need to Know

➤ International adoptions are an increasingly popular choice for American adopters.

➤ International adoption is affected by trends in foreign adoption policies.

➤ International adoptions are not necessarily faster or easier than U.S. adoptions.

➤ Children adopted from orphanages should be given full health and medical checkups.

Part 3
Finding Your Child

It's meant to be! That's how most people feel when they've adopted a child. That doesn't mean they expected a child to fall into their laps. They learned as much as they could about their child before making a commitment. This part will show you what you need to know about birthparents and their children.

The home study investigation and the wait for approval can drive the average person into fits of fear. Don't let that happen to you. In this part, you'll find out what the home study involves and how to survive it—and the waiting afterwards.

This part also includes issues faced by adoptive singles, gays and lesbians, disabled people, and older adoptors. They certainly can and do adopt!

Getting to Know You: The Home Study

Amy cleaned the dust bunnies from underneath the bed, scrubbed the floors, and polished items that hadn't seen Lemon Pledge in months. (Or maybe longer.) And yet she still thought it wasn't good enough. Then she had an idea: She'd pretend she was her mother, doing an inspection. And she went back to work.

Amy was preparing for a *home study*, a process in which potential adoptive parents are evaluated for their fitness as parents. Many people mistakenly think that a home study is primarily an inspection of their home (and so, it had better be so clean it could pass a military inspection). But a home study is far more than that.

Adopterms
The *home study* is a process that includes interviewing prospective parents, talking to them in their homes, checking their references and reviewing medical, financial, and other relevant information. Criminal records checks and child abuse clearances are also usually performed. The home study might take a week, a month, or longer or shorter, depending on the agency.

The home study can include interviews, visits to the home, checking references, and reviewing medical, financial, and other relevant information. It's a scary idea to many people, who balk at having to "prove their worthiness" to a total stranger. But remember: If perfection were required to adopt a child, there would be no adoptive parents and no adoption!

This chapter covers the basics of why home studies are done, what they are like, and how to survive your own home study.

Why Have a Home Study?

Why do agencies perform home studies? For one thing, home studies are required in many states (and are always required in international adoptions). But home studies are performed for several other primary reasons:

➤ To evaluate the prospective adopter's desire and commitment to adopt. This is particularly important when a couple is applying to adopt; both people must equally want a child. If one partner is just "going along" with the adoption plan to make the other partner happy, the resulting adoption will not be fair to the child, who needs a complete, committed family.

➤ To explore the reasons why the prospective adopter wants to adopt. Some adopters may still be grieving over an infertility problem. Others have lost young children—an agonizing loss—and are seeking a replacement child. The adopters must have sound reasons for wanting to adopt: They have accepted their infertility and are eager to become parents. Or they want to give a child who's "already here" a happy home life. There are lots of other good reasons, too.

➤ To evaluate the prospective adopter as a possible parent. How can a social worker know if you'd be a good parent if you've never had a child before? She can't. She has to go by the information you provide and the information she obtains from your references. (I'll talk more about references later in this chapter.)

➤ To educate the prospective adopter about adoption (and possibly about the child he or she is seeking to adopt). With some agencies, this aspect may be small or non-existent; other agencies provide reading lists, arrange meetings with birthparents and adopted adults, and more to help the prospective adopter understand adoption.

➤ To give the prospective adopter a chance for self-evaluation. The home study practically forces prospective adopters to evaluate themselves as future parents. They engage in a learning process that can be scary, but also personally fulfilling.

➤ To check background, criminal records, and financial resources.

Real Life Snapshots

The social worker walked around slowly, frowning hard at the grass. What was wrong, the prospective adoptive mom thought? Was there something wrong with the grass? It was mowed, it was green. What could it be? The wannabe mom sighed and restrained herself from blurting out to the social worker, "You don't like the grass? We'll change it!"

That prospective adoptive mom was *me*. And I would have redone the grass if I thought the social worker wanted me and my husband to do that. But she didn't. Instead, she was probably lost in thought, thinking about some other problem. Who knows? We passed the home study investigation. Nearly everyone "makes it through." And others who decide they probably don't fit the criteria drop out of the process before they can be turned down.

Get Your Application In

Once you've selected an adoption agency (see Chapter 6), you don't just jump into the home study the next day. First, you have to fill out an application and pay a small fee ($50–$100) to process it.

What's involved with application? The agency needs to know basic information: who you are, where you work, if you have kids already and how old they are, and so forth.

The following pages contain an Adoption Information Sheet used by The Gladney Center in Fort Worth, Texas.

Adoptinfo
During the home study process, as you are asked many questions, the birthmother will also be responding to numerous questions and providing information on her own circumstances. In addition, if the birthfather is available, social workers will contact him to find out how he feels about adoption and to obtain medical and social information on him.

T H E

GL🌲DNEY

C E N T E R

2300 Hemphill Street, Fort Worth, Texas 76110

.ADOPTION INFORMATION SHEET

<u>Please Note</u>: This Information Sheet is an opportunity for you to share information about your family to enable us to place you in our adoption program which will best meet your needs. Please complete **all information and return this form with a $50.00 processing fee and current family photo.**

I. FAMILY INFORMATION:

Names: _____

Home Address: _____

Home Phone Number: _____

	MALE	FEMALE
Date of Birth:	_____	_____
Race/Ethnicity:	_____	_____
Weight and Height:	_____	_____
Educational Background:	_____	_____
Occupation:	_____	_____
Employer:	_____	_____
Office Phone:	_____	_____
*Net Annual Income:	_____	_____
Religious Affiliation:	_____	_____
Date of Present Marriage	_____	_____
(If less than 3 yrs. indicate length of relationship)	_____	_____
Ages of Children by Present Marriage:	_____	_____
Adopted or Biological?	_____	_____
Number of Previous Marriages:	_____	_____
Ages of Children by Previous Marriages:	_____	_____
Who has custody?	_____	_____

II. MEDICAL INFORMATION

Have you had medical treatment for infertility? _____
If yes, summarize diagnosis: _____

_____

List all past and present significant medical conditions. _____

_____

Have you had treatment for emotional, psychiatric, or substance abuse problems? _____
If yes, please explain. _____
Have you had individual or marriage counseling? _____
If yes, please explain: _____

* If you will be working with the Agency Assisted Program, the greater of either this amount, or the financial information provided with your application will be used in determining your agency fee.

III. PLACEMENT PREFERENCES

Prioritize your interest (1,2, or None), Domestic versus International Adoption: Domestic: ＿＿＿ International ＿＿＿
Check the race/ethnic backgrounds of a child which would be acceptable to you.

1. **DOMESTIC ADOPTION:** (If applicable) <u>Full</u> <u>Half</u>

Hispanic	＿＿＿＿	＿＿＿＿
Anglo	＿＿＿＿	＿＿＿＿
Asian	＿＿＿＿	＿＿＿＿
Black	＿＿＿＿	＿＿＿＿
* Native American	＿＿＿＿	＿＿＿＿

* Subject to U.S. Indian Child Welfare Laws

Comments: ＿＿＿＿＿＿＿＿＿＿＿＿＿＿＿＿＿＿＿＿＿＿＿＿＿＿＿＿＿＿＿＿＿

<u>**Would you accept a domestic infant with a medical problem?**</u> ＿＿＿＿

If yes, Correctable: ＿＿＿＿ or Non-correctable: ＿＿＿＿

2. **INTERNATIONAL ADOPTION:** (If applicable) Infant-12 months ＿＿＿＿ 13+ months ＿＿＿

China ＿＿＿ Guatamala ＿＿＿ Mexico ＿＿＿ Russia ＿＿＿ Vietnam ＿＿＿

<u>**Would you accept a foreign infant with a medical problem?**</u> ＿＿＿＿

If yes, Correctable: ＿＿＿＿ or Non-correctable: ＿＿＿＿

IV. OTHER INFORMATION

Have you been convicted of a felony or misdemeanor? ＿＿＿＿

If yes, please explain: ＿＿＿＿＿＿＿＿＿＿＿＿＿＿＿＿＿＿＿＿＿＿＿＿＿＿＿

Have you ever been found guilty of a crime or pled guilty or nolo contender to a criminal charge, in order to qualify for deferred adjudication? ＿＿＿＿

If yes, please explain: ＿＿＿＿＿＿＿＿＿＿＿＿＿＿＿＿＿＿＿＿＿＿＿＿＿＿＿

Are you acquainted with anyone who has adopted a child through Gladney? ＿＿＿＿

If yes, whom: ＿＿＿＿＿＿＿＿＿＿＿＿＿＿＿＿＿＿＿＿＿＿＿＿＿＿＿＿＿＿＿

Are you acquainted with anyone associated with Gladney? ＿＿＿＿

If yes, whom? ＿＿＿＿＿＿＿＿＿＿＿＿＿＿＿＿＿＿＿＿＿＿＿＿＿＿＿＿＿＿＿

Are you a Gladney adoptee, birth parent, or adoptive parent? ＿＿＿＿

If yes, which?＿＿＿＿＿＿＿＿＿＿＿＿＿＿＿＿＿＿＿＿＿＿＿＿＿＿＿＿＿＿＿

Describe your community involvement: ＿＿＿＿＿＿＿＿＿＿＿＿＿＿＿＿＿＿＿＿＿

＿＿＿＿＿＿＿＿＿＿＿＿＿＿＿＿＿＿＿＿＿＿＿＿＿＿＿＿＿＿＿＿＿＿＿＿＿＿＿

＿＿＿＿＿＿＿＿＿＿＿＿＿＿＿＿＿＿＿＿＿＿＿＿＿＿＿＿＿＿＿＿＿＿＿＿＿＿＿

＿＿ ＿＿＿＿＿＿＿＿＿＿＿＿＿＿＿＿＿＿＿＿＿＿＿＿＿＿＿＿＿＿＿＿＿＿＿＿＿

List a personal reference ＿＿＿＿＿＿＿＿＿＿＿＿＿＿＿＿＿＿＿＿＿＿＿＿＿＿＿

I understand that this is a preliminary form and not an application to adopt. I affirm that the information provided is true and correct to the best of my knowledge. I further understand that failure to provide true and correct information may result in the rejection of my application. The $50.00 processing fee is **non-refundable**.

Signed: ＿＿＿＿＿＿＿＿＿＿＿＿＿＿＿＿＿＿＿＿ Date: ＿＿＿＿＿＿＿＿＿＿＿＿

Signed: ＿＿＿＿＿＿＿＿＿＿＿＿＿＿＿＿＿＿＿＿ Date: ＿＿＿＿＿＿＿＿＿＿＿＿

Reprinted with permission of The Gladney Center, Fort Worth, Texas.

Adopterms

An adoption *social worker* or *caseworker* is a person who performs a home study. The social worker might not have a degree in social work but might have a degree in psychology or some other related area.

Some social workers are *independent contractors* to adoption agencies, which contract out the home study process to them.

Getting On Your Case

If you pass the very preliminary application stage, then the agency can move you into the more involved home study phase. The home study will be performed by a social worker or caseworker assigned to your case.

One sad truth is that social workers rarely receive much, if any, training on adoption and related issues in graduate school. As a result, the just-hired social worker doing your home study may know *less* about adoption that you do. Generally, a new social worker in this situation will be supervised by a more experienced social worker, and you will both learn the process together. If, however, you have some concerns about your social worker, you can always ask her for a joint meeting with her supervisor. Better to try to work with her first before going over her head so as not to alienate her.

Home Sweet Home

Although the check of your residence is not the most critical issue in a home study, a social worker will (or should) examine your home, to see if it is reasonably clean and safe and if there is a place (or a plan for a place) for the child to room in. Social workers normally don't look inside your kitchen cabinets to see if your pots and pans are neatly arrayed, nor will they check your medicine cabinet to see if you have any interesting drugs in there.

Another reason social workers want to see you in your home is to get a feel for how you and your family members interact with each other in the comfort of your own home.

While your home doesn't have to be picture perfect for the visit, it should appear to be a safe place for a child. Here are a few things you should check before the social worker comes to your home:

➤ Fix any safety hazards, such as cords lying around. If you have stairs, make sure you have a plan to gate them off so they are safe for a young infant or toddler.

➤ Make sure you have at least one smoke detector on every floor.

➤ Make sure any unsafe objects (medicines, guns) are locked up. Make sure you have a plan to lock up poisonous household chemicals and other hazards.

➤ If you have a swimming pool, make sure you have a plan to have it fenced and gated for controlled access (if it isn't already).

Real Life Snapshots

One couple told me a funny story about their first home study: There were strange noises coming from another room, and the social worker wondered aloud what was going on. The couple assured him that the sounds were coming from their cat, who liked to climb in and out of paper bags. But the worker wasn't sure—he said the noises sounded like a child to him—and he demanded to take a look. Result: one cat and one red-faced social worker!

Visiting Hour

When the social worker comes to your home, keep in mind that she or he is a professional with a job to do. This is not a friend or family member stopping by. So should you offer any refreshments? Sure, offer something to drink. On the other hand, don't bring out fancy little appetizers that you spent hours preparing or a huge gloppy chocolate cake or other messy items.

What can you expect to be asked about? Usually the questions fall into the categories of why you want to adopt (and if you're infertile, the worker will probably want to explore this issue), what you do for a living, what your hobbies are, and any other questions that might give the social worker a picture of who you are. Here are some questions that you may be asked (and not in this order!):

➤ When did you start thinking about adoption? Why?

➤ Are you infertile? How do you know?

➤ How did you and your spouse (if you're married) meet each other? What drew you together then? How has your relationship changed?

➤ Have you gathered any information about adoption? What have you learned?

➤ Do you both (if a couple) want to adopt?

➤ How do you think a child would change your career? Your marriage? Your life in general?

➤ What do you have to offer a child?

➤ Do you know anything about birthparents? If so, what do you know?

➤ How do you feel about birthparents?

➤ Do your parents and other relatives know you want to adopt? Why or why not? If they know, how do they feel about it?

➤ Do you think adopted children should be told about being adopted? Why or why not?

➤ How will you afford the adoption fees?

➤ What is the greatest advantage to adopting a child? What is the greatest disadvantage?

➤ What are your hobbies and interests? Will you need to adapt them in some way after you adopt? If so, how?

➤ How will you feel if the adopted child turns out to be very different from you?

➤ What would be a "perfect" adoption experience, for you?

➤ Do you think you will continue fertility treatments at the same time you seek to adopt? If so, why?

Familybuilding Tips
During the social worker's visit, don't assume that any one tiny detail will derail you. Here's one way to look at it. If *you* were a social worker and you visited a potential adopter, and she had a few dirty dishes in the sink, would you turn her down just because of that? Now, be fair! (Some people hide their dirty dishes in the stove. Hopefully, they remember this after the social worker leaves...)

Now think about how someone else would reasonably evaluate you. This should help you relax a little, hopefully!

Be friendly and polite but remember that this is an evaluation process. Answer questions honestly—many adoption professionals say they hate it when applicants lie to them, and sometimes this can be a reason to turn an applicant down.

This does not mean you should bare your most personal secrets (for example, you tried marijuana once when you were 16). You should, however, be forthright about matters that can be checked (for example, you were arrested and charged for it, and it's on your record) or that continue to cause you problems.

The biggest "enemy" in the home study process is probably your own fear. Tracy and Steve, an adoptive couple I know, remember how they didn't have milk in the house when the social worker came over: He thought she had bought milk and she thought he had. But neither did. So when the social worker asked for milk with her tea, oops!

Both were convinced they had failed. Tracy thought that this lapse would be seen as a failure to communicate in her marriage and a lack of competence at running a household. "We actually agonized about this for days and didn't relax until we got the okay weeks later!" says Tracy. "Now we joke about it, and the social worker, who we still know, claims she didn't even remember asking for milk—she prefers lemon!"

Your Other Children

If you already have other children, expect the social worker to ask about them and to interview them, if they are old enough. (Over age five may be old enough.) If you have adult children, the social worker will probably want to talk to them, too.

The best way to prepare your children is to *tell* them that you want to adopt and why you want to adopt. And to assure them that you will still love them and not provide exclusive attention to the adopted child. (Note: Adult children need to know this too!)

Your Pets

I'm not kidding here: The social worker will want to see any pets you have to determine their compatibility with children. This is probably a good time to take a hard look at whether you really want to keep Brutus, your pet pit bull. (I know I am risking the wrath of pit bull lovers everywhere, who swear they are the nicest, kindest creatures on God's green earth. But you'll have to ask yourself: How badly do you want to adopt?)

Don't worry that the social worker is a dog person and you love cats or hamsters or whatever. If your pets look well cared for, relatively clean and happy, that should be enough. Just keep them from jumping all over the social worker when she visits.

> **Familybuilding Tips**
> Many pet-owning adoptive parents have told me that their social workers wanted proof that their pets had had their shots. One prospective parent complained that she kept her cats indoors all the time, so she hadn't got them any shots. Too bad, the social worker said; if she wanted to adopt, the cats would get their injections. Not surprisingly, the cats got their shots.

Testing, Testing

Some agencies and attorneys require hopeful adopters to take a psychological test. This test is given by a psychologist, and its purpose is to rule out any serious psychological problems. (Presumably, if you have any, you already know about them.)

I have heard some prospective adopters say they won't go to agencies or lawyers who require psychological testing or even just an interview with a psychologist. Why? They fear that some imaginary problem could be attributed to them, forever destroying their chance at adoption.

Adoptinfo

What if you don't "pass" a psychological evaluation? Does this go on some permanent record somewhere? No—at least not one that an adoption agency can access. The therapist will keep a record. If your insurance company paid for the evaluation, it will also have a written record. What information is released by the therapist to the insurance company varies considerably. Your insurance company should not release this confidential information without your permission. Keep in mind that most states have laws regarding confidentiality of medical and psychological records.

Let's look at the "forever" angle for a moment, because I have heard this fear voiced many times by people who want to adopt. Too often, they think they have one chance and one chance only to adopt a child. If they are turned down in their home study, they reason, they'll never ever adopt a child.

I have known people who were turned down by an adoption agency, and they did some serious introspection and soul-searching. If they couldn't understand why they were turned down and their desire to adopt was still intense, they applied to another agency. And later they did successfully adopt a child. Unfortunately, denials occasionally are based on personality conflicts between a social worker and prospective adopters. Another social worker will see how wonderful you would be for a child, as happened in the case I've described. So don't think in terms of "never" or "one and only." These are negative and self-defeating modes of thinking.

This Is Your Life

Many agencies and some attorneys will ask you to write a few pages about yourself. They want to know who you are as a person, according to you. This exercise also forces you to think about yourself in different ways: As a parent, as a provider, as a spouse. You may have taken these roles for granted; now you must explore them. This information is often shared with birthmothers as they select the family they want for their child. In a confidential adoption, identifying information will be deleted.

The autobiography (which is sometimes done in a resume format) does not have to reveal your deepest darkest secrets. You can reveal them if you want to, but remember, this isn't Oprah and you don't get extra points for agonizing. Here are a few pointers for preparing an autobiography:

➤ Write it yourself. Some people ask others (spouses or friends) to write their autobiography for them. This is a bad idea. Even a professional writer would have great difficulty capturing the spirit of who *you* are, why you want to adopt, and so forth. Also, this document should not be overly polished and slick—somehow, it's less believable that way.

➤ Type it. Do not hand in a sloppy, handwritten document.

➤ Add photos, if you want. Some agencies request a photo of you and your family to append to the autobiography. If you think open adoption is okay (see Chapter 16), then this should not be a problem. On the other hand, if you want a confidential adoption, it doesn't make sense to submit a photo and I advise against it. It might inadvertently be provided to birthmothers. If the agency insists on a photo—and I don't know why they would, in a confidential adoption—make it clear this is for "agency staff eyes only."

➤ If you do decide to attach photos, you can use a candid snapshot. Some people have a professional photographer take their pictures, but this is not necessary or expected.

Familybuilding Tips

If you do submit a photo of your family to the adoption arranger, make sure you're wearing your "Sunday best" and are smiling! Grim features have no place here. If you have a pet, try to get it in the picture too. (Yes, I *know* it's hard to get pets to sit still! But it's worth it.)

Your Adoption Resume

Resume-like writeups work well for some people, who create a one- or two-page resume of their family, sometimes including a photograph on top.

Beyond the basic format, however, an adoption resume should not sound like a job resume. The adoption resume should convey the idea that you are a healthy, happy family and would make good adoptive parents. Of course, it should also be clear that you and/or your spouse are employed and can financially support a child.

How much detail you include is up to you; however, I suggest avoiding including things like your annual income. Or your beach home in Bermuda, if you are so fortunate! If you flaunt your affluence, you may attract scammers (see Chapter 9).

If you have other children, you could mention their ages and how they feel about having a new sibling. You could even talk about the family dog or cat! A lot of birthmothers are attracted to families with pets.

Familybuilding Tips

The most important thing you should convey in an adoption resume is why you want to adopt (beyond being infertile, if that's the case) and why you think you would make good parents. Any past experience with children is good to mention.

It's also good to mention anyone in your extended family (don't name names) who is favorable to adoption. It's nice to think of people who are eager to become grandparents through adoption. Many birthmothers fear that the child will not be accepted by the adoptive family, so if your family is pro-adoption, mention it!

Backup Material

As part of the home study, you'll need to amass lots of information for your social worker. The specific documents you need to gather may be determined by state law. (If you are adopting a child from another country, the U.S. Immigration and Naturalization Service requires very specific information; see Chapter 11.) The information you will need to provide includes financial information and personal information.

Here are some of the financial materials you may be asked to provide:

➤ Income tax statements (In the case of international adoption, the past three years of returns are now required.)

➤ Pay stubs to verify your wages

➤ Savings account passbooks

➤ IRA information

➤ Debt information (balances on your credit cards, loans, and so on)

Here are some of the personal materials you may be asked to provide. (You may need originals or certified copies of some documents.)

➤ Your marriage certificate

➤ Certificate of divorce, if you are divorced

➤ The results of a physical examination performed by your doctor

➤ Names of references the social worker can contact

I'll explain some of these personal requirements in more detail.

Getting Physical

The adoption arranger wants you to get a physical exam because she wants to know if your life expectancy is normal and if you have any known (or unknown) serious medical problems. At your physical, your doctor will probably check your main body systems: heart, lungs, and so forth. You will probably also need to get some lab work, such as a complete blood count or a urinalysis. Often the social worker or agency will specify which medical tests they want performed at your physical. You may be checked for specific illnesses, such as hepatitis or HIV. You do *not* have to be a perfect specimen of manhood or womanhood, but you should be healthy and well enough to parent a child.

Your physical exam might not be covered by insurance because, theoretically, it might not be necessary. So find out ahead of time if it will or will not be covered.

Checking Your References

Most agencies and attorneys will ask you for the names of personal references. They want people who will vouch for your good character and the likelihood that you'll make a good parent. Often, they will ask your references to write letters on your behalf. Here are a few do's and don'ts about references:

➤ Don't give out anyone's name without checking with the person first. Some people don't like the idea of writing adoption references, for a number of reasons: They don't like the idea of adoption. They don't like the idea of *you* adopting. They may feel uncomfortable writing a reference in the fear that what they say will get you turned down. So always ask first.

➤ Do try to give the names of people who are parents themselves. They don't have to be adoptive parents, but it's easier for parents to write about child care than it is for people who don't have kids.

➤ Do try to give references who can be reached locally. (Or at least who live somewhere in your state.) If you've lived in the area a few years and you can't think of anyone local who is willing to give you a personal reference, your social worker will wonder why.

➤ Do convey the seriousness of these letters to you. Tell your chosen references that they should consider this as serious as if they were giving you a reference for a bank loan you're applying for. I don't think too many people would joke around to a bank official. Nor should they to a social worker.

➤ Do make sure your references understand what's expected of them: to verify that they think you're good parent material. Toward that end, any child care experience you've had which they can discuss is good. Your nurturing qualities should be emphasized. Your good upstanding character is important to note. Also, they should avoid any jokes! Sometimes humor helps, but you just never know.

Real Life Snapshots

Kelly, an adoptive parent I know, decided to read her reference letters before they were mailed to the adoption agency. Good thing she did: "One letter was from my oldest friend, but she wrote about her mother's death, then her own divorce, and then her father's illness and subsequent death. The gist was that I had always been there for her. But the letter was really depressing and of course entirely irrelevant to our needs."

She explained to her friend what was needed, and her friend rewrote the letter. "She wrote a lovely letter about our friendship through the years and our positive relationship with her son."

The other reference was mean-spirited. "It said how cynical and jaded we were... and that our real salvation would be in having someone to call us Mommy and Daddy." Kelly found someone to replace this reference. Later, the writer said she wrote the letter as a gag; she thought Kelly was joking about adoption.

Does this mean that you should read what people write before they mail their letters? That's up to you. Many people might not want you to read what they've written, even if it's very positive. Also, the agency might disapprove of your screening your references. However, Kelly is convinced that those initial references could have caused problems and certainly would have delayed her home study process.

I guess the bottom line here is, throughout the entire home study process, sincerity shines through. You, your family, and your references should always strive to be positive but truthful. Accentuate the positive, eliminate the negative. And don't mess with Mr. In-between.

The Least You Need to Know

➤ Home studies are more than a check of your house.

➤ Be prepared for the home visit: Make sure your house is clean, safe, and welcoming to a child.

➤ If you write an autobiography or resume, be sure to emphasize why you want to adopt.

➤ Make sure you know, and provide, all of the documentation your social worker asks for.

➤ Choose your references carefully, and make sure they know what's expected of them.

Chapter 13

Special Interests: The Non-Traditional Parent

In This Chapter

➤ Adoption for single parents

➤ Adopting if you're gay or lesbian

➤ Adopting if you're disabled

➤ Adopting as older parents

➤ Adopting transracially

Lana and Ted, in their late 40s, wanted to adopt a child but figured they were "too old." Then they read a story about other latter-day Baby Boomers adopting from Russia. They investigated and found out it was possible. Today, Lana and Ted are the proud parents of a Russian baby girl.

At age 39, Lucy's "biological clock" was screaming for a baby. Unfortunately, because of a medical problem, Lucy couldn't have children. Plus, she wasn't married. But everything clicked into place when Lucy overheard a single adoptive mom talking about how singles *could* adopt. Lucy couldn't miss the beaming face of the proud mother and her cute little boy. Today, Lucy is the mom of an adorable biracial daughter.

Adoption Alert
Some nontraditional parents have reported that they are offered ill children to adopt. Sometimes ill children are offered to nontraditional parents (as well as traditional parents), because it's hard for the agency to find any parents at all for the child.

A nontraditional parent usually does has less of a tough time adopting a special needs child, so if you want one, you shouldn't hesitate to adopt one. But if you don't want to adopt a special needs child, be sure to be upfront about this and stick to your position. Don't be "guilted" into adopting a child that has needs you don't think you can cope with.

When many people think of new adoptive parents, they envision Mom and Dad, a healthy heterosexual couple, probably in their thirties, with their same-race adopted child. But the fact is that adopters don't always fit this profile.

This chapter covers the "nontraditional parent," whether single, gay or lesbian, disabled, or older than average. Also included is information about adopting across racial lines—a hotly debated practice.

Single with Children

Every state in the U.S. allows single people to adopt. As a result, marital status is not a legal barrier to adopting a child anywhere. At least, not officially. Many adoption agencies and attorneys, however, still perceive the married couple as the ideal choice for the children they place. So sometimes the single man or woman drops to the end of the adoption line when it comes to priorities—depending on who the adoption arranger is. Smart singles do their homework!

Let's back up for a moment and address one issue that seems to baffle some people: why singles choose to adopt kids.

Single Adoptions: Pros and Cons

Single men and women want to adopt for many of the same reasons that married people want to (wanting a child to love, wanting to give a child a family, not being able to get pregnant, and so on.) But why don't they wait until they're married? Here are some reasons:

➤ They have no desire to marry, but don't wish to forego parenthood.

➤ They might like to marry but they haven't yet and they're afraid they might not ever find the right man or woman. They do want to become parents.

➤ They may be gay or lesbian and marriage isn't an available option.

➤ They are divorced and don't believe they will remarry—yet they don't wish to forego parenting.

➤ They are infertile and want to become parents.

➤ They want to provide homes for children who need them.

Real Life Snapshots

Dr. Jerri Ann Jenista, a pediatrician and mother of five adopted children, offered readers some helpful and humorous hints to single parenting in *The Handbook for Single Adoptive Parents*. (Chevy Chase, Maryland: The National Council for Single Adoptive Parents.) Here are just a few:

"Good friends, especially other single parents, are a must. These are the people who will bail you out when you need to go Christmas shopping without children or you are in the hospital with pneumonia."

"Reliable day care is the key to survival. Approval for additional children should be sought from your day care provider, not your adoption agency or your family."

"The plumbing, electrical and heating systems in your house are always in a merely temporary state of good repair."

"Sleeping in their clothes, eating pizza for breakfast, putting away their own laundry and not having a TV does not harm children."

And lastly, my favorite:

"Your kids won't care if you have a spotless house, brand new clothes or gourmet meals. But they will remember the 105 times you played Chutes and Ladders, all the books you read together, and the Ninja Turtle costume you made out of a cardboard box."

Some critics of single parent adoption (and single parenting in general) say that singles should not be allowed to adopt kids. If you're single and you want to adopt, it's critical that you understand their arguments (even though you probably adamantly oppose most or all of them). Here are a few objections you may come across—and some powerful counter-arguments:

➤ A child needs two parents so that one can fill in for the other when one is too tired, sick, and so on.

This is one of the strongest arguments against single adoptive parenting. Child rearing is very difficult, and it can be especially tough when 100 percent of the work falls on one parent. For this reason, it's important for singles who want to adopt to identify family members, friends, or others who can pitch in on a regular as well as an emergency basis.

➤ A child needs to be raised by parents of both sexes.

Many people agree that it's important for girls to have adult males to relate to and for boys to have adult females to relate to. Singles argue that this person does not necessarily have to be a parent; it could be a close friend or family member of the opposite sex.

Familybuilding Tips

Adoption experts say that single males have a much more difficult time adopting than do single females. This is in part because several unspoken assumptions work against single males who want to adopt: that they are gay, that they can't be good parents, or that they might even be pedophiles.

Hope Marindin, editor of *The Handbook for Single Adoptive Parents* (see Appendix H for ordering information), says that sometimes agencies believe that males who wish to adopt are pedophiles. She advises men who feel that this may be an unstated problem to offer to take a psychological test such as the Minnesota Multiphasic Personality Inventory or to agree to an interview and evaluation by a psychologist of the agency's choice.

➤ If the single parent becomes ill or dies, the child will be orphaned.

When single men and women adopt, they are usually well aware that they need to plan for the unhappy contingency that they could become ill or very ill. Most agencies and attorneys want to know who (friends, family members, or others) can provide backup in the case of emergency. Singles who want to adopt should seriously consider this issue. (They should also periodically revisit it after they adopt. Former potential caregivers may move away or become ill or die themselves, necessitating a new plan.)

➤ The single person will probably have to work to support the child and thus cannot be an at-home parent.

The fact that most single adoptive parents must work is not a strong argument, because most parents in two-parent couples are employed. With a two-parent family, however, it is true that one parent can fill in for the other if one has to travel, becomes ill, and so forth. This kind of tag-team arrangement isn't easy for the single person, who must make special arrangements anytime the usual daycare arrangements fail.

➤ The stereotypical poverty-stricken, single biological parent is often confused with the single adoptive parent, maybe on welfare; however, single *adoptive* parents are overwhelmingly working people who support their children.

Some single adopters say that their pet peeve is being confused with single biological parents who are divorced. Divorced parents may face a number of obstacles single parents don't have to deal with: animosity from their former spouses, reduced incomes, and insecurity with their new status as single parent. On the other hand, divorced singles may also be able to rely on their former spouses when a crunch time comes.

Tips for Single Adopters

How do you apply for adoption if you're single? Here are a few suggestions:

➤ Join an adoptive parent group. Join a singles group if one is available in your area; if not, don't shy away from a couples group. You don't necessarily have to fit a "mold" to gain from a group.

➤ Investigate agencies and nonagency adoption arrangers in your area (see Chapters 6 and 7).

➤ Prepare for possible objections to you as a single adopter and arguments you can offer to counter them.

➤ Read *The Handbook for Single Adoptive Parents*, an excellent resource for single adopters. (See Appendix H for ordering information.)

Adoptinfo

In a 1991 study published in *Families in Society: The Journal of Contemporary Human Services*, researchers studied about 800 adopters, all who had adopted children with special needs, including 139 single adoptive parents.

They found that the average income of the single adoptive parent was about $21,300. At about that time, the income level for the average single parent in the U.S. was about $13,500. Thus, although many of the single adopters were not wealthy, neither were they poor.

Over half had some college education, were college graduates, or had Master's degrees and above.

Gay and Lesbian Adopters

It's impossible to know how many adopters are gay or lesbian. First of all, adoption statistics of any kind are extremely difficult to come by. It may well be true that more gays and lesbians are probably seeking to adopt, as societal acceptance increases. Another problem with knowing how many gay or lesbian adopters there are is that some don't reveal their sexual orientation, often because they fear that they'll be turned down or because they want to retain their privacy.

Most state laws don't specifically address whether gays may or may not adopt. Only two states—Florida and New Hampshire—specifically ban homosexuals from adopting children.

161

Adoptinfo

Gay and lesbian organizations, some adoption groups, and some adoption Web sites offer information on which agencies are amenable to applications from gays and lesbians and which are not. Organizations for single adoptive parents may also be aware of friendly and un-friendly agencies or attorneys.

The Gay and Lesbian Parents Coalition International offers an adoption packet for $25, which includes information on gay and lesbian adoption issues. They can be contacted at 4938 Hampden Lane #336, Bethesda, MD 20814. (Phone: 301-907-2647.)

However, even if state law allows gays or lesbians to adopt children, many private adoption agencies and attorneys still turn away gay and lesbian applicants—often stating other reasons for their refusal. Some sectarian (religious) agencies oppose gays and lesbians adopting children outright. In addition, often birthparents select the adopting parents, and most prefer a married heterosexual couple.

As with single parent adopters, gay and lesbian adopters should understand—and be prepared to counter—the arguments made against their right to adopt. Here are some reasons critics argue against gay and lesbian adoptions:

➤ They feel that only heterosexual couples should adopt.

Many people continue to believe that a two-parent, mother-and-father family is the best. Gays and lesbians who are in committed relationships argue that they can provide a two-parent family. But as of this writing, no state allows gays and lesbians to actually marry and create a legal marital relationship. One way to show commitment could be to state (if this is true) that you have been involved in a relationship with the same person for two or more years and that you both intend for this relationship to continue. If you co-own a home or condominium or share other important financial arrangements, this could be seen as another indication of a commitment—just as such traits are seen as a sign of stability in a heterosexual person.

Another important point to make is that adoption is not a right, like the right to vote. Instead, the primary goal of adoption is, or should be, to place the child with the best possible parents. Those who object to homosexuality believe that the best placement is with a two-parent, heterosexual couple.

➤ They see homosexuality as morally wrong.

This is a matter of personal viewpoint. It's not surprising that people who hold such beliefs would be opposed to the idea of gays and lesbians adopting children. Others, who view homosexuality as an acceptable personal choice, will likely be more receptive to the idea.

➤ They believe that gays and lesbians may abuse their children.

Studies indicate that gays and lesbians do not abuse their children more than heterosexual parents (in fact, some studies suggest that heterosexual biological fathers and stepfathers are more likely to be abusive than gay fathers). So this issue seems invalid.

➤ They believe that children will be embarrassed by having parents who are gays or lesbians.

It may well be true that children of gay or lesbian parents might have trouble explaining their situation to friends—although supporters of gay and lesbian adoption argue that this does not mean we should institutionalize stigma. Of course, the main issue and point of adoption is to consider the best interests of children, rather than to destigmatize gays and lesbians.

➤ They believe that gay and lesbian parents will encourage their children to become gays and lesbians.

This suggestion is often made by people who object to homosexuality in general. However, it does not appear that gay and lesbian parents seek to "transform" their children into homosexuals.

➤ Some foreign governments are opposed to gays and lesbians adopting internationally.

In that case, gays and lesbians who wish to adopt from those countries often conceal their sexual orientation from the orphanage and foreign officials.

> **Adoptinfo**
>
> OH.
>
> Those who argue against the "embarrassment" argument cite the 1984 case of *Palmore v. Sidoti*. In this case, a noncustodial biological father opposed having his child (who was white) live with his wife, who had married a black man. The U.S. Supreme Court ruled that although it might be difficult for the child to live in a mixed-race family, race alone could not be held as a constraint to child custody and that the courts could not sanction stigmatizing of race.
>
> Some proponents of gay and lesbian adoption believe that the principle of not allowing racial stigma to prevail should also be extended to sexual orientation. Others argue that race and sexual orientation are two completely different issues, and this particular argument is likely to continue.

Some people take a "halfway" approach to the issue of homosexuals adopting. They believe that gays and lesbians should be able to adopt if they already have a relationship with the child. (For example, if they are related to the child or if they are a foster parent to the child.) In those cases, they believe it's preferable to reduce the losses the child has already suffered by keeping the child with someone familiar.

However, people who take the halfway approach are generally not in favor of placing a "new" child with a known gay or lesbian couple—for any or all of the reasons stated earlier.

Tips for Gay/Lesbian Adopters

Here are a few suggestions for gays and lesbians who seek to adopt:

Adoption Alert

Do not assume that because your friend, who you think is openly gay or lesbian, has adopted through an agency or attorney that this then means the agency or attorney will accept an application from other gays or lesbians. (Unless your friend tells you this is true.) Why not? Because your friend may have chosen to not reveal his/her sexual orientation. Some people withhold this information.

➤ Read about adoption in general as well as the experience of homosexual adopters. Several of my previously published books may help with general information: *There ARE Babies to Adopt* and *The Encyclopedia of Adoption,* a reference book. The Child Welfare League of America has also published a 1995 booklet, *Issues in Gay and Lesbian Adoption*, which may be of interest.

➤ Locate parent groups sympathetic to gays and lesbians. How? Well, one way is to simply ask them. But if the idea of asking outright makes you nervous, you could first question whether they have any single members. If they do, then the next question could be if gays and lesbians or "alternative lifestyles" are welcome in the group.

➤ Understand your state laws. In most states, if there are two homosexual partners, only one is allowed to adopt; the other is usually required to give up her or his parental rights for the adoption to happen.

However, increasing numbers of states are now recognizing *second parent adoptions*, in which a homosexual can become the legal adoptive parent of his or her partner's biological child.

➤ Locate agencies or attorneys that will accept you as a potential adopter. As with parent groups, you may wish to first ask the agency or attorney if they accept single applicants. If they do not, they probably would not be accepting of gays or lesbians adopting; so the questions can end there. If they do accept singles, the only way to really know if they will accept gays and lesbians is to ask. You could be somewhat oblique: "Have you ever had any gays and lesbians apply?" And see what kind of response you get.

Parents with Disabilities

Moving on to another category of non-traditional adopters, let's talk about disabled people who wish to adopt children. What could a disabled person possibly offer an adopted child? First of all, the disabled person may be a very loving, kind, and accepting person, important traits in an adopter. It's also true that sometimes disabled people adopt children with similar disabilities.

One mom who has been in a wheelchair all her life adopted a child with a disability requiring a wheelchair. The mom can identify with the child's problems, and she knows how to cope with them, practically and psychologically. But she also knows the importance of discipline and won't put up with any nonsense—no "poor me" stuff works with her! She is probably a far better "fit" than the average nondisabled person.

A lot of people are surprised to learn that vibrant and perfect health is not always a requirement to adopt. What is the main issue is if you have a normal life expectancy and if you are healthy enough to parent a child. Of course, most adoption arrangers want to place children with parents who will be able to raise them to adulthood, which pretty much excludes people who have terminal cancer or other life-threatening illnesses.

But people who are able to master their disabilities can apply to adopt. People with a variety of illnesses or impairments have succeeded at adoption. It isn't necessarily easy—non-traditional parents often have to "try harder"—but it is often possible.

In general, social workers will look at the severity of the disability as well as the type of child the disabled person wants to adopt. For example, a person who has difficulty moving around might find it very hard to parent an active toddler. Thus, the person should be prepared to discuss how he or she plans to keep up with a whirlwind of a child.

> **Adopterms**
>
> *Second parent adoption* refers to the adoption of one person's biological child by his or her homosexual partner. Some people have compared it to stepparent adoption, in that one parent is a biological parent and the other seeks to create a legal relationship with the child. Usually, the person who wishes to adopt has a parent-like relationship with the child already.
>
> People who desire second parent adoptions want the rights and protections that lawful parenthood brings. For example, if the custodial parent becomes incapacitated or dies, the nonadoptive partner may be unable to claim custody of the child—even if the two have had a continuously strong and positive relationship.

Mental Illness

Many people who have been treated for psychiatric illnesses (such as depression) are fearful that their medical histories may prevent them from adopting. When it comes to adoption, are psychological problems evaluated differently than physical ones?

What's important to most social workers is the nature of the illness and its current status. For example, most social workers will not have a problem with an applicant who was once depressed over a personal or professional setback but who has since recovered. Most social workers also do not object to applicants who take medication for depression. However, most social workers would hesitate to place a child with an applicant who has been suicidal, or has suffered a recent severe depression.

A past psychosis presents the most serious problem. (A psychosis is a break with reality; often a person who becomes psychotic requires temporary hospitalization in a psychiatric facility.) Again, the nature of the illness, when it occurred, and the applicant's current status are most relevant. The primary exceptions to this are the most severe psychiatric illnesses, such as schizophrenia or multiple personality disorder. Although these illnesses can be controlled with medication, many people with these illnesses have relapses. For this reason, they are usually not considered good choices as adoptive parents.

Real Life Snapshots

Several years ago, I was contacted by a woman who had suffered from multiple personality disorder. She had recovered, and at the time was a successful professional. She had letters from her psychiatrist attesting to her health and ability to function. She wanted to know if she had any chance to adopt.

My answer was that she should try, but to expect a very rocky road, because her illness was a psychotic disorder. (As opposed to a temporary problem of depression or anxiety.) Since mental illness can often be exacerbated or recur from stress, many social workers would be afraid to place a child with her. In addition, social workers share the common prejudices of the general population about mentally ill people. She indicated that she would probably not pursue adoption.

Tips for Disabled Adopters

If you are disabled and want to adopt, here are some strategies to improve your chances:

➤ Understand that you may encounter some resistance from agencies and attorneys. Don't take it personally.

➤ Explore different avenues of adoption: agency or nonagency, U.S. or international, infant or older child.

➤ Don't be apologetic about your disability, but do be open about your limitations. Be prepared to discuss how you can accommodate them.

➤ Be patient with silly questions you may be asked.

➤ Be up-front about whether you want to adopt a healthy child or a child with special needs. If you don't want to adopt a child with special needs, you don't have to.

Real Life Snapshots

Pat and Denise are both disabled—Denise had polio and Pat was born with spina bifida—and they successfully adopted a healthy biracial child several years ago.

In an article in *Accent on Living* magazine, Denise offered the following advice to disabled adoptive parents: "Be up-front about your disability and about the fact that you have the ability to be a parent. Address any issues before they worry about them, such as how you're going to handle child care. These are questions the social worker might not be inclined to ask but might make a lot of assumptions about your inability to do them."

"Older" Parents

As Baby Boomers age, the definition of how old is "too old" to adopt is changing. (To paraphrase an old joke, many Boomers think that "middle age" is about five years older than however old they are.)

Many men and women in their late 40s and beyond find that childbearing is not an option. Yet they still eagerly wish to be parents. Adoption is a good answer for some of them.

Here are some advantages that older parents may bring to an adoption:

➤ They may have more emotional maturity than younger parents.

➤ They may be more financially stable than younger parents.

➤ They may have more stable values than younger parents.

➤ They may have more time or patience for their children than younger parents.

Here are some disadvantages to older adopters:

➤ They may be less vigorous than younger adopters. Agencies and attorneys can investigate the health of the prospective adoptive parents to determine whether they seem to have enough energy and commitment to parent a child.

Adoptinfo

Older parents may actually have an advantage when they seek to adopt older children or children with disabilities. The reason? Many older adopters have grown children and are already experienced parents. Of course, children with special needs can be very challenging. But older parents may have the patience and the time to give the kids what they need: love, attention, and reasonable structure.

Familybuilding Tips
Some foreign countries with over-loaded orphanages have relaxed their age requirements so more children can be placed. In these countries, 50- or even 60-year-olds are able to adopt infants.

One fascinating example is China. There is a *minimum* age limit of 35. If you are under 35, as of this writing you can't adopt a child from China.

➤ They may have less patience and understanding than younger adopters. On the other hand, many younger people may be very impatient, while older adopters may be more willing to stop and listen.

➤ They may seem more like grandparents than parents. Yet in our society today, we see many people who have delayed childbearing and who have biological children while in their late 30s or even 40s. Nor is it important for every parent to look as if he or she stepped off a magazine cover: What's important is the love and commitment they give to a child.

➤ They may become ill or die before the child is fully grown. These days, the average life expectancy for many people is well into the late 70s and beyond. What social workers can do is look at the health history of the prospective adopters' own parents and grandparents. At what age did they die? What did they die from? How was their general mental and physical health?

Many agencies, however, do set upper age limits (although those limits seem to be generally creeping up). In the past, the maximum age limit was around 40; today, many agencies will accept parents who are 40 to 45 years old and sometimes even older.

The Truth About Transracial Adoption and Transracial Adopters

Adopterms
Transracial adoption alludes to an adoption in which the adoptive parent is not of the same race as the adopted child. Although parents of all races can (and do) adopt children of all races, the term is most frequently used to describe adoptions of black or biracial children by white parents.

Although many people want to adopt a same-race child, there are others who choose to adopt a child of another race. They may have unique problems in adopting in a *transracial adoption*. (Discussed in Chapter 3.)

The transracial adoption of black children by white parents is a hotly debated subject. Some organizations are adamantly opposed to it; the National Association of Black Social Workers, for example, calls transracial adoption "racial genocide." In addition, there is still great animosity towards transracial adoptions among most public agency social workers (despite state and federal laws which have sought to overcome this refusal to place children cross-racially for adoption).

Those who oppose transracial adoption believe that children of other races cannot develop an ethnic identity or sense of racial heritage when they are raised by white parents. They argue that these children will feel inferior, or will not be comfortable with their own racial culture.

Some studies suggest that this may not be the case. Rita Simon and Howard Altstein have been studying a group of black children adopted by white families since 1971. Their results (published in *In the Best Interests of the Child: Culture, Identity and Transracial Adoption*, Free Association Press, 1994) suggest that the majority of children have strong self-esteem and a positive sense of their identity.

Although Simon and Altstein found that most of the transracially adopted children have done well, they don't deny that transracial adoptions can cause problems. Unfortunately, racial slurs and inequalities still happen at all levels in our society. Transracially adopted children may be subjected to teasing and may sometimes feel like they don't fit in. (It is also likely that the parents in Simon and Altstein's' study were especially sensitive to racial issues and took care to deal with them as effectively as possible.)

As previously mentioned, social workers in public agencies are generally opposed to transracial adoptions. As a result, if you are interested in transracial adoption, your best bet will primarily be private adoption agencies or attorneys. Or you may wish to adopt through an international adoption agency; for example, Americans for African Adoptions, an adoption agency in Indianapolis, Indiana, places mostly black children from Africa.

Adoption Alert

Special laws govern the adoption of any child who has parents, grandparents, or even great grandparents who are Native American. The Indian Child Welfare Act of 1978 treats all Native American lands as if they were separate countries within the U.S. As a result, adoptions are handled differently. In most cases, the consent of the birthparents alone is not enough to adopt a child—you must also obtain the consent of the tribe.

Adoptions have been stopped in their tracks and even overturned after years when a tribe has complained that the Indian Child Welfare Act was not complied with.

(If you are part Native American yourself, or eligible for tribal membership, the way to adopt an Indian child may be considerably eased.)

The Least You Need to Know

➤ Singles can adopt, but it takes more work. Single adopters must prove that they have a network of people who will take care of the child at times when they themselves cannot.

➤ Laws and policies on gays and lesbians adopting are evolving. Gays and lesbians who are interested in adopting should work with supportive agencies or attorneys.

➤ Disabled people who want to adopt kids should be ready to discuss how they'll handle their disability.

➤ Adoption is possible for people over age 45.

➤ Transracial adoption is hotly controversial but still possible. Private agencies or attorneys are the best arrangers for these adoptions.

Getting Emotional

You've applied to an adoption agency and they've approved your application. Congratulations! You're awash with emotions: excitement, fears, and hopes for the future. And guess what—you're not alone. Your family and friends also care about what happens to you. How will your adopting a child affect them? Lots of ways! Once you become a parent, everything will change: get-togethers, holiday plans, nights out, and how you spend your time with your new family.

Remember that however long it took you to reach the decision to adopt, you finally made it. By the time you tell your family and friends about it, you will have adjusted to the idea. But the others may well be at "Start" in terms of their interest and knowledge about adoption. What they need from you is information, and what you need from them is support. You also may already have adopted or biological children in your family, and they'll have many questions and issues as well.

This chapter will talk about the attitudes of your family and friends toward adoption as you go through the process, before you even receive information on a particular child you might adopt.

How Do Your Parents Feel?

If you have no children now and you plan to adopt, you can bet that your lifestyle will change. Your parents probably realize it! They know parenting isn't for sissies (not that you are one). Here are a few issues that might concern your parents and some thoughts that might be running through their minds:

➤ How will your relationship with them change?

After you adopt a child, you'll have to make some major shifts and changes in your relationships with your parents and friends. You'll learn that parents must (usually) put their children ahead of other people outside the immediate family.

➤ Will you need and want their help with the adoption, or should they try to step back and wait until you ask?

Most people assume that a woman who has just given birth needs plenty of extra help because she is so exhausted from the childbirth. This same reaction doesn't always happen when a newborn baby is adopted; parents are far less likely to extend offers for help to the new adoptive parent.

Yet adoptive parents with a new baby can become extremely exhausted, too. Taking care of a new baby is hard work, whether it was born to you or adopted by you. Those 2 a.m. feedings and the 24-hour-a-day responsibility can all get pretty daunting. A little help if you can get it, especially at the beginning, can help you catch up on sleep and get a new outlook.

It can be a very good idea to tell your parents that you would like their help when the baby comes, even before you are told about a child you might adopt. Another advantage of having your parents help you with child care is that they will become emotionally involved with the child. You will probably find yourself drawn closer to your parents, too. Don't expect all to be perfect, however! There may be a few disagreements about what's best for the child. But remember, *you* are the parent and you may need to assert yourself in that role.

➤ Will you have a really long wait for your child? Will the adoption go through smoothly or will there be problems ahead?

Your parents may have some concern when you tell them that you plan to adopt a child. First, they may be convinced that you'll have to wait some incredibly long period to adopt—and that will be terribly difficult for you. Assure them that your plan is to adopt much sooner than that and you have developed a good strategy to reach that goal.

➤ Will the birthmother change her mind about the adoption?

Tell your parents that it's true that a minority of birthmothers change their mind about adoption, but in most states, when the birthparents sign their consent to an adoption, it is either irrevocable or they only have a brief period of time to change their minds.

If you are adopting a child from another country, explain to your parents that the orphanage (or other organization or individual) has custody of the child, and it would be very difficult for the foreign birthmother to rescind her consent.

If you are adopting a foster child, explain that the state or county did a formal "termination of parental rights," and the biological parents are not allowed to interfere with that court order.

➤ How should they explain this to others in the family?

You may think that you receive far too many probing questions about adoption, but you probably don't realize that when people hear from your parents themselves or from others that you are planning to adopt, your parents get interrogated, too! Tell your parents what you want them to know and be sure to emphasize that you want to create a family. You might want to add that you hope to be good parents like they were. Also tell them what information you want shared, and what is "off the record." (And if something is *really* off limits, maybe you shouldn't share it with your parents in the first place.)

> **Familybuilding Tips**
> Some parents can be tremendously supportive in the preadoption phase, clipping articles, cheerleading you when you're down, and keeping their eyes and ears open for the latest information. Of course, this can be carried too far, and if your parents and friends are burdening you with adoption information, it's perfectly okay to tell them to lay off—you've got enough.

➤ How will other children you already have be affected, your parents may wonder. (Such as their other grandchildren.) And what will this child be like? What if he turns out to have problems? Or what if she just doesn't fit in with the family?

If they express such fears, or hint at them, you might tell them that children don't come with warranties, whether born to you or adopted. And if they persist, you might gently mention a few people who are biological relatives and yet they have had serious problems. Biology is no guarantee of a happy parental experience and adoption does not foredoom one to an unhappy experience! Parenthood is a challenge, either way.

Familybuilding Tips
You can bet that if you do tell family members you're planning to adopt, you and the adoption will be very hot topics of the day.

Resist the common prospective adopter tendency to tell all to anyone who asks anything. Put your brain in gear before your mouth starts moving. Why? Because the sad fact is that people tend to remember anything "bad" that you have to say, and if it has something to do with you or with the child, maybe you wouldn't want them remembering or repeating it later on.

What if you're a single person and your mom thinks your plan to adopt a child is the craziest idea she's ever heard? You might think about circumstances in the past when she disapproved of actions you took, and then they turned out okay.

You might also want to try to determine the underlying fear. Does your mom think she'll be constantly trapped into on-call babysitting? You can reassure her by telling her you've developed a childcare plan. Or she might think adopting will prevent you from ever marrying. Remind her that single people do get married. And that in 5 years, you'll be 40 anyway, whether you adopt or not.

Your Friends and Family

In addition to your parents, others will react to your plan to adopt. Your siblings may think it's a great idea or really dumb, and you'll see by how they regard you and treat you during the adoption process. (Do not, however, assume they are disapproving if they make no or few comments. They may be preoccupied with their own life issues.)

As with your parents, if siblings express dismay about you adopting, you could remind them of decisions you made in the past that they were skeptical of but that worked out. Or decisions *they* made that everyone questioned but ultimately proved positive. Then tell them that this is a decision you are making and that you believe will work out for your family. Closed for discussion, done deal.

If you already have children, this new child (or children) will become their sibling(s). They may have some powerful positive and negative feelings about this:

➤ They may fear you'll favor the new child over them.

Whether you think it's an issue or not, it's a good idea to reassure the children already in your home—or even your adult children who have left home—that they still are very important to you and always will be. No one can "replace" them. You want to adopt another child (or children), but the new child will have a different relationship with you.

Also be sure to tell them that love isn't like a pie that must be divided up because there's only so much. You can love the family that you have now, and you can love a child whom you adopt too without diminishing the love for the ones who "came first."

➤ They may worry that you'll spend less time with them.

Let's be realistic about one aspect that will probably change—your time. Especially if you are adopting an infant, your time will be more in demand than it was in the past. You'll need to be sure that once you do adopt and are over the initial adjustment stage, your other children—and your spouse!—still receive loving attention.

Your family and children may especially worry if the child you plan to adopt is disabled. Won't this take too much time and energy out of you—and them? How long will it take to figure out exactly what the child needs and how to provide it? Will the disabled child become the center of attention *because* of the disability? As you can see, there are many things to think about here!

➤ They may worry that the household workload will increase.

Guess what? They're right! At least in the early days and until you get settled, you may find yourself calling on your children to help you with the new baby or older child. However, they should not be expected to sacrifice all their time and energy to the child whom *you* chose to adopt.

If you think you will really need extra help, you should consider your options even before you receive a referral for a child. Should you find a baby-sitting cooperative in your neighborhood or start one yourself? Should you check out daycare programs? (If you work, you definitely should decide ahead of time whether you will continue to work, how long you'll take off after you adopt your child, and other work-related issues.)

Be sure to keep in mind the possible reactions of the newly adopted child to whatever plans you make. A two-year-old adopted from another country, who speaks another language, may not adapt very well at first to a daycare center, to your children, or to you. She probably needs at least a few weeks with you before she can be placed in another new and strange environment. It's a bad mistake to hold off on thinking about these issues until after you adopt.

➤ Children already in the family may consciously or unconsciously wonder about their place in the family, for example, no longer being "the baby" or "the big kid." Again, reassure them of your love. And when the child comes, make sure you still have "alone time" with them so they continue to feel special.

➤ They may wonder what their friends will think. (I'll talk about how to explain adoption to others in Part 4.) Others have strange ideas about adoption sometimes, based on TV shows or things they've heard. Yet most people don't believe in vampires that they see on TV shows. Tell them that just as vampires are mythical, the idea that all adoptees are disturbed is also a myth. Just because you see it on TV doesn't make it "real."

➤ If adopted themselves, they may have new questions about their birthparents. If nonadopted, they may have questions about their births. Answer the "old" adoptee's questions honestly and openly, and reassure them of your continuing love. And talk to nonadopted kids about their births and how important they are and always will be to you.

Real Life Snapshots

After my husband and I were approved to adopt, we began thinking about names for the baby that would come someday. (More information on naming is offered in Chapter 18.) We involved the two children already in our family, then ages six and seven.

We all pored over name books, looking at the meanings of different names, and also seeing if the name sounded right with our last name. We finally selected a boy name and a girl name, since we didn't know if our new baby would be male or female. Of course, my husband and I had veto power over some of the silly names the kids chose!

This task took many hours and also helped the children feel that they were important to the future adoption. And they were!

Of course, your children may exhibit many positive and excited feelings about the new child. They may be eager to hug the new baby or show the new older child the ropes. Children can be very affectionate and helpful—but don't expect that kind of behavior 100 percent of the time or you will be disappointed. You'll also see jealousy, boredom, and other common reactions to a new person—and rival—in the family. This is normal.

The Least You Need to Know

➤ Most adoptive parents' own parents worry about adoption, but most become very proud grandparents.

➤ Your relationships with others will change when you adopt. Make sure you have a childcare plan in place before you adopt.

➤ Children already in your home need reassurance that you'll still pay attention to them after the adoption.

➤ If possible, involve family members in looking forward to the adoption with you.

Chapter 15

What You Should Know About a Child You May Adopt

In This Chapter

➤ Basic medical information you need to know

➤ Birthfamily background you should ask for

➤ Does the child have "good genes?"

➤ Checking out prenatal care

How do you first learn about a child who may become *your* child? Sometimes the call with the information comes as the result of a birthmother who has chosen your resume and you as the potential parents to her child. Or maybe the social worker has gotten word of the child she thinks would be just right for your family, so she contacts you. Or you may have been thumbing through a state photolisting book and suddenly, there he is, a child who tugs at your heartstrings. The first inklings of a contact are made in many different ways—the first word of a child that you may be able to adopt. But how do you know whether to follow your head or heart? I recommend following both! And this chapter will provide you with practical guidance on the "head" part.

On the "downside," many times when people adopt, they feel like they have little or no control over the process. They don't like this helpless feeling. So they try to find out as much information about a child and/or the birthmother as possible, to decide whether or not to adopt. This is a good thing.

They may be especially concerned about heredity. Medical and scientific advances have made us increasingly aware of how heredity affects our "predispositions" for various physical traits, health, even talents and personality traits.

This chapter covers genetic predispositions as well as environmental and medical factors that you should know about if you're thinking about adopting a child.

Vital Statistics

When the agency or attorney tells you about a child that's already been born, you should be sure to ask plenty of questions about the child's health and her environment to date.

Here's a sampling of questions you might ask:

➤ When was the child born? (If unknown, approximately when? Who determined this and how did they come up with that date?)

➤ How much did the child weigh as an infant?

➤ What was the head circumference of the child as an infant? If not available, what is the child's head circumference now? (The child's head size is relevant to a physician. A head size that is too small in relation to the child's age or body can mean a problem with brain development.)

➤ Does the child appear to be developmentally on track?

➤ Is the child shy or outgoing? Noisy or quiet?

➤ Does the child have any siblings? Where are they?

➤ What illnesses has the child had and at what age? What treatments did she receive?

➤ What is the child's best feature? Biggest problem area?

If the child is older than two, you might also consider asking the following questions:

➤ Where has the child lived since birth? In how many homes or with how many different caregivers?

➤ What major experiences have happened to the child—positive or negative?

➤ Does the child have any siblings? Where are they?

➤ Has the child been physically or sexually abused? Has the child been neglected?

➤ Has the child received any therapy? If so, from whom?

Deep Background

Aside from those basic questions, it's important to obtain as much medical background information about the birthparents (and extended birthfamily) as you can. Unfortunately, much of the information you receive may be sketchy. If a child was abandoned, for example, there's no way to know the medical history of the birthfamily.

When the birthparents are available, though, the adoption arranger will usually provide them with a questionnaire about their medical histories. The arranger should also ask for information from the birthparents' parents, if possible.

I strongly recommend that any health information provided on the birthparents and their parents be reviewed by a medical doctor before the adoption is finalized, so that the physician can give an evaluation on possible risks and problems.

Born in the USA

The medical information on a U.S.–born child is only as good as whatever information the birthparents supply to your adoption arranger. The amount of information available may vary due to state law. Some states require very specific medical information from birthparents, while many others leave the amassing of information up to the arranger.

Familybuilding Tips

Usually, the primary source of medical information an adoption arranger receives will be from the birthmother (or pregnant woman) herself. She will generally provide all her current medical information.

But think about this. Were you in pretty good shape when you were 18 or 21? Probably you were healthier then than now! The point is that most birthmothers have not yet encountered serious health problems that they may suffer as they age, including those that may have a genetic basis, such as diabetes and arthritis. So what you really should know are the health conditions of the birthparents' *parents*.

For example, Wyoming law requires medical history including "all available information regarding conditions or diseases believed to be hereditary, any drugs or medication taken during pregnancy by the child's natural mother and any other information which may be a factor influencing the child's present or future health."

The state of Michigan, however, gets much more specific and requires the following: "An account of the health and genetic history of the child, including an account of the child's prenatal care; medical condition at birth; any drug or medication taken by the child's mother during pregnancy; any subsequent medical, psychological, psychiatric, or dental examination and diagnosis; any psychological evaluation done when the child was under the jurisdiction of the court; any neglect or physical, sexual, or emotional abuse suffered by the child; and a record of any immunizations and health care the child received while in foster or other care."

Adoptinfo

Here's an interesting innovation in adoption law: In 1996, Pennsylvania passed legislation to create an Adoption Medical History Registry.

According to the law, a Pennsylvania birthparent may fill out an Adoption Medical History Information form, which remains on file should the adopted child seek information as an adult. In addition, the form can be updated if the birthparent later develops health problems that the adopted child should know about. The information is voluntary and is only disclosed to adoptive parents or adoptees over age 18. It is also completely anonymous.

Adoption Alert

Information on birthmothers and birthfathers is usually more difficult to obtain in international adoptions. In some cases, the agency may not even know who the birthmother is. And you can usually forget about any information at all on the birthfather.

However, I believe it's a good idea to ask for this information so that when it *can* be amassed, adoption arrangers will work to provide it to you.

And that's not all! Michigan also requires information on: the health and genetic history of the child's biological parents and other members of the child's family; the parents' health at the time of birth; a summary of the parents' medical and psychological histories at the time of placement; and information on the hobbies, special interests, and school activities of the child's family. This law appears to be one of the most, if not the most, comprehensive. But most other states, although they may require medical and genetic information, leave the details up to the adoption arranger.

Children in Foster Care

If you adopt a foster child in the U.S., the medical information you receive will only be as good as is supplied in the case records.

Since foster children generally receive inadequate healthcare, I think that children who have lived in foster homes for more than a year also need a thorough exam. It's also a good idea to provide whatever medical records you can obtain to a medical expert before the adoption is complete, to ensure that any known medical problems can be dealt with by your family and by your doctor.

Health Issues Overseas

As mentioned in Chapter 11, obtaining background medical information can be an especially difficult problem in international adoptions, because the orphanage may know nothing about the child prior to his or her arrival. Also, sometimes children from other countries have illnesses that are not seen often in the U.S. In addition, children who have lived in orphanages for more than a few months can be severely impacted by the orphanage experience. The longer the child lives in an orphanage, the higher the probability that there will be health or psychological problems later on.

If the agency does not provide you with enough information, ask the agency to ask their facilitator or the orphanage director for more. (See Chapter 11 for more information on international adoptions.)

Listen Up!

I've noticed that some eager adopters seem deaf to the medical information that they're given. Social workers report that sometimes even when adopters are told of a child's possible health problems, they don't necessarily "hear" the information. They are too anxious to adopt to really consider the ramifications of what they're being told.

For this reason, some agencies list possible risks in writing and require adopters to sign these forms in front of a notary.

Good Genes, Bad Genes

Most of us don't think about any of the "bad" genes that might "run in" our families. And yet, we all have positive and negative *genetic predispositions*. Some people inherit a predisposition for high blood pressure, for example. Many experts believe there are inherited predispositions for certain psychiatric problems as well.

When people have biological children, they can't selectively choose the "good" genes that they want and de-select the ones they don't. (Not yet!) It's pretty much a roll of the genetic dice. Yet adopters want as much genetic information as they can obtain, because they want to control what they will and will not deal with in a child. The birthfamily information you receive from the arranger can help you better understand what runs in the child's family.

However, keep in mind that although there may be a family history for a particular problem, the birthparents may never actually develop the problem, and the adopted child may not develop it, either. But it's still good information to know.

If you would have difficulty dealing with a particular condition or illness, for whatever reason, be sure to make this clear to the adoption arranger.

> **Adopterms**
> A *genetic predisposition* refers to a probability that a child will inherit some feature that occurred in the biological family, from something as simple as blue eyes to far more complicated issues such as alcoholism and mental illness.

> **Familybuilding Tips**
> Not having adequate medical or genetic background information is a key complaint of older adoptees. You can head off this problem by seeking this data now. Not only will you be able to use the information, but also you can relay it to your child when he or she grows up.

Baby on the Way: Prenatal Info

If the child is not yet born, whatever information you can gain about the birthmother and about the child's prenatal condition is important. Researchers are discovering that prenatal conditions have an enormous impact on children's later mental and physical development.

Here are a few prenatal conditions that can affect a child:

➤ Is the birthmother receiving adequate prenatal care? This means care in the first or early second trimester of her pregnancy, when she is seen at least monthly by an obsetrician or, if low risk, by a family practitioner.

➤ Is the birthmother eating right?

Because unborn children receive all their nutrition from their birthmothers, the birthmothers' diet is crucial. Is the birthmother eating plenty of vegetables, fruits, whole grains, and dairy products? Good. Is she eating a steady diet of junk food and nothing else? Not so good.

➤ Is the birthmother abusing alcohol?

Most physicians advise pregnant women to stop drinking alcohol altogether during the pregnancy; alcohol use can damage the developing fetus. At its most extreme, this damage can lead to Fetal Alcohol Syndrome (FAS), which causes severe neurological damage.

➤ Is the birthmother abusing drugs (legal or illegal)?

Abuse of illegal drugs (such as marijuana, heroin, and cocaine) during pregnancy can adversely affect the child's physical and mental development. The birthmother's gynecologist will probably check for drugs and should report any signs of drug use to the agency or attorney. This may not be possible because of patient confidentiality unless the birthmother signs a release. Ask the agency or attorney if they obtain such releases.

Also, remember that many legal drugs and medications can be dangerous to a developing fetus, and so should not be taken by pregnant women. If the birthmother is getting adequate prenatal care, she will be aware of these restrictions.

➤ Is the birthmother under severe stress?

What is the birthmother's general emotional and psychological state? While it's inevitable that an unplanned pregnancy will cause some amount of stress, high levels of depression or anxiety will not be good for her or the developing fetus.

Real Life Snapshots

Before Carla and Bob adopted their baby, they asked the birthmother numerous questions about her medical history and those of her parents, the birthfather, and his parents. They collected as much data as they could (far more than the social worker had ever sought). When they were finally satisfied, they decided to adopt the child. He grew up extremely healthy.

Several years later, Carla and Bob had a biological child. Unfortunately, he was born prematurely and suffered numerous complications for the first two years of his life. At that point, Carla wryly remembered her careful questioning of the birthmother and her fears about adopting an unhealthy child. She'd had no idea she could have a very sick biological child. The moral of this story is that with kids, either adopted or biological, no matter how careful you are, you can't ensure there will be no problems.

How to Say No

Why would you want to say "no" to an adoption arranger who's offering you a child? There are many reasons. Perhaps the child has a medical problem that you feel you can't deal with. Or you feel you just don't have enough information about the child.

If you feel that a referral for a particular child is *not* right for you, it's a good idea to explain to the arranger, as tactfully as possible, why you don't feel comfortable accepting this child. If the arranger pressures you to adopt the child anyway, I recommend that you consider finding another adoption arranger.

Most prospective parents are terrified to "turn down" a child, convinced the adoption arranger will never offer them another. The reality is that if the agency does indeed place the kind of child you seek, it will probably offer you another child. An agency would only decide not to work with you if you turned down, say, three or four healthy children for reasons that don't make sense to the arranger.

Real Life Snapshots

Todd and Vicky had applied to adopt through an attorney and were completely stunned when they were called a month later and told of a baby that was just born. Did they want to adopt her? They felt unready and scared, and they turned the child down. After that, they agonized that God would punish them by never ever giving them another chance to adopt.

Well, He didn't. Punish them, I mean. They adopted another child about six or seven months later. They felt, as most adoptive parents do, that the child they adopted was the child who was meant for them.

The Least You Need to Know

➤ If you are considering adopting a child who is already born, find out as much as possible about the child's birth size and current physical development.

➤ Try to obtain information on the child's biological grandparents, as well as the birthparents.

➤ If you are considering adopting a child who is not yet born, find out about the birthmother's health and prenatal care.

➤ Don't feel pressured to adopt a child you are not sure about.

Chapter 16

What You Should Know About Birthmothers

In This Chapter

➤ How do birthmothers choose adoption arrangers, and why should you care?

➤ What are the pros and cons of meeting birthmothers?

➤ What should you ask and *not* ask a birthmother?

➤ What if you and the birthmother don't wish to meet?

➤ Why do some birthmothers change their minds about adoption? What patterns should you look for?

When you're concentrating on your own goal of adopting a child, it can be difficult—nearly impossible—to understand why a woman would contemplate placing a child for adoption. And yet it is important to understand not only why women choose adoption, but how they choose the adoption arranger, whether an agency or attorney.

You also need to realize that birthmothers have fears and concerns about adopters—hey, they watch TV too! (Adopters are sometimes the bad guys on television, sadly.) Some birthmothers wish to meet prospective parents and some do not. This chapter takes a look at adoption from a birthmother's perspective and explains why you need to try to look through her eyes.

Choice of Adoption Arranger

I'd first like to talk about *why* birthparents choose agency adoption (and particular agencies), or private adoption (and particular attorneys). If you know why the birthmother chose a particular agency, attorney, or third party, this can give you another piece of the puzzle to help you decide if you want to adopt her child.

Here are some reasons why birthmothers choose agencies:

➤ They're young and their parents chose the agency for them.

There are both pros and cons to young birthparents whose own parents bring them to the agency (from a prospective adopter's viewpoint). It's good that the parents know about the pregnancy and believe that adoption is the right path. However, if the young (under age 18) birthmother herself is not committed to the decision to place her child for adoption, she may change her mind.

➤ They called the agency and the social worker seemed understanding and kind.

Younger birthmothers are probably more likely to turn to adoption agencies than attorneys, because they need more emotional "hand-holding" than do adult women. Thus, if they believe the agency social worker is understanding, they may decide to stay with the agency. Conversely, these women may be frightened of lawyers, or may feel that placing through an attorney is not quite acceptable or is in some way "cold."

➤ The adoption agency had an attractive ad in the Yellow Pages when the birthmother checked the phone book under "adoption." The birthmother may be drawn to emotional appeals.

➤ Some birthmothers don't know about non-agency adoptions and think agencies are the only way to go.

➤ The agency said they could choose the adopting parents from resumes of approved families, and this sounded good. The opportunity to choose the adoptive parents is a very attractive one to many birthmothers.

➤ They may be suspicious that if they use a lawyer, their needs won't truly be represented.

Some women are suspicious of lawyers who handle adoptions; they think the lawyers might be trying to "sell" babies.

➤ They heard about the agency from a friend, or saw an ad and called the agency.

I think that most birthmothers can find an agency that does meet their needs *if* they do some checking around. The trouble is that they (as do many adoptive parents) may call one agency, not like what they hear, and erroneously decide that all agencies are the same. Most birthmothers, however, will be satisfied with their first contact. Birthmothers who do a great deal of "shopping around" for an adoption arranger may be setting the adoption up for failure because they're finding something wrong with every contact.

Choosing an Attorney

As discussed in Chapter 6, in some states, lawyers can handle private adoptions from start to finish; in other states, the birthmother and prospective adoptive parents must find each other first and then come to the attorney to handle the legal work. In many cases, two attorneys must be hired; one for the birthmother and one for the adopters.

From a birthparent's perspective, there are pros and cons to arranging the adoption through a lawyer rather than an agency. Here are several reasons why birthmothers choose a non-agency adoption:

➤ They do not want to apply for welfare benefits.

Some adoption agencies require birthmothers to apply for welfare programs (such as Aid to Families with Dependent Children, Food Stamps, and Medicaid), although other agencies can and do pay for the birthmother's medical and living expenses through funds provided by the adoptive parents.

With a private adoption, if state law allows (and most states do), the adopting parents can pay the birthmother's medical bills. In some states, it is also legal for the adopting parents to pay for the birthmother's living expenses, such as rent, heat, electricity, and so forth. This may also be done by agencies as a "pass through" of expenses to the adoptive parents.

➤ They may want to live independently during their pregnancy, and if they can receive living expenses from the adopters, this is an achievable goal.

➤ They want an open adoption or a confidential adoption.

If a birthmother doesn't like the idea of open adoptions but the agency promotes them, she may choose a non-agency adoption for more privacy. On the other hand, if the agency is heavily into confidentiality and the birthmother wants more openness, she may turn to a private adoption. (See Chapter 18 for more on open versus confidential adoptions.)

➤ They want a certain kind of family to adopt their child (for example, a family of a particular religion or racial background).

If an agency does not have the kind of family a birthmother wants, she may choose a private adoption to have more choices.

➤ They don't want counseling.

Some birthmothers turn away from agency adoptions because they *do not* want counseling by a social worker, therapist, or anyone else. However, in more and more private adoptions, counseling is an offered option which the birthmother can take or leave.

➤ They don't know what adoption agencies are available in their area.

I've heard some birthmothers tell me that they aren't aware of local agencies that provide adoption services because the word "adoption" is not in their name. For example, Catholic Social Services and the Children's Home Society are two agencies that arrange adoptions. But because the word "adoption" is not in their name, some birthmothers might not think to contact them.

Meeting a Birthmother

Some agencies or attorneys (or other adoption arrangers) think it's a good idea for a woman to meet the people who want to adopt her child. Some arrangers recommend a meeting on a first-name basis, while others favor full disclosure.

On the other hand, some adoption experts don't like the idea of meetings occurring before consent is signed because they worry that it could interfere with the birthmother's decision—making her feel pressured into the adoption. They prefer that meetings occur after the birthmother makes up her mind about adoption, independently of knowing the couple. (Others say that the birthmother needs to meet the couple to know if adoption is the right choice for her.)

The argument that the birthmother may be less likely to change her mind if she meets the couple is actually used as a "selling" point by some open adoption advocates, who tell adopters that the birthmother will then know them and won't want to hurt them.

The most important point to keep in mind for *you* is that most people are filled with trepidation about meeting a birthmother and this is normal. It doesn't necessarily mean that a meeting would be wrong for you. However, if everything in you screams "No!" do not allow yourself to be pressured into a meeting.

You may also end up meeting a birthmother if you go your own way and advertise (see Chapter 7).

If you think it's stressful to meet the woman who might give you her child—you're right. It's also stressful for *her*. It's also okay to not meet, if that is your choice.

There are some common fears that many birthmothers have of meeting adoptive parents, and it's a good idea to consider the thoughts a pregnant woman might have before meeting *you*, should you both choose to meet:

> ➤ They (the adopters) will be smarter than me and I might say something stupid.

> ➤ They'll think I'm too fat.

> ➤ They'll think I'm a slut.

> ➤ They'll think I'm a drug addict.

> ➤ I'll probably hate them and they'll hate me, too.

> ➤ What if they're abusive?

> ➤ I'm scared.

As you can see, the stress is certainly not one-sided. Of course, when you want a child so intensely, it may be very hard for you to understand how someone *could not* want a child. It can be far too easy to assume that anyone who doesn't want to parent a child must be unkind or cold. Give her a chance! She might be the mother of the child you parent.

Adoption Alert

I've seen many people who are seeking to adopt become irrational and scared when faced with the idea of meeting a real live birthmother. I call it "Rapture of the Adoption." It's similar to "rapture of the deep" in that the adopter has plunged to unknown depths far too fast to handle what's going on. This can also happen with *no* meeting; for example, if the arranger tells you about a child and says you have one day to decide.

If you reach this stage, you may feel out of control, silly, scared, overwhelmed, and excited. Keep your wits about you. Don't agree to adopt a child unless you have seriously considered the idea. Don't let Rapture of the Adoption overtake you.

Questions to Ask

Here are some questions I suggest that the adoption arranger should be sure to ask the birthmother. You may wish to ask some of these questions yourself. You should also add your own questions to this list as well.

> ➤ When is your baby due?

> ➤ When did you start thinking about adoption?

> ➤ Are you working with an agency or attorney? (If you've met her through you own advertising.)

> ➤ Are you feeling all right?

> ➤ How does the birthfather feel about the pregnancy? How does he feel about adoption?

> ➤ How do your parents feel about the pregnancy?

> ➤ How did you choose this agency/attorney/facilitator?

> ➤ Do you have a plan for your life, after the baby is born, either job-wise or educationally?

➤ What do you like to do in your spare time?

➤ Do you know anybody who placed a baby for adoption? Do you know any adopted people?

Questions to Avoid

There are some questions you *should not* ask the birthmother, because they might make her very uncomfortable. This doesn't mean you never ask these questions, either directly or through an intermediary. Just don't ask them in your first encounter with the birthmother.

Here are some of the "don't ask" questions in your first talk with the birthmother:

➤ Are you sure you really want the baby adopted and you won't change your mind?

➤ Have you taken any drugs during your pregnancy?

➤ Did the father refuse to marry you?

➤ Were you raped?

➤ How many times have you been pregnant?

➤ How many men might be the father?

Interviewing Tips

If you decide to interview and screen birthmothers yourself, whether in person or by phone, you need some basic interviewing tips. Here are a few:

1. Try to avoid pre-conceived notions about the birthmother as poverty-stricken, unintelligent, or anything else. Research indicates the opposites are generally true and that she is more likely to be middle class and of normal intelligence. Listen with an open mind.

2. If you have any questions that might be sensitive in nature, don't ask them first. You need to build up a little trust. (Don't ask them last, either. You might never get to them.) Some sensitive questions can be deferred to the birthmother's attorney or social worker. The best idea is to start with simple small talk. The weather is nearly always a safe topic. "It's not the heat, it's the humidity!"

3. The way you word questions is important. For example, don't phrase questions in a way that implies the answer (for example, "You're not working now, are you?" implies that the expected answer will be "no.") Don't ask the question in a way that implies the "right" answer.

4. After you ask a question, wait for the response. Don't answer for the birthmother or try to rush her.

5. If the birthmother backs off from answering a particular question, ask other questions. Then reword and revisit the original question, and you may get your answer. For example, if you asked, "Do you think prenatal care is important?" the birthmother may have shied away from the question because she hasn't been to a doctor yet. You could later ask, "Have you decided what doctor you plan to see?" By rephrasing the question and also asking it later, you are more likely to receive an answer. However, if the second try doesn't work, back off.

6. At the end of the talk, ask the birthmother if there's anything important that you haven't discussed. As a writer, I have found that this simple question often gets me extremely valuable information.

7. Understand that some birthmothers are not emotional or "sharing" kind of people, and they won't want to be your close friend. This doesn't mean they're not serious about adoption. Their primary concern is if you would be good parents to the child; and if you seem to be good candidates, then they're satisfied.

Questions for *You*

Don't expect to be the only one asking questions when you speak with a birthmother. In most cases, she'll have a few questions to ask you! Some of these questions may be appropriate and some may not be. Here are a few questions you should be prepared to answer:

➤ How long have you been married?

➤ Can't you have children?

➤ Why do you want to adopt?

➤ What does your family think of adoption?

➤ Do you have any pets?

➤ How long have you been thinking about adopting?

➤ What religion are you?

➤ Will the adopting mother work after the baby is born? If so, what kind of childcare arrangements do you favor?

There are also questions that you *should not* answer. Some of these may be answered later by your adoption arranger and some are just no one's business. Even if you *want* to answer them, resist this impulse!

Adoption Alert

If you have identified a birthmother and she asks you for money, it's far better to refer her to your agency or attorney. Do the same if any other person asks, such as the birthfather, his parents, and so on.

Any exchange of money could be construed as "baby selling" by a third party and is also a pretty dumb idea. You won't get a receipt, and the payment could be denied later on. (Note that I'm not talking about $10 for bus fare and a sandwich. I'm talking about significant amounts. Although watch out for constant nickel and dime stuff.) Don't make this mistake.

Here are some questions that a birthmother might ask and that you *should not* answer:

➤ What's your address? You may want to provide this information later, but *do not* provide it in your first encounter, which, by the way, should be in a public place like a restaurant or park. Not a fancy restaurant either because that might make her (or you) too nervous. Go for the mid-range.

➤ Who do you (and your spouse) work for? Don't get too specific, at least not at First Contact. It's okay to say, for example, that you're an engineer and your husband's a plumber. It's better to not say that you work for XYZ Electronics at 95 Maple Street. You don't want people contacting you at work except for the adoption arranger.

➤ How much money do you make? A birthmother who asks you this right away may be a scammer (see Chapter 9)—or a naive person who doesn't know what to ask you. Either way, tell her that you make enough to support your family and to support a child.

➤ How much money will you give me? This is another sign of a possible problem or a naive person. Tell the birthmother that you have to refer all financial aspects to your social worker or attorney. If you are pressed very hard on the money issue, do not pursue this adoption. There will be other opportunities.

Real Life Snapshots

After advertising her desire to adopt, Alicia was contacted by a 15-year-old girl in another state, who wanted her to fly out to meet her. Alicia was ready to jump on the next plane out.

Ask yourself: If a 15-year-old girl who was a stranger from another state asked you to drop everything and fly there to meet her, would you? Without consulting with her parents, her attorney, or some other representative? I wouldn't, especially knowing what I know about the high probability that this young teenager will change her mind. (Her age is a negative factor.)

As stated elsewhere in this book, I think most adopters should first look within their own state to adopt a child. And they should retain the services of a competent and honest adoption agency or attorney. They should also try hard to retain their own common sense.

"Dear Birthmother . . ."

Another way for the birthmother to get to know you is to write a "dear birthmother" letter that explains why you want to adopt. (This is similar to the adoption resume discussed in Chapter 12.) Often adoption agencies or attorneys show these letters to pregnant women considering adoption. It's a kind of sales pitch and can be a tough letter to write.

Basically, a "dear birthmother" letter is written by the potential adoptive couple or (usually) by the potential adoptive mom. The letter explains why the writer wants to become a parent and describes herself and her family. Often the letter includes positive and comforting words to the birthmother.

Adoptinfo

OH.

The "dear birthmother" idea rose into prominence with the book *Dear Birthmother: Thank You For Our Baby* by Kathleen Silber and Phyllis Speedlin after its publication in 1982.

This is a book that describes open adoption very positively and includes warm and realistic letters between adoptive parents and birthmothers.

Dear birthmother letters can get very emotional and can be very difficult to write. If you write one that makes you burst into tears, it's probably a good letter. Of course, you do *not* want to appear an emotional basket case either. You want to convey the strength of your desire to adopt and at the same time show that you're emotionally stable and would be a good parent. Show it to your spouse, of course. But be sure to also show it to someone who is less emotionally involved (*not* your partner and *not* your parents). A trusted friend or someone you respect may be a good choice. Make sure they have a positive emotional reaction.

Birthmothers Who Change Their Minds

Probably the most intensely felt fear of adopters is that the birthmother will make an adoption plan—and then flip-flop and decide to raise the child herself. Anecdotally, I'm estimating that at least two-thirds of birthmothers who pursue or continue to pursue adoption into the third trimester do *not* change their minds about adoption.

But you should ask each adoption arranger about what their experience has been. If Agency A says that 95–100 percent of their birthmothers go through with it, this doesn't sound right. Even the best arrangers have some birthmothers who change their minds. Conversely, if Agency B says only 10 percent proceed with the adoption, something is wrong—with their policy, procedures, or elsewhere. It's not your job to figure out what they're doing wrong. Move on.

> **OH.** **Adoptinfo**
> It's very important that a birthmother feel that the adoption decision is hers and that she was not forced into it by others—her parents, the birthfather, or anyone else. A study reported in a 1996 issue of *Clinical Social Work Journal* revealed that those birthmothers who felt pressured into adoption suffered significantly higher levels of grief than those who felt unpressured. In addition, a greater level of grief was associated with the birthmother feeling ashamed or guilty.

Women who are in their second or third trimesters are better "risks" for adopters because a woman still in her first trimester may be going through many emotional issues, receiving pressure from the birthfather and others, and the baby may not seem entirely "real" to her. Later, after she feels the baby, it kicks and so forth, she can be more reality-based. If she still is considering adoption then, that is a sign of potential commitment, although no guarantee.

It's also true that a woman usually gives signals that she's ambivalent; for example, she has no plan for her life after the birth. A good counselor should spot those clues.

Various studies have researched the common characteristics of birthmothers most likely to change their minds about adoption. Here's a list of those characteristics:

➤ The birthmother is under age 17.

➤ She has no immediate or future career/life plans.

➤ She lives in a big city.

➤ She was brought up by a single mom.

➤ She is non-religious.

➤ She lives with the birthfather.

➤ Her mom disapproves of adoption.

➤ She lives with her parent(s).

➤ She is a high school dropout.

➤ Her mother or father have no education beyond high school.

➤ She (or her parents) are on welfare.

➤ She has friends who are single parenting and urging her to do the same.

➤ She has a very difficult delivery of her child.

You may think that some of these factors would lead the birthmother *to* adoption rather than away from it. For example, a birthmother who is 15 is not in a good emotional or financial position to raise a child. But in many cases, she has not achieved the maturity to realize this. Also, she may be strongly influenced by her peers, and if her other friends are parenting babies, she may choose parenting, too. (If she has friends who've placed their babies for adoption and are comfortable about that choice, that's a positive sign for you.)

Conversely, a 20-year-old woman is more mature and may decide that adoption is the best course for her child. She is less likely to be influenced by others.

Education appears tied with the decision to place for adoption; the less educated the birthmother is, the more likely she will choose parenting over adoption. This may be because if a woman has no career goals (which is more likely with less-educated women), she may see parenting as a default choice. By "career goal," I don't mean the birthmother must be an aspiring brain surgeon. Wanting to be an X-ray technician or a hair stylist are career goals, too.

The reason for changing one's mind after a difficult delivery can be speculated on. Perhaps the birthmother has become worried about and attached to the child. Perhaps she fears she won't have more children in the future.

Other factors are easier to understand. A woman who was raised by two parents is more likely to believe that

> **Adoption Alert**
> Do not assume that if "your" birthmother falls into one or two of my "likely to change her mind" categories, then all is lost. Few people fit every one. But if she fits most of the high-risk categories, proceed with caution. On the other hand, if she is the exact opposite—she was raised by two parents, not on welfare, and so forth, she can still change her mind. It's just less likely. Remember that nothing is 100 percent certain.

her child should have two parents, while a woman raised by a single mom is more likely to think single parenting is okay. Also, if the birthmother is already on public assistance, she may not see a problem with single parenting; whereas, if the birthmother is very opposed to going on welfare, as many are, she may see adoption as a better choice.

A woman who is religious may believe that God has called her to place her baby for adoption, and she may also see adoption as a means to atone for having a baby when unmarried. (Yes, there are still people who think nonmarital childbearing is a sin.)

What to Do If It Happens to You

If she's going to change her mind, when does it happen and what should you do if she does?

During early pregnancy and even through the second trimester, the pregnancy may seem unreal to a pregnant woman, especially if she is in a crisis situation. (This is one reason why some adoption arrangers don't like to work with women in their first trimester. There are too many psychological issues to work through first before the woman can decide for or against adoption.) Do not count heavily on adopting the baby of a woman who is now two months pregnant. She has many physical and psychological issues to go through before she can really decide.

When birthmothers who have truly committed to adoption do change their minds, it's usually either close to the birth or just after childbirth. Sometimes the imminence of birth makes the birthmother face the issue of adoption versus parenting for the first time. In other cases, the birth itself has an impact. She may experience a change of heart after seeing the child. Or she may be affected by others, such as the birthfather or her relatives, who want the child to stay with the biological family. Very few women decide months after a child is born and with an adoptive family that they want the child back from the adoptive family—although it can happen.

OH.

Adoptinfo

In many states, when a birthparent consents to an adoption, the consent is either irrevocable or can only be revoked for a brief period. (Check the State Adoption Law Chart in Chapter 10 for more information.)

If you're really worried about a birthmother changing her mind, it's a good idea to look into adoption termination insurance, discussed in Chapter 6. But the reality is, even if you lose not one penny, there's no insurance for the emotional pain. It hurts, and it hurts bad. I have heard from adopters whose adoption fell through that they would "never ever" think about adopting a child again. It was too painful, too scary, too hard. Clearly, they needed time to grieve. Do you know what happened later? After a few months, they decided to adopt and they ultimately did adopt a child.

How the Birthparents' Parents Feel

Often the birthmother's parents have a profound impact on her decision to place or not place her child for adoption. As a result, it's also a good idea to try to understand where their heads are at.

Although birthparents don't always tell their own parents about the impending adoption—or even about the pregnancy—when their parents do know, they are bound to have their own reactions, fears, and concerns. Here are some common issues among the birthparents' parents:

➤ Will the child be safe? Will he or she be loved?

No scientific studies have been done on what the primary concerns of a birthparent's family are, but my "take" is that most are concerned about whether the child will be safe and loved.

The safety angle is a concern because many people are worried about child abuse. The agency (if you are using one) should tell birthparents to let their parents know that adopters are thoroughly screened by social workers in most cases.

They also may need reassurance that the child will be loved. Knowing that the adopters tried for five years to create a biological child and then considered adoption for another two or three years could help illustrate the couple's intense commitment to parenthood. Non-identifying (or identifying, in the case of open adoption) information can also help the birthparents' family feel that the adoption is a good choice for the child.

➤ Will this be my only grandchild (if there are no others in the family)? Will my child have other children later on?

No one can know for sure whether the birthmother will marry and have more children in the future. But many do. Had she chosen to parent her child as a single parent, the probability of marriage in her future would be diminished. Conversely, some studies indicate that birthmothers are more likely to marry than single mothers.

The Least You Need to Know

➤ It's important to avoid stereotyping birthmothers.

➤ Birthmothers have questions about adopters.

➤ Birthmothers have different coping styles; don't generalize that all are weepy.

➤ Most birthmothers don't change their minds about adoption, but there are patterns to consider.

➤ If possible, convey reassurance to the birthparents' parents that you will provide a safe and loving family for the child.

Chapter 17

Playing the Waiting Game

In This Chapter

> ➤ Dealing with nosy family and friends

> ➤ How to cope with your social worker

> ➤ Keeping a positive attitude

> ➤ Battling adoption jitters

> ➤ What if you get turned down

You're pretty certain you'll be approved by the adoption arranger. Your child will be coming soon, and everything is all set. Now things should be easy, right? But you feel like you are slowly going crazy. Every day you wonder, will it be today? Will it be tomorrow?

Waiting time is crazymaking for many adopters. They want the baby born *now*. They want the orphanage to release the child *now*. They want the foster care system to send the child to his new home *now*. But they feel they have no control over when anything will happen. All they can do is wait.

Actually, there *are* things you can do. Like think about a name for your child. Plan where her room will be. And pay some attention to *yourself*—remember, for the next 18 or so years, you'll be very busy attending to the needs of this other person!

This chapter shows you how to survive the "I got those waiting-for-my-new-child-to-come-home blues."

All in the Family

Your immediate family (your spouse and any children you may already have) and your extended family (your parents, your spouse's parents, your siblings, and others you're close with) will probably make you wild during the wait to get approved to adopt.

This may not be very comforting, but people do it to pregnant women, too. Most pregnant women in their last trimester swear they are asked 20 times a day when they are due and why they haven't had the baby yet.

When people know that you're planning to adopt a child, they too will ask you repeatedly when the child will be coming. They're really not trying to drive you crazy—usually what they're doing is trying to show interest and caring. You can tell them you're very excited and anxious but haven't heard anything, but as soon as you do, you'll tell the whole world. They'll probably hear your whoops of joy in Australia! This should stave off the questions for a while.

If you're faced with people telling you that you *can't* adopt, just tell them that the agency you're working with has approved you and does think you'll get your baby sometime. You can joke and say that it'll probably be sometime before you're eligible for Social Security. Later, when your baby does come, say that you're so fortunate, it worked out that you were able to adopt sooner than you expected.

If people ask you personal questions that you would rather not answer, you can be vague and say that you're not sure about that. If the questions are insulting from your perspective, such as how you possibly want to raise someone else's problem, you could then say that you regard all children as blessings and will be thrilled when you can become a parent. Keep in mind that it is not necessary for you to share intimate details of your life.

Curious Co-workers

People outside your family—the people you work with and basically anybody who knows that you're adopting a child—can drive you bananas as well. They'll ask you how it's going and may also ask you probing questions that you'd rather not answer. You don't have to! Tell them what you want to tell them and then change the subject if that works for you. You can also say you are so pleased that they are really interested in your adopting a child. And you'll be happy to let them know if any newsbreaking event occurs and the stork suddenly drops off a child. Gentle and positive humor works well with most people.

Surviving Your Social Worker

Most adopters are at least a little afraid of their social worker—whether they admit it or not. After all, the social worker giveth—and the social worker can taketh away. Most social workers are compassionate people who want adopters to succeed. But they are human and they have human flaws. Here are a few dos and don'ts on dealing with your social worker as you wait:

➤ Don't call the social worker daily or even weekly unless you have a specific problem or issue to discuss.

➤ Don't call the social worker early on Monday morning or late on Friday afternoon. (Actually, try to avoid calling anyone at these times—most people are not at their best then.)

➤ Don't expect the social worker to be the supreme authority on adoption. Hopefully, she'll have read a few books and know something. But don't depend on her for all information.

➤ Do treat the social worker with respect and courtesy at all times.

➤ Do try to see the process from the social worker's view—she's in charge of placing children and wants them to go to the best family.

Most social workers are very nice people, but once in a while a social worker gets heady with power and can jerk you around a little. Here's an example of minor "jerking around," although the social worker might not see it that way. It's Thursday and you have an appointment for her to come for a visit next Thursday. She calls you and says her schedule is a mess next week but she has some free time tomorrow. So can she come then instead of next week? This means you have a day to clean—rather than a week.

So what do you do? If you have a valid reason (needing extra cleaning time doesn't count) for her to *not* come, then tell her so. If you have an appointment with your dentist for a root canal and may not feel well, that is a good excuse. (Do not suddenly arrange for a root canal to avoid the social worker. Not worth it.) Or if you have an important business or family event already scheduled, explain this. Otherwise, get out the mop and broom now!

Here's an example of major jerking around. Terri was talking to the social worker at a followup visit and holding and hugging the baby. Suddenly, the worker said, "You know, she's not your baby until *I* say that she's your baby!" Terri burst into tears. The worker then said, "Well, I didn't say I wouldn't approve you," and Terri cried more. What happened? The social worker approved the family. Either she was having a bad day or she was on a power trip (or both), but she was unfair to the new mom. Terri told the agency director about it later, and the worker was reprimanded.

Sometimes it's personal. Dana says when the social worker found out that her father was an alcoholic, she insisted that Dana agree to have nothing to do with him after the adoption. The social worker was estranged and unforgiving of her own father's alcoholism. Said Dana, "She had a hard time accepting I had come to terms with my father's problem and argued with me about whether he should be in my life." Dana wasn't about to disown her father, and she stuck to her guns. The adoption went through.

Generally, you can put up with minor annoyances. But if things get bad, and you truly believe that she is not being fair to you, take action. Ask the social worker if she has a problem with your application or if you have offended her in any way. Tell her that you truly want to adopt and you are genuinely committed to being a good parent.

If that doesn't work, you have the option of talking to her supervisor or the agency director. You may be able to get a different social worker assigned to your case.

> **Adoption Alert**
> Rarely, a social worker may be a perfectionist who turns down applicants for no good reason. If she does this too much, her adoption agency would go out of business. For this reason, problem social workers usually don't last long with any agency.

Despite these lapses of judgment just referred to, most social workers are very nice and normal people! Hold that thought in your mind because it's the truth.

Even the best adoption agency or attorney finds that sometimes people get angry or feel like they're being left out of decisions. For the large part, this is because the process of adoption is incredibly anxiety-inducing.

Remember, your adoption arranger can't share every minute detail with you. On the other hand, if you've heard nothing for weeks or months, it's probably time to give your adoption arranger a friendly call to find out how things are going. Sometimes there are glitches in the adoption process. Don't expect everything to zoom through, problem-free. Things happen.

On the other hand, if you feel like nothing is going right, and there are far too many errors or omissions in the process, you may be right. See Chapter 9 for information on dealing with adoption scammers.

Waiting Dos and Don'ts

The wait is the hardest of all for *you*, the future adopter. Sure, other people can aggravate you with interminable questions, but you have an awful lot of questions, hopes, and fears yourself. So how do you manage to get through these days, weeks, or even months of waiting?

Adoption obsession is very common for the person who has been approved and is waiting for a referral. It can be very debilitating and enervating.

It's not really a good idea to become obsessive while you wait to receive your referral for a child or the approval for a particular child. There are some things you can do to distract yourself during this waiting period:

➤ Maintaining a positive mental attitude is probably the most important advice I can offer. Sure, we all have doubts and fears. But try not to agonize over every problem that maybe might happen.

➤ Keep a journal of your thoughts and how you feel about the adventure that lies ahead. You certainly do not have to be a professional writer to express your feelings and frustrations, your ups and downs. Many people find that the very act of writing down their thoughts frees them from considerable anxiety. It may also jog your unconscious into producing solutions to particular problems.

> **Adopterms**
> *Adoption obsession* refers to constantly thinking about adopting a child. It usually occurs in first-time adoptive parents, although people adopting a second or third child may also experience it. A "little" obsession is beneficial, because it leads you to pursue different opportunities and to learn as much as possible. Just don't let it overtake your life!

➤ Read books about parenting and adoption (but don't go overboard). You may also wish to review children's books about adoption as well. (See Chapter 5 and Appendix H for specific resources.) Keep in mind that most authors have biases, whether they realize it or not. Some see adoption as an idyllic experience; others think adoption is a problematic institution that should be radically changed. The reality is probably somewhere in the middle.

➤ Meet and talk to parents, adoptive and nonadoptive. An effective adoptive parent group can be really helpful, because it allows you to see people with children they've adopted. You can learn the tactics they used to succeed, and the dos and don'ts of adoption.

➤ Take an exercise class or renew an old hobby. Staying involved with our interests makes us happy, and children derive benefit from happy parents. Hopefully you will maintain your hobbies and interests even after your child comes home. After all, don't you want to help your child develop her own interests? She may even share some of yours!

> **Adoption Alert**
> Keep in mind that sometimes parent groups deteriorate into a kind of "gripe session" where members mostly come to complain about the woes of adoption or how tough it is to deal with their children's problems. Avoid those groups. (Fortunately, they are rare.)

Here are some things you should *not* do while you wait for an approval:

➤ Try to keep the obsessing down to a tolerable level. Easy to say, but hard to do. Distract yourself.

➤ Don't worry about negative stories others tell you about adoption. Everyone will know a horror story, just as everyone has a medical horror story when you are facing surgery.

➤ Don't make any other major life changes unless you have to. Adopting a child is big enough!

➤ Don't quit your job (if that's an option for you) unless you know for sure a child is coming or unless you're looking for a good reason to quit anyway. Some people, believe it or not, quit their jobs after they're approved for adoption so they can devote their time to getting ready. That may be okay if you will be adopting within a month or two. But what if the wait lasts longer—as long as a year? You can find yourself with a lot of extra time on your hands.

Losing Your Nerve

People never get cold feet and decide that they really *do not* want to adopt, do they? Sure they do! As you get closer to the goal of adoption, you or your spouse may get panicky and fearful. Can you really be good parents? Can you deal with all the changes that will come with parenthood—or with parenting yet another child?

Adoption Alert
If you find yourself obsessing over adoption for more than a few months, ask yourself what the problem is. Is it fear that you won't succeed? Fear that you will have trouble parenting? Or something else? Make sure you are sure of the adoption before you proceed.

I like to compare the fear of adopting your first child to the fear many of us felt when we decided to get married. Getting the pre-marital jitters doesn't mean that you don't love your future spouse. What it means is that you're planning a major life change—and that can be frightening.

You don't need nerves of steel like Superman to adopt, but it's important to understand that there will be ups and downs in the process. If you know this is normal, it will make the experience much easier. Here are some ways to cope with the emotional highs and lows:

➤ Meet other people who have recently adopted. They can understand.

➤ Give yourself a set time to worry about problems that arise. When that time is over, order yourself to think about other things.

➤ Consider renewing a hobby you enjoyed in the past but have neglected.

➤ If you are religious, try meditation or prayer.

➤ Remind yourself that there is a child at the end of this maze and it's all worth it.

A little fear is normal. Of course, if you have very serious doubts, and you are wondering if your motives are good ones, then you should think carefully before making this major step—for your sake and for the child's sake.

What to Do if You Are Turned Down

Rejection doesn't happen much in adoption, because most families who think they may get rejected by an agency drop out of the home study process before it ends. But once in awhile, a family is surprised by their rejection. Here are a few reasons why prospective adopters may not be approved for adoption:

➤ The social worker is being unreasonable. (See "Surviving Your Social Worker" at the beginning of this chapter.)

➤ The social worker feels you are still yearning for a biological child.

Few people completely lose their sadness about not being able to have a biological child. But they should work through the issue when they apply to adopt. And if the prospective parents have lost a pregnancy or a child, they need time to grieve this loss. Adopted kids should never be "replacement kids."

If your social worker believes that you still need to work on grief issues, at least consider the possibility that she may be right. If you still think she's wrong, talk to her about it. Realize that the social worker may not change her mind; you may need to apply to another agency or attorney. The good news is that you will be prepared to deal with issues of infertility, grief and loss, should the new social worker bring them up.

Real Life Snapshots

Noreen and Tom applied to their local adoption agency and were very excited about finally having a child. Noreen had suffered four miscarriages; that's why she and Tom applied to adopt.

Unfortunately, the agency turned them down. They were not given a reason why. For several years, they felt like something was wrong with them.

Then they moved to another state, and decided to try again. They applied to a new adoption agency, were approved, and brought home their baby son about a year later.

Were Tom and Noreen better people later on? Or was the first social worker wrong? I don't know. What I do know is that if Tom and Noreen had given up, they wouldn't have their son today.

➤ You lied to the social worker about something serious—such as a previous drug offense.

Lying really aggravates most social workers. This does not, however, mean that you must confess every infraction that you ever made. The social worker is not there to give you absolution. She's a person evaluating you as a prospective parent. So when it comes to important issues that would reflect on your ability to raise a child, don't lie.

If you have any criminal history, this will usually disturb the social worker even when it doesn't relate to parenting issues; for example, a white-collar crime such as tax evasion.

➤ Your references weren't strong—or they were negative.

I've discussed the importance of references in Chapter 12. A bad reference might not completely derail your adoption, but it could delay you for months. So don't underestimate the importance of references.

In nearly all cases, your references will be so glowing you'd be embarrassed to read them. But if you've given someone's name without his knowledge, or if you've given the name of someone who (unbeknownst to you) believes adoption is a bad institution, you could be asking for trouble.

➤ You have a serious or life-threatening medical problem.

If you have a serious medical problem, you may get turned down. This does not (or should not) include disabilities such as being wheelchair-bound or other chronic problems that will not radically shorten your lifespan.

Is this fair? After all, thanks to medical progress, many serious illnesses can be controlled. The problem is, social workers are supposed to consider the best interests of a child. All other things being equal, they would rather place a child with a healthy family than with one who is not.

If you are rejected for this reason, you may want to reapply to the agency or another agency in a year or two, with a letter from your physician describing your state of health and the prognosis.

The Least You Need to Know

➤ If you feel your social worker is being unreasonable, discuss your concerns with her supervisor or the agency director.

➤ The waiting period is difficult, but remember that adoption will be worth the wait.

➤ Keeping a journal, practicing your hobbies, and reading about adoption can help you through the waiting period.

➤ Last-minute fears about adoption are nearly universal.

➤ If you are rejected by an agency, try to find out why. You may be able to re-apply later on.

Part 4
Raising Your Adopted Child

Too many people think that once the adoption is official, they can forget about it forever. Not true! Issues still can and will come up.

For example, your parents and friends will almost inevitably ask questions that you might not want to answer. So what do you do? You read this part first.

Your child will also have questions about adoption, and you need to be prepared to answer them—whether your child is 3, 13, or 33! This part includes a chapter on explaining adoption to children of all ages.

Chapter 18

Congratulations! We've Got a Child for You!

In This Chapter

➤ What you can do to clinch an adoption

➤ Getting ready for your child

➤ The difference between open, semi-open, and confidential adoptions

➤ Finalizing an adoption

Sue and Tom knew in their minds and their hearts that Cara was due any day now and that she had chosen them to parent her child. But when "The Call" came that Cara was in labor, they were stunned, nervous, excited, and scared—a broad range of emotions in one fell swoop!

Maureen had applied to adopt a foster child through the county social services agency. It had been six months since she'd been approved, and she wondered if she would *ever* receive a referral to a child. An hour later, the social worker called: They were thinking that Missy, an eight-year-old girl, might be a good fit with Maureen. Would she like to arrange a meeting? Maureen was so excited. She was maybe going to be a mom!

This chapter explains what to do when you finally find a child who is right for you.

Sealing the Deal

I don't think there's any secret formula or any magic incantations you can say to be certain the adoption goes through. But here are some tactics that may work for you:

➤ If you're religious, prayer may help. Not all adoptive parents are religious, and you don't have to be a member of an organized religion to adopt. But many adopters who are religious report that their faith helps them tremendously. If you are not religious, try meditation.

➤ Show the social worker you're truly committed. Promptly fill out the forms you're given, arrange for your physical examination(s), and read any books she recommends.

➤ Compliment your adoption arranger. Not in a fake way—most people can tell when you're being nice only because you want something. But you can achieve the same goal more honestly by finding something that you genuinely like about your arranger, and complimenting her on it. Most people enjoy genuine admiration. And when your adoption arranger feels favorably towards you, she's more likely to go the extra mile for you.

Familybuilding Tips

One fascinating effect of finding something positive about another person is that, as you emphasize what you like about the person, you will probably find yourself liking him or her even more! Then the other person responds positively to you, and the relationship is further reinforced.

This is a good tactic to use in adopting. (And in life.)

➤ Show your gratitude to your adoption arranger. If you are given a referral to a child, write a thank-you note expressing your joy, your hope, and your thanks for her help. Almost no one does this! I wonder why . . . I think it's very effective.

➤ Get into a PAM—*a positive adoption mindset.* When you hear about a child you might be able to adopt, you must be realistic and understand that sometimes things don't work out. Still, be positive. Imagine yourself picking up your child. Think about how excited you'll feel. Imagine happy occasions with the child. Allow yourself to feel truly parental. I believe that a positive adoption mindset can subconsciously enable you to work through many barriers that may pop up. (Not all, but many.)

➤ Get ready for your child. I'll discuss this in the next section.

Getting Ready for Your Child

Getting ready to bring a child home involves actions you should take, as well as mental and emotional adjustments you will need to make.

Here are some actions you can take before your child comes home:

➤ Choose a name for the child.

➤ Get the child's room ready.

➤ Check on health insurance.

➤ Decide whether you will stay at home with the child or not.

➤ Identify part-time or full-time child care. (Even a stay-at-home parent needs a break now and then.)

The Name Game

Another possible occupation is to consider a name for your child. (If you don't know whether the child will be a boy or a girl, then choose names for both genders.) Here are a few issues to consider in naming a child—or changing names:

➤ The child's ethnic background.

➤ The age of the child. If the child is two or over, her name is part of her identity, and it might be a bad idea to change it. (Some adopters make the child's first name her middle name, so it's not lost altogether.) My view is that if the name of the child would cause embarrassment or taunting, perhaps it should be modified.

Sometimes when adoptive parents adopt an abused child, they want to wipe out all the pain of the past and give the child a "clean slate." To do so, they decide to change the child's first and middle names. They see it as a claiming tactic and as a loving act. The problem is that the child may come to the family with nothing but himself and his identity—a part of which is his name.

➤ Naming the child after someone in the family. *Namesaking* is very popular with many adoptive parents.

Adopterms

A *positive adoption mindset* (PAM) is an attitude and feeling that you will succeed with this adoption and you will become a parent.

How is a PAM different from the adoption mindset discussed in Chapter 2? The adoption mindset refers to a goal-oriented state of mind in which you can develop a successful adoption plan. But when you reach the PAM stage, you have already found your child and are waiting for the adoption to go through.

Adopterms

To *namesake* a child is to name the child after someone within your family. Often the first name of a favorite relative is used, but sometimes a family last name is used as a first name, such as "Adams" or "Brooks."

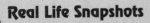

Real Life Snapshots

Timmy, a very smart newly adopted child, told his new Mom that he wanted to change *her* name. What did she say? She told him that by adopting him, she'd gained the best name possible: Mommy.

A Room of One's Own

Getting the child's room ready can mean a paint job and buying new furniture or simply rearranging the room and supplying it with a few toys and decorations. In my family's case, we built an addition to our house so we could have an extra bedroom. At this point, your child's room should be clean and safe and pleasant. And don't forget the childproofing, for infants and toddlers who are adopted. (Covering wall sockets, removing dangerous or breakable objects, and so forth.) But it won't be really anything—until after your child comes home.

Have Health Insurance

Finding out about health insurance coverage is important. Federal laws now require most companies to cover employees' adopted children from the moment they are placed in the home, regardless of any "pre-existing conditions" they may have.

Adoptinfo

OH.

The Health Insurance Portability and Accountability Act of 1996 is a federal law which states that "pre-existing" conditions (health problems a child had before entering your family) cannot be excluded from insurance coverage. This was not always the case.

In a few states—such as Florida—health coverage starts with birth for couples who are adopting an infant. (But it does not cover prenatal care or delivery of the child.) Find out what the coverage is according to your state law.

Be sure to tell your insurance company that you are adopting a child as soon as the child arrives in your family. You don't have to wait for the adoption finalization—in fact, you should not.

Consider Childcare

Before the child comes home, you should decide whether you or your partner will stay home with the child and, if so, for how long. The Family and Medical Leave Act requires that employers of more than 50 people allow workers to take off up to 12 weeks of unpaid leave for the birth or adoption of a child. You don't have to take the whole 12 weeks—a few weeks may be sufficient for you, depending on your situation.

Do keep in mind that most children need some exclusive time with their new parents, so try to budget at least a few weeks if you can. (This is not always possible.) Also remember that if you are adopting a child of any age from another country, the cultural transition can be very shocking and upsetting for awhile—you may need to allow more time.

If both you and your partner will be returning to work, you will also need to arrange a workable child-care plan.

"Open" or "Closed"?

As you prepare to finalize an adoption, you will also need to think about whether it will be *confidential*, *semi-open*, or *open*. Everyone seems to have different definitions for the terms. For our purposes, I prefer the following definitions.

➤ A *confidential* adoption refers to an adoption in which the adopter and the birthparents do not know each other, nor do they ever meet. Instead, all the arrangements and paperwork occur through a middleman, usually an adoption agency or an attorney. Some people call this a *closed* adoption, although I prefer the terms *confidential* and *traditional* because they sound non-judgmental. (*Closed* sounds so negative.) A confidential adoption doesn't mean that the adopters and birthparents know nothing about each other. What it means is they have no identifying information about each other.

➤ Usually, *semi-open* refers to an adoption in which the adopters and birthparents meet once or twice and on a first-name-only basis. In addition, they may agree to exchange pictures and letters on an annual or fairly infrequent basis through the adoption arranger. (If your adoption arranger advocates a semi-open adoption, be sure to ask for an exact definition of her terms.)

Adopterms

In a *confidential adoption*, neither the adopter nor the birthparents know each other, nor do they meet. In a *semi-open adoption*, the adopters and birthparents may meet once or twice, and may exchange information through the adoption arranger. In an *open adoption*, there is a full exchange of information (including first and last names) between the adopting parents and the birthparents. They may or may not decide to have a continuing relationship after the adoption.

Adoptinfo

In an open adoption, often the adoption arranger creates a contract that spells out what is expected of each side; for example, how often photographs and letters will be exchanged, and how they will be exchanged (either directly or through the adoption arranger).

If one side reneges on the agreement, the other may be able to take the matter to court, depending on which state the parties live in. However, in most cases, the contracts do not appear to be enforceable. But parties should be encouraged to act in good faith.

➤ In an *open* adoption, as I define it, the adopters and the birthparents both know each other's full names. (It is not open if only one side has identifying information about the other.) They may agree to exchange photos and letters directly, without using the agency or attorney as a middleman. Sometimes a semi-open adoption later becomes an open adoption, if both parties decide that they want it that way.

Many wannabe adopters don't realize that they have more choices than they know. For example, if they want an open adoption, but their agency does not advocate open adoptions, they can choose another agency.

Conversely, if they want a confidential adoption, they should not feel unduly pressured into agreeing to an open adoption. Adopters who agree to an open adoption against their wishes may later find it difficult to fulfill their side of the agreement (for example, sending the birthmother letters and photos). This is terribly unfair to both the birthmother and the child. Agreeing to an open adoption when they don't want one is also unfair to the adopters themselves.

Open Up

Entire books have been written about open adoptions, but I can only dwell on them for a few pages at most. But because open adoptions are so frequently discussed, it's a good idea to consider the pros and cons of "openness."

> **OH.** **Adoptinfo**
> Some studies indicate that open adoption is a better choice for everyone involved, while others point away from that conclusion.
> A 1996 study reported in *Child Development* found that all the children studied "reported positive levels of self-esteem, curiosity about their birthparents, and satisfaction with the openness situation" regardless of whether their adoptions were closed, semi-open, or open. What this apparently means is that the child's sense of security in his adoptive family is more important than contact with the birth family.

The exact definition of open adoption varies from agency to agency. For many agencies, open adoption means that the birthmothers choose pre-approved families from five or six resumes or autobiographies. They may meet the adoptive families on a first-name basis, or they may not.

Some (not many) agencies encourage a complete disclosure of identities between birthparents and adopting parents, as well as an ongoing close relationship. Agencies that support fully open disclosures believe that an open adoption is a better way for both adoptive parents and birthparents—as well as the children. Agencies that don't support open adoption feel just as strongly that continued contact is not a good idea for any of the parties.

The pros and cons of open adoption have been endlessly debated by social workers and attorneys. It appears that those who support open adoptions are completely committed to them; those who believe in confidential adoptions seem equally convinced that open adoptions are catastrophic. As a result, it's an either/or proposition with little room for compromise, and adopters need to deal with an agency that they feel comfortable with. Table 18.1 presents some classic differences.

Table 18.1 Open Adoption Pros and Cons

Pros	Cons
Your child will never have to search for birthparents.	Your child may never wish to search for birthparents.
The adult child may be able to establish a relationship with birthparents.	The birthparents may want more or less contact than the adoptee wants.
The minor child may be able to have a positive relationship with birthparents.	An unstable birthparent could cause problems.
You may feel more relaxed about the adoption knowing exactly who the birthmother is.	You may feel less of a sense of entitlement and see yourself as not a "real mother."
You gain more "extended family."	Do you really want more extended family?
The birthmother may be less likely to change her mind about the adoption because she knows you.	Open adoption may attract birthmothers who don't really want their babies adopted—and see open adoption as "halfway."
The birthmother wouldn't want mind about the adoption to change her because it would hurt you too much.	The birthmother might feel she should have input into childrearing or threaten to change her mind if her wishes aren't fulfilled.

Bottom line: Before you finalize an adoption, make sure you understand what level of openness is expected of you, and are comfortable with any future obligations you agree to.

Finally! Finalization Day

Whether they admit it or not, most adopters breathe an inward sigh of relief when a judge says that the child is legally theirs. The adoption just doesn't seem "real" to most adopters until a judge decrees that it is.

The official process is called *finalization*, and it usually occurs in a courthouse (either in the courtroom or in the judge's chambers). It's a really good idea to have retained an experienced attorney to handle finalization to make sure it's done right. This is *not* the time to cut corners.

Familybuilding Tips
It's very important that adoptive parents and birthparents agree to terms that they feel they can comply with. Some adoptive parents agree to anything, just so they can "get the baby." Then they don't follow through. Others made sincere agreements but find that what they agreed to is too difficult with raising a new family—such as weekly letters to the birthmother. (Do *you* write weekly letters to anyone? E-mail doesn't count.) This mistreatment has led to heartbreak and anger among birthparents.

Adopterms
A *finalization* of an adoption refers to the legal process wherein a child is declared to be the lawful child of the adopters, who now have all the rights and obligations of any parent.

An *adoption decree* is a statement which grants the adopters full parental rights. It is usually given to the adoptive parents after the finalization.

The finalization process varies, but you are given a date and time and place to appear. The judge may ask several questions and review papers that have been drawn up. Many family court judges say that they adoption finalizations are one of the few judicial proceedings they really enjoy—they enjoy playing a part in creating a family.

If you have other children, you may wish to bring them to the courthouse—assuming that you think they'll be well-behaved. (Most children are awed in the presence of a judge. But not all!) This is a momentous day for them, too, and it's good if you can make them a part of their sibling's formal entry into the family. Many families also plan a formal or informal celebration after the courtroom finalization.

Subsequent to the adoption finalization, you will receive an *adoption decree*, which officially states that you are the parents of the child. You will also later receive an amended birth certificate, which lists your names as the parent(s). (Note: these are very important papers. Be sure to keep them in a safe place.)

Adoption Redux: Readoption

In the case of intercountry adoptions, some countries issue a final adoption decree to the adoptive parents while they are in the country. But the parents may seek a *readoption* in their home state later on.

Why? There are several reasons why a family might choose to readopt. For one, some countries (such as China and Romania) do not change the child's last name on the adoption decree, which can be confusing to others. For another, a foreign-looking document may be challenged by some people such as school authorities who have never seen such a document. The family who readopts may believe that a U.S.–issued birth certificate would be a lot more credible to the average bureaucrat—and they're probably right. A readoption also may protect from possible legal changes overseas that might retroactively affect adoptions finalized in the foreign country.

Readoption procedures are not uniform from state to state (or even from county to county within a state). Some areas make it a lot tougher than others. It's a good idea to find out ahead of time (before you adopt) what the procedure is in your area so that research will be already done by the time you return. Ask your agency for information on readoption and check with your adoptive parent group for assistance.

Bringing Home Your Child

The day you finally bring home your child can be a mixture of euphoria, tiredness, confusion and a host of other emotions. You may have waited for this day for years. Even if it's only been months, those were very intense months indeed!

It's a good idea to take photographs or videotape the event. Your child may be a tiny baby now, but when she grows up, she'll want to see what everyone looked like on that very important day (and what she looked like, too)!

Many families prefer to wait until the finalization to announce their new child, but it's really your own choice. You may wish to send handwritten announcements, or you may decide to order special adoption announcements.

Special announcements are advertised in adoption publications such as *Adoptive Families* or *Roots & Wings*. (See Appendix H for their addresses.)

Adoption announcements are also sold by Tapestry Books, a mail-order bookstore that concentrates on adoption books and pamphlets. It also provides a free catalog. (Call 1-800-765-2367.)

Familybuilding Tips
Some families celebrate two special days for their adopted children: their birthday and "Adoption Day."

Should you celebrate both? My feeling is that the child's birthday is most important and should never be subordinated to the day she arrived in your family. However, go ahead and celebrate both days for a while, if you like. Keep in mind that as children grow older, they may not like the idea of celebrating Adoption Day. In addition, if you have biological children, they may be jealous that the adopted child gets two special days and they only get one.

Also remember that some adoptive parents make too much of adoption and consequently cause their children to feel embarrassment or isolation. Do what works best for your child, not you.

Adopterms
A *readoption* is a term used in the case of families who have finalized an adoption in another country and then choose to readopt the child in their home state. This may be easy or difficult, depending on where they live.

Adoptinfo

Are there any other ways to go besides readoption? Jean Erichsen-Nelson, director of social services for Los Niños International Adoption Agency in The Woodlands, Texas, says that the Immigration and Naturalization Service may agree to use the family last name on citizenship papers when they are issued—although this is not equal to a legal name change.

Another option, says Erichsen-Nelson, is to obtain an Affirmation of a Foreign Adoption Decree. You would have to find out whether such an option is available in your state. But if it is, it would probably be less expensive than a readoption.

The Least You Need to Know

➤ While you wait for the adoption to be finalized, prepare for the child's arrival: Arrange a room, and investigate health insurance and day care.

➤ Make sure you are comfortable with the choice of open, semi-open, or confidential adoption.

➤ Make sure you save your child's birth certificate and adoption decree in a safe place.

➤ If you finalize an international adoption, you may wish to readopt the child in the U.S.

Chapter 19

Here's Johnny! Introducing Your New Child

In This Chapter

➤ What are adoption rituals?

➤ What should you tell people about your adopted child?

➤ "Positive adoption language" and why it matters

➤ Explaining transracial adoption

Some people throw a big party and invite all their friends and relatives when they bring home their newly adopted child. Others wait a few days, a few weeks, or even a few months and then gradually introduce the child to new people. Others hold special ceremonies or rituals, such as a candle-lighting ceremony, with other adoptive parents. Or, in the case of an open adoption, a ceremony that they've created with the birthparents. They may also tie in their adoption celebration with religious rituals such as christenings, naming ceremonies, or other rituals. And still others celebrate the day they finalize the adoption.

What's the best and most successful way to introduce your child to her new family? And does an adopted child need any more introduction than a birth child? This chapter covers these and other issues that come up when you adopt a child of any age.

Adoption Rituals

Although it may be "instant love" for you and your child, don't expect an immediate positive response from other family members, including your siblings, your parents, and your other children (if you have them). Your family will need time to get to know the child. And don't expect immediate love from the child either. Are you wild about all *your* relatives? How'd you like to be six years old and confronted with a horde of new people? It might be pretty scary.

> **Adopterms**
>
> An *adoption ritual* is a ceremony that acknowledges that a child has been (or will be) adopted into the family. Some people choose to incorporate mention of adoption into a traditional religious ceremony; others prefer to create special religious or non-religious rituals that celebrate adoption.

Sometimes the introduction of your adopted child to the family can be eased with a special *adoption ritual*. The adoption ritual can be religious, secular, or even one you design yourself.

Why do parents celebrate an adoption ritual? They may feel they need something beyond the usual christening or bris religious rituals, one that acknowledges the uniqueness of adoption. In addition, if the child is an older child, she may benefit from a ceremony that indicates that this family is her forever family. Rituals can also help solidify these concepts in the minds of children and adults.

> **Real Life Snapshots**
>
> Since 1961, the Adoptive Parents Committee (APC) in New York City has celebrated its own annual candle-lighting ritual for new adopters.
>
> At the beginning of the (non-sectarian) APC ceremony, a poem is read. Then the candle-lighting begins. Families proudly display their children as they bring them to the stage.
>
> Part of the ceremony includes the lighting of the "Wish Candle" by a couple who has been trying to adopt. They represent all the other potential adoptive parents, and will, hopefully, light a candle for their own adopted child a year later.

Some rituals include the birthparents as well as the adoptive parents. For example, Diane was a birthmother I knew who wanted an open adoption. She and the adopters arranged a ceremony in which she formally handed the child to the couple and read a statement she had made. Afterward, the couple read promises that they were making to Diane and to the child. Everyone who attended the ceremony said there was a lot of beaming—and also some sniffling.

Some people choose to hold their adoption rituals shortly after the child is placed in their family; others delay until the finalization, when they feel the adoption is truly official. How *you* feel may be entirely different, so when you hold your adoption ritual (if you choose to have one) is up to you.

Religious Rituals

If you are Christian, you may wish to christen your child shortly after he arrives in your home. In my case, our minister asked us if we wanted to wait until finalization, but we didn't want to. So our baby was christened about a month after arrival into our home.

Real Life Snapshots

Debra Smith, former director of the National Adoption Information Clearing-house, and her husband Gary chose a formal Jewish ceremony to celebrate the entry of their son and daughter into their family.

First Justin, age four, had a ceremonial *bris* (religious circumcision) and Talia, two, had a naming ceremony. Both children were immersed in a ritual bath.

Then the Smiths and their children were honored by being allowed to bless the Torah. The rabbi offered a special blessing to the children and then gave them their Hebrew names. Said Smith, "We said that the children will learn from their Jewish family members and they will also bring special talents and abilities to us from their birthfamilies."

Whether adoption is mentioned or not at the religious ceremony is up to you (but if you are adopting a child of another race or country, it may be obvious that the child was not born to you). You may wish to bring up adoption in the course of the ceremony because adoption is a positive familybuilding option that you should be proud to be a part of.

In *Designing Rituals of Adoption for the Religious and Secular Community* (Resources for Adoptive Parents, 1995), Mary Martin Mason describes rituals that could be used by Christians, Jews, and those who wish a non-sectarian approach.

Of course, not everyone feels that there is a need for a special ritual associated with adoption. They believe that adoption is a means for bringing a child into a family, and although they don't deny the fact of adoption, neither do they create a special ritual. Instead, they rely on the same rituals used by parents whose children were born to them, such as christenings or family parties and so forth.

Adoption Q & A

You may be extremely surprised at what people ask you about your child. For example, they may ask you if the child's birthmother used drugs or was an alcohol abuser. Or how much the child "cost." If the child had been born to you, no one would dare ask you those questions.

Here are some of the most common questions people ask new adoptive parents—in the way that they ask them—so get ready to cringe:

➤ Are you sure you can keep her?

Most people have heard of those few headliner media cases where adopted children were sent back to their birthparents. So when they ask if you'll be able to "keep" the child, in most cases, the sentiment behind the question is sincere caring and concern for you.

If you want to explain your state law—for example, that consent is irrevocable after so many days—go ahead. If you're not comfortable with this, you can simply say that everything is fine.

> **Familybuilding Tips**
>
> When your family first meets your new child, it's nearly inevitable that someone will say, "Why didn't her 'real mother' want her—she's so cute!"
>
> Try not to go ballistic every time this happens. Your family members need time to learn, too. And realize that some of these remarks are meant in a positive way.
>
> Of course, I'm not saying that you should let every comment go by. As a parent, you should stick up for your child! What I'm saying is, pick your battles wisely.

➤ She's so cute! How could her real mother give her away?

When people wonder aloud how the birthmother could ever "give up" such an adorable child, explain that birthmothers usually make the adoption decision before the child is born. Physical beauty (or the lack thereof) is usually not a factor; other reasons are the driving force. Whether you share those reasons—and I strongly advise caution before you blurt them out—is up to you.

➤ Are you sure the mother didn't have any diseases or use drugs?

This line of questioning is intrusive and unfair. When a woman gives birth to a child, her relatives wouldn't think of asking her if anything is wrong with her health. So why assume that just because a child was adopted, the birthmother was unhealthy? To answer, you can simply say that the child is healthy and you feel very blessed.

Real Life Snapshots

Sometimes you may feel like you *want* people to know your child was adopted, especially if you are worried you might get blamed for a child's problem. For example, Tracey adopted a baby with fetal alcohol syndrome (FAS). Often she finds herself explaining that the baby was adopted because she doesn't want people assuming that it was she who was alcoholic and caused the baby's medical problems.

Adoptive parents like Tracey may need to work on how they feel about their child's illness and if it is really important to tell everyone that it wasn't they who made their children sick.

➤ How much did you pay for him?

This is one of the most annoying questions that new adoptive parents report. It makes your child sound like a commodity, not a human being.

It's illegal to buy or sell children. What you paid were adoption fees, and whether you tell people how much they were or not is up to you. Remember, though, that there are heavy expenses associated with having a biological child as well.

My advice is to limit the number of people to whom you divulge the amount you paid. Some people may attach a mental price tag to the child forever. This is not the way your child should be regarded.

If, however, people inquire about fees because they sincerely want to adopt, you can give them a "ballpark figure" or you can refer them to your agency or attorney or to the local adoptive parent group.

➤ She'll probably be really good in math (to the mother of a newly adopted Asian infant).

When we think of racist assumptions, most of us think of negative ones. But there are also some "positive" ones as well, such as assuming children of a certain race will naturally be smart. In my opinion, the best thing to say is, "Some children are good at math and science and some aren't as good, so we'll just have to wait and see."

Think Before You Speak

One common mistake new adoptive parents make is to tell everyone every minute detail about the baby. I know one woman who is very sorry she mentioned that her baby was born with traces of cocaine in her bloodstream—people still remember this years later.

Real Life Snapshots

"My mother-in-law will never forget that I told her Sharon's birthmother did have a drug problem," sighs Julia. "Every time Sharon gets a cold or even misbehaves a little bit, my mother-in-law has to bring it up. She says, 'Do you think this has something to do with the cocaine?' I really regret telling her!"

It would have been better if Julia had not told her mother-in-law about the birthmother's drug use. But it's too late for that. Instead, Julia needs to face the problem head-on, before Sharon gets older and starts wondering herself. (Sharon is three.)

Julia should tell her mother-in-law very clearly that Sharon is a healthy child and that there is no indication that her birthmother's drug use has hurt her. She should also say that the subject is closed, permanently. If her mother-in-law attempts to bring it up again, Julia should respond only with silence. Her mother-in-law will get the picture.

Adopterms

Entitlement refers to the feeling that the adopter is worthy and ready to take on all the responsibilities and obligations of parenthood. Everyone assumes that biological parents are entitled to parent their children. But adoptive parents must "prove their worthiness" (in most cases) by undergoing a home study and answering numerous questions about themselves.

Feelings of entitlement don't always come the first few days or weeks after the adoption. But as the parents take on care-giving tasks, this feeling usually does evolve.

It is really not necessary to share private information about the child with everyone, including your parents. "My mother-in-law will never forget that I said my baby's mother wasn't sure which of two guys was the father," says Sue, an adoptive mom. "I don't want that to reflect on my daughter. I wish I had just kept my mouth shut."

Yet many adoptive parents think that they have to answer even the most insensitive questions. Perhaps this is because they don't yet feel a full sense of "entitlement" to their child; perhaps also because they've already had to share so much of their personal life with the social worker or attorney. Remember: You do not have to. In fact, it's better if you don't.

Positive Adoption Language

Back in Chapter 4, I mentioned the importance of avoiding adoption "slanguage" when speaking of birthparents. Now that you're an adopted parent yourself, you may be especially sensitive to negative phrases and words.

Here's a sampling of words and phrases that may have a negative connotation, along with more positive substitutes:

Table 19.1 Adoption Language

Negative Adoption Language	Positive Adoption Language
Real mother, natural mother	Birthmother, biological mother, genetic mother
Real father, natural father, "sperm donor"	Birthfather, biological father, genetic father
Give away, give up, put up for adoption	Place for adoption, chose adoption
She kept her baby	She chose to parent her baby
Fake mother, foster mother**	Adoptive mother, mother
A child of their own, their real child	Their biological child
Foreign adoption	International adoption, intercountry adoption
Mixed race child, mulatto	Biracial child

** *"Foster mother" is an appropriate term when used correctly: to describe a woman who is providing temporary care to a child. When it is used to describe an adoptive mother, it is inaccurate and is also seen as a disparagement.*

As an adoptive parent, you may hate the suggestion that a mother is only "real" if she gives birth. What if you, as an adoptive parent, are the one who gets up every night to feed, change, and watch over your child? Those nights will seem pretty "real" to you and to your child. And they are.

Does this mean that the birthparents are then "unreal?" One birthmother says that people ask her if she feels like she's not the real parent of her child who was adopted. She answers that she doesn't feel like an "un-mother." But she understands and accepts that her daughter was parented by a Mom and Dad who both love her very much. To her, they are all "real."

It can be tremendously frustrating when you learn positive adoption language and you hear even your close family and friends using those old, bad words. Try not to get too angry! They don't have adopted children, so they might not understand. After they get to

Familybuilding Tips
Want to teach people to use positive adoption language without lecturing them? Try "modeling." If you are speaking with someone who keeps using the phrase "real" or "natural" mother, for example, respond by using the word "birthmother."

Rather than verbally battering the other person, use the term "birthmother" whenever you can. After a while, you will usually find the other person using the term, too!

You can use this technique with such simple words and phrases as "birthmother," "birthfather," and "placed for adoption." See if it works for you!

know your child, you may be surprised to find your family being outraged by negative comments others make about adoption and adopted kids.

Special Situations: Transracial Adoption

Back in Chapter 13, when I discussed transracial adoption, I mentioned that studies suggest that most transracially adopted children adjust well to their adoptive families. I think that family members in these situations don't see each other as "black" or "white" or "biracial"; they see each other as individuals, with many similarities among themselves.

Outsiders, however, may not understand. How do your family members react when you adopt a child who looks very different from them and from you? They may be shocked and upset, or they may be accepting and positive. (Or shocked and upset at first and accepting and positive later.) You may be hurt by comments about why you couldn't have a child of "your own."

Luckily, time seems to be a factor—as your extended family members become used to your child and get to know him as a person, they will likely become more accepting and loving.

But there still may be some family members who cannot or will not accept your child. If you feel that your child is being treated negatively by certain relatives, you may have to adjust or curtail your visits. Before you take such a drastic step, however, confront the issue head on with the offending relatives, away from the child. Maybe there is something about the adoption or the child that they don't understand or that confuses them, and you can clear it up. Give it a try—communication is often a problem between extended family members, and it's best to resolve it when you can.

While family and friends may become supportive and understanding of your adoption, strangers or acquaintances may not. You may be especially annoyed when strangers ask you intrusive questions like where you "got" your Chinese child. Although most people are probably not trying to annoy you or violate your privacy, you still may not feel like answering them.

You could say the child was adopted from China, but if they persist, wanting to know what agency she was adopted from and other details, you could ask why they want to know. The answer might be that they are interested in exploring adoption themselves or they know someone who is. In that case, you might wish to provide information or recommend a parent group. If it's just nosy busybody stuff, you could say the child was sent from God, as all children are. (If you are religious.)

And as your child grows older (older than two or three), she'll start listening to what you tell people about her. Maybe you don't want to be so forthcoming about her adoption anymore. So what should you say?

Here are a few choices:

➤ Tell them you can't talk now.

➤ Give them the name and phone number of your parent group.

➤ If it's someone important to you who you know, ask them to call you later.

➤ Tell them that *you* will call them later, if the person is known to you. If the person is a total stranger and wants to offer his phone number—and you're willing to do so—then you could call her later and have a parent group representative call them later.

Real Life Snapshots

When Mona was asked where did she "get" her baby from, she said, "Texas." But the person said, "No, I mean, what country, since I know from TV that there are no white babies in American and you can only adopt mixed race crack-addicted ones."

Mona, a quick thinker said, "Well, he's actually Swedish and came from a small town, called Nordstrom's" the name of a popular department store in Texas. The other person foolishly believed her.

➤ Tell them that you really are in a rush and just don't have time to talk about anything.

➤ Sometimes people will say that you are "wonderful" for adopting this "poor little orphan." Saying that you are blessed to be the parent of your child is true and, if said in your child's presence, will make your child feel good, too.

Keep your sanity intact by remembering that the most important thing is to educate yourself, listen to the advice of others, choose what works for you, and follow your own gut-level instincts. Do what is right for your child and for your family.

The Least You Need to Know

➤ Decide for yourself the best way to introduce your new child to your family.

➤ Give your family a chance to get used to your adopted child—and vice versa.

➤ Adoption rituals or ceremonies can be meaningful and helpful.

➤ Keep negative information about a child or birthfamily to yourself unless it's necessary to tell others.

Chapter 20

Using the "A" Word

In This Chapter

➤ When do you explain adoption to a child?

➤ Explaining adoption to young children, school children, and teenagers

➤ Answering sensitive adoption questions

➤ Explaining special situations

Lois was going through old papers in the attic when she noticed a document that said something about "adoption" and starting reading it. To her shock, she realized the document referred to *her*. Thirty-five years ago, she'd been adopted—a fact she'd never known. Lois felt bewildered, betrayed, and shaken to the core.

This chapter is about talking to your child about being adopted. So why begin with a story about an adopted adult? To make an important point: There are still people out there who think the best thing to do is to pretend that an adopted child was born to you. Don't be one of them. Adoptees almost always find out about their adoptions anyway. And when they find out as adults (or worse, as adolescents), they may be shattered.

Your child will have questions about adoption as he grows up. I think the biggest mistake adoptive parents make in explaining adoption is either talking about it too much or not talking about it at all, as if it's a bad thing. This chapter will show you how to strike a balance.

Explaining Adoption: Like Explaining Sex?

Many people have compared explaining adoption to explaining the "facts of life." How can talking about adoption possibly compare to talking about sex? Here are a few ways:

➤ You can't talk about adoption just once—as the child gets older, he'll have newer and tougher questions.

➤ The child's level of understanding of adoption becomes more sophisticated as the child grows up.

➤ Talking about adoption can be hard for adoptive parents, especially the first time. Talking about sex can be tough, too.

Why is it so hard for many adoptive parents to discuss adoption with their kids? Here are some reasons:

Adoptinfo

The discomfort some adoptive parents have when discussing adoption reminds me of a quotation I read in *Dialogues About Adoption: Conversations Between Parents and Their Children* by Linda Bothun (Swan Publications, 1994). When Carin presented her daughter Ashley, age eight, with yet another adoption book, Ashley said, "I don't need that book. *You* need that book."

➤ It brings up memories of the pain of their infertility.

➤ They worry that it will make the child feel unwanted.

➤ They may not have much information to share.

➤ The adopters may feel like "second class" parents.

➤ They may prefer to avoid the negative emotions an adoption discussion would bring up.

➤ They're afraid they can't explain adoption so the child can understand it, so they delay and often worry about it.

The fact is, you have to talk about adoption because your child needs to hear about it from you. The following sections will give you advice on what to say and when to say it.

What to Tell—and When

Many experts agree that three or four is the youngest age at which a child can begin to have any concept of being born to a different mother. This is the earliest time to begin discussing adoption in little detail but very positive terms. As your child grows, you can tailor the information you give to fit the child, both individually and developmentally.

We can break down the ages and stages into several parts:

➤ Early childhood: ages 3–5

➤ School-age child: 6–12

➤ Adolescent: ages 13–18

➤ Adult adoptees

Keep in mind that these stages are *not* cast in granite. For example, an explanation described here for "early childhood" might still work for a seven- or eight-year-old. Or it might be too simplistic for a more mature five-year-old. When discussing adoption, consider your child's emotional and intellectual maturity.

Early Childhood

A simple story about adoption can suffice for the child who is three or four. Most children like to hear their "adoption story." When my son was little, he loved his story. He wanted to be told again and again how Mommy and Daddy ran around the house when they heard he was born and how they called everyone. And how when they saw him Mommy was so excited she jumped up and down like a little girl. And how she told Daddy to drive extra extra careful on the way home with him.

Your child's story won't be the same—it'll be unique. Here are a few details to include:

➤ How you felt when you first learned about your child

➤ How you felt as you waited for the child to enter your family

➤ Your reactions when you learned the child would be coming

➤ What it was like when you first saw your child, in person

➤ What were the reactions of others in your family—your spouse, other family members, the child's siblings, and so on

➤ What the first few days with the child were like

Adoptinfo

Some people advise new parents to tell their infants, "You're my beautiful adopted baby." Others disagree because infants don't understand adoption. Also, this constant repetition can make some parents fixate on the "adopted" part rather than the "beautiful baby" part.

As psychiatrist Denis Donovan, author of *Healing the Hurt Child*, says, "Babies have no need to 'know' about adoption. They need love, care, nurturance, safety, and challenge."

The good news about explaining adoption to preschoolers is they like to hear about it and generally react very positively. In *The Psychology of Adoption,* psychologist David Brodzinsky explains: "They generally are told about being adopted in the context of a warm, loving, and protective environment. Thus the emotional climate surrounding the telling process is one which fosters acceptance and positive self-regard."

Familybuilding Tips
Children, especially younger ones, can be amazingly resilient. One minute, five-year-old Tamara is upset that she didn't grow in Mommy's tummy. Then, while Mommy is agonizing over whether she said the "right thing," Tamara is running out the door to play with her neighbor. On the other hand, sometimes issues and concerns *do* bother children. If you sense your child is upset, a little careful probing can often reveal what's going on.

Another reason why they feel positive is they can't really understand adoption yet! This doesn't mean that when they *do* understand adoption, they'll feel badly about it. It just means that you should not assume your three-year-old child has accepted adoption for life just because he is happy hearing the adoption story now. There will be other questions as your child grows up.

In fact, while you may feel that you should talk about adoption to your three- or four-year-old, your child doesn't really need to hear about it much. As the authors of *Talking with Young Children About Adoption* (Yale University Press, 1993) say: "Adopters and adoptees are often out of phase with each other regarding worries, concerns, and pain around adoption. For parents these worries and concerns surface before adoption and are often strongest during the child's toddlerhood, when the issue of beginning to talk with their children about adoption is often negotiated with some trepidation and sadness." But your young child may not even understand or care.

You can also supplement the personal adoption story with one or two books about adoption. I strongly recommend *Tell Me Again About the Night I Was Born* by Jamie Lee Curtis, a charming and beautiful book.

Information Overload

Some parents go overboard when they explain adoption to their young children. They buy five or six (or more!) books about adoption. They talk about adoption constantly. They press the child to ask questions. In their over-eagerness to discuss the subject, these adoptive parents can make their children tense and distressed.

Real Life Snapshots

Be careful that you don't overburden your preschool child with too much adoption talk. Adoptive mom Lindsey found this out the hard way. She'd discussed adoption frequently with her five-year-old son, Jason, because she wanted him to accept being adopted. But his behavior began to deteriorate, and she could not figure out why.

One day he began sobbing over nothing. He said he was afraid she was going to have him adopted. Apparently he thought all the talk about adoption was preparation for his leaving!

A child psychiatrist told Lindsey the constant references to adoption were making him feel alienated from his parents. The doctor said it was okay to talk about adoption if the subject came up—but that Lindsey should stop focusing on it. Once Lindsey laid off, Jason's behavior improved.

Here are a few points to keep in mind:

➤ Select one or two adoption story books. Read them to your child. If she likes them, read them again. If she doesn't like them, put them away.

➤ Don't obsess if your child doesn't seem to "accept" her adoption. Give the kid a break: She's four years old.

➤ If your child asks a question when you don't feel ready to answer—such as why her mother "didn't want" her—try not to clutch up. Take a deep breath, and answer. If you really don't feel up to it, tell her you'll talk about it after dinner or tomorrow or some other definite time. And make sure you talk to her then.

➤ Take your child to adoptive parent group parties where other adopted children attend. At one party, an amazed eight-year-old told me that almost *all* of the children at the party were adopted! She had thought she and her brother were the only ones.

"Why Did Mommy Give Me Away?"

Kids often do *not* use "positive adoption language" and instead use what they hear on TV, in daycare, or other places. So don't jump down your child's throat if she uses words like "give me away," "real mother," and so forth. *You* use the appropriate terminology, and after awhile your child will model on you.

The whys of the adoption choice by birthparents is probably the toughest question your child will ask you. I can't tell you how many adoptive parents answer, "Because she loved you." I think this answer is too simplistic for a young child. Think about it. You love your child, too. Does this mean that you might have her adopted? Does love equal leaving someone? That's the way your child may perceive it.

The point is, the birthmother may have loved the child plenty, but that is not the sole or even primary reason why she chose adoption. So what are some valid explanations that your child can understand—ones that don't put the birthparents down? Here are a few that might work for you:

➤ "Your birthmother wanted you to have both a mommy and a daddy and not just one. She couldn't provide two parents."

An older child may ask *why* wasn't a daddy around? But for most small children, it won't occur to them. If it *does* occur to the child, you could state that neither the birthmother nor the birthfather were ready to be parents, and they wanted someone who was ready and very excited and happy to be the parents—you!

It may also be a good idea to mention that the decision was made before the child was born, if that is the case, so that the child will know there was nothing wrong with *him*. (This is more likely to be a concern in an older child, but some children are precocious.) Instead, it was the birthparents who just weren't ready or able to be parents.

➤ "Your birthmother didn't feel ready to be a parent, but she wanted you to have good parents who were ready."

➤ "Your birthmother had problems that she couldn't fix, and she knew you needed parents who were ready to be parents."

For young children, I would not provide elaborate explanations on what the "problems" were. If the birthmother was young, that's understandable to kids. But I'd try to avoid stressing the point if she was a drug addict, alcoholic, and so on. Instead, be more vague, saying she was sick and knew she couldn't be a good mom so she decided that someone else who could be was a good idea.

➤ "Your birthmother was poor and also not ready to be a parent, and she knew that she couldn't provide what you needed. She knew that you would be well-cared for with us."

I would not make a huge deal about the poverty thing (although it is true in most cases of intercountry adoption) because some bright children might wonder why you didn't give the mother money so she *could* be a parent. Another (and possibly more compelling) reason for the birthmother choosing adoption was the cultural stigma against unwed motherhood. I would avoid this explanation because it's too difficult for most young children to understand. You could say that you never had a chance to meet her and the decision was made before then.

Your "Chosen Child?"

Chosen child or *special child* are two phrases some parents like to use when discussing adoption with their young children. It's understandable: All parents think their children are special! But if you use these expressions with your adopted child, she may grow up believing that because she was "chosen" or "special," she must be extra good or do really well in school. You don't want your child to feel she must constantly prove her worthiness. So don't make a big deal about her being a chosen child.

School-age Children

As children grow, they start to ask even tougher questions about adoption. For example, if the birthmother was poor, why didn't someone give her money so she could be a parent? Or, if she wasn't ready to be a parent, why didn't someone teach her what she needed to know? And why did she think a child had to have two parents? Lots of kids have just their mom or dad. And on and on.

The thing is, while school-age children have the intelligence to ask these tough questions, they often still see the world in terms of black and white. People are either good or bad. You're either starving or you're not hungry at all. If there's a problem, somebody should fix it.

You probably can't explain the difficult social problems that lead some birthparents to choose adoption. You can, however, admit the obvious: The world can be an unfair place sometimes. And problems like teenage pregnancy, drug or alcohol abuse, poverty, and bigotry need to be worked on. But the birthmother couldn't solve her problems, and the people she knew didn't know how to solve them, either.

And here's a tough thing to admit: You don't know how to solve these problems, either. What you do know is that you wanted to adopt a child and when you learned about your child, you knew you wanted to be his parent.

Adopterms
In the past, adoptive parents were told to tell a child she was a *chosen child* so that the child would feel special and important. Today most experts believe that overemphasizing being "chosen" can be problematic and is not advisable.

Adoption Alert
Some adopted adults decide to seek out their birthparents when they grow up. Realizing this, some adoptive parents mention the possibility of a search in their adoption explanation. I think this is a bad idea. If you constantly emphasize the "other parents," they may loom large in your child's mind (some young children fear being kidnapped by their birthparents). Secondly, the decision to search should be up to the adoptee, not you.

Of course, if your child brings up the issue himself, you can tell him that you are not opposed to a search (if that's true). See Part 5 for more information about searching.

Here's another facet that's tough for adoptive parents to accept: Although the preschool child may (and usually does) blithely accept whatever cheery explanation of adoption you offer, the older child is more skeptical and may feel sad for his birthmother. He will have his feelings hurt if classmates and friends ask him why his "real mother gave him up."

How can you make the pain go away? It helps to accept and acknowledge your child's feelings. If your child says he's sad about his birthmother not knowing how to be a parent, admit it is sad. Avoid over-stressing the positives, like how great adoption is. All the emotions associated with truly understanding adoption are not positive ones. And that's okay.

What if your child is teased about being adopted? Sometimes it's because the teasers are feeling inadequate themselves. In *Talking With Young Children About Adoption*, the authors cited the teasing of Teddy, who was told by other children that he didn't have to listen to his mother when she said to put his seat belt on because she wasn't his real mother. Said Teddy, "What do you think she is, a cartoon character?" The author later discussed the incident with her child, who said, "Gary is jealous. He doesn't have a father, and I do, so he's attacking my adoption."

Of course, not all children react so matter-of-factly. Here are some important points to convey to your child:

➤ Kids tease other kids about a lot of things: wearing glasses, being thin, being chubby, not doing well at math, or not being good at baseball. And sometimes if they can't think of anything else, they'll choose adoption.

➤ Convey to your child that *you* are a real parent, and you will always love him and be his real parent. He's real and you're real. You're not a "cartoon character" and neither is he.

➤ You might tell your child that he can tell his friends they can see you and touch you and hear you. This means you exist. This may sound silly, but I think it makes an important point.

➤ Do understand that sometimes teasing hurts. If you were teased because you're a "mere" adoptive parent and told you weren't "real," you'd be mad, too! The sad news is that we can try to protect our children, but sometimes the teasing happens anyway. If they're prepared for it, however, they'll have a little psychological armor that they wouldn't have had otherwise. So that's your job.

Teenagers and Adult Children

It's important that children know they were adopted before they reach adolescence; it's too turbulent a time to suddenly surprise them with the news. But even if your teenage child already knows, he may still have questions.

In fact, although you may be fully comfortable with the adoption by the time your child is a teenager, your child may be more curious about it than ever. As the authors of *Talking with Young Children About Adoption* say: "By their children's adolescence [adoptive parents] have often reached a deep love of comfort and satisfaction about adoption and truly feel that it was 'no big deal'…yet the adolescent may question everything about adoption and need to acknowledge and work through a host of positive and negative feelings about it."

Why talk to teenagers or adult children about adoption? There are several reasons:

➤ They may have unresolved questions or issues and be afraid to ask you.

➤ They may wish to search for birthparents but not hurt your feelings.

➤ They may have forgotten the information you've given them before.

➤ They may have misunderstood information.

➤ Some information, such as medical or genetic background, will be helpful to them if they have biological children.

Bringing up the subject of adoption with an older child might be awkward. Try saying something like, "Joyce, I know you know you were adopted, but I'm wondering if you have any questions you want to talk about. A lot of people do. But of course, not everyone does." Then listen. Maybe your child won't want to talk about it right away. (Or ever!) Or maybe she needs time to frame her questions—rather than blurt them out as children do.

It might also be a good idea to review what you've told her in the past and update it to the adult version.

Sensitive Situations

In many cases, parents can tell their children that birthparents made a positive choice to place them for adoption. But sometimes the situation was not so upbeat or easy to explain. Here are a few situations that make "telling" problematic for some adopters:

➤ You have an open adoption and the child already knows the birthparents.

➤ The child was the result of a rape, or the child of a birthparent with severe problems, such as drug addiction or mental illness.

➤ The birthparent's parental rights were involuntarily terminated by the state (usually in a foster child situation) because the parents were abusive or neglectful or because they abandoned the child.

Open Adoption

Many people think that if an adoption is open (and especially to the extent that the child actually knows and has met with his birthparent), then there is no need to explain. After all, the child knows who you are and knows who the birthmother is, right?

Wrong. Even in an open adoption, children need explanations about why they were adopted and what adoption is. Here are some issues that may come up:

➤ Why the child doesn't live with his birthmother. As I said before, most preschool children readily accept whatever you say, so at that point you can simply explain that his birthmother was not ready to be a parent.

As your child grows older, he may wonder *why* she wasn't ready and how come he doesn't get to see her all the time. Then, you may want to explain more about the birthmother's circumstances. You'll also want to emphasize the permanency of adoption.

➤ If the birthmother is raising other children, why didn't she parent your child? This is a tough one. Remind your child that the birthmother wasn't ready to be a parent at that point in time. It was *not* his fault, nor did she think he was "bad." She just couldn't handle a child.

If the birthmother already had children when she placed your child for adoption, she must have felt unready to parent more than one child. If she had children after your child was placed, she was older and may have felt more capable of parenting.

➤ If the child becomes angry with you, he may threaten to live with the birthparents. You need to explain, as calmly as possible, that *you* are his legal parent. He may not choose to live with anyone else until he grows up.

➤ Why you, not the birthparents, make parenting decisions. Because you are the legal parents, you make parenting decisions. In some open adoptions, the birthmother may provide input—but it is the adoptive parents who decide what is to be done.

Unfit Birthparents

Are there some things children should not be told? My opinion is that it's a bad idea to tell small children that they are the product of rape or that their birthmother was psychotic. This is tough information for anyone at any age to grasp and to accept.

So when do you tell them, if ever? I'm going against the grain here, but I think the child should be an adult (or nearly an adult) before hearing painful and sensitive truths. Certainly she should know well before she is old enough to search for her birthparents—finding out the circumstances of his birth then would be extremely traumatic.

If the problem was something like alcoholism or drug addiction, it's a good idea to tell your child as a young adult or perhaps as early as age 10 or 11. Remember, children are very judgmental at that age. Try *not* to chime in if your child condemns her birthmother for her "bad" behavior, but explain that some people have a problem with substances.

But if this is the case, and you do share information, be sure you know what your child is learning about substance abuse in school. If he is told that alcoholism is hereditary, he may feel doomed. You need to reassure him that it *can* be hereditary but certainly that is not always true.

Real Life Snapshots

Jennie says her daughter's birthmother was a crack addict who was also HIV-positive. How did she explain that to her adopted daughter?

Jennie told her daughter that her birthmother was very sick. When the birthmother learned that there was a special medicine (AZT) she could take during pregnancy to keep her baby from getting sick too, she did it. She took the awful-tasting medicine and she got into a special program to help her baby be as safe as possible. But she knew that she was too sick to be a good parent. So she chose adoption.

This is a good explanation because it's true. It doesn't romanticize the birthmother but it doesn't demonize her either. It makes her sound like a real person—which she was.

Foster Children

If you've adopted a foster child, usually the birthparent's rights were involuntarily terminated because of abuse, neglect, or abandonment.

When you've adopted a child who was abused or badly neglected by a birthparent, it can be extremely hard to work up any positive feelings or sympathy for the birthparents. In fact, you may be very angry at what they've done to your child. It's not easy to forgive someone who has hurt your child so badly.

But if you don't try to find it in your heart to somehow accept what has happened, you could end up hurting your child. Many children think that what their parents did was their fault. They also sometimes think that if their birthparents were "bad," then they might grow up to be bad, too. So never say an unkind word about the birthparents to your child.

This doesn't mean you can only say sweet things about the birthparents. Try instead to convince yourself (and your child) that the birthparents simply could not be good parents. Maybe nobody ever taught them how. Maybe they couldn't overcome their problems or they didn't realize they had problems. Don't excuse their problems or depict them as "victims." While you don't want to condemn them, neither do you want the child to think their behavior was okay.

With the child in foster care, the birthparents were given a chance to solve their problems. But they did not. For whatever reason, they weren't capable of being good parents. So the child was placed with someone who was ready and capable: You.

The Least You Need to Know

> ➤ It's important to tell your child he was adopted, preferably before he starts school.

> ➤ Younger children will be happy with a simple story about their adoption. Older children and teenagers may be given more details.

> ➤ Don't tell the child that her birthmother chose adoption only "because she loved you." Explain that the birthmother was not ready to be a parent.

> ➤ Don't say negative things about the birthparents to your child.

> ➤ Don't discuss sensitive issues like abuse or neglect with young children. Save this information for when the child is a young adult.

Chapter 21

As They Grow

In This Chapter

➤ How are adoptees like and unlike their adoptive parents?

➤ Common fears of adopted children

➤ Bad behavior: disciplining the adopted child

➤ Coping with serious problems

Carol was worried that something was seriously wrong with Maria, the child she'd adopted from Romania at the age of three. Three months after the adoption, Maria was nearly obsessional about food. Sometimes she overate to the point of gorging. She also hid food in her closet. Was Carol a bad mother?

As discussed in earlier chapters, most adopted children grow up to be healthy adults. But some adopted children, like biological children, will need medical or psychological treatment; others won't.

This chapter discusses common physical, emotional, and behavioral issues that may occur after the adoption.

Your Kid Doesn't Look Like You—Deal with It!

Some adopters have difficulty accepting a child who looks very different from what they envisioned. (Most adopters don't have a problem with the fact that their kids probably won't look like them. The people who have the "problem" are usually strangers outside the family.)

> **OH.** **Adoptinfo**
> Back in 1976, Michigan researchers looked at a large sample of adoptive and nonadoptive families to see if there were any physical similarities between parents and children. They found significant similarities between the biological parents and their children, which was no surprise. But although the significance was less, the researchers *also* found significant similarities in the stature and weight of the adopters and their children.

How we view ourselves and each other affects how we act and even how happy we are with each other. In 1980, researcher Lois Raynor studied adopted adults and their adoptive parents and reported her findings in *The Adopted Child Comes of Age*. She found that the more they saw themselves as similar to each other, the happier they were. For example:

➤ Of adopted adults who said they were "very much like" their adoptive parents, 97 percent said their adoption experience was satisfactory.

➤ Of adopted adults who said they were "unlike" their adoptive parents, 52 percent said their adoption experience was satisfactory.

➤ Of those adoptive parents who thought their adopted children were "like" them in appearance, interests, intelligence, or personality, 97 percent were happy with the adoption experience.

➤ Of those adoptive parents who thought their adopted children were "unlike" them in appearance, interests, intelligence, or personality, 62 percent were happy with the adoption experience.

The important thing to note in Raynor's study is that it did not matter whether the adoptee and adoptive parent actually seemed similar to outsiders! Adoptive parents and their children who saw similarities between each other were happier with each other, regardless of whether anyone else saw those similarities. One suspects that if a similar study were done on biological children and their parents, the happier ones would also be those who found similarities in each other.

This may explain why the majority of people who were transracially adopted feel positively about adoption. For example, a black child and a white parent look very different to outsiders. But happy transracial adopters and adoptees probably concentrate on their shared traits, and they perceive themselves as similar to one another.

But what if the person who doesn't like it is your adopted child herself? Eventually adopted children do notice physical differences between themselves and their parents, whether it's skin color, ethnic appearance, or some other characteristic. Your child may say that she wishes her skin was the same color as yours or that she had curly hair like yours, instead of straight hair. She will also realize (by the age of five or six) that other people notice that she doesn't look much like you.

It's best to not deny there are differences or try to avoid the topic. Tell your child that not all biological children resemble their parents—some look very different. But do acknowledge the physical differences between you. And do realize that it is positive that your child wishes she could look like you. You might share with her that you wish she had been born from you and your spouse, but that it wasn't possible.

> **Familybuilding Tips**
> Many adoption experts urge adopters to acknowledge and accept the differences between themselves and their children. I think this is good advice for any parent, since it helps to see your children as individuals. However, some parents go overboard and tend to concentrate on those differences. Try to do both: Acknowledge the differences and celebrate the "samenesses." Achieve a balance.

Remember, too, that sometimes adopted children do resemble their adoptive parents. Just because someone is not genetically "yours" does not mean she will have nothing in common with you.

Different Strokes for Different Folks

There are other potential differences beyond physical appearance. For example, you may have trouble understanding why your child isn't more athletic/bookish/outgoing/musical, like you are. If you love to party, you may have trouble understanding a child who is shy.

Scientists are intensely interested in discovering the inherited basis for a broad array of medical problems and even behavioral predispositions. So it's understandable if you wonder about the affect of heredity and environment on your adopted child. In fact, one rather humorous tendency among some adoptive parents is to unconsciously blame any health or behavioral problems the child may have on heredity, while taking credit for positive achievements of the child.

Of course, this isn't even close to being true. Most people are a product of their heredity and their environment, and it's impossible to sort out which is the driving force.

Real Life Snapshots

Sandy's son Todd is not performing very well in school, but she's doing her best to give him the help he needs. She doesn't know why he's having so much trouble. But sometimes she secretly wonders if it's because his birthparents were poor students, too. Or maybe it's because he's adopted?

Change the scenario. Sandy's son Todd just graduated summa cum laude from Harvard Medical School. He's brilliant and has a great future ahead of him. Sandy knows in her heart that the wonderful environment she and her husband Jim have provided have made this special graduation day—and Todd's stellar future—a possibility.

What's important to keep in mind here is to avoid laying *too much* blame on heredity because often there are many actions that you can take to correct problems a child has. The best thing to do is to encourage various interests in your child and see what "works." Maybe your daughter will love ballet just like you did; maybe she'll prefer field hockey. Maybe your son wants to be a benchwarmer at the football game like you were; maybe he longs to be the star quarterback. What you should do is tailor your parenting and lifestyle to meet the needs of your child.

Common Fears of Adopted Children

All children have fears, no matter how good a parent you are. Adopted kids have the normal fears of the dark and monsters under the bed. But, adoptive children may have special fears (especially if they were adopted after age one or two). Here are some of those fears:

➤ Fear of separation/fear of losing parents

➤ Fear of being kidnapped by birthparents

➤ Fear of what other people will think about being adopted

➤ Fear of repeating the mistakes of the birthparents (suicide, drugs or alcohol abuse, early pregnancy)

➤ Fear that biological siblings or birthmother are suffering or have died

If your child exhibits any of these fears, it's a good idea to be supportive and let her know that you will always be there when you're needed.

Problem Child

Do adopted kids ever have emotional or psychological problems? Sure they do. Sometimes they hit a temporary rocky road; other times they may need professional help. Probably the biggest time when kids experience trouble is during adolescence, generally a difficult time for most children. In this section, I'll look at some of the most common problems some adopted children face.

> **Adoptinfo**
> Studies suggest that adopted children who most frequently need help are those who are adopted after age two.

"You're Not My Real Mom"

"I hate you! You're not my real Mom! My real Mom would never be as mean as you are!" The first time you hear these words from your child, it can be a shattering experience. You may wonder about your competence and if your child loves you at all.

The good news is that in most cases, your child doesn't mean what she said. She's had an emotional outburst because she's mad you didn't buy her the CD she wanted. Or you wouldn't let her do what "everybody else" is doing. Or you are punishing her for a wrongdoing.

You should handle outbursts like this exactly as a biological parent would. Evaluate if you were right or wrong. Are you being fair? Is the punishment appropriate for the crime? If you feel you've done everything right, hold your ground. If you cave in every time the "real parent" charge comes up, your child will use it repeatedly.

So what you can say is that you are her real Mom, in the first sentence. And then say that you have decided that it's important for her to do what you've said. Say you love her and you feel sad that she's angry, but you'll talk about it later. (You might also add that parents who raise biological children don't let their kids do whatever they want, either.) Then take a deep breath, shed a few tears in private, and move on. (Your child may, too. She may be surprised at her own outburst.)

> **Adopterms**
> An *adoption issue* is a problem that preoccupies and distresses an adoptee and that is related to adoption. For example, fear that a birthparent might kidnap the child is an adoption issue.
>
> So what *is not* an adoption issue? Any problem not related to the adoption. For example, a child who is temperamentally shy. Or a child who hates his teacher. Remember that many problems adopted kids have have nothing to do with the fact that they were adopted.

Discipline Disasters

Sometimes adopters are so thrilled they've finally adopted a child that when the child misbehaves later on—as children invariably do—they let the behavior go because they are unwilling to discipline their child. But if any parent, adoptive or nonadoptive, lets a child rule the household, that parent is in trouble.

Other adopters don't feel a sense of entitlement to be a full and complete parent to the child. They imagine the birthmother thinking of them as bad parents for losing their tempers and yelling. The truth is that if the child *had* remained with the birthmother, she would probably punish him for his misbehavior, too. Since you are parenting the child and she's not, it's your job.

> **Familybuilding Tips**
> The authors of *The Adoptive Family in Treatment* discuss a problem sometimes inadvertently caused by adopters who overly coddle their child—the creation of a little prince or princess who rules the household.
>
> Parents need to realize that they, not the child, are in charge. Don't let your child run wild and take charge of your family. Even though you wanted this child for so long and you love her intensely, you do her no favors by constantly giving in to her demands. The cold cruel world won't do that.

"Echo Response"

Sometimes a child adopted at an older age can display what therapist Claudia Jewett calls an *echo response*. This refers to hypervigilant behavior based on fears the child has developed from past experiences. For example, Jewett counseled a child who would never get into blue cars (although other color cars were okay). Through questioning the child, Jewett learned that the state social services cars had always been blue. The child associated blue cars with being taken away and put in yet another foster home. Understanding and desensitization can work to solve these kinds of problems.

Food Fights

If "food is love," then an early-life shortage of food can be interpreted very strongly and negatively by some children. Actually, food problems are fairly common among kids who are adopted after infancy, particularly older kids from other countries. Here are a few food issues:

➤ Extreme pickiness about foods. Kids who've lived in an orphanage, group home, or other place where they didn't always get enough to eat—or got extremely bland food—need to get used to the many new foods you serve.

➤ Gorging on food. Food gorging can really upset parents, especially when a child gorges to the point of vomiting. This is not a sign of bulimia; usually, the adopted child who gorges wants to be sure that he or she will have enough food to eat, unlike the past. Food gorging is especially common if the child was malnourished. The problem is nearly always temporary.

➤ Hoarding and hiding food. This is a common problem for children who never knew where their next meal was coming from. They need time to learn that food is plentiful in their new home. Remember Maria from the beginning of this chapter? After her parents discovered her hoarding food, they told her she could have her own kitchen shelf stocked with foods she liked. For awhile, Maria repeatedly checked the cabinet to make sure the food was there. After awhile, she stopped looking—and hoarding.

Serious Trouble

This section is about more serious behavioral and psychological problems that some adopted children sometimes have, problems that are difficult for them and for their parents. They may stem from earlier abuse or from a lengthy stay in foster care.

Troubled adopted children (like troubled nonadopted children) will often display observable signs that they need help. The following list shows a few possible indicators.

If your child exhibits just one or two of the problems described below (with the exception of the last three items on the list), your child may have a temporary problem. But if three or more of these problems show up, or any of the last three, your child needs professional help.

➤ Sudden loss of appetite or extremely increased appetite

➤ Change in sleep habits (needing too little sleep or sleeping all the time)

➤ Serious drop in grades

➤ Frequent lying or evasion

➤ Deteriorating personal hygiene

➤ Obsession with fears and worries

➤ Loss of interest in hobbies or friends

➤ Lack of friends

➤ Association with undesirable friends

➤ Persistent "orphanage behavior," such as rocking or head-banging that occurs beyond the toddler years

Adoptinfo

If your child is exhibiting problematic symptoms that are not causing imminent harm to himself or others, don't rush to the nearest psychologist or psychiatrist. Instead, start with your pediatrician. Ask the doctor to give your child a complete physical examination. If all is well with your child physically, your doctor may advise you to seek the help of a mental health professional.

Adoption Alert

Keep in mind that after placement and for at least several months, older adopted children will nearly always act out. This is normal. They are testing you. If they're bad, will you still want them? As you discipline the bad behavior, make sure you always show that you still love the child.

➤ Slow physical or mental development

➤ Physical violence or attacks

➤ Antisocial behavior such as stealing, starting fires, or harming animals

➤ Self-injurious behavior (cutting or harming oneself)

➤ Substance abuse

Getting Help

It's important to find a sympathetic, knowledgeable therapist to help you and your child. Some therapists are biased against adoption in general; they attribute all problems to the adoption itself. Others think adoption is completely irrelevant and look for some other cause, without realizing that some children are genuinely confused and troubled by their adoptive status.

Psychiatrist Steven Nickman has bluntly stated that sometimes mental health professionals can make already-existing problems worse for adopted children. Nickman cites several problems that therapists may display when treating adopted children:

➤ Not understanding the difference between adopting a child from foster care or from an orphanage and adopting a newborn infant. That is some big difference!

➤ Not understanding the difference between confidential adoption and open adoption.

➤ Not recognizing or acknowledging the bond that exists between the parents and the adoptee; not perceiving similarities between the parents and adoptee.

➤ Providing inappropriate therapy. The therapist may insist on working exclusively with the child and shutting the family out, or may ignore the child's previous history.

So how do you find a qualified therapist? Don't be afraid to ask your pediatrician or other physicians for recommendations. You can also contact a local teaching hospital and request a referral. Your network of friends and family might also be able to help.

OH.

Adoptinfo

Some research indicates that adopted children are more likely to see therapists than nonadopted kids. Does this mean adopted kids are more troubled than nonadopted kids?

Not necessarily. For one thing, many studies include abused children and children who were adopted after years in foster care, whose problems most likely stem from their early life experiences. Also, some biased therapists may be more likely to find problems in adopted kids than in nonadopted kids. Finally, adoptive parents are more likely to take their children to therapists when they see signs of a possible problem.

Remember, the majority of adolescents who were adopted as infants do well.

248

Adoption Experts

A therapist who identifies herself as an "adoption expert" is more likely to see adoption as problematic. But a therapist who knows nothing about adoption may not understand the conflicts that can occur in an adopted child. Try to choose someone who is experienced in childhood or adolescent problems and who is neither fixated on adoption as inevitably *the* problem or someone who blithely ignores it.

Whichever type of expert you choose, ask the following questions as a screening tool:

➤ How many adopted children have you treated? If you feel it's important that the therapist have experience in treating adopted kids, then if she has only treated one or two adoptees, she wouldn't work for you.

➤ Of the adopted children you've treated, in how many cases was the main problem related to adoption? If the therapist says 95–100 percent of the adoptees she treated had problems directly related to adoption, seek another therapist. Adoptees may have life problems and distresses that are related to adoption and *not* related to adoption. If the therapist sees an "adoption monster" behind every adoptee, she'll miss important information needed to help a child.

➤ Do you think adopted children are often very disturbed by being adopted? If the therapist says that some children are distressed about adoption, that's okay. If she says all adoptees or the overwhelming majority are distressed, this reveals a bias related to the example given in the preceding bullet item.

Adoptinfo

OH.

A 1993 issue of the *Journal of Child Psychology and Psychiatry* studied adopted and nonadopted children referred for therapy. Researchers found that adoptive families had more supportive resources than nonadoptive families.

Said the researchers, "Adoptive mothers rated themselves as significantly closer to their own families and perceived their husbands to be closer to in-laws than did biological mothers. Adoptive fathers reported feeling close to their in-laws and perceived their wives to be closer to their in-laws than biological fathers. Adoptive mothers also felt that there were more family members who could be called upon for help than did biological parents."

➤ Do you think adopted children are rarely disturbed about being adopted? If the therapist thinks adoption never bothers kids, then she could miss something important, as well. In fact, it's unlikely you'll receive this answer from a therapist. If you do, I'd seek out someone else.

➤ Do you have any connection to adoption—are you an adoptive parent, adopted person, or birthparent? Or do you perform adoption evaluations? It's okay if the therapist has a connection to adoption—if you think it's okay. It's best to know what her bias might be. For example, if she is a birthmother who thinks adoption scars everyone involved, obviously she would be the wrong person for you. Conversely, if she's an adoptive parent who believes in some sort of Adoption Nirvana, just say no to her!

When a Problem Is Too Hard

Some adopters decide they simply cannot handle severe physical, emotional, or psychiatric problems that show up in their adopted child. What happens when a child's behaviors fall too far short of the parents' expectations?

Researchers at the University of Southern Maine identified several stages of an impending adoption failure:

1. In the first stage, *diminishing pleasures*, the joys of parenthood were far overwhelmed by the hardships.

2. Next, the parents want the child to change his behavior, but he can't or won't change. The parents may begin complaining how difficult this child is. It's a good idea for the parent to gain feedback and support from an adoptive parent group at this point.

3. At the *turning point* stage, an event causes the parents to feel they can no longer parent the child. The child may exhibit frightening or cruel behavior, or he may run away repeatedly. The parents start to imagine what life would be like if the child were no longer part of the family.

4. The *deadline* stage is just what it sounds like: The parents give the child an ultimatum. If the child doesn't do what the parents ask, they take steps to take the child away from the family.

Sometimes the adopters ask the agency or attorney to take the child "back" and place him with another family. In other cases they request that the state social services department take over the child's case (however, if they do so, they usually lose control over what happens to the child). These situations are referred to as *disrupted adoptions*. They are extremely rare for children placed in infancy. If an intercountry adoption disrupts, then the adoptive parents must find another placement. This can be very difficult. In the extremely unlikely event it happens to you, contact an experienced adoption agency for help.

Keep in mind that disrupted adoptions are rare. Some factors that may lead to disruption are prior severe abuse, multiple homes, and foster homes—although children who fit this "profile" can do well and should not be ruled out as adoptive "candidates."

Adoption researcher Victor Groze estimates that only about 2 percent of all adoptions fail. Of course, the best plan is to work on resolving the problem well before it reaches the latter stages and before the parents and the child give up on working together.

Bottom line, although the large majority of adopted children turn out just fine, sometimes they will experience serious medical or psychiatric problems. If that happens, then of course you will need to seek

Adopterms
A *disrupted adoption* generally refers to an adoption that fails before finalization, although many people also use the term for any failed adoption. (Some people use the term *dissolution* for adoptions that fail after finalization.) How adoption disruptions are handled depends on state laws.

treatment for the child. First, get the child a physical examination to rule out a readily treatable problem. Then, if the problem may be behavioral or psychiatric, seek out a competent therapist. Finally, take into account your own needs as a human being. Don't blame yourself and don't obsess on the problem. You're one of the good guys!

The Least You Need to Know

➤ You and your child probably won't look alike or act alike—but you can still accept differences and find common interests.

➤ Most adopted kids are fine. If temporary emotional problems do surface, it's best to deal with them without making a big deal out of them.

➤ Don't spoil your adopted child. Remember that you are in control.

➤ Hoarding food and overeating sometimes occur with newly adopted orphans. These problems usually go away.

➤ If your child shows signs of a serious behavioral or psychiatric disorder, contact a therapist.

Chapter 22

If Birthparents Remain in Contact

In This Chapter

➤ Dealing with a "middleman"

➤ Handling parenting conflicts with the birthparents

➤ What to do if birthparents drop out of contact

➤ What to do as your life situation changes

Annie had been telling everyone she knew that she wanted to adopt. One day her friend Charlotte called. She knew a young woman who was pregnant and wanted her baby adopted. She was a good person in a bad situation—her boyfriend had walked out on her when he found out she was pregnant. She was due in about three weeks. Would Annie like to meet her?

Tom and Lola have an open adoption relationship with Sheila. But lately she has been calling a lot and "dropping by" rather frequently. They feel like something is up, and they don't feel comfortable with Sheila. They wonder what to do.

Open adoptions (described in Chapter 18) are offered to adopters and birthparents today. But they don't work equally well for everyone. If you have chosen an open adoption, this chapter will show you how to create a beneficial relationship with the birthparents and your child.

Dealing with a "Middleman"

As explained in Chapter 18, in many cases an open adoption is facilitated by a "middleman"—usually an agency worker or attorney. The middleman may help initiate the adoption (by introducing you to the birthparents and helping you develop a successful relationship) or may get involved after you've found suitable birthparents (to legally finalize the adoption).

If you have a "semi-open" adoption (one in which occasional meetings with the birthparents are arranged through the middleman), you will always have the middleman in the middle of your contact. There are advantages and disadvantages to this kind of arrangement:

Pros	Cons
Avoids direct contact with the birthparents.	You may want direct contact.
Having a middleman retains your privacy.	Having a middleman leads to slower communication.
The middleman can present requests or messages to and from the birthmother.	The messages or requests may get distorted in the interim.
The middleman can offer counseling to you and the birthparents.	You may not want counseling.

Real Life Snapshots

Sometimes contact between birthparents, adoptive parents, and the adopted child can startle others. When birthmother Sue was planning her wedding, she asked adoptive parents Hal and Jenna if their daughter Bonnie could be the flower girl. They thought it was a charming idea and agreed. There was a lot of talk among family members about whether or not this was appropriate—but it worked for them. Bonnie was thrilled to have an important part in the wedding.

Making Direct Contact

Maybe you prefer the direct approach. You want to be able to call or write the birthmother directly, and you want her to be able to contact you directly as well.

If direct contact is a concept that works for you and the birthparents, fine! But if you decide to "manage" the open adoption on your own, with no third-party intervention or assistance, realize that you may make mistakes. Hurt feelings can result in myriad issues. Open adoption proponents compare these misunderstandings to those that occur in any extended family.

Sometimes you may not even realize that you're making a mistake or error in judgment with the birthparents—which an intermediary might be able to point out to you. So it's clearly a tradeoff of whether direct contact or contact through an intermediary works best for all concerned.

> **Adoptinfo**
>
> OH.
>
> If you do have an open adoption experience, you are far more likely to have contact with the birthmother than the birthfather. Birthfathers seem far more reticent about maintaining contact, although some do create a relationship with adopters and adoptees.

If Problems Occur

Although your relationship with the birthparents may be great, sometimes problems develop later on. If you think about it, relationships with family members (including your own parents) aren't always an evenly flowing fount of joy. So it's not surprising if problems occasionally surface with an open adoption.

Even very strong proponents of open adoption emphasize that relationships between adoptive parents and birthparents can change, sometimes quite a bit, after the adoption. One of the most difficult adjustment periods appears to be the first year after the adoption. Over the following pages, I'll discuss a few things that can go wrong.

> **Familybuilding Tips**
>
> No matter how well you get along with the birthparents before the adoption, it's a good idea to put your expectations and plans in writing. These contracts are discussed in Chapter 18.

The birthmother may want to step back for awhile and *not* see the child or the adoptive parents. This may be hard for the adopters to understand, and the birthmother may not wish to explain. For example, she may find contact painful, and yet she does not want the adopters, whom she likes, to feel responsible for her pain. Social workers should explain this ahead of time to adopters so that they are not alarmed if they presume that an open adoption means that everyone is always happy. Most proponents of open adoption report that there are adjustments to be made and this needs to be understood ahead of time.

Birthparents Drop Out of Sight

Once adopters agree to an open adoption, they are often very enthusiastic about it. Which is why it is hard for new adopters to understand that often, after a year or two, birthparents who were in constant contact before start calling and writing less (or even drop out of sight altogether).

In other cases, the birthmother may seek regular contact with you after the placement. She may express a desire for contact with you as much as contact with the child. Some adopters have joked that they feel like they adopted the child *and* the birthmother. This is more likely to be true if the birthmother is emotionally needy. Counseling may help her learn how to make other contacts and fulfill her emotional needs in a variety of ways—including contact with you.

At the risk of sounding like a soap opera cliché, sometimes the birthparents pull away because they are "getting on with their lives." They can see that you are doing a good job as parents and the child is safe and happy. They still care about the child but are moving into other areas of their own lives.

> **Familybuilding Tips**
> Holidays may cause conflicts in the first few years of an open adoption. Will you allow the birthparents to see the kids on special days like birthdays, Christmas, Hanukkah, and so forth?
>
> You can liken this issue—and many other conflicts that people in an open adoption go through—to the learning curve of a newly married couple over the first year together. What most newly-weds learn to do is negotiate and compromise.
>
> Similarly, you can negotiate issues like holiday and birthday visits with the birthparents. Make sure everyone accepts the solution and understands what their responsibilities are.

But adopters may have trouble dealing with this. "Doesn't she care anymore? What am I supposed to tell my child?" said adoptive mom Nancy, who was used to the monthly calls or visits from birthmother Becky. After a while, Becky's contacts became less and less frequent. Nancy feels hurt and worried and doesn't understand what is going on.

Nancy needs to understand that Becky has her own personal needs. She could ask Becky if there is a problem, and Becky may or may not let her know. In the meantime, Nancy needs to learn to accept this decreased contact and not make too much of it so that her son, Corey, won't become upset or think he's done something wrong.

Birthparents Are Overinvolved

Sometimes birthparents (especially young and immature birthparents) become oppressively demanding. If this is the case, it usually happens within the first few months or year of placement, when you all are struggling to define your roles. Of course, you should be flexible and negotiable about changes; however, always keep in mind what is best for your child.

Here are a few issues you and the birthparents should agree on beforehand:

➤ Whether or not the birthmother will be allowed to spend time with the child alone. Don't agree if you think that it would be unsafe to allow it (for example, if the birthmother has a drug or alcohol problem).

➤ What the child should call the birthmother.

➤ What to do with birth relatives, primarily birthgrandparents. Will they too be involved with the open adoption, or will your child's relationship be mostly with the biological parents?

I like what the authors of *The Open Adoption Experience* say about boundaries: " . . . open adoptions do not require that you live without rules or by someone else's set of rules . . . An adoptive family can and should have appropriate boundaries about its relationship with the birthfamily. The difference between open adoption and confidential adoption is not that there are no longer boundaries but that there are boundaries where there used to be walls."

Adoption Alert
An open adoption relationship, at least in the first year, is not the same as getting along with extended family because of the very nature of adoption. Birthmothers need to resolve all the problems that led to the adoption and grieve the loss of their child and make sense of their role. Adoptive parents need to feel secure as parents and bond with their child. Neither party can "fix" the problems of the other. If there is serious conflict, it is critical that you seek a third party to help everyone address the issues.

Whatever the issue, make it clear that *you* are the parent with the ultimate and final say over the childrearing and that this is not a co-parenting arrangement.

Birthparents Want Too Much Contact

The birthparents may want more contact than is comfortable for you, especially in the beginning of an open adoption. As new adopters, you may be tired from caring for the child, or you may just want to be left alone for awhile. You probably don't want the birthmother dropping in whenever she feels like it or constantly calling you. She may need to learn—by you telling her tactfully—that you have a life and a right to privacy.

The birthparent may then assume that you are "reneging" on your agreement. Birthparents and adopters can become quite upset with each other at this point. The problem is that the relationships are still so new and they need to be worked on.

Real Life Snapshots

Adopters Corinne and Ted felt that open adoption was the right choice for them and Ava, the birthmother. But a month after baby Leda was born, things started to unravel. Ted and Corinne were exhausted new parents. On a few occasions, Ava called them and they forgot to return her calls.

On her end, Ava was anxious. Corinne and Ted had seemed so nice! But now they didn't seem that friendly. Maybe she had been deceived, just so they could get her baby. Maybe she should see an attorney.

Ava eventually did get through to Corinne and Ted and told them that she was angry. They got peeved as well. After more disagreements, Corinne and Ted decided to hire an adoption mediator, and Ava agreed to participate in mediation.

The mediator explained what the strains of new parenthood were like to Ava and also helped her work through her own anxiety and fears about adoption. She helped Ted and Corinne understand Ava's fears. Finally, the mediator sat them all down and worked out a plan they could live with. Of course, mediation cost Ted and Corinne money. But they felt it was worth every penny.

Your Life Changes

As we move on through life, things change; sometimes for the better and sometimes not. For example, you may get divorced (although studies indicate that adoptive parents have a lower divorce rate than nonadoptive parents). Or you may find yourself facing health or financial problems.

When you're in difficult straits, you may find yourself cutting back on contact with the birthparents. Maybe it's because you're just too tired or upset to talk to them. Or maybe it's because you're afraid they will be disappointed in you. Most birthparents do realize that life situations change. And if they don't realize it, they will need to accept it.

The Birthparent's Life Changes

You may have stayed about the same, but perhaps the birthparent's life has improved or worsened. If the birthmother had a problem with drugs or alcohol, she may have recovered and really turned her life around. You may need to re-evaluate her as she is now, rather than as she was when you first met her.

On the other hand, the birthmother may have developed some problems. Remember that you can always renegotiate how much time you allow her to spend with your child.

More Than One Child

One problem can occur when you have adopted more than one child. No matter how hard you try, the open adoption arrangement with one birthmother cannot be exactly equal to the arrangement with the birthmother for the other child. One birthmother may be very responsive to the child, while the other birthmom sends a card once a year and that's about it. So the parents may feel upset for the child who has been "shortchanged" in the open adoption.

No matter how hard we want to equalize the situation for our children, it's impossible for their lives to be on an exactly even footing. And children need to learn that life will not provide equal opportunities for all. The open adoption experience will be different, even when both birthmothers are very enthusiastic participants.

Adoptinfo

Some people argue that open adoption may be harmful for children. In one study, researchers found no harm done to the children involved in open adoptions. But neither did they find any benefit in open adoption as opposed to confidential adoption. The children in each situation fared about the same in terms of development and happiness.

Many more studies are needed to affirmatively state that open adoption is the best way to manage an adoption. In the meantime, numerous social workers strongly believe that open adoption is more humane than confidential adoption. Perhaps as many social workers see open adoption as detrimental.

Real Life Snapshots

Rachel is a birthmother who sends cards and gifts to her son and calls him once in awhile. But she knows that his brother, not her biological son but also an adopted child, does not have an open adoption with his birthmother. Rachel says she thinks that it must make him sad that his birthmother never contacts him, and she feels kind of like a "surrogate birthmother" to him. She always remembers her son's brother on his birthday and at holiday time.

The Least You Need to Know

➤ Open adoptions take work, but proponents believe they are worth every effort.

➤ Adoptive parents and birthparents sometimes disagree. This is normal.

➤ It's a good idea to get your open adoption agreement in writing so everyone understands the terms and conditions up front.

➤ The first year of an open adoption involves adjustments for all.

Part 5
If Your Adult Child Searches

There's constant disagreement about how many adult adoptees search for their birthparents; it's enough to know that some of them do. If your child grows up and wants to search, there are plenty of issues for your family to face. This part covers why and how adoptees search—and what to do if birthparents are found.

The bottom line is that whether or not they decide to search for birthparents, nearly all adopted children still need the love of the parents who adopted them. Read this part to enlighten yourself on a much-talked-about (and little-understood) topic.

Chapter 23

Why Do They Search?

In This Chapter

➤ Which adoptees are most likely to search for birthparents?

➤ What do adoptees hope to find by searching?

➤ Common search myths and realities

➤ How do you feel about the search?

Some adoptees are drawn to—even obsessed by—the desire to seek out their birthparents. But many adoptees say it's no big deal and they do not search.

Why do some adopted adults search while others have no interest? And does searching for biological parents mean that an adoptee doesn't love the adoptive parents? This chapter discusses the major reasons why some adoptees seek to find their birthparents.

Who Searches?

To *search*, in adoption terminology, means to seek out a biological relative. Most searchers try to locate their birthmothers, sometimes followed by a search for the birthfathers. Some searchers try to find birth siblings as well.

Adopterms

To *search* means to seek out a biological relative. Usually, the relative is the birthmother, sometimes followed by the birthfather. Some adoptees search for birth siblings as well.

Adoption Alert

What if your minor child (under age 18) tells you that she doesn't want to wait until she's 18 to search? Should you get involved in the search for her birthparents?

My view is that unless there is some compelling reason to start now, the search should be delayed until your child is an adult. Children under age 18 are not ready for the turmoil that a reunion can sometimes generate. (In fact, sometimes people who *are* 18 are still unready).

Here are the primary traits of most searchers:

➤ Most are female.

➤ Most are in their childbearing years (whether male or female). Having their own child can propel them into thinking intensely about what their own birth must have been like and wonder what their biological mother was like. They may also worry about possible inherited diseases.

➤ Many are well-educated. A well-educated person would consider it possible to find a birthparent; a less-educated person might not know how to begin a search.

➤ Many are "only children" in the adoptive family. If the adoptee is an "only child," he may wonder if he has any siblings out in the world. If he grew up with siblings, whether biological or not, the desire for sisters and brothers may have been fulfilled. (Certainly he would not idealize siblings, having lived with them!)

➤ Many have very little information on what their birthmother looks like, what her medical history is, and what kind of personality she has. This can spur adoptees into searching. (Lack of medical history is especially frustrating to some adoptees.)

➤ Some report learning late (in adolescence or adulthood) about their adoption, or learning about it in a traumatic way. This might also spur an adoptee into searching, but not always.

➤ Some people are more curious by nature than others and need to know everything they can about virtually every subject. Information about their biological family members is no exception.

Real Life Snapshots

Tom, age 18, and his father were having a heated quarrel when Tom's father spat out that Tom was adopted. Stunned, Tom left home and moved in with a friend for several days. His father found him, apologized, and begged forgiveness. Tom did forgive his father, but he wondered what else his father had withheld from him, despite his father's protestations that now Tom knew "everything."

Despite all this, Tom has never searched for his birthmother and has no desire to do so. He thinks his parents were wrong in not telling him about the adoption when he was a child, but he doesn't think that a search is the right answer for him.

Why Do They Search?

Over the next few pages I'll talk about some of the main reasons adopted adults give when asked why they decide to search for birthparents.

Roots

Probably one of the easiest motives to understand is sheer curiosity. Maybe the adopted person doesn't resemble her adoptive parents or anyone in the family—and wonders if she looks like anyone in her biological family. She may feel very different because she is of a different ethnic background.

She may wonder about similarities beyond physical ones. Does her birthmother share any of her interests? Is she athletic or musical? Does she hate to get up early, too? What's her pet peeve? What's her favorite holiday? Stuff like that.

Personality traits may also be inherited. Is the birthmother an introspective, shy type or a bouncy, gregarious person? Is she the first one to try something new, or does she like to stick with the tried and true? These are a few more issues the adopted adult may wonder about—and probably has wondered about for years.

Adoptinfo

Researchers Kowal and Schilling found several major reasons why adoptees search. The most prevalent (24%) was birth, pregnancy, or the adoption of a child. One subject stated, "As I rocked my newborn son in my arms, I wondered who had rocked me."

Other causes included: encouragement of another person; medical problems in themselves or their children; and a change in the relationship with the adoptive parents. Another precipitant was a "life-cycle marker"—the timing of a particular birthday or the time in general seemed right to the adopted person.

Medical History

Many adoptees want medical background information for themselves, as well as for any children they have (or may have). They may wonder if their birthfamilies have any history of heart disease, cancer, or other illnesses that have a genetic link.

For some adopted adults, the desire for medical information is really a subterfuge. It's the socially acceptable reason they offer for searching. However, the real reason they search is for one of the other reasons listed here.

Adoptinfo

Researchers Kowal and Schilling studied the information adoptees were looking for when they searched. Their findings: 75% of the adoptees studied wanted medical history; 71% wanted information on the personalities of their biological parents; 68% wanted a physical description of their biological parents; 66% wanted the names of their birthparents. More than 50% also sought the following information: ethnic background; their own early medical history; the hobbies of their birthparents; the reasons why their adoption occurred; the marital status of their birthparents; the educational level of birthparents; and the birthparents' occupations.

Why Adoption?

Many adoptees report that they want to know *why* they were adopted. No matter how carefully told and truthful the adoption story was, some adopted people feel that they need to hear it from the person they were born to: Why did she choose adoption?

Many adult adoptees will learn that the decision was not a "choice" but more of a societal mandate. Women in the 1950s through the 1970s (and earlier) were considered bad if they parented a child as unwed mothers. So adoption was considered the right thing to do. Of course, for many women it was the right thing to do, while others had doubts and regrets.

Search for Siblings

Some adopted adults I've talked to say they really want to meet their siblings—if they have any. Especially if they are "only" children, they wonder if there are any brothers or sisters out there. Their sibs are often a lot closer to them in age than their birthparents, so they may share more things in common than they do with the birthparent.

Adoptive Parents Are Gone

Adopted adults who have never done anything about searching may find themselves interested when an adoptive parent dies. This close link is gone, and they may wish to see if they can find the woman who created them and perhaps forge a relationship with her. In other cases, the adopted person may have been interested in searching for a long time but was afraid the adoptive parents would be upset or offended. (And sometimes they are.) So the adoptee did not search until the adoptive parents died.

Finally, some adoptees seek out their birthmother simply to thank her for having chosen adoption. They may worry that she feels guilty about it.

Unrealistic Expectations

There are other, more negative motivations that apparently lead a few adopted adults to search.

Some adopted adults believe that their personal problems stem primarily (or solely) from adoption. This viewpoint is more often heard from adoptees who are estranged from their adoptive families; but it may still occur even if the adoptee and adoptive parents are on good terms.

Here's how blaming adoption for everything can work: The person has a problem, maybe a lot of problems. She thinks her problems all relate to adoption in some way. (If she had not been adopted, she would have gone to a different school, had a different job, married a different person, and so on.)

Adoptinfo

I could find no studies on the relationships of adult adoptees with biological siblings. Anecdotally, however, it does appear that biological siblings are generally accepting of the adopted adult.

Sometimes, however, siblings who were parented by the birthmother are not in the same socioeconomic strata as the adoptee. In that case, they may be jealous of the advantages that the adoptee obtained—an affluent life, a college education, a good job, and so forth.

Adoption Alert

Experts warn that the adoptee who thinks that all her problems will be solved by meeting her birthmother is setting herself up for a bad fall.

Although hopefully the end result will be a successful meeting with the birthparent and the evolution of a happy relationship, life still does go on, with all its daily problems and issues. It's important for the adopted adult to keep this fact in sight.

Real Life Snapshots

In their article on the search process in a 1986 issue of *Social Casework: The Journal of Contemporary Social Work*, researchers Auth and Zaret described a patient, K, who "blamed all the shortcomings in her life on that fact that she had been deprived of ever knowing her birth mother."

K's parents supported her in the search process, and she also received counseling. Fortunately, by the time K did meet her birthmother, she no longer expected her birthmother to be a fairy godmother with a magic wand and was able to see her as a real person, with good and bad points.

Many adopted adults do not receive good counseling, however, and thus it can be very distressing to give up the image of the perfect mother when they meet a flesh-and blood-person instead.

OH. Adoptinfo

Psychiatrist and adoptee Robert Andersen analyzed adoption searchers in a 1989 article in *Child Welfare*. He says adoptees may view the search as an adventure or as therapy. Searchers who see the search as an "adventure" view it as an exciting experience.

Searchers who see the search as "therapy," on the other hand, may feel incomplete until they are made "whole" through the search. Although this view is more popular, it is also more problematic; finding birthparents will not solve all an adoptee's problems.

Based on this reasoning, the only corrective action the adoptee can think of is to seek out her birthmother and create a strong relationship with her. The problem with this "answer" is that no birthmother, no matter how loving and caring, can erase all life's problems. The adoptee is bound to be disappointed—unless she adjusts her thinking to conform more with reality. An adoptee who feels unwhole will not resolve an identity crisis through meeting a birthparent, even if this may seem true at the euphoric first few meetings.

In fact, the birthparent and reunion the adoptee hopes for may be nothing like the reality. Table 23.1 lists some unrealistic search fantasies and the more common realities.

What Are You Afraid Of?

Many adoptive parents have powerful negative feelings about the idea of an adoption search. Should they feel guilty? I don't think so. I think they should feel—human. But frankly, they don't have much to worry about.

Table 23.1 Search Expectations versus Search Realities

Expectation	Reality
Birthparent will be beautiful, glamorous, famous, or rich.	Birthparent may be none of those things.
First meeting will be euphoric. It will be like a fairy tale come true.	First meeting may be positive or negative. (The birthparent may even refuse the meeting.)
Birthparent will welcome adoptee with open arms and unconditional love.	Birthparent may accept or deny parenthood. The birthparent may reject the adoptee.
Adoptee will control meeting.	Birthparent may surprise the adoptee by bringing extended family.
Adopted person can control the relationship.	Birthparent may want more or less than the adoptee wants.
Birthmother will identify the birthfather.	Birthmother may refuse to identify.
Adoptee will have new extended family.	Birthmother may be unwilling to tell extended family.
Birthparent will be a lot like adoptee.	Birthparent may be very different.
Adoptive parents will understand the need to search.	Adoptive parents may not accept/understand.
Birth siblings will accept adoptee with open arms into their lives.	Siblings may be jealous of adoptee.
Adoptee's life problems will end.	Life problems usually continue.
Adoptee and birthmother will have smooth relationship.	Relationship may be rocky.
Birthparent will want same kind of relationship adoptee wants, whether intense, at arm's length, and so on.	Birthparents' needs may be very different from adoptee's needs.

Whether they admit it or not, adoptive parents whose children search often feel jealousy and even anger toward the birthparent. The adoptive parents may feel that they've done all the hard work of parenting—and now this interloper, the birthparent, will take over. This is rarely the case—but the fear is there.

One adoptive mom I know found the search painful and scary, even though she struggled to be supportive of her child's need to search. Other adoptive parents are more philosophical and accepting. And there are adoptive parents who actively launch the search to locate the birthparents themselves, in an attempt to gain information the child can have when she is grown up.

OH. **Adoptinfo**

As many as half of all searchers don't tell their adoptive parents about the search until it's over or they're well into it. Most are afraid of hurting their adoptive parents.

Remember, it isn't inevitable that your child will search—most don't. Questions about birthparents' medical history may only mean your child wants information rather than contact. Be careful not to assume your child wants to search so that it becomes a self-fulfilling prophecy. Many adoptees express a feeling that they are expected to search and are concerned something is wrong since they don't want to. On the other hand, don't blind yourself to the possibility that your child may wish to search.

Here are some other common responses of adoptive parents when they learn that their adult child has searched—or plans to search:

➤ Fear of abandonment

➤ Anxiety and fear for the adopted person—she might get hurt

➤ Feeling rejected

➤ Support and hopeful attitude

➤ Remembrance of infertility issues and the reasons for adopting

OH. **Adoptinfo**

It's hard to find information about how adoptive parents feel when children search. Many parents remain silent—whether they feel happy, sad, or ambivalent. It may not be "politically correct" for the adopters to admit to being upset, but that's a normal human reaction.

Many adoptees who are sensitive to the feelings of their parents report that they don't search for birthparents until their parents are very old or have died.

Fear of Abandonment

Many adoptive parents worry that if the adoptee likes the birthparents better, he may devote all his spare time to them and forget he was ever adopted.

Does this make any sense? Of course not. No adopted person, whether they had a great, mediocre, or even terrible relationship with his adoptive parents, can forget that he was adopted and that he was parented by the adopters. You might forget where you parked your car. You might forget what day it is. You don't forget who raised you.

Still, it may be true that when the adoptee first locates a birthparent, the birthparent will receive the lion's share of attention. Usually, though, after the excitement fades, the adoptee's relationships with both the birthparents and the adoptive parents comes back into balance.

You'll Like Them Better than You Like Us

Adopters often fear that their children will like the birthparents better than they like the adoptive parents. Why? One reason is that the adoptee has no history of bad times with the birthparents. They didn't yell at Susie for smoking in the shed. They didn't tell Jimmy that if he wanted a car, he'd have to save his own money for it.

Real Life Snapshots

When Alicia met her birthmother Barbara, adoptive mom Ellen had reservations. "I worried if my relationship with Alicia would change. Would she want to do more things with Barbara than with me?" Ellen feared that Barbara would be more attractive and appealing, that she would lose time with Alicia, that Alicia would be rejected by Barbara, and that Alicia would be disappointed in Barbara.

In reality, the reunion was a happy one. She advises adoptive parents in this situation "to feel confident in their relationship with their child. When the newness of the relationship with the birthmother wears off, they remember who loved them and raised them. Nothing can replace the relationship of a mother and child."

She also says adoptive parents should be helpful, supportive, and willing to listen. Ellen says the best part of a search is, "The child is closer to you now than before, and you don't have to worry about birthparents anymore, now that you know them."

First, realize that most birthparents are normal people who probably would have parented the child in the same ways you did. They would have sent Susie to her room for smoking, too.

And remember the flip side. The birthparents didn't see Susie play the lead fairy in the school play. They didn't sew her dress and create her gorgeous wings, which she treasured. Nor did they see Jimmy win a science fair prize. Or help him catch his first bass. You did.

Another reason is that the birthparents are usually younger than the adoptive parents (sometimes 10 or as even 20 years younger) so they are much closer in age to the adopted person. As a result, they may have more in common with the adoptee.

Adoption Alert

Many adoptive parents are scared and apprehensive about an adopted adult's search. But some actually press their child to search. I don't think this is a good idea.

If your child wants to search, then be supportive. But don't pressure her and try to take over this important aspect of your child's life. Let your child decide if and when to search for a birthparent.

Finally, some adoptive parents fear that the genetic similarities of the birthparents will prove irresistable to the adoptee.

It's very common for adopted adults and birthparents to explore mutual likes and dislikes when they first meet. If the relationship progresses, though, your child will begin to realize that although she and her birthmother share traits, they are also unalike in some ways as well.

It's notable that most adoptees take great pains to insist that they love their parents and that their search was not initiated because they didn't think the adopters were "good enough." They weren't looking for better parents. They just wanted to know the people who were responsible for their creation.

Adoptees Who Don't Search

There is great disagreement about how many people actually search for birthparents, but it does appear to be a minority of all adoptees. So what about the ones who don't search?

Adoptinfo

Some studies indicate that adult adoptees who search are more likely to see adoptive parents as different from them than adult adoptees who choose not to search. This does not mean that searchers don't love their parents; in most cases, they do love them. But they may not feel like they are similar to them. Hence, they search in the hopes that the birthparent is similar to how they perceive themselves. Of course, it doesn't always work out; sometimes adoptees and birthparents are very different.

Many report that they don't like to tell people they were adopted because the first thing many people say to them is, "So have you found your mother yet?" And if they say that they don't want to, people look at them askance.

In other cases, many times adopted adults find the identifying information they need—and then decide not to contact their birthparents. They may delay for months or even years, for a variety of reasons: fear, ambivalence, confusion, or insufficient desire to continue.

Some adopted adults have asked me if they were strange because they didn't search or didn't contact their birthparents. I told them I didn't know if they were strange, but if they were, it probably had nothing to do with not searching. My suggestion to all adoptees is: If you want to search and contact your birthparents, go ahead. If not, don't. Follow your own heart and do what's right for you and not what your friends, spouse, adoptive parents, or anyone else says.

The Least You Need to Know

➤ Adoptees have different reasons for searching. Many want to understand where they come from or find out why they were placed for adoption.

➤ Some adoptees think finding their birthparents will solve their problems. They need to understand that this is not the case.

➤ Adoptive parents should realize that just because a child searches, it does not mean that he or she does not love them.

➤ Not all adoptees search. Each adoptee must decide what is right for himself or herself.

Chapter 24

How Do They Search?

In This Chapter

➤ What's the hardest part of finding a birthparent?

➤ Using state registries

➤ Using search groups and private investigators

➤ Searching on the Internet

Finding a birthmother or birthfather is usually a lot more complicated than paging through a phone book. Why? Many adoptees have no idea what their birthmother's first or last name was or now is. (She may have married or divorced since the adoption.) Furthermore, in most states, the adoptee's original birth certificate is sealed (confidential), and the new birth certificate lists the adoptive parents' names as parents.

Getting Involved

If your adopted child decides to search, you may wish to get involved. In fact, the authors of *The Adoptive Family in Treatment* say that therapists should encourage families to become involved when a search occurs. "The impact of the search, whatever the outcome, will be felt throughout the family, and the support of the family system makes the search process itself far more bearable for the searcher," they say. I recommend, however, that the person who takes the lead, in deciding to search and determining how to search and whether or not a reunion occurs with a birthparent, should be the adopted adult. Not you.

If you do decide to take an interest or get involved in your child's search, I've included this chapter to give you a brief overview of searching tactics and techniques. There are entire books devoted to searching; I will only touch on some basics here.

It's important to keep in mind that searching for birthparents was not considered acceptable in the past and was actively discouraged. It has only been in the past 15–20 years or so that birthmothers have been told at the time of adoption that the adopted adult might search for them someday. It's also true that most professionals (and most laws) are careful to ensure contact is made only when the birthmother consents to contact. Some adoptees and adoptee groups, however, believe that it is their right to search for birthparents and contact them, whether the birthparents want contact or not.

The Right To Search?

Should adoptees be able to find their birthparents if they so choose? The entire issue of an adoptee's right to know versus a birthparent's right to privacy is a heated one.

Some adoption rights groups, such as the Adoptees Liberty Movement Association (ALMA) in New York, have asserted that the adoptee has the right to know who her birthmother is—although she cannot force her birthmother into an ongoing relationship.

Others believe that birthparents should not have to respond to the inquiries of children they've placed for adoption if they don't wish to. They may be embarrassed about the adoption or angry about the circumstances surrounding it. Or they may feel they have closed the door on the past.

The existence of birth siblings raise even more complicated issues. Does an adoptee have the right to contact siblings by birth when her birthmother opposes this contact? Or do siblings have the right to search for an adopted biological sister when their mother is against the idea? Such tough calls are hotly debated.

For this reason, the search for birthparents can be a difficult one, as many states and private organizations do not allow the release of confidential birth information.

Stating Your Case: State Registries

Over half the states in the U.S. have some sort of state registry that adopters may be able to use to find information about their birthparents (and vice versa). These registries are generally managed by the state social services department (usually located in the state capital or in the state vital statistics branch). I'll explain the different kinds of registries over the following pages.

(Keep in mind that because not everyone is aware of the state registries, and because not everyone chooses use them, searchers should not rely on the state registry alone but should also register with other organizations mentioned later in this chapter.)

Mutual Consent

If both an adopted adult (over 18 or, in some states, over 21) and a birthparent register in a state with a *mutual consent registry* (also known as a *voluntary consent registry*), identifying information will be provided to both.

The following states offer mutual consent registries (some states with registries may be missing from this list):

Arkansas	Michigan
Colorado	Missouri
Connecticut	Nevada
Florida	Ohio
Georgia	Oregon
Hawaii	Rhode Island
Illinois	Texas
Louisiana	Vermont
Maine	West Virginia

Adopterms
If both the adopted adult and the birthparent register with a *mutual consent* or *voluntary consent* registry, identifying information will be released to both parties.

Confidential Intermediaries

Some states provide a *confidential intermediary* system. In this system, the adopted adult can request identifying information on the birthparents. The confidential intermediary locates the birthparents and asks for their permission to release identifying information. If they consent, the adoptee is given their names.

States that offer confidential intermediary systems, according to information provided by state officials and attorneys, are (not all states responded to my question, so some states with confidential intermediary systems may not be listed):

Arizona	Vermont
Michigan	Wisconsin
Minnesota	Wyoming
North Dakota	

Adopterms
A *confidential intermediary system* is a system whereby one person, usually the adoptee, requests that a search be made for the birthparent. The birthparent will be identified, contacted, and asked if she or he wants contact. If the birthparent agrees, the identifying information is provided to the adoptee.

Note that some states offer both a mutual consent registry and a confidential intermediary system. They

Adopterms
Open records refers to a system wherein the adult adopted person can merely request his original birth certificate and it will be provided.

Adoptinfo
Some states vary their laws by *when* the adoption occurred and make the rules different before a certain date and after it. For example, in Vermont, a mutual consent must be obtained from birthparents and adoptees in order for identifying information to be released *if* the adoption occurred before July 1, 1986. But if the adoption was finalized after that date, identifying information will be released to the adoptee unless the birthparent filed a request for nondisclosure with the Vermont Adoption Registry.

do this because the birthparents may not have registered in a mutual consent registry—or for other reasons. If that is the case, the adopted person can then request the confidential intermediary to determine if the birthparents will agree to be identified.

Open Records

Open records refers to a system wherein the adult adoptee can merely request his original birth certificate with the names of his biological parents, and it will be provided. At present, Alaska, Kansas, and, very recently, Tennessee use this system. Legislative battles are occurring in other states where some favor open records and others are opposed.

Many adoption groups are eager to institute open records laws, so that adopted adults in any state can gain access to their original birth certificates for the asking. This information won't help adoptees who are seeking medical or social information but who do not wish to make contact with the birthparent in order to gain this information. Instead, the original birth certificate provides only the identifying information on birthparents.

Petitioning the Court

Many states do not have mutual consent registries, confidential intermediary systems, or open records; in those states, if an adoptee wants to open his birth records, he must obtain a court order to do it. To obtain a court order, the adoptee must convince a judge it's a good idea for the records to be opened.

An adoptee who chooses to go before a judge should be prepared to state why he needs to see his records. If there is a medical necessity (for example, the adopted person needs a bone marrow transplant), most judges would agree to open the records but generally will try to discreetly obtain the information from birthparents and their consent before releasing information to the adoptee. Sheer curiosity, on the other hand, is often not convincing enough to a judge.

Documentation—such as a letter from a physician, psychologist, or counselor stating that the adoptee needs the information to deal with issues he's struggling with—might help. It's also a good idea for the adoptee to prepare counter-arguments for every reason why a judge would say "no."

Judges hold varying opinions on whether or not adoptees should have access to their birth records. Adoptees who wish to approach a judge should consult an attorney in their state of birth about the best way to do so.

I'm All Grown Up! Contacting the Agency

Another way that some adopted adults find birthparents is by asking the adoption agency that originally arranged the placement. The agency may have a policy to release information if the birthparent agrees.

Adoptees who are interested should speak with the agency director or social worker. If the contact says no, he or she may still be a source of good information about alternate search methods.

The theory is if the agency has a policy to provide identifying information, things will work out well. However, the implementation isn't always effective.

Adoptinfo

Some states ask birthparents to think about the possibility of an adoptee search when the adoption is finalized. In Delaware and Arizona, birthparents and adoptive parents sign affidavits stating whether they grant or deny the release of identifying information when the child grows up. In Pennsylvania, if birthparents consent, the information is released when the adult adoptee asks for it.

Be sure to check the most recent adoption laws in your state.

Adoptinfo

There is a variety of books on searching. *Searching for a Past: The Adopted Adult's Unique Process of Finding Identity* by Jayne Schooler (Pinon, Colorado Springs, CO, 1995) emphasizes both the practical and emotional aspects of searching.

There are also general "people-finding" books, such as *Researching Public Records* by Vincent Parco (Citadel Press, 1994) or *How to Locate Anyone, Anywhere* by Ted L. Gunderson (Plume, 1996).

Real Life Snapshots

Several years ago, Pennsylvania adoptee Carol Sandusky sued the Cumberland County Children Services because a social worker gave her personal information to a biological sister—even though Sandusky had told the social worker that she did not want that information released.

Sandusky also learned more than she wanted to know about the circumstances surrounding her birth. The biological sister offered Sandusky graphic descriptions of how Sandusky had been abused by her biological parents before she was adopted.

Sandusky ultimately lost her lawsuit because a judge ruled the statute of limitations on the allegations had run out; however, she publicly stated her anger at the violation of her privacy.

Hiring Magnum, PI?

It's possible to hire someone else to do the legwork and find the information. Private investigators, search consultants, and search organizations are all available to perform searches—for a fee.

Adopterms

A *search group* is an organization that assists adoptees and birthparents with the search process. They may provide information, or they may actively involve themselves in the process. There are hundreds of search groups nationwide.

There are numerous search support groups nationwide, and there's probably a group near you. *People Searching News* offers a listing of hundreds of groups for $13. They also offer many books and articles on searching. You can find them on the Internet at http://www.findme-registry.com/catalog.htm.

No one should be hired without a thorough interview first. Here are some questions to ask:

➤ How many adoption searches have you performed?

Go with someone who knows what he or she is doing. If the person has performed only 5 or 10 searches in 10 years, stay away! On the other hand, if the person says she's performed 10,000 searches (or some other ridiculous number), be wary. Use common sense.

➤ About how long does it take to find the information?

The longer the person drags out your "case," the more the bill might be. Find out the typical timeframe.

➤ Do you have to break any laws to get it?

Although it's rare, search consultants have been arrested for illegal searches of government databases. An adoptee should not be connected with anyone performing criminal acts. So if the searcher hesitates when you ask how she plans to obtain the information, go elsewhere.

➤ What are your fees? What is the upper limit of your fees?

You don't want an open-ended search that might ultimately cost you thousands of dollars. Find out up front what the fees are and what you will get for your money. Get it in writing, too.

➤ Do you have contracts for adoption searches? Can I see one?

Ask to see a sample contract the investigator or agency uses. Read it over carefully and see if it seems reasonable to you. If possible, show it to your attorney before you sign it.

Before you engage the services of a PI or search consultant, ask for references from other customers. Also, check with the Better Business Bureau. Your local search groups may also have an opinion of the person's work.

Other Search Methods

Besides tapping into state registries, petitioning the court, or hiring a PI, there are a number of other ways adoptees can begin their search. Here are a few of the most common:

➤ Register with the International Soundex Reunion Registry (ISSR) in Carson City, Nevada. This valuable resource has helped thousands of people locate each other. Both the adoptee and the birthparent must be registered in order for a match to take place. For information, contact: International Soundex Reunion Registry, PO Box 2312, Carson City, NV 89702-2312. Phone: 702-882-7755.

➤ Use Internet resources.

There are many online registries available. For example, thousands of people have registered with America Online's registry, which launched in late 1996. Within the first six months of operation, the registry was responsible for at least 40 reunions. (The keyword on AOL is "adoption.")

Many adoptees also use the Internet to personally advertise their desire to find their birthparents. The Internet also houses many public records and databases, which makes it a convenient search tool for adoptees.

➤ Advertise in classifieds. A typical ad will announce that an adoptee with such-and-such a birthdate is searching for a birthmother. Some adoptees advertise in the area of their birth or where they think the birthparent might reside.

➤ Try a personal investigation.

The adoptee could try to reconstruct what is known about her birth: For example, what hospital was she born in? Who were the attending physicians? Individuals at the hospital may be willing to provide information. The problem with this is that medical records and documents are held as confidential in virtually all cases, and thus doctors and nurses would be violating state confidentiality laws if they provided such information. People have sued medical staff for releasing just such information.

Adoptees can also tap into public databases and computerized phone records for more information.

Real Life Snapshots

In 1997, a wire release reported that Colorado adoptee Carolyn Donahower found her birthfather very rapidly in the privacy of her own home by using her computer.

Donahower knew her birthfather's name and also suspected that he might be living in Kansas. She used Select Phone, a CD-ROM program of business and residential phone listings, and found a match. She left a few phone messages. "The next morning, my birthfather called me and we spoke for the first time in 30 years."

Bottom line: In many cases, adopted adults can locate their birthparents if they are still living. But whether their birthparents will agree to see them and whether a meeting will occur is a whole other story—which is why the next chapter is devoted to this subject.

It's also important to consider the impact of the search on the person "found." Contact may completely disrupt a person's life and cause them great distress. On the other hand, many searches result in happy and successful relationships, and the individuals involved are very pleased about the reunion. Keep in mind that your life will be changed, *and* other lives will also be changed if and when you choose to search.

Real Life Snapshots

I was once involved in a search to find my cousin. This isn't an adoption story, but I hope it illustrates what determination can achieve.

No one in the family knew Roger's phone number, address, or employer. Since his last known address had been in my county, I first double-checked that he had no phone listing there.

Then I did some fancy footwork. I dressed in a business suit, drove to the nearest large city, found the government offices, and asked to see the Postmaster. I was very authoritative and was allowed in. (If you act like you're entitled to information, often you'll be given it.)

The Postmaster gave me the latest county directory to page through—and there Roger was! But his old address and phone number were listed. There was a small breakthrough, though: This directory included an employer.

I called the employer and was told that Roger hadn't worked there in years. Using a combination of convincing and pleading, I got to talk to someone who had known him. He gave me the name of another company that Roger may have worked at. I called the other company and went through the same thing. Was I doomed to follow this guy through his resume?

Finally, at the third employer, success! I reached Roger. Mission accomplished.

The Least You Need to Know

➤ The adoptee's right to search is hotly debated; thus finding birthparent information can be difficult for many adoptees.

➤ Some states will help with mutual consent registries or confidential intermediaries.

➤ Some adoption agencies will help searchers; others will not.

➤ The Internet is a new resource for many searchers, as is the Adoption Forum on America Online.

➤ Be careful when choosing a private investigator or search agency.

Reunions

So your child has located his birthmother and is ready to make contact. What will happen next? Will the reunion be a joyous one?

No one really knows how many first-time meetings with birthparents go well. And even if the meeting is euphoric, it's impossible to guess how the long-term relationship between adoptee and birthparent will play out. However, many adoptees who have searched for birthparents state that they're glad they searched, even when the outcome wasn't what they hoped for.

This chapter talks about reunions, both good and bad.

Making Contact

How should an adoptee contact his birthparent? It's not a good idea to appear on someone's doorstep and say, "Hi! I'm your son that you placed for adoption 30 years ago." That's an unfair way to approach a birthparent.

Instead, if a child wants to make contact, he could try a phone call. And he shouldn't be distressed if the birthparent hangs up. It could be just shock or fear. He should try again a few hours or days later, when the birthparent has had a chance to recover from the excitement. If there is still a hostile reaction, even when the adoptee says something like, "May I call later if this is a bad time," then back off.

Others say that a letter without a return address is a better idea. The letter should be simple and state that if no further contact is desired, the adoptee will honor this. Some favor a follow-up phone call to the letter, in case it was not received. But if the birthparent does fail to respond, a non-response is tremendously frustrating to the adoptee. Does this mean that the birthparent didn't receive the letter or that she doesn't want to respond? Sometimes, even when a birthmother says point-blank to an adoptee that she does not want a relationship, the adoptee pursues one.

Adoptinfo

One study, done on 82 adopted adults in South Africa and reported in *Maatskaplike Werk/Social Work* in 1992, suggests that the majority of reunions may have positive outcomes. One problem, however, is that such studies rely on voluntary responses, so we don't know if people who had a good experience are more likely to respond.

In the study, 48% of all the adopted adults said the reunion results were rewarding and positive. 28% had mixed feelings and the remaining 24% were disappointed.

Real Life Snapshots

Hal wasn't looking for his birthmother and really never had any inclination to do so. But she had been looking for him and finally made contact—the day before his Bar exam. Hal was rattled. He called his parents, and they came unglued as well. The next day, Hal flunked the Bar exam.

Would he have failed it anyway? Nobody knows. In any case, his parents were furious and decided they hated Barbara for hurting their son on such an important day in his life. For her part, Barbara was sorry that her timing was so bad.

Assuming your child gets beyond the initial contact, what kind of relationship is he looking for? Counselors Patricia Auth and Shirley Zaret, in their 1986 article on the search process for *Social Casework: The Journal of Contemporary Social Work*, wrote about the five primary outcomes to a search for birthparents. They are

Adopterms
A *reunion* refers to a face-to-face meeting of the adopted person and the birth relative.

1. A one-time meeting that works out well. Both birthparent and adoptee agree that they don't need any further meetings.

2. A continuing relationship with the birthparents, although the adoptive parents remain the "real" parents as far as the adoptee is concerned. The birthparents are accepted as if they were newly met extended family members.

3. A continuing relationship with the birthparents, who become the primary parents to the adoptee. This probably doesn't happen often.

4. An inability to locate the birthparents. This can cause anger, frustration, and distress.

5. The birthparents reject the adopted adult. This can cause confusion, anger, worry, and other feelings of hurt and dismay. Counseling may help if this scenario occurs.

Reunion Rejection

As mentioned above, the reunion may not be at all what the adoptee has pictured. Because unhappy reunions can be so shattering, I'd like to talk about some of the negative possibilities.

Rejection by a birthparent can be difficult or even impossible for an adopted child to take. But the adopted child has no idea what the birthparents' circumstances are, and can't predict how the birthparent will react to contact.

The adoptee should not take rejection personally; his birthmother doesn't even know him, so she can't hate him or even dislike him. The birthmother may have any number of reasons for not wanting a relationship. Maybe she doesn't want to reopen old wounds. She may be embarrassed about the "mistake" she made so many years ago. She may feel that it would be unfair to the adoptive parents to create a relationship with the adult child.

The adoptee should realize that the birthparent may not even have told her family about him. Adults who are searching today were adopted 20 or more years ago, when many birthmothers were maligned for being pregnant out of wedlock. As a result, many are still ashamed of the situation and may have denied the adopted person's existence for years.

Not every birthparent wants to immediately integrate the adoptee into her extended family—even if she is eager to meet the child herself. (Anecdotally, it appears that most siblings are welcoming and positive to the "new child," at least at first. Some birthsiblings, however, may be jealous of the adoptee, who may have grown up with more financial advantages than the biological children did.) Birthsiblings may also be at a difficult time in their lives, such as adolescence.

Real Life Snapshots

Lori was thrilled when she met her birthmother, Sue. But when Lori told Sue she wanted to meet her adult half-siblings, Sue was adamantly opposed. Sue felt her other children would think her a bad person for having had a child adopted.

Lori argued that almost nobody felt that way anymore; although her half-siblings would probably be initially shocked and maybe a little upset, they'd be excited to find out they had another sister out there. But Sue still refused.

Lori's friends offered differing opinions. Some said she should respect her birthmother's wishes. Others said that since the siblings were adults, if Lori wanted to meet them, she should do so, whether her birthmother liked it or not. But if she did that, she risked destroying her relationship with her birthmother.

The birthparent might not be what the adoptee expects. The adoptee who secretly wishes her birthmother is a movie star can be shattered to learn that her mother is mentally ill or a criminal.

Real Life Snapshots

Tom found out that his birthmother was severely mentally ill, and had been since his birth. But he still thinks that he should have been raised by her. How could his very ill birthmother possibly have parented Tom in her confused state of mind? Answer: She could not.

Monique found that her birthmother was a violent and manipulative woman. Monique decided after several meetings that she would limit contact for her own safety and mental health.

Finally, the birthparents may be dead. If the adoptee is in her 40s or younger, hopefully her birthparents will still be living. But sometimes they are not. This can be shattering for the adopted person, who may blame herself for not beginning her search earlier. She must be reminded that in the past, she was not ready to search.

Many Happy Reunions

In many cases, the birthmother may welcome the contact and find great joy in meeting the person she gave birth to. She may be thrilled to see how well her "baby" has grown up. She may delight in introducing the adopted child to her family.

Despite the initial euphoric reunions that may occur, the adoptee and birthparent need time to work out a relationship that suits them both. This can be hard! Here are some possible outcomes:

➤ The adoptee and birthparent develop a friendly relationship.

The best reunions are ones in which the birthparent is a mature, well-adjusted adult who is delighted to meet the adoptee. She accepts the adoptive parents, although she may wish to develop her own special relationship with the adult child, realizing that sometimes it takes time to reach an equilibrium in a relationship.

➤ They become extremely close.

Both parties develop a strong, lifelong relationship. This is a good outcome—although adoptive parents may become jealous if they feel shut out. In some cases, the adoptee and birthparent may relocate to be near each other and may spend a great deal of time together. The adoptee may call the birthmother "Mom" (although this doesn't happen very often when the adoptive parents are alive, unless the adoptee has broken contact with them).

➤ They drift apart.

Even with a very intense and joyous initial meeting, sometimes the adoptee or birthparent pulls away, often leaving the other person hurt and confused.

The adoptee may decide that he simply doesn't want any more contact for an extended period. This doesn't mean that the birthmother has done anything wrong (although she may agonize that she has). She may feel that she gained her child back only to lose him again.

The birthmother may drift away for a variety of reasons: her embarrassment, an inability to handle the intense emotion, family pressure, or other issues. Or she may feel that she has nothing in common with the adoptee and not wish further contact. (Or the adoptee may feel this way.) This can be very painful to the adoptee.

Adoption Alert

If one person pulls away from the relationship, the other should keep in mind that subtle or direct pressure usually doesn't work. Unwanted phone calls, letters, and visits can antagonize the person who is reluctant to continue the relationship. Instead, it's better to accept the other person's decision while still keeping the channels of communication open.

I recommend that both birthparent and adoptee think about how much contact they want from the other and discuss it with each other. Both should realize that neither can force more contact or closeness than the other will allow.

➤ They have a falling out.

Sometimes, the birthmother and adoptee may argue or disagree over something very important to both of them (for example, the birthmother wants a stronger relationship than the adoptee wants).

Real Life Snapshots

Several years ago, I was contacted by a euphoric birthmother who had recently been contacted by her birthchild. She had actually decided to move a thousand miles away so she could live in the same city as her daughter.

I cautiously asked her if she had told her daughter she planned this move. "Oh no," she told me. "I want it to be a surprise." I tried to convince her to take it slow and also to tell her daughter so she could gauge her reaction. But she would not.

Before an adoptee or birthmother makes any radical life choices, each should listen to what the other person wants and needs.

How Does the Family Feel About the Reunion?

One group not commonly considered when an adult adoptee is seeking or planning a reunion is his own family—his spouse and children. It is easy for the adoptee to get caught up in the excitement of the search to the point of obsession. Understandably, family members may feel shut out.

What has this got to do with you, the adoptive parents? You may hear complaints from your child's spouse or children about the search obsession. They may be afraid to talk to your child directly about their concerns lest they be seen as jealous and overbearing.

If your child seems obsessed by the reunion to the point of neglecting his own family, I suggest using concrete examples, rather than a lecture, to make him realize what he's doing. (For example, the time he missed his daughter's dance recital to meet with his birthmother.) Other than that, remember that the adoptee is the one who must ultimately decide how much time to devote to the birthfamily.

How Do You Feel About a Reunion?

Very few studies have been done on how adoptive parents feel about adoptees searching for birthparents. However, one study by Phyllis R. Silverman and others, reported in a 1994 issue of *Social Work*, studied the views of the adoptive parents when a reunion occurs.

The researchers found that the adoptive parents' responses to the reunion idea generally fell into one of three categories: "accepting and open" (open), "divided in their reaction" (divided), and "closed and rejecting" (closed).

The researchers found that all of the adoptive parents, open or not, expressed some degree of fear and apprehension. They were mostly worried about their family being threatened and their child getting hurt. Aside from that commonality, however, reactions varied:

➤ "Closed" families saw the search as disloyal and a betrayal. One set of adoptive parents threatened to cut off the adoptee's funds for college unless he severed contact with his birthparents. Another adoptee was disowned by her parents when they learned of her search efforts.

➤ In a "divided" family system, the hallmark reaction was ambivalence. Families in this group were suspicious and tried to convince the adoptees not to search. Adoptees who searched coped with this attitude by not alluding to the search very much.

➤ In the "open" system, the adoptive parents and birthparents formed close relationships with each other. The adoptive parent saw the reunion as an opportunity and not a threat. Parents who fit this category said they felt closer to their children after the reunion. The authors noted, however, that the parents' openness to a reunion was no guarantee of a happy outcome.

Ideally, you and the birthparents can form a civil, if not friendly, relationship. This may not be possible if you are distressed by fear and anxiety. Or if you and the birthparents just plain don't like each other. Don't feel you have to "love" your child's birthparents; you don't. On the other hand, try to avoid putting them down and making your child feel like she's trapped in the middle.

Real Life Snapshots

Joyce Greer is an adoptive mom who went public with how she felt when her daughter searched for her birthparent. In a "My Turn" article in *Newsweek*, Greer wrote:

"The more my daughter's relationship developed with her other mother, the more frightened I became of losing her. The thought absolutely terrified me. For a while, I could not control my jealousy . . .

"To make matters worse, my daughter was then pregnant with 'our' first grandchild. Not only would I have to share my daughter and son-in-law, whom we love very much, but I'd be required to relinquish part of my special status as Grandma."

The story has a "happy ending" as far as Greer is concerned. Greer found Marilyn, the birthmother, to be a wonderful person. A year from the search, they are still evolving their relationship. Greer strongly recommends that before adoptees search, they and their adoptive parents should work through all possible outcomes that they can imagine, so they are prepared for anything.

The Last Word

What's the bottom line on reunions? Although it's true that adoptees who create a positive relationship with their birthparents are initially quite fascinated by them (understandably so), things usually settle down, and they find a balance between their relationship with their adoptive parents and their birthparents. Sometimes they become very close with their birthparents; other times, they drift apart as the demands of daily life take over and their interest wanes.

The best outlook for a reunion *is not* a "perfect" one—since the ideal is unreachable. But it is instead a relationship in which the birthparents and adopted adults feel comfortable with each other; hopefully, the adoptive parents can grow to accept the relationship, too.

Most birthparents realize that the adoptive parents have dedicated the child's lifetime to making her happy and secure and loved. Hopefully, a positive relationship will include acceptance and respect for all parties. You don't have to love each other; but you just might develop a wonderful rapport together.

The Least You Need to Know

➤ Birthparents should be initially contacted in a letter or phone call—not by a surprise visit.

➤ Adopted children should not take rejection by a birthparent personally.

➤ Both the adopted child and the birthparent will have to decide how much contact they want.

➤ Adoptive parents should support their child's relationship with a birthparent, and not worry that it will destroy their relationship with the child.

Selected Adoption Agencies

This listing does not include all the adoption agencies that exist; there are hundreds more.

In addition, listing of an agency in this book does not guarantee the quality of that agency. I cannot guarantee that you will be happy with any of the agencies listed here (although I hope that you will be). Agency directors and boards of directors change; be sure to screen an adoption agency thoroughly before contracting for its services to adopt a child. Read Chapters 6 and 9 carefully, and use your common sense, when choosing an adoption agency.

Alabama

Lifeline Children's Services, Inc.
2908 Pump House Rd.
Birmingham, AL 35243

Villa Hope
4 Office Park Circle, Ste. 218
Birmingham, AL 35223-2512

Alaska

Catholic Social Services
Bishop Whalen Center
3710 E. 20th. Ave.
Anchorage, AK 99503

Arizona

Arizona Children's Home
P.O. Box 7277
Tucson, AZ 85725-7277

Catholic Community Services
690 E. 32nd St.
Yuma, AZ 85365

China's Children
8776 E. Shea Blvd., #B-3A, Box 216
Scottsdale, AZ 85260

Christian Family Care Agency
1102 S. Pantano Rd.
Tucson, AZ 85710

Dillon Southwest
P.O. Box 3535
Scottsdale, AZ 85271-3535

LDS Social Services
235 South El Dorado
Mesa, AZ 85202

Arkansas

Adoption Services, Inc.
2415 N. Tyler
Little Rock, AR 72207

Children's Homes, Inc.
1502 E. Kiehl Ave., Ste. B
N. Little Rock, AR 72120-3000

California

Across the World Adoptions
399 Taylor Blvd., Ste. 102
Pleasant Hill, CA 94523-2200

Adopt A Special Kid (AASK)
2201 Broadway, Ste. 702
Oakland, CA 94612

Adopt International
121 Springdale Way
Redwood City, CA 94062

Adoption Horizons
302 4th. St., Fl. 2
Eureka, CA 95501

Adoption Options
5101 Glen Verde Dr.
Bonita, CA 91902

Adoption Services International
2021 Sperry Ave. #41
Ventura, CA 93003

Adoptions Unlimited
P.O. Box 462
Chino, CA 91710

African Cradle
509 13th. St., Ste. 5
Modesto, CA 95354

Bay Area Adoption Services
465 Fairchild Dr., Ste. 215
Mountain View, CA 94943-2251

Bethany Christian Services
3048 Hahn Dr.
Modesto, CA 95350

God's Children
P.O. Box 320
Trabuco Canyon, CA 92679

Heartfelt Adoption
10649 Charbono Way
Rancho Cardova, CA 95670

LDS Social Services
791 S. Pepper Ave.
Colton, CA 92324

Life Adoption Services
440 West Main St.
Tustin, CA 92680

Vista Del Mar
3200 Motor Ave.
Los Angeles, CA 90034-3740

Colorado

Catholic Charities
1020 Upham St.
Lakewood, CO 80215

Chinese Children Adoption
1100 W. Littleton Blvd. #206
Littleton, CO 80120-2249

Hope's Promise
309 Jerry St. #202
Castle Rock, CO 80104-2442

LDS Social Services
3263 Fraser St., Ste. 3
Aurora, CO 80011

Worldwide Children's Connection
3525 Lowell Blvd.
Denver, CO 80121

Connecticut

A Child Among Us
2410 New London Turnpike
South Glastonbury, CT 06073

Catholic Charities
238 Jewett Ave.
Bridgeport, CT 06606

Catholic Family Service
478 Orange St.
New Haven, CT 06511

Lutheran Social Services
2139 Silas Deane Hwy., Ste. 201
Rocky Hill, CT 06067-2336

Thursday's Child
227 Tunxis Ave.
Bloomfield, CT 06002

Wide Horizons for Children
34 Connecticut Blvd.
E. Hartford, CT 06108

Delaware

Adoptions From the Heart
18-A Trolley Square
Wilmington, DE 19806

Catholic Charities
4th & Greenhil Ave.
Wilmington, DE 19805

Children's Choice, Inc.
262 Chapman Rd.
Newark, DE 19702-5412

District of Columbia

Adoption Center of WA
1990 M ST. NW, Ste. 380
Washington, DC 20036

Adoption Services Information
   Agency/ASIA
7720 Alaska Ave. NW
Washington, DC 20012

American Adoption Agency
1228 M St. NW, 2nd Fl.
Washington, DC 20005-5197

International Children's Alliance
1101 17th. St. NW, Ste. 1002
Washington, DC 20036

Florida

A Bond of Love Adoption
2520 S. Tamiami Trail
Sarasota, FL 34239-4501

Adoption By Choice
4102 W. Linebaugh Ave. #200
Tampa, FL 33624-5239

Children's Home Society
P.O. Box 5616
Jacksonville, FL 32247-5616

Children's Home Society
212 Pasadena Pl.
Orlando, FL 32803-3828

Children's Home Society
314 S. Missouri Ave.,
Ste. 101
Clearwater, FL 34616

LDS Social Services
950 N. Orlando Ave., Ste 360
Winter Park, FL 32789-2254

Life for Kids
315 N. Wymore Rd.
Winter Park, FL 32789

Lifelink Child & Family Services
1031 S. Euclid Ave.
Sarasota, FL 34237-8124

Shepherd Care Ministries
5935 Taft St.
Hollywood, FL 33021

Georgia

Georgia AGAPE, Inc.
3094 Mercer University Dr., #200
Atlanta, GA 30341

Hope for Children, Inc.
1507 Johnson Ferry Rd., Ste. 190
Marietta, GA 30062

LDS Social Services
4823 N. Royal Atlanta Dr.
Tucker, GA 30084

Lutheran Ministries of GA
756 Peachtree St. NW
Atlanta, GA 30308

New Beginnings Adoption and
Counseling Agency
1316 Wynnton Court, Ste. A
Columbus, GA 31906

Hawaii

Hawaii International Child
P.O. Box 240486
Honolulu, HI 96824-0486

LDS Social Services
1500 S. Beretania St., Ste. 403
Honolulu, HI 96826

Idaho

Boise Children's Family Center
319 Allumbaugh St. #319
Boise, ID 83704-9208

LDS Social Services
10740 Fairview, Ste. 100
Boise, ID 83713

Illinois

Bensenville Home Society
331 S. York Rd.
Bensenville, IL 60106

Catholic Charities
651 West Lake St.
Chicago, IL 60661

Children's Home & Aid Society
910 2nd. Ave.
Rockford, IL 61104

The Cradle
2049 Ridge Ave.
Evanston, IL 60201-2794

Lutheran Social Services
1144 Lake St.
Oak Park, IL 60301

New Beginnings Adoption Agency
5875 N. Lincoln Ave.
Chicago, IL 60659-4614

New Life Social Services
3525 W. Peterson, Ste. 215
Chicago, IL 60659

St. Mary's Services
717 W. Kirchoff Rd.
Arlington Hts., IL 60005

Sunnyridge Family Center
2 South
426 Orchard Rd.
Wheaton, IL 60187

Indiana

Americans for African Adoptions
8910 Timberwood Dr.
Indianapolis, IN 46234-1952

Bethany Christian Services
6144 Hillside Ave #10
Indianapolis, IN 46220-2474

Catholic Charities
315 E. Ashington Blvd.
Ft. Wayne, IN 46802

Childplace
2420 Highway 62
Jeffersonville, IN 47130

Coleman Adoption Service
615 N. Alabama St., #419
Indianapolis, IN 46204-1434

Iowa

Bethany Christian Services
6000 Douglas, Ste. 230
Des Moines, IA 50322

Bethany Home
1706 Brady St. #207
Davenport, IA 52803-4708

Heart International Adoptions
5335 Merle Hay Rd., Ste. B
Johnston, IA 50131

Kansas

Adoption by Gentle Shepherd
6405 Metcalf, Ste. 318
Overland Park, KS 66202

Lutheran Social Service of Kansas and
Oklahoma
1855 North Hillside
Wichita, KS 67214

Special Additions, Inc.
10985 W. 175th St.
Olathe, KS 66062-9464 (also in Kansas
City)

Kentucky

Adoptions of Kentucky
One Riverfront Plaza, Ste. 1708
Louisville, KY 40202

A Helping Hand Adoption Agency
P.O. Box 8336
Lexington, KY 40533

Mary Kendall Home
193 Phillips Ct.
Owensboro, KY 42303-3771

Louisiana

Children's Bureau of New Orleans
Plaza Tower
1001 Howard Ave., Ste. 2800
New Orleans, LA 70113

Special Delivery Adoption Service
8772 Lake Quarters Rd.
Baton Rouge, LA 70809

St. Elizabeth Foundation
8054 Summa Ave., Ste. A
Baton Rouge, LA 70809

Volunteers of America
360 Jordan St.
Shreveport, LA 71101

Maine

International Adoption Services Centre
P.O. Box 55
Alna, ME 04535

Maine Adoption Placement Service
P.O. Box 772
Houlton, ME 04730-0772

St. Andre Home
283 Elm St.
Biddeford, ME 04005

Maryland

Adoption Options
6123 Montrose Rd.
Rockville, MD 20852

Adoption Service Information Agency
(ASIA)
8555 16th. St., Ste. 603
Silver Spring, MD 20910

Adoptions Together, Inc.
6 Sudbrook Lane
Baltimore, MD 21208

Associated Catholic Charities
19 W. Franklin St.
Baltimore, MD 21201

The Barker Foundation
7945 MacArthur Blvd., Ste. 206
Cabin John, MD 20818

Bethany Christian Services
1641 Rte. 3 N., Ste. 205
Crofton, MD 21114

Cradle of Hope Adoption Center
8630 Fenton St., #310
Silver Spring, MD 20910-3803

Creative Adoptions, Inc.
10750 Hickory Ridge Rd., #109
Columbia, MD 21044

LDS Social Services
Amber Meadows Prof. Building
198 Thomas Jefferson Dr., Ste. 13
Frederick, MD 21702

World Child
1400 Spring St., Ste. 410
Silver Spring, MD 20910

Massachusetts

Adoption Resource Canter at Brightside
2113 Riverdale St.
W. Springfield, MA 01089

The Alliance for Children
40 William St., Ste. G80
Wellesley, MA 02181-3902

Catholic Charities
55 Lynn Shore Dr.
Lynn, MA 01902-4903

Concord Family Service
111 Old Road to Nine Acre Corner
Concord, MA 01720

Lutheran Social Services
416 Belmont St.
Worcester, MA 01604

Michigan

Adoption Associates
1338 Baldwin St.
Jenison, MI 49428-8937

AIAA
626 Jenks Blvd.
Kalamazoo, MI 49006-3075

Bethany Christian Services
32500 Concord Dr. #250
Madison Hts, MI 48071-1118

Bethany International Services
901 Eastern Ave. NE
Grand Rapids, MI 49503

Catholic Social Services
4925 Packard Rd.
Ann Arbor, MI 48108-1521

Family Adoption Consultants
P.O. Box 50489
Kalamazoo, MI 49005

Lutheran Adoption Services
21700 NW Hwy, Ste. 1490
Southfield, MI 48075

MARE
P.O. Box 6128
Jackson, MI 49204

Spaulding for Children
16250 Northland Dr., Ste. 120
Southfield, MI 48075

Minnesota

AIAA
3080 Shields Dr., #101
Egan, MN 55121

Bethany Christian Service
3025 Harbor Lane #223
Plymouth, MN 55447

Children's Home Society
2230 Como Ave.
St. Paul, MN 55108

Crossroads Adoption Service
4620 W. 77th, Ste. 105
Minneapolis, MN 55435

HOPE Adoption & Family
421 S. Main St.
Stillwater, MN 55082

Lutheran Social Services
2414 Park Ave.
Minneapolis, MN 55404-3713

New Horizons Adoption Agency
P.O. Box 623
Frost, MN 56033

Mississippi

New Beginnings
P.O. Box 7055
Tupelo, MS 38802

Missouri

Children's Hope International
9229 Lackland Rd.
St. Louis, MO 63114

Christian Family Services
8039 Watson Rd., Ste. 120
St. Louis, MO 63119-5325

Dillon International
610 Martin Pointe Ct.
Ballwin, MO 63011-1762

Gift of Love Adoption Services, Inc.
1 Mid Rivers Mall Dr., Ste. 140
St. Peters, MO 63376

Love Basket
4472 Goldman Rd.
Hillsboro, MO 63050

Lutheran Family & Child Services
4201 Lindell Blvd., Ste. 400
St. Louis, MO 63108-2915

Refuge Maternity Home
499 Walnut St.
Winfield, MO 63389

Small World Adoption Foundation
1270 Fee Fee Rd.
St. Louis, MO 63146

Special Additions, Inc.
201 W. 135th St.
Kansas City, MO 64145-1201

Nebraska

Nebraska Children's Home Society
3549 Fontenelle Blvd.
Omaha, NE 68104

Nebraska Children's Home Society
P.O. Box 2181
21 East 20th St.
Scottsbluff, NE 69363

New Hampshire

LDS Social Services
131 Route 101-A
Amherst Plaza, Ste. 204
Amherst, NH 03031

New Jersey

Adoptions From the Heart
451 Woodland Ave.
Cherry Hill, NJ 08002

Catholic Social Service
2830 Marlton Pike
Camden, NJ 08105-2164

Children of the World
685 Bloomfield Ave., Ste. 201
Verona, NJ 07044

Children's Home Society of
New Jersey
929 Parkside Ave.
Trenton, NJ 08618-2898

Golden Cradle
1050 N. Kings Hwy., #201
Cherry Hill, NJ 08034-1909

Lutheran Social Ministries
120 Route 156
Yardville, NJ 08620

Small World Ministries
257 West Broad St.
Palmyra, NJ 08065

Nevada

LDS Social Services
513 S. Ninth St.
Las Vegas, NV 89101

New Mexico

Adoption Resources of Santa Fe
58A Old Agua Fria Rd. West
Santa Fe, NM 87505

Chaparral Adoption Agency
1503 University Blvd. NE
Albuquerque, NM 87102

Christian Placement Service
1356 New Mexico 236
Portales, NM 88130-9411

Family and Children's Services
1503 University Blvd.
Albuquerque, NM 87102

LaFamilia Placement Services
707 Broadway NE, Ste. 103
Albuquerque, NM 87102

Rainbow House International
19676 Highway 85
Belen, NM 87002

New York

Catholic Family Center
25 Franklin St.
Rochester, NY 14604

Child & Family Adoption Center
234 Main St.
New Paltz, NY 12561-1113

Children of the World
27 Hillvale Rd.
Syosset, NY 11791-6916

Community Maternity Services
27 North Main Ave.
Albany, NY 10022

Family Focus
54-40 Little Neck Parkway, Ste. 3
Little Neck, NY 11362

Family Service of Westchester
One Summit Ave.
White Plains, NY 10606-3011

New Life Adoption Agency
430 E. Genessee St., Ste. 301
Syracuse, NY 13202

Parsons Child and Family Center
60 Academy Rd.
Albany, NY 12208-3103

Spence-Chapin
6 E. 94th. St.
New York, NY 10128

VIDA
354 Allen St.
Hudson, NY 12534

North Carolina

Carolina Adoption Services
106 E. Northwood St., Ste. 7
Greensboro, NC 27401

Catholic Social Services
621 W. 2nd St.
Winston-Salem, NC 27106

Christian Adoption Service
624 Matthews-Mint Rd., #134
Matthews, NC 28105

The Gladney Center
P.O. Box 1902
Mount Airy, NC 27030

Lutheran Family Services
P.O. Box 12287
Raleigh, NC 27605

Victoria Adoption Center
3803-B Computer Dr., Ste. 201
Raleigh, NC 27609

North Dakota

Catholic Family Service
1223 S. 12th. St.
Bismarck, ND 58504

Ohio

AASK Midwest, Inc.
1025 S. Reynolds Rd.
Toledo, OH 43615

Adoption by Gentle Care
17 Brickel St.
Columbus, OH 43215

The Beech Brook Spaulding Adoption
Program
3737 Lander Rd.
Cleveland, OH 44124

Bellefaire Jewish Children's Bureau
22001 Fairmount Blvd.
Cleveland, OH 44118

International Adoption Consultants
13 Park Ave. West, Ste. 508
Mansfield, OH 44902

Oklahoma

Cradle of Lawton, Inc.
902 NW Kingswood Rd.
Lawton, OK 73505

Deaconess Home
5300 N. Grand Blvd., Ste. 210
Oklahoma City, OK 73112

The Gladney Center
6403 N. Grand Blvd., Ste. 104
Oklahoma City, OK 73118

LDS Social Services
4500 South Garnett, Ste. 425
Tulsa, OK 74146-5201

Small Miracles International
107 Mid America Blvd. #3
Midwest City, OK 73110

Oregon

ASIA of Oregon
17647 Hill Way
Lake Oswego, OR 97035-5415

Cascade International Children
1425 NE Irving, Ste. 250
Portland, OR 97232

Holt International Children's Services
P.O. Box 2880
Eugene, OR 97402

Journeys of the Heart
P.O. Box 482
Hillsboro, OR 97123

Orphans Overseas
10226 SW Park Way
Portland, OR 97225

PLAN International Adoption
P.O. Box 667
McMinville, OR 97128

Pennsylvania

Adopt-A-Child
Maxon Towers, Ste. L-111
6315 Forbes Ave.
Pittsburgh, PA 15217

Adoption Horizons
899 Petersburg Rd.
Carlisle, PA 17013

Adoption Unlimited
2770 Weston Rd.
Lancaster, PA 17603

Adoptions From the Heart
76 Rittenhouse Place
Ardmore, PA 19003
(Agency also has offices in Lancaster,
Harrisburg, Allentown, and
Greensburg, Pennsylvania)

Bethany Christian Services
694 Lincoln Ave.
Pittsburgh, PA 15202

Catholic Charities Adoption
P.O. Box 3551
Harrisburg, PA 17105

Children's Adoption Network
130 Almshouse Rd., Ste. 403
Richboro, PA 18954

Children's Aid Society
1314 DeKalb St.
Norristown, PA 19401

Choices Adoption Agency
527 Swede St., Fl. 2
Norristown, PA 19401-4806

International Assistance Group
21 Brilliant Ave., Ste. 201
Pittsburgh, PA 15215

International Families
518 South 12th. St.
Philadelphia, PA 19147

Kaleidoscope of Family Services
355 W. Lancaster Ave.
Haverford, PA 19041

Lutheran Children and Family Service
1256 Easton Rd.
Roslyn, PA 19001

Marian Adoption
3138 Butler Pike
Plymouth Meeting, PA 19462

St. Joseph's Center
2010 Adams Ave.
Scranton, PA 18509

Three Rivers Adoption
307 Fourth Ave., Ste. 710
Pittsburgh, PA 15222-2102

Tressler Lutheran Services
836 S. George St.
York, PA 17403

Welcome House Foundation
Green Mills Farm
Perkasie, PA 18944

Rhode Island

Catholic Social Services
433 Elmwood Ave.
Providence, RI 02907

Jewish Family Service
229 Waterman St.
Providence, RI 02906-5212

South Carolina

Children Unlimited
P.O. Box 11463
Columbia, SC 29211

Christian World Adoption
270 West Coleman Blvd.
Mt. Pleasant, SC 29464

Tennessee

Bethany Christian Services
4719 Brainerd Rd., Ste. D
Chattanooga, TN 37411-3842

Catholic Charities of TN
30 White Bridge Rd.
Nashville, TN 37205-1401

Heaven Sent Children
316 W. Lytle St #214
Murfreesboro, TN 37130

Porter-Leath Children's Center
868 N. Manassas St.
Memphis, TN 38107-2516

Small World Ministries
401 Bonnaspring Dr.
Hermitage, TN 37076-1147

St. Peter Home and Adoption Service
1805 Poplar Ave.
Memphis, TN 38104

Williams-Illien Adoptions
3439 Venson Dr.
Memphis, TN 38135

Texas

About Life Adoption Agency
4131 N. Central Expressway
Dallas, TX 75204-2102

Adoption Resources Center
8600 Wurzbach Rd., Ste. 1110
San Antonio, TX 78240-4334

Andrel Adoptions, Inc.
3908 Manchaca Rd.
Austin, TX 78704

Associated Catholic Charities
P.O. Box 66508
Houston, TX 77266

Bright Dreams International
2929 Carlisle St., Ste. 255
Dallas, TX 75208

Buckner Adoption
5204 S. Buckner Blvd.
Dallas, TX 75227

Christian Homes of Abilene
P.O. Box 270
Abilene, TX 79604

Cradle of Life Adoption
245 N. 4th St.
Beaumont, TX 77701-1920

The Gladney Center
2300 Hemphill
Fort Worth, TX 76110

Homes of St. Mark
3000 Richmond Ave. #570
Houston, TX 77006

Hope Cottage Adoption Center
4209 McKinney Ave.
Dallas, TX 75205-4543

International Family Services
700 S. Friendswood Dr, Ste. B
Friendswood, TX 77546

LDS Social Services
6120 Earle Brown Dr.
Brooklyn Center, MN 55430-2123

Lee & Beaulah Children's Home
1100 Cliff Dr.
El Paso, TX 79902

Los Niños
P.O. Box 9617
The Woodlands, TX 77387

Methodist Mission Home
6487 Whitby Rd.
San Antonio, TX 78240

New Life Children's Services
19911 SH 249
Houston, TX 77070

Smithlawn Home and Adoption
Agency
P.O. Box 6451
Lubbock, TX 79493

Southwest Maternity Center
6487 Whitby Rd.
San Antonio, TX 78240-2131

Utah

A Act of Love
195 W. 7200 S. #223
Midvale, UT 84047

LDS Social Services
National Headquarters
10 East South Temple St., Ste. 1200
Salt Lake City, UT 84111

Virginia

Bethany Christian Services
291 Independence Blvd. #542
Virginia Beach, VA 23462-5473

Catholic Charities
820 Campbell Ave. SW
Roanoke, VA 24016

Children's Home Society of VA
4200 Fitzhugh Ave.
Richmond, VA 23230-3829

Commonwealth Catholic Charities
1512 Willow Lawn Dr.
P.O. Box 6565
Richmond, VA 23230-0565

Frost International Adoptions
5205 Leesburg Pike, Ste. 205
Falls Church, VA 22041

United Methodist Family Services
3900 W. Broad St.
Richmond, VA 23230

Washington

Adoption Advocates International
401 East Front St.
Port Angeles, WA 98362

Americans Adopting Orphans
12345 Lake City Way NE, Ste. 2001
Seattle, WA 98125

Bethany Christian Services
19936 Ballinger Way NE, Ste. D
Seattle, WA 98155

Catholic Community Services
100 23rd Ave. South
Seattle, WA 98144-2302

Faith International Adoptions
535 E. Dock St. #208
Tacoma, WA 98402

New Hope Child & Family Agency
2611 NE 125th, Ste. 146
Seattle, WA 98125

WACAP
P.O. Box 88949
Seattle, WA 98138

West Virginia

Burlington United Methodist
Rte. 4, Box 240-B
Keyser, WV 26726

Wisconsin

Adoption Services, Inc.
911 N. Lynndale Dr., Ste. 2C
Appleton, WI 54914-3086

Bethany Christian Services
2312 N. Grandview Blvd.
Waukesha, WI 53188

Evangelical Child & Family Agency
1617 S. 124th St.
New Berlin, WI 53151-1803

Lutheran Social Services
1101 W. Clairemont Ave., Ste. 2H
Eau Claire, WI 54701

Special Children, Inc.
910 Elm Grove Rd. #2
Elm Grove, WI 53122-2531

Special Needs Adoption Network of
    Wisconsin
1126 S. Main St., Ste. N509A
West Allis, WI 53214

Wyoming

Catholic Social Services
P.O. Box 1026
Cheyenne, WY 82003

Global Adoption Services
1425 S. Thurmond St.
Sheridan, WY 82801-5547

Selected National Adoption Organizations

The following national adoption organizations provide information and support on adoption and adoption-related issues. Some specialize in a particular area, such as children with special needs, whereas other organizations provide information on all children. Contact the organizations for more information. Note that these are only a sampling of the many groups which directly or indirectly deal with adoption.

Adoptive Families of America (AFA)
2309 Como Ave.
St. Paul, MN 55108
800-372-3300 or 612-645-9955

Formed in 1967, AFA is the largest adoptive parent group in the U.S., with members nationwide. Also an educational and advocacy organization, AFA tracks federal and state laws and adoption issues. Offers advice and information to current and prospective adoptive parents. Publishes *Adoptive Families* magazine.

American Academy of Adoption Attorneys
P.O. Box 33053
Washington, DC 20033-0053
202-832-2222
E-mail: www.adoptionattorneys.org

The American Academy of Adoption Attorneys was formed in 1990 to improve adoption laws and practice in the U.S. and abroad. Membership by invitation. Members have completed at least 50 adoptions, 10 of which were interstate placements.

International Concerns for Children
911 Cypress Dr.
Boulder, CO 80303
Web site: http://www.fortnet.org/icc/

This organization offers information and help on international adoption. Publishes the *Report on Intercountry Adoption*, which is updated 10 times per year and offers valuable and timely information. Cost is $20. Also offers a photo-listing of children with special needs from other countries. Cost is $25.

National Adoption Center
1500 Walnut St., Ste. 701
Philadelphia, PA 19102
Voice: 800-TO-ADOPT or 215-735-9988
Web site: http://www.nac.adopt.org/

This organization provides information and agency referrals to people interested in adopting children with special needs. Also works to promote public awareness of the children. Provides a photo-listing service of "waiting children," both in print and online.

National Adoption Information Clearinghouse
P.O. Box 1182
Washington, DC 20013
888-251-0075 or 703-352-3488
Web site: http://www.calib.com.naic/index.htm

The National Adoption Information Clearinghouse offers a broad array of adoption information for adoptive parents, adoptees, and birthparents, much of which is free of charge.

National Council For Adoption
1930 17th St. NW
Washington, DC 20036
202-328-1200
Web site: http://www.ncfa-us.org

National advocacy and information group comprised of agencies and individuals. Provides information and assistance on all adoption-related areas. Lobbies on adoption issues and answers media queries about a broad array of adoption topics. Publishes several newsletters, including *National Adoption Reports* and *MEMO*.

National Council for Single Adoptive Parents
P.O. Box 15084
Chevy Chase, MD 20825
No phone

An information service for single people who want to adopt or who have adopted. Publishes a helpful guide on single-parent adoption: *The Handbook for Single Adoptive Parents* (1997). Cost is $20. Order from the above address.

North American Council on Adoptable Children (NACAC)
970 Raymond Ave., Ste. 106
St. Paul, MN 55114-1149
612-644-3036

The NACAC concentrates on laws, issues, and policies related to adoptive placements of children with special needs. Provides information and assistance. Holds an annual conference in either the U.S. or Canada. Publishes an informational newsletter.

RESOLVE, Inc.
1310 Broadway
Somerville, MA 02144-1731
617-623-0744 (helpline)
Web site: http://www.resolve.org/

This is the headquarters of the national infertility information group. They also offer information on adoption. RESOLVE has chapters nationwide. (See Appendix E for a listing of parent groups.)

Stars of David International, Inc.
3175 Commercial Ave., Ste. 100
Northbrook, IL 60062-1915
800-STAR-349 or 847-509-9929
E-mail: StarsDavid@aol.com
Web site: http://www.starsofdavid.org/

Stars of David is an information and support network for Jewish and interfaith adoptive families with 30 chapters nationwide. Holds an annual conference.

Tapestry Books
P.O. Box 359
Ringoes, NJ 08551
800-765-2367
Web site: http://www.webcom.com/~tapestry/

Tapestry Books is a mail-order book business which offers virtually every adoption book. They also offer a free catalog.

Selected List of Adoption Attorneys

All attorneys listed here are members of the American Academy of Adoption Attorneys. Listing in this appendix does not constitute endorsement of any particular individual listed; you should carefully screen any attorney you are considering working with.

Alabama

David P. Broome
P.O. Box 1944
Mobile, AL 36633-1944

Bryant A. Whitmire, Jr.
New South Federal Savings Bank Building
215 North 21st. St., Ste. 501
Birmingham, AL 35203

Alaska

Sharon L. Gleason
510 L St., Ste. 306
Anchorage, AK 99501-1952

Arizona

Michael J. Herrod
4725 North 19th. Ave.
Phoenix, AZ 85015

Scott E. Myers
3180 East Grant Rd.
Tucson, AZ 85716

John Neff Nelson
1600 South Fourth Ave., Ste. C
Yuma, AZ 85364

Kathryn A. Pidgeon
Exodyne Business Park
8433 North Black Canyon Highway, Ste. 100
Phoenix, AZ 85021-4859

Kelly A. Sifferman
7000 North Sixteenth St., Ste. 120-419
Phoenix, AZ 85020

Mary L. Verdier
2800 N. Central Ave., Ste. 1400
Phoenix, AZ 85004

Daniel I. Ziskin
3309 North Second St.
Phoenix, AZ 85012

Arkansas

Eugne T. Kelley
222 West Walnut St.
Rogers, AR 72756

California

G. Darlene Anderson
127 East Third Ave., Ste. 202
Escondido, CA 92025-4201

David H. Baum
16255 Ventura Blvd., #704
Encino, CA 91436-2312

Timothy J. Blied
4100 Newport Place Dr., #800
Newport Beach, CA 92660-2422

D. Durand Cook
8383 Wilshire Blvd., Ste. 1030
Beverly Hills, CA 90211-2401

Douglas R. Donnelly
926 Garden St.
Santa Barbara, CA 93101

Marc Gradstein
1204 Burlingame Ave. #7
Burlingame, CA 94010-4126

Randall B. Hicks
6690 Alessandro Blvd., Ste. D
Riverside, CA 92506

Allen C. Hultquist
707 Broadway, #1111
San Diego, CA 92101

George Maricic
P.O. Box 2367
Rancho Cucamonga, CA 91729-2367

Diane Michelsen
3190 Old Tunnel Rd.
Lafayette, CA 94549-4133

Linda S. Nunez
513 East 1st., 2nd. Fl.
Tustin, CA 92680

David Radis
1901 Avenue of the Stars,
    20th Floor
Los Angeles, CA 90067

Jed Somit
1440 Broadway, #910
Oakland, CA 94612

Janis K. Stocks
1450 Frazee Rd., Ste. 409
San Diego, CA 92108

Ronald Stoddart
1698 Greenbriar Lane, #201
Brea, CA 92821

Felice Webster
4525 Wilshire Blvd. #201
Los Angeles, CA 90010

Marc D. Widelock
5401 California Ave., #300
Bakersfield, CA 93309

Nanci Worcester
Adoption Center of Northern
California
210 Magnolia Ave. #2
Auburn, CA 95603

Colorado

W. Thomas Beltz
Adoption Choice Center
729 South Cascade Ave., Ste. 2
Colorado Springs, CO 80903

Melinda L. Garvert
5585 Erindale Dr., #202
Colorado Springs, CO 80918-6969

Susan Beth Price
769 West Littleton Blvd.
Littleton, CO 80120

Connecticut

Pamela Nolan Dale
58 Kane Ave.
Stamford, CT 06905

Janet S. Stulting
One American Row
Hartford, CT 06103-2819

Delaware

Ellen S. Meyer
521 West St.
Wilmington, DE 19801

District of Columbia

Mark T. McDermott
1300 19th. St. NW, #400
Washington, DC 20036

Leslie Scherr
815 Connecticut Ave. NW, Ste. 500
Washington, DC 20006-4004

Peter J. Wiernicki
1300 19th. St. NW, #400
Washington, DC 20036

Florida

Bennett S. Cohn
205 Sixth St.
West Palm Beach, FL 33401

Linda W. McIntyre
98 Southeast Sixth Ave., Ste. 1
Delray Beach, FL 33483

Mary Ann Scherer
Oakridge Professional Bldg., Ste. 200
2734 East Oakland Park Blvd.
Ft. Lauderdale, FL 33306

Michael A. Shorstein
402 Dupont Center
1660 Prudential Dr. #402
Jacksonville, FL 32207

Susan Stockham
2520 S. Tamiami Trail
Sarasota, FL 34239

Cynthia Stump Swanson
500 E. University Ave., #C
Gainesville, FL 32601

Jeanne Trudeau Tate
PO Box 2231
Tampa, FL 33601

Georgia

Rhonda L. Fishbein
17 Executive Park Dr., Ste. 480
Atlanta, GA 30329

Richard A. Horder
1100 Peachtree St., Ste. 2800
Atlanta, GA 30309-4530

Irene A. Steffas
4187 Kindlewood Court
Roswell, GA 30075-2686

Hawaii

Laurie A. Loomis
1001 Bishop St.
2010 Pacific Tower
Honolulu, HI 96813-3544

Idaho

Alfred E. Barrus
1918 Overland Ave.
PO Box 487
Burley, ID 83318

Illinois

Daniel Azulay
One East Wacker Dr., #2700
Chicago, IL 60601-2001

Shelley Ballard Bostick
20 N. Wacker Dr., #3710
Chicago, IL 60606

Victoria Bush-Joseph
Civic Opera Building
20 N. Wacker Dr., Ste. 3710
Chicago, IL 60606

Deborah Crouse Cobb
6100 Center Grove Rd., Ste. 5
Edwardsville, IL 62025-3301

H. Joseph Gitlin
111 Dean St.
Woodstock, IL 60098

Susan Grammer
PO Box 111
Bethalto, IL 62010-0111

Theresa Rahe Hardesty
7513 North Regent Place
Peoria, IL 61614

John C. Hirschfeld
Burnham Athenaeum Building
306 West Church St.
PO Box 6750
Champaign, IL 61826-6750

Richard A. Lifshitz
120 North LaSalle St., #2900
Chicago, IL 60602

Carolyn B. Smoot
208 North Market St.
PO Box 1234
Marion, IL 62959

Glenna J. Weith
C-U Station
116 N. Chestnut St., Ste. 230
Champaign, IL 61820

Sally Wildman
180 N. LaSalle St., Ste. 2401
Chicago, IL 60601

Indiana

Timothy J. Hubert
25 NW Riverside Dr.
PO Box 1287
Evansville, IN 47706-1287

Joel D. Kirsh
401 Pennsylvania Pkwy., #370
Indianapolis, IN 46280-1390

Steven M. Kirsh
401 Pennsylvania Pkwy., #370
Indianapolis, IN 46280-1390

Iowa

Lori L. Klockau
402 S. Linn St.
Iowa City, IA 52240

Ross S. Randall
3112 Brockway Rd.
PO Box 1020
Waterloo, IA 50704-1020

Kansas

Martin W. Bauer
220 West Douglas, 300 Page Court
Wichita, KS 67202-3194

Jill Bremyer-Archer
PO Box 1146
McPherson, KS 67460-1146

Allan A. Hazlett
1608 SW Mulvane St.
Topeka, KS 66604-2746

Richard A. Macias
901 N. Broadway
Wichita, KS 67214-3531

Kentucky

Elisabeth Goldman
118 Lafayette Ave.
Lexington, KY 40502

W. Waverley Townes
730 West Main St., #500
Louisville, KY 40202

Louisiana

Edith H. Morris
1515 Poydras St., Ste. 1870
New Orleans, LA 70112

Maine

Judith Berry
28 State St.
Gorham, ME 04038

Maryland

Jeffrey Ewen Badger
PO Box 259
Salisbury, MD 21803-0259

Dawn Oxley Musgrave
Adoptions Together, Inc.
6 Sudbrook Lane
Baltimore, MD 21208

Carolyn Thaler
29 West Susquehanna Ave., Ste. 205
Towson, MD 21204

Massachusetts

Susan L. Crockin
The Chatham Center
29 Crafts St., Ste. 500
Newton, MA 02160

Herbert D. Friedman
265 Franklin St.
Boston, MA 02110

Karen K. Greenberg
144 Gould St.
Needham, MA 02194-2317

Michigan

Herbert A. Brail
930 Mason St.
Dearborn, MI 48124

Monica Farris Linkner
Adoption Law Center
3250 Coolidge Highway
Berkley, MI 48072

Minnesota

Jody O. DeSmidt
121 S. 8th. St., #1550
Minneapolis, MN 55402-2815

Steven L. Gawron
2850 Metro Dr., #429
Bloomington, MN 55425

Amy M. Silberberg
15511 Afton Hills Dr. S
Afton, MN 55001

Judith D. Vincent
Mill Place, Ste. 240
111 Third Ave. South
Minneapolis, MN 55401

Wright S. Walling
121 S. Eight St., Ste. 1550
Minneapolis, MN 55402-2815

Mississippi

Lisa Milner
2000 Deposit Guaranty Plaza
PO Box 23059
Jackson, MS 39225-3059

Missouri

Mary Beck
104 Hulston Hall
Columbia, MO 65211

Sanford P. Krigel
4550 Belleview
Kansas City, MO 64111

Allan F. Stewart
120 S. Central, Ste. 1505
Clayton, MO 63105

Elizabeth Karsian Wilson
401 Locust St. #406
PO Box 977
Columbia, MO 65205-0977

Nebraska

Lawrence I. Batt
400 Continental Building
209 South 19th. St., Ste. 400
Omaha, NE 68102-1757

Nevada

Rhonda L. Mushkin
601 East Charleston Blvd.
Las Vegas, NV 89104

New Hampshire

Margaret Cunnane Hall
37 High St.
Milford, NH 03055

New Jersey

Donald C. Cofsky
209 Haddon Ave.
Haddonfield, NJ 08033

Robin A. Fleischner (also licensed in
    New York)
159 Millburn Ave.
Millburn, NJ 07041

Elizabeth A. Hopkins
766 Shrewsbury Ave.
Tinton Falls, NJ 07724

James Miskowski
PO Box 387
45 North Broad St.
Ridgewood, NJ 07450

Steven B. Sacharow
Commerce Center
1810 Chapel Avenue West, 3rd Floor
Cherry Hill, NJ 08002-4609

Toby Solomon
354 Eisenhower Parkway
Livingston, NJ 07039

Deborah Steincolor
329 Belleville Ave., Ste. 2N
Bloomfield, NJ 07003

New Mexico

Jane G. Printz
1200 Pennsylvania NE
Albuquerque, NM 87110-7410

New York

Anne Reynolds Copps
126 State St., 6th Floor
Albany, NY 12207

Robin A. Fleischner (also licensed
in New Jersey)
11 Riverside Dr., #14 MW
New York, NY 10023

Gregory A. Franklin
95 Allens Creek Rd.
Building 1, Ste. 104
Rochester, NY 14618-3227

Michael S. Goldstein
62 Bowman Ave.
Rye Brook, NY 10573

Flory Herman
5350 Main St.
Williamsville, NY 14221

Frederick J. Magovern
111 John St., #1509
New York, NY 10038-3001

Cynthia Perla Meckler
8081 Floss Lane
East Amherst, NY 14051

Christine Mesberg
28 Hilltop Rd.
Waccabuc, NY 10597

Brendan C. O'Shea
102 Hackett Blvd.
Albany, NY 12209

Douglas H. Reiniger
630 Third Ave.
New York, NY 10017-6705

Kristina Rende
350 Theodore Fremd Ave., #300
Rye, NY 10580

Benjamin J. Rosin
630 Third Ave.
New York, NY 10017-6705

Golda Zimmerman
430 E. Genesee St., Ste. 203
Syracuse, NY 13202-1103

North Carolina

W. David Thurman
801 East Trade St.
Charlotte, NC 28202

Ohio

James S. Albers
88 North Fifth St.
Columbus, OH 43215

Margaret Blackmore
536 South High St.
Columbus, OH 43215

Susan G. Eisenman
338 South High St.
Columbus, OH 43215

Ellen Essig
105 East Fourth St., #900
Cincinnati, OH 45202

Carolyn Mussio Franke
3411 Michigan Ave.
Cincinnati, OH 45208

Jerry M. Johnson
400 West North St.
Lima, OH 45801

Mary Smith
1200 Edison Plaza
300 Madison Ave.
Toledo, OH 43604-1556

James E. Swaim
318 West Fourth St.
Dayton, OH 45402

Oklahoma

Barbara K. Bado
1800 Canyon Park Circle, #301
Edmond, OK 73013

Cynthia Calibani Butler
208 SW 3rd St.
Lawton, OK 73501

John O'Connor
15 West 6th St., Ste. 2700
Tulsa, OK 74119-5423

Jack H. Petty
6666 NW 39th Expressway
Bethany, OK 73008

Peter K. Schaffer
204 N. Robinson Ave., #2600
Oklahoma City, OK 73102-7095

Oregon

John Chally
825 NE Multnomah, Ste. 1125
Portland, OR 97232-2148

Catherine M. Dexter
The Pittock Block
921 SW Washington, Ste. 865
Portland, OR 97205

John R. Hassen
P.O. Box 670
129 N. Oakdale, Ste. 1
Medford, OR 97501

Sandra L. Hodgson
825 NE Multnomah, Ste. 1125
Portland, OR 97232-2148

Susan C. Moffet
The Pittock Block
921 SW Washington, Ste. 865
Portland, OR 97205

Robin Elizabeth Pope
1834 SW 58th. Ave., Ste. 101
Portland, OR 97221

Laurence H. Spiegel
P.O. Box 1708
4040 SW Douglas Way
Lake Oswego, OR 97035

Pennsylvania

Richard J. Amrhein
70 East Beau St.
Washington, PA 15301

Craig Bluestein
200 Old York Rd.
Jenkintown, PA 19046

Barbara Casey
527 Elm St.
P.O. Box 399
Reading, PA 19603
And at . . .
368 Thornbrook Ave.
Rosemont, PA 19010

Steven G. Dubin
1018 State Rd., Ste. 102
Southampton, PA 18966

Debra M. Fox
355 West Lancaster Ave.
Haverford, PA 19041

Tara E. Gutterman
4701 Pine St., #J7
Philadelphia, PA 19143

Deborah Lesko
5032 Buttermilk Hollow Rd.
West Miffin, PA 15122

Martin Leventon
355 West Lancaster Ave.
Haverford, PA 19041

Samuel J. Totaro, Jr.
Ste. 100
Four Greenwood Square
3325 Street Rd.
Bensalem, PA 19020

Rhode Island

Doris Licht
1500 Fleet Center
Providence, RI 02903

South Carolina

Richard C. Bell
1535 Sam Rittenberg, #C
Charleston, SC 29407

L. Dale Dove
125 Hampton St.
P.O. Box 10112
Rock Hill, SC 29731-0112

Thomas P. Lowndes, Jr.
P.O. Box 214
128 Meeting St.
Charleston, SC 29402

Stephen A. Yacobi
408 N. Church St., #B
Greenville, SC 29601

Tennessee

Paul M. Buchanan
Third Floor Noel Place
200 Fourth Ave. North
P.O. Box 198985
Nashville, TN 37219-8985

S. Dawn Coppock
PO Box 1422
Knoxville, TN 37901-1422

Michael Jennings
130 Jordan Dr.
Chattanooga, TN 37421-6731

Texas

Vika Andrel
3908 Manchaca Rd.
Austin, TX 78704

Gerald A. Bates
500 Throckmorton St., #1404
Fort Worth, TX 76102

Karla Jill Boydston
2300 Hemphill
Fort Worth, TX 76110

Carla M. Calabrese
311 N. Market St., #300
Dallas, TX 75202-1846

David Charles Cole
8340 Meadow Rd., #231
Dallas, TX 75231

Heidi Bruegel Cox
2300 Hemphill
Fort Worth, TX 76110

Susan I. Paquet
1 Austin Place
Weatherford, TX 76086

Melody Brooks Royall
13430 Northwest Freeway, #650
Houston, TX 77040

Mel W. Shelander
245 N. Fourth
Beaumont, TX 77701

Ellen A. Yarell
1980 Post Oak Blvd., #1720
Houston, TX 77056

Utah

Les F. England
P.O. Box 680845
Park City, UT 84068-0845

Virginia

Jennifer Brust
2000 N. 14th. St., #100
Arlington, VA 22201

David T. Daulton
Plaza One building, Ste. 804
550 East Main St.
Norfolk, VA 23510

Robert H. Klima
9257 Lee Ave. #201
Manassas, VA 22110

Betsy H. Phillips
Irongate at Spring Hill
Route 4, Box 179 P
Rustburg, VA 24588

Nancy D. Poster (also licensed
  in Maryland)
9909 Georgetown Pike
P.O. Box 197
Great Falls, VA 22066

Ellen S. Weinman
15 South College Ave.
Salem, VA 24153-3833

Washington

Rita L. Bender
1301 Fifth Ave., 34th. Floor
Seattle, WA 98101

Mark Demaray
1420 Fifth Ave., Ste. 3650
Seattle, WA 98101-2387

J. Eric Gustafson
222 North Third St.
P.O. Box 1689
Yakima, WA 98907-1689

Michele Gentry Hinz
1420-5th Ave., Ste. 3650
Seattle, WA 98101-2387

Margaret Cunniff Holm
201 W. 5th, Ste. 301
Olympia, WA 98501-1114

Albert G. Lirhus
1122 Denny Bldg.
2200 Sixth Ave.
Seattle, WA 98121

West Virginia

David Allen Barnette
P.O. Box 553
Charleston, WV 25322-0553

Wisconsin

Lynn J. Bodi
3 S. Pinckney St.
P.O. Box 1784
Madison, WI 53701-1784

Carol M. Gapen
3 S. Pinckney St.
P.O. Box 1784
Madison, WI 53701-1784

Stephen W. Hayes
735 N. Water St., #1000
Milwaukee, WI 53202

Judith Sperling Newton
3 South Pinckney St.
P.O. Box 1784
Madison, WI 53701-1784

Victoria J. Schroeder
394 Williamstowne
Delafield, WI 53018

Wyoming

Peter J. Feeney
P.O. Box 437
Casper, WY 82602

State Public (Government) Adoption Agencies

Each state has a central adoption office based in the state social services headquarters. These offices are primarily concerned with the adoption of foster children, but in most cases, state adoption personnel are also aware of adoption laws and proposed changes to laws. State personnel probably can't recommend individual adoption agencies but may be able to tell you about complaints or allegations against specific agencies. If the individuals you contact cannot answer your question, ask if they know of an organization or group who might know the answer.

Alabama

Alabama Office of Adoption
Department of Human Resources
50 N. Ripley St.
Montgomery, AL 36130
205-242-9500

Alaska

Alaska Division of Family and
   Youth Services
Box 110630
Juneau, AK 99811-0630
907-265-5080

Arizona

Arizona Department of Economic Security
P.O. Box 6123
Phoenix, AZ 85005
602-542-2359

Arkansas

Arkansas Department of Human Services
Division of Children and Family Services
P.O. Box 1437, Slot 808
Little Rock, AR 72203-1437
501-682-8462

California

Adoptions Branch
California Department of Social
   Services
744 P St., M/S 19-69
Sacramento, CA 95814
916-445-3146

Colorado

Colorado Department of Social
   Services
1575 Sherman St., 2nd Floor
Denver, CO 80203
303-866-3209

Connecticut

Department of Children and Families
505 Hudson St.
Hartford, CT 06106
203-238-6640

Delaware

Delaware Division of Child Protective
   Services
1825 Faulkland Rd.
Wilmington, DE 19805
302-633-2655

District of Columbia

District of Columbia Adoption and
   Placement Resources
Department of Human Services
609 H St. NE, 3rd Floor
Washington, DC 20002
202-724-8602

Florida

Florida Department of Children &
   Families
1317 Winewood Blvd.
Tallahassee, FL 32399
904-487-2383

Georgia

Georgia Department of Human Resources
Division of Family and Child Services
2 Peachtree St. NW, Ste. 414
Atlanta, GA 30303
404-657-3560

Hawaii

Hawaii Department of Human Services
810 Richards St., 4th Floor
Honolulu, HI 96813
808-586-5698

Idaho

Department of Health and Welfare
Division of Family and Community
   Services
P.O. Box 83720
Boise, ID 83720-0036
208-334-5700

Illinois

Department of Children & Family Services
406 East Monroe St.
Springfield, IL 62701-1498
217-524-2411

Indiana

Division of Family and Children
Bureau of Family
   Protection/Preservation
402 W. Washington St., Room W364
Indianapolis, IN 46204-2739
888-204-7466

Iowa

Iowa Department of Human Services
Hoover State Office Building, 5th Floor
Des Moines, IA 50319
515-281-5358

Kansas

Kansas Department of Social and
   Rehabilitative Services
300 SW Oakley St., West Hall
Topeka, KS 66606
913-296-8138

Kentucky

Kentucky Cabinet for Human
   Resources
275 East Main St., 6th Floor
Frankfort, KY 40621
502-564-2147

Louisiana

Louisiana Department of Social
   Services
Office of Community Services
P.O. Box 3318
Baton Rouge, LA 70821
504-342-2297

Maine

Department of Human Services
11 State House Station
August, ME 04333-0011
207-287-5060

Maryland

Maryland Department of Human
   Resources
Social Services Administration
311 West Saratoga St.
Baltimore, MD 21201
410-767-7423

Massachusetts

Massachusetts Department of Social
   Services
24 Farnsworth St.
Boston, MA 02210
617-727-0900

Michigan

Michigan Department of Social Services
235 S. Grand Ave.
P.O. Box 30037
Lansing, MI 48909
517-373-4021

Minnesota

Adoption Unit, Minnesota Department
   of Human Services
444 Lafayette, 2nd Floor
St. Paul, MN 55155
612-296-3740

Mississippi

Mississippi Department of Social
  Services
750 North State St.
Jackson, MS 39202
601-359-4500

Missouri

Missouri Division of Family Services
P.O. Box 88
Jefferson City, MO 65101
314-751-2502

Montana

Montana Department of Public
  Health & Human Services
1400 Broadway, Cogswell Building
P.O. Box 8005
Helena, MT 59620
406-444-5919

Nebraska

Nebraska Department of Social
  Services
P.O. Box 95026
Lincoln, NE 68509
402-471-9331

New Hampshire

Department of Health and Human
  Services
Children, Youth and Families
6 Hazen Dr.
Concord, NH 03301-6522
702-486-7650

Nevada

Office of Adoption, Nevada Children and
  Family Services
6171 W. Charleston Blvd., Bldg. 15
Las Vegas, NV 89158
702-486-7650

New Jersey

New Jersey Division of Youth and
  Family Services
50 East State St., CN 717
Trenton, NJ 08625
609-292-9139

New Mexico

CYFD/SSD/Children's Bureau
Placement Services Section
P.O. Drawer 5160
PERA Building, Room 252
Santa Fe, NM 87502
505-827-8456

New York

New York State Department of
  Social Services
40 North Pearl St.
Albany, NY 12243
518-474-2868

North Carolina

North Carolina Department of
  Human Resources
325 North Salisbury St.
Raleigh, NC 27603
919-733-3801

North Dakota

North Dakota Department of
Human Services
State Capitol
600 East Blvd.
Bismarck, ND 58505
701-328-4805

Ohio

Department of Human Services
Adoption Services Section
65 East State St., 5th Floor
Columbus, OH 43266-0423
614-466-9274

Oklahoma

Oklahoma Department of
Human Services
P.O. Box 25352
Oklahoma City, OK 73125
405-521-2475

Oregon

Oregon Department of Human
Resources
State Office for Services to Children
and Families
Human Resources Building
500 Summer St. NE
Salem, OR 97310-1017
503-945-5689

Pennsylvania

Department of Public Welfare
Office of Children, Youth and Families
P.O. Box 2675
Harrisburg, PA 17105-2675
717-787-7756

Rhode Island

Rhode Island Department of Children
and Their Families
610 Mt. Pleasant, Building 5
Providence, RI 02908
401-457-4548

South Carolina

Department of Social Services
P.O. Box 1520
Columbia, SC 29202-1520
803-734-6095

South Dakota

Department of Social Services
Richard F. Kneip Building
700 Governors Dr.
Pierre, SD 57501-2291
605-773-3227

Tennessee

Tennessee Department of Human Services
400 Deaderick St.
Nashville, TN 37248
615-741-5935

Texas

Texas Department of Protective and
Regulatory Services
Agency Mail Code E-557
701 W. 51st St.
P.O. Box 149030
Austin, TX 78714-9030
512-438-3412

Utah

Department of Human Services
Division of Child and Family Services
120 North 200 West, Ste. 225
Salt Lake City, UT 84103
801-538-4080

Vermont

Vermont Division of Social Services
103 South Main St.
Waterbury, VT 05671
802-241-2131

Virginia

Department of Social Services
Theater Row Building
730 East Broad St.
Richmond, VA 23219-1849
804-692-1273

Washington

Department of Social and Health
    Services
Children's Administration
14th. & Jefferson
P.O. Box 45713
Olympia, WA 98504-5713
360-902-7968

West Virginia

West Virginia Department of
    Human Services
Capitol Complex, Building 6, Rm.
B850
Charleston, WV 25305
304-558-7980

Wisconsin

Department of Health and Family Services
Division of Children and Family Services
1 West Wilson St.
P.O. Box 8916
Madison, WI 53708-8916
608-266-3595

Wyoming

Department of Family Services
Hathaway Building, Third Floor
Cheyenne, WY 82002
307-777-3570

Selected Adoptive Parent Groups

Adoptive parent groups are self-help groups for people who want to adopt. The majority of these groups are managed by volunteers who simply want to help others.

I've done my best to verify all information here; however, keep in mind that addresses and phone numbers are subject to change. Some groups provided phone numbers and others did not.

Alabama

Alabama Friends of Adoption
P.O. Box 19025
Birmingham, AL 35219-9025
205-290-0375

Parents Adopting Children Together
301 Deer Run Rd.
Auburn, AL 36830

Single Adoptive Parents Support
Subgroup
2407 Titonka Rd.
Birmingham, AL 35244

Alaska

Anchorage Adoptive Parents
Association
550 W. Seventh Ave., Ste. 1320
Anchorage, AK 99501
907-276-1680 or 907-345-4472
Fax: 907-276-8016
E-mail: spzget@alaska.net

Valley Adoptive Parents Association
P.O. Box 931
Palmer, AK 99645

Arizona

Advocates for Single Adoptive
    Parenting (ASAP)
10105 E. Via Linda, #103-198
Scottsdale, AZ 85258
602-951-8310 or 602-273-6055

Getting International Families
    Together
16053 N. 47th Dr.
Glendale, AZ 85306

Arkansas

Miracles
111 Devon Court
Jacksonville, AR 72076

River Valley Adoption Support Group
1005 W. 18th Terrace
Russellville, AR 72801-7025
501-967-1641

California

Adoption Assistance and Information
    Group
16255 Ventura Blvd., Ste. 704
Encino, CA 91436-2313
818-501-6800

Adoption Network
32392 Pacific Coast Highway
Laguna Beach, CA 92677-3300

Families Adopting in Response (FAIR)
P.O. Box 51436
Palo Alto, CA 94303
415-856-3513

For the Children
13074 Larkhaven Dr.
Moreno Valley, CA 92553-5689
909-956-4240

Hand in Hand
874 Phillip Ct.
Eldorado Hills, CA 95762

Intercountry Adoption Network (ICAN)
9830 Canedo Ave.
Northridge, CA 91324
818-772-8356

Open Door Society of Los Angeles
12235 Silva Pl.
Cerritos, CA 90701

Orange County Adoptive Parent
    Association
39 Foxborn
Irvine, CA 92714-7524
714-786-6494
Fax: 714-786-5125
E-mail: BUS4WE4@aol.com

River Valley Adoption Support Group
16255 Ventura Blvd., Ste. 704
Encino, CA 91436-2312
818-501-6800

Single Adoptive Parents of Los Angeles
7259 Balboa Blvd. #18
Van Nuys, CA 91406
818-901-9519
Web site: http://home.earthlink.net/
    ~sreben/index.html

South Bay Adoption Support Group
24662 Soquel-San Jose Dr.
Los Gatos, CA 95030-9226
408-353-2995
Fax: 408-353-3166
E-mail: lilsnee@silverspoon.com

Together Expecting A Miracle (TEAM)
1300 Astoria Place
Oxnard, CA 93030
805-485-4677

Colorado

Colorado Parents for All Children
780 E. Phillips Dr. S
Littleton, CO 80122

Colorado Parents for All Children
971 Burns Rd.
Colorado Springs, CO 80918

Connecticut

Adoptive Parents Exchange Group
6 Putnam Park Rd.
Bethel, CT 06801-2221

International Adoptive Families
433 Quarry Brook Rd.
South Windsor, CT 06074-3598

Latin American Parents Association of
Connecticut, Inc.
P.O. Box 523
Unionville, CT 06085
203-270-1424

Delaware

Adoptive Families with Information
and Support (AFIS)
P.O. Box 7405
Wilmington, DE 19803
302-239-6232

District of Columbia

North Virginia FACE
103 15th St. N.E.
Washington, DC 20002-6505

Interracial Family Circle
P.O. Box 52391
Washington, D.C. 20009
202-393-7866
Web site: http://www.jaguNET.com/
~spectrum/ifc

Florida

Lifeline for Children
P.O. Box 17184
Plantation, FL 33318
954-979-1314

Parents Adoption Lifeline, Inc.
536 Inlet Rd.
North Palm Beach, FL 33408
561-433-8200

People Adopting Children Everywhere
(PACE)
P.O. Box 560293
Rockledge, FL 32956
407-639-8895

Special Needs Adoptive Parents, Inc.
(S.N.A.P.)
15913 Layton Court
Tampa, FL 33647
813-978-8183

Georgia

Adopted Kids & Parents
4137 Bellflower Ct.
Roswell, GA 30075

Georgia Adoptive Parents
1722 Wilmont Dr. NE
Atlanta, GA 30329

Georgia Council on Adoptable
Children
3559 London Rd.
Chamblee, GA 30341-2041
770-986-0760

Hawaii

Adoptive Families of Kauai
1702 Makoi St.
Lihue, HI 96766
808-246-0844
E-mail: soltysik@gte.net

333

Forever Families
7719 Waikapu Loop
Honolulu, HI 96825
808-396-9130
E-mail: Foreverfam@aol.com

Idaho

Families Involved in Adoption
P.O. Box 612
Priest River, ID 83856-0512

Illinois

Adoptive Families Today
P.O. Box 1726
Barrington, IL 60011-1726
847-382-0858

All-Dopt
727 Ramona Pl.
Godfrey, IL 62035
618-466-8926

Central Illinois Adoptive Families
(CIAF)
2206 Oakwood Ave.
Bloomington, IL 61704
309-662-3349
E-mail: oggieco@aol.com

Chicago Area Families for Adoption
1212 S. Naper Blvd.
Naperville, IL 60540

Child International
4121 Crestwood Dr.
Northbrook, IL 60062-7544
847-272-2511
Fax: 847-509-9740

Children of Eastern European Regions
(CHEER)
138 Clara Place
Elmhurst, IL 60126
630-834-5161

DeKalb Adoptive Families
303 N. Second St.
DeKalb, IL 60115-3236
815-758-4307

Families with Children from Vietnam
210 Magnolia Dr.
North Aurora, IL 60542
E-mail: Kward0601@aol.com

Fox Valley Adoption Support Group
1111 Adobe Dr.
Aurora, IL 60506-1603

Illiana Adoptive Parents (IAP)
P.O. Box 412
Flossmoor, IL 60422

Single Adoptive Parent Support Group
P.O. Box 578478
Chicago, IL 60657

Stars of David
3175 Commercial Ave., Ste. 100
Northbrook, IL 60062-1915
847-509-9929
E-mail: StarsDavid@aol.com

Uniting Families Foundation
95 W. Grand Ave., Ste. 206
P.O. Box 755
Lake Villa, IL 60046
847-356-1452
Fax: 847-356-1584
E-mail: UnitingFam@aol.com

Indiana

Adoptive Family Network
306 Sharon Rd.
W. Lafayette, IN 47906

Families Through International
Adoption
971A South Kenmore Dr.
Evansville, IN 47714

OURS Through Adoption
RR 3, 104 S. Water St.
Monroeville, IN 46773-9301
219-623-3166

Iowa

Adoptive Families of Greater Des
Moines
1690 Northwest Dr.
Des Moines, IA 50310

Cedar Valley Adoption Group
118 N. Eighth St.
Osage, IA 50461

Iowans for International Adoption
31496 Iron Bridge Rd.
Spragueville, IA 52074-9758

Kansas

International Families of Mid-America
6708 Granada Rd.
Prairie Village, KS 66208

Parents by Choice
6100 W. 58th St.
Mission, KS 66202

Kentucky

Adoptive Parents Guild
1888 Douglas Rd.
Louisville, KY 40205

Families & Adoptive Children Together
150 Ridgemont Rd.
Paducah, KY 42003
502-554-0203

PACK, Inc.
139 Highland Dr.
Madisonville, KY 42431-9154
502-825-2158 (Call after 8 p.m. EST)

Louisiana

Adopt Older Kids, Inc. (A-OK)
818 Briarwood Dr.
New Iberia, LA 70560

Adoptive Couples Together
P.O. Box 1311
Kenner, LA 70063

Maine

Adoptive Families of Maine
17 Pike St.
Augusta, ME 04330

Adoptive Families of Maine
129 Sunderland Dr.
Auburn, ME 04210

Maryland

Adoptive Families and Friends
1440 Hunting Horn Lane
Frederick, MD 21703
301-695-2574
E-mail: msecula@solarex.com

Children in Common
3335 Governor Martin Ct.
Ellicott City, MD 21043
410-203-9613

Families Adopting Children
    Everywhere (FACE)
P.O. Box 28058
Northwood Station
Baltimore, MD 21239
410-488-2656

Latin American Parents Association
P.O. Box 4403
Silver Spring, MD 20914-4403

Rainbow Families
128 E. Lynbrook Place
Bel Air, MD 21014-5415
410-838-3858

Massachusetts

Latin American Adoptive Families
23 Evangeline Rd.
Falmouth, MA 02540

Open Door Society of Massachusetts,
Inc.
1750 Washington St.
Holliston, MA 01746-2234
800-93ADOPT (in-state)
Fax: 508-429-2261

Single Parents Adopting Children
Everywhere (SPACE)
6 Sunshine Ave.
Natick, MA 01760

Michigan

Adopt
6939 Shields Ct.
Saginaw, MI 48609

European Adoptive Families
of MI
P.O. Box 87894
Canton, MI 48187
313-981-6534
E-mail: EAFofMI@aol.com

Families of Latin Folks (FOLK)
P.O. Box 15537
Ann Arbor, MI 48108

The Family Tree Support Group
27821 Santa Barbara Dr.
Lathrup Village, MI 48076-3355
248-557-3501

Greater Lansing OURS by Adoption
(GLOBA)
P.O. Box 25161
Lansing, MI 48909
E-mail: cordess@voyager.net

Latin American Families Through
Adoption (LAFTA)
608 Marcelletti Ave.
Paw Paw, MI 49079-1219
616-657-6498

Michigan Association of Single
Adoptive Parents (MASAP)
7412 Coolidge Ave.
Center Line, MI 48015-2049
810-758-6909

PACE
P.O. Box 8423
Holland, MI 49422-8423

West Michigan Friends of Adoption
7635 Yorktown St.
Richland, MI 49083
616-629-9037

Minnesota

Families of Multi Racial Adoptions
2057 Roe Crest Dr.
Mankato, MN 56003-3434

Families Supporting Adoption
11462 Crow Hassan Park Rd.
Hanover, MN 55341-9404

Northland Families Through Adoption
518 Lagarde Rd.
Wrenswall, MN 55797

Missouri

Adoption Today
5350 Casa Royale Dr.
St. Louis, MO 63129-3007
314-894-4586

Families Through Korean Adoption
1350 Summit Dr.
Fenton, MO 63026
E-mail: Chris72247@aol.com

Single Mothers By Choice
4320 Genessee
Kansas City, MO 64111

Montana

Adoptive Families of Montana
1499 Cobb Hill Rd.
Bozeman, MT 59715

Families for Adoptable Children
P.O. Box 485
Anaconda, MT 59711

Nebraska

Families Through Adoption
1619 Coventry Lane
Grand Island, NE 68801-7025
308-381-8743
E-mail: lerickso@genie.esu10.k12.ne.us

Open Hearts Adoption Support Group
4023 S. 81st St.
Lincoln, NE 68506

Nevada

Southern Nevada Adoption
Association
1316 Saylor Way
Las Vegas, NV 89108
702-647-0201

New Hampshire

Open Door Society of New Hampshire
P.O. Box 792
Derry, NH 03038
603-679-1099
E-mail: ODSNH@aol.com

New Jersey

Adoptive Parents Committee—New
Jersey Chapter
P.O. Box 725
Ridgewood, NJ 07451
201-689-0995

Adoptive Single Parents of New Jersey
107 Maple St.
Haworth, NJ 07641
201-387-1236

Concerned Persons For Adoption
P.O. Box 179
Whippany, NJ 07981
908-273-5694

Latin American Adoptive Families
(also address for Stars of David
South Jersey)
205 Meadow Lane
Woodbury, NJ 08096
609-384-2764
E-mail: laafnjpa@aol.com

Today's Adoptive Families
30 Manchester Way
Burlington, NJ 08016
609-386-7237

New Mexico

Parents of Inter Cultural Adoptions
P.O. Box 91175
Albuquerque, NM 87199

New York

Adoptive Families of Older Children
149-32A Union Turnpike
Flushing, NY 11367
718-380-7234

Adoptive Parents Committee
(Headquarters)
P.O. Box 3525
Church St. Station
New York, NY 10008-3525
212-304-8479

Adoptive Parents Committee
Hudson Region Chapter
P.O. Box 245
White Plains, NY 10605-0245
914-997-7859

Adoptive Parents Committee—Long
Island Chapter
P.O. Box 71
Bellmore, NY 11710

Born In My Heart
c/o The Northport East Northport
School District
The Parent Center/Community
Services
Laurel Avenue School
Northport, NY 11765
516-754-6385 or 516-757-9245

The Council of Adoptive Parents
P.O. Box 964
Penfield, NY 14526
716-383-0947
Fax: 716-387-9841
E-mail: tlsavini@naz.edu

Families Interested in Adoption
53 Harlem Rd.
West Seneca, NY 14224-1821
716-827-7845

New York Singles Adopting Children
(NYSAC)
P.O. Box 472
Glen Oaks, NY 11004
212-254-1696

Parents Network for Post-
Institutionalized Children
374 Oak St.
Patchogue, NY 11772

Richmond Adoptive Parents, Inc.
P.O. Box 020665
Staten Island, NY 10302

Southern Tier Adoptive Families
3617 Lome Dr.
Endwell, NY 13760
607-748-4172
E-mail: VSNZ43A@Prodigy.com

Western New York Single Adoptive
Parents
73 Cleveland Dr.
Kenmore, NY 14223

North Carolina

Adoptive Families HEART TO HEART
456 NC Hwy 62 East
Greensboro, NC 27406
910-674-5024

Capital Family for Adoptions
108 North Drawbridge Lane
Cary, NC 27513

Coastal Hearts of Adoption
6002 McLean St.
Emerald Isle, NC 28594
919-354-5826

North Carolina Adoption Connections
P.O. Box 4153
Chapel Hill, NC 27515-4153
919-967-5010

North Carolina Center for the
    Advancement of Adoption
    Education
P.O. Box 2823
Chapel Hill, NC 27515-2823
919-967-5010

Stars of David
Wake County Jewish Federation
12804 Norwood Rd.
Raleigh, NC 27613
919-676-6170

Tri-Adopt
P.O. Box 51192
Shannon Plaza
Durham, NC 27717

North Dakota

Adoption in Our Heart
2578 Willow Rd. NE
Fargo, ND 58102

Families and Friends of Adoption
1814 Lewis Blvd.
Grand Forks, ND 58201

Ohio

Adoptive Families of Greater
    Cincinnati
4 Revel Ct.
Cincinnati, OH 45217-1916

Adoptive Families Support Association
P.O. Box 91247
Cleveland, OH 44101-3247
216-491-4638

Families Thru Adoption
426 Goosepond Rd.
Newark, OH 43055-3137

New Roots
P.O. Box 14953
Columbus, OH 43214
614-470-0846

Open Adoption Support Group
541 Brandwynne Court
Dayton, OH 45459-3015
937-436-4614
E-mail: debsykes@bright.net

Rainbow Families of Toledo
1920 S. Shore Blvd.
Oregon, OH 43618
419-693-9259

Southeast Ohio Adoptive Family
    Support Group
P.O. Box 75
Athens, OH 45701

Oklahoma

Adopt A Special Kid (AASK)
c/o Adoption Support
P.O. Box 25
Harrah, OK 73045
Fax: 405-454-1179

Adoptive Families Support Association
    (AFSA)
1301 Charlton Rd.
Edmond, OK 73003
405-359-0812
E-mail: SafTMom@aol.com

Oregon

Adoptive Families Unlimited
P.O. Box 40752
Eugene, OR 97404
541-688-1654
E-mail: adoptfam@aol.com

Northwest Adoptive Families
Association
P.O. Box 25355
Portland, OR 97225-0355

Rogue Valley Adoptive Families
1156 Conestoga Drive
Grants Pass, OR 97527
541-471-3608
E-mail: Turnbull@chatlink.com

Pennsylvania

Adoptive Families with Information
and Support
RR#1, Box 23
Landerburg, PA 19350

Families Through Adoption
4109 Kingswood Ct.
Harrisburg, PA 17112

Families With Children From Asia
Pat & Bob Steele
3111 N. Second St.
Harrisburg, PA 17110-1302
717-233-0755
E-mail: rsteele@epix.net

International Adoptive Families
402 Pebblecreek Dr.
Cranberry Township, PA 16066-5652

Single Adoptive Parents of Delaware
Valley
1415 Arline Ave.
Roslyn, PA 19001

South Carolina

Piedmont Adoptive Parents
24 Willowood Dr.
Spartanburg, SC 29303
864-578-3571

South Dakota

Adoptive Families of Black Hills
3701 Reder St.
Rapid City, SD 57702-2242

Families Through Adoption
P.O. Box 851
Sioux Falls, SD 57101

Tennessee

Mid-South Families Through Adoption
6151 Ashley Rd.
Arlington, TN 38002

OURS of Middle TN
3557 Bethlehem Rd.
Springfield, TN 37172
615-643-3426
E-mail: 74532.3114@compuserve.com

Texas

Adopting Children Together
P.O. Box 120966
Arlington, TX 76012-0966
817-467-4778

Austin Kids from All Cultures
4508 Sinclair Ave.
Austin, TX 78756
512-467-9177

COAC-Dallas
P.O. Box 141199
Dallas, TX 75214-1199

Interracial Family Alliance of Houston
P.O. Box 16248
Houston, TX 77222
281-586-8949

Vermont

The Chosen Children from Romania
P.O. Box 401
Barre, VT 05641-0401
802-479-2848
Fax: 802-476-3445

Vermont Families Through Adoption
16 Aspen Dr.
Essex Junction, VT 05452

Virginia

Adoptive Families Hand in Hand
P.O. Box 1175
Culpepper, VA 22701

Association of Single Adoptive Families
P.O. Box 3618
Merrifield, VA 22116-3618
804-798-2673

Blue Ridge Adoption Group
c/o Commonwealth Catholic Charities
820 Campbell Ave. SW
Roanoke, VA 24016

Families for Russian and Ukrainian
Adoption
P.O. Box 2944
Merrifield, VA 22116
703-560-6184

Korean Focus for Adoptive Families
1906 Sword Lane
Alexandria, VA 22308
703-974-2663
E-mail: mmp@bellatlantic.net

Romanian Children's Connection
1206 Hillside Terrace
Alexandria, VA 22302

Washington

Adoptive Families Network of S. Puget
Sound
P.O. Box 112188
Tacoma, WA 98411-2188

Adoptive Families United
1537 NE 92nd St.
Seattle, WA 98115
206-527-0425

Clallam County Adoptive Parent Support
Group
226 West 13th St.
Port Angeles, WA 98362
360-452-2785

Families with Children from China
c/o Corp Serve, Inc.
1001 Fourth Ave., Ste. 4500
Seattle, WA 98154
206-323-0886
E-mail: Jstrabuk@gj.com

Friends in Adoption Support Group
P.O. Box 659
Auburn, WA 98071-0659
206-343-3153

Goldendale Adoptive Parents
Association
409 Pine Street Extension
Goldendale, WA 98620
509-773-5737

Heart to Heart (Christian Adoption
Alliance)
1010 Lone Tree Ct.
Bellingham, WA 98226
360-734-4074

Kitsap Adoption Group
5219 NE Falcon Ridge Lane
Poulsboro, WA 98370
360-697-2997

West Virginia

AFFA
P.O. Box 2775
Charleston, WV 25330-2775

Wisconsin

Adoptive Families of Greater
  Milwaukee, Inc.
15385 Glenora Court
New Berlin, WI 53151
414-860-0940

Adoptive Parent Group of Southern
  Wisconsin
1408 Vilas Ave.
Madison, WI 53711
608-251-0736

Interracial Families Network of Family
  Enhancement
2120 Fordem Ave.
Madison, WI 53704
608-241-5150

Lakeshore Adoptive Families
1616 Jasmine Dr.
Manitowoc, WI 54220
414-683-1843

The Ties Program
Adoptive Family Travel Programs
11801 Woodland Circle
Hales Corners, WI 53130

US/Chilean Adoptive Families USCAF
2041 North 107th St.
Wauwatosa, WI 53226
414-257-0248

Wisconsin Association of Single
  Adoptive Parents
4520 N. Bartlett Ave.
Milwaukee, WI 53211-1509
414-962-9342
E-mail: lglass@csd.uwm.edu (Lauren K.
  Glass)

Wyoming

Northern Wyoming Adoptive Parents
P.O. Box 788
Basin, WY 82410
307-568-2729
Fax: 307-765-2793
E-mail: johnsonp@mailnwc.whecn.edu

RESOLVE Groups

RESOLVE, Inc., a nationwide organization with chapters in most states, provides information and assistance to people who are infertile and seek help on issues of infertility, including adoption. They offer a newsletter, referrals to physicians, and other services. Its headquarters are located at RESOLVE, Inc., 1310 Broadway, Somerville, MA 02144-1731. Its national help line is 617-623-0744.

Alabama

RESOLVE of Alabama
3325 Lorna Rd. #2179
Birmingham, AL 35216-5463
205-982-9654

Alaska

RESOLVE of Alaska
P.O. Box 243234
Anchorage, AK 99524
907-566-0022

Arizona

RESOLVE of the Valley of the Sun
P.O. Box 54214
Phoenix, AZ 85078
602-995-3933

Arkansas

RESOLVE of Northwest Arkansas
P.O. Box 4492
Fayetteville, AR 72702
501-444-2186

California

RESOLVE of Greater Los Angeles
P.O. Box 15344
Los Angeles, CA 90015
310-326-2630

RESOLVE of Greater San Diego
P.O. Box 86543
San Diego, CA 92138-6543
619-595-3988

RESOLVE of Northern California
312 Sutter St., 6th. Floor
San Francisco, CA 94108
415-788-6772
Helpline: 415-788-3002

RESOLVE of Orange County
P.O. Box 50693
Irvine, CA 92619-0693
714-859-0580

Colorado

RESOLVE of Colorado
P.O. Box 61096
Denver, CO 80206
303-469-5261

Connecticut

RESOLVE of Fairfield County
P.O. Box 16763
Stamford, CT 06905-6763
203-329-1147

RESOLVE of Greater Hartford
P.O. Box 370083
West Hartford, CT 06137-0083
860-523-8337

District of Columbia

RESOLVE of Washington, DC Metro
    Area, Inc.
P.O. Box 39221
Washington, DC 20016
202-362-5555

Florida

RESOLVE of Fort Lauderdale
P.O. Box 16262
Ft. Lauderdale, FL 33318
954-749-9500

RESOLVE of the Palm Beaches
20423 State Rd. 7, Ste. 247
Boca Raton, FL 33498
407-336-4420

Georgia

RESOLVE of Georgia
Box 343
2480-4 Briarcliff Rd.
Atlanta, GA 30329
404-233-8443

Hawaii

RESOLVE of Hawaii
P.O. Box 29193
Honolulu, HI 96820
808-528-8559 or 808-742-8885

Illinois

RESOLVE of Illinois
318 Half Day Rd., #300
Buffalo Grove, IL 60089-6547
773-743-1623

Indiana

RESOLVE of Indiana
6103 Ashway Court
Indianapolis, IN 46205
317-767-5999

Kansas

RESOLVE of Kansas City
P.O. Box 414603
Kansas City, MO 64141
913-791-2432

Kentucky

RESOLVE of Kentucky
P.O. Box 22825
Lexington, KY 40522-2825
502-589-4313

Louisiana

RESOLVE of Louisiana
P.O. Box 55693
Metairie, LA 70055-5693
504-454-6987

Maine

RESOLVE of Maine
P.O. Box 10691
Portland, ME 04104
207-772-4783

Maryland

RESOLVE of Maryland
P.O. Box 5664
Baltimore, MD 21210
410-243-0235

Massachusetts

RESOLVE of the Bay State, Inc.
P.O. Box 1553
Waltham, MA 02254
617-647-1614
Fax: 617-899-7207

Michigan

RESOLVE of Michigan
P.O. Box 2185
Southfield, MI 48037
810-680-0093

Minnesota

RESOLVE of the Twin Cities, Inc.
1021 Bandana Blvd. East, Ste. 228
St. Paul, MN 55108
612-659-0333

Missouri

RESOLVE of St. Louis
P.O. Box 131
Hazelwood, MO 63042
314-567-8788

Nebraska

RESOLVE of Nebraska
P.O. Box 24527
Omaha, NE 68124-0527
402-449-6875

New Hampshire

RESOLVE of New Hampshire
12 Bayshore Dr.
Greenland, NH 03840
603-427-0410

New Jersey

RESOLVE of New Jersey
P.O. Box 4335
Warren, NJ 07059-0335
908-679-7171

New Mexico

RESOLVE of New Mexico, Inc.
P.O. Box 13194
Albuquerque, NM 87192
505-266-1170

Nevada

RESOLVE of Northern Nevada
P.O. Box 9749
Reno, NV 89507-9749
702-852-3205

New York

RESOLVE of Capital District
P.O. Box 12901
Albany, NY 12212
518-464-3848

RESOLVE of New York City
P.O. Box 185
Gracie Station, NY 10028
212-764-0802

North Carolina

RESOLVE of Triangle, Inc.
P.O. Box 5564
Cary, NC 27511
919-477-2360

Ohio

RESOLVE of Ohio
P.O. Box 770725
Lakewood, OH 44107
1-800-414-OHIO
E-mail: resolveohi@aol.com

Oklahoma

RESOLVE of Oklahoma
4041 NW 33rd
Oklahoma City, OK 73112
405-949-8857

Oregon

RESOLVE of Oregon
P.O. Box 40717
Portland, OR 97240
503-762-0449

Pennsylvania

RESOLVE of Philadelphia
P.O. Box 0215
Merion Station, PA 19066-0215
215-849-3920

RESOLVE of Pittsburgh
P.O. Box 11203
Pittsburgh, PA 15238-0203
412-921-3501

Rhode Island

RESOLVE of the Ocean State
P.O. Box 28201
Providence, RI 02908
401-421-4695

South Carolina

RESOLVE of Upstate South Carolina
204 Fernbrook Circle
Spartanburg, SC 29307-2966
864-542-9092

Tennessee

RESOLVE of Tennessee
4770 Germantown Rd., Ext, Ste. 327
Memphis, TN 38141
902-541-5360

Texas

RESOLVE of Central Texas
P.O. Box 49783
Austin, TX 78765
512-453-2171

RESOLVE of Dallas/Fort Worth
16831 Thomas Chapel Dr.
Dallas, TX 75248
214-250-9061

RESOLVE of Houston
P.O. Box 441212
Houston, TX 77244-1212
713-975-5324

RESOLVE of South Texas
P.O. Box 782052
San Antonio, TX 78278
210-967-6771

Utah

RESOLVE of Utah
P.O. Box 57531
Salt Lake City, UT 84157-0531
801-483-4024

Vermont

RESOLVE of Vermont
P.O. Box 1094
Williston, VT 05495
802-657-2542

Virginia

RESOLVE of Virginia
P.O. Box 70372
Richmond, VA 23255-0372
804-751-5761

Washington

RESOLVE of Washington State
P.O. Box 31231
Seattle, WA 98103-1231
206-524-7257

Wisconsin

RESOLVE of Wisconsin
P.O. Box 13842
Wauwatosa, WI 53213-0842
414-521-4590

The Complete Idiot's Guide to Ado

Todd J. Ochs, M.D.
841 W. Bradley Pl
Chicago, IL 606
773-975-5989
Fax: 773-97

Karen
Inter

**Sele
Inte
Adc
Exp**

There are several international adoption medical experts (all of them pediatricians) in the U.S. who can answer most medical questions and who may be willing to review medical records and/or videotapes of children for a small fee. Here is a selected list of the most prominent physicians. Listing of a physician in this book does not guarantee the quality of that physician.

Andrew Adesman, M.D.
Evaluation Center for Adoption,
  Ste. 139
Schneider Children's Hospital
269-01 76th. Ave.
New Hyde Park, NY 11040
718-470-4000

Jane Ellen Aronson, M.D.
International Adoption Medical
  Consultation Services
Winthrop Pediatric Associates
222 Station Plaza North
Mineola, NY 11501
516-663-4417
E-mail: jaronmink@aol.com

Deborah Borchers, M.D.
4452 Eastgate Blvd., Ste. 202
Cincinnati, OH 45245
513-753-2820

Jerri Ann Jenista, M.D.
551 Second St.
Ann Arbor, MI 48103
313-668-0419
Fax: 313-668-9492

Dana Johnson, M.D., Ph.D.
Box 211 UMHC
C-432 Mayo Building
420 Delaware St., SE
Minneapolis, MN 55455
612-626-2928
Fax: 612-624-8176
E-mail: johns008@maroon.tc.umn.edu

Laurie Miller, M.D.
NEMC No. 286
750 Washington St.
Boston, MA 02111
617-636-8121

...3-3902

...5-5989

...lness, M.D.
...nationally Adopted Children's
Healthcenter
11100 Euclid Ave.
Cleveland, OH 44106
216-844-3224 or 216-844-3230
800-755-6601 (outside OH)
E-mail: IACHC@po.cwru.edu

Nina Scribanu, M.D.
3307 M St. NW, Ste. 410
Washington, DC 20007
202-687-8635

Sarah Springer, M.D.
Lisa Nalven, M.D.
Adoption Resource Center of
Pittsburgh
1709 Boulevard of the Allies
Pittsburgh, PA 15219
412-575-5805

Selected Adoption Publications

There are a variety of magazines, newsletters, and other publications, ranging from the very simple typewritten one composed by a harried parent to very professional-looking publications prepared by a small staff. The subjects that are covered range from the specific (local, single parenting, children adopted from China, and so on) to general information of interest to adoptive parents, adopted people, or birthparents.

It's impossible to list them all, so I've selected a small sampling for you here of the publications that I think would most interest readers nationwide. These publications are primarily oriented to the adoptive parent.

Adopted Child
P.O. Box 9362
Moscow, ID 83843
208-882-1794

This monthly newsletter features one topic per issue. Yearly subscription is $22.

Adoption/Medical News
Adoption Advocates Press
1921 Ohio St. NE
Palm Bay, FL 32907
407-724-0815

A four-page newsletter edited by Jerri Ann Jenista, M.D., on medical issues of interest to adoption professionals, adoptive parent groups, and others. (Featured issues include AIDS, fetal alcohol syndrome, attention deficit disorder, low birth-weight babies, and so on, as well as information on children adopted from particular countries: Russia, China, and so on.) Ten issues, $36.

Adoptive Families
2309 Como Ave.
St. Paul, MN 55108
800-372-3300 or 612-645-9955

Bimonthly magazine for adopting and adoptive parents. Full-color with articles on a variety of adoptive parenting issues and issues of interest to adoptees and birthparents. Covers federal and state issues on adoption and new resources. Six issues, $24.95.

The Handbook for Single Adoptive Parents
National Council for Single Adoptive Parents
P.O. Box 15084
Chevy Chase, MD 20825

Includes information valuable to singles who wish to adopt. Information on questions many singles have: how to adopt, parenting the child, dealing with challenges, personal experiences, and so on. Many resources for singles are listed. Cost is $20.

The *Handbook* contains information for singles interested in adopting, parenting the child, and dealing with challenges that may come up. Personal experiences are also offered, as well as a valuable listing of resources for singles.

National Adoption Reports
National Council For Adoption
1930 Seventeenth St. NW
Washington, DC 20009
202-328-1200
Web site: http://WWW.NCFA-us.org

A monthly newsletter packed with the latest federal and state news and information on adoption. The annual subscription rate of $24 per year for this monthly newsletter is included in $50 membership dues.

Report on Intercountry Adoption
International Concerns for Children
911 Cypress Dr.
Boulder, CO 80303-2821
303-494-8333 (Voice and fax)
Web site: http://www.fortnet.org/icc

Important annual listing of the latest information on international adoption. It includes lists of agencies, criteria for adopting parents, descriptions of children in various countries, and essays on adoption. Valuable for adopting parents and adoption professionals. Updated 10 times per year. Yearly subscription, $20.

ROOTS & WINGS
ROOTS & WINGS Publications
P.O. Box 577
Hackettstown, NJ 07840
908-637-4259
E-mail: adoption@world2u.com
Web site: http://www.adopting.org/rw.html

Quarterly magazine with adoption articles for and by adoptive parents, adoptees, and birthparents. Covers a broad range of issues. Yearly subscription, $19.95.

Adopterms Glossary

Adoptee refers to the person who was adopted. Some people prefer the terms "adopted child," or "adopted adult."

Adoption refers to the complete transfer of parental rights and obligations from one family to another family. The adoptive family assumes all the legal obligations and responsibilities of the family that a child was born to, and the birthfamily no longer has these rights and obligations.

Adoption agencies are organizations licensed by the state to place children with adoptive families. They are usually staffed by social workers.

Adoption attorneys are lawyers who arrange adoptive placements. Some attorneys specialize in adoption.

Adoption cancellation insurance is insurance that prospective parents take out to cover financial losses they would incur if a birthmother changed her mind about adoption.

Adoption facilitators or **adoption consultants** help adopters identify birthmothers, write adoption resumes, deal with birthmother meetings, and so forth. Some adoption consultants are social workers; some are not licensed in any capacity. Adoption facilitators are not allowed to work in all states.

Adoption issues are problems that preoccupy and distress an adoptee or anyone else connected with the adoption and that are related to adoption.

Adoption mindset is a goal-oriented attitude in which the adopter not only wants to adopt a child, but *needs* to adopt a child. The adopter is fully prepared to act on this need.

Adoption obsession refers to constantly thinking about adopting a child.

Adoption-readiness is an attitude in which the adopter feels ready to explore adoption.

Adoption ritual is a ceremony that acknowledges that the child has been (or will be) adopted into the family. Adoption rituals may be religious or secular.

Adoptive parent group, sometimes called an **adoptive parent support group**, is a group of people who meet to socialize and/or to discuss issues related to adoption.

Adoptive parents are people who are approved to become parents to a child. Some adoptive parents are related to the child, while many are not.

Agency adoption is arranged by workers at a licensed adoption agency. This term usually refers to private adoption agencies, rather than state or county public agencies.

Biracial is a term for a child who has biological parents of different races.

Birthfather is a man who, with a woman, conceives a child who is later adopted or for whom an adoption is planned. He may also be called the **biological father.**

Birthgrandparents are the parents of the birthmother or birthfather. They may or may not become involved in the adoption.

Birthmother is a woman who gives birth to a child whom she subsequently places for adoption.

Black market adoption refers to an adoption that is arranged outside the law and usually involves very large sums of money paid to an attorney, agency worker, or other individual.

Chosen child is a term once used on adopted children, to make them feel special and important. Today most experts advise against using this term. Many adoptees also advise against this terminology.

Confidential adoption refers to an adoption in which neither the adopter nor the birthparents know identifying information about each other. Some people use the term "closed adoption," which is considered negative.

Confidential intermediary system is a system in a state whereby the adoptee can request that a search be made for a birthparent. The birthparent will be identified, contacted, and asked if she or he wants contact. If the birthparent agrees, identifying information is provided to the adoptee.

Consent to an adoption means that the birthmother and, hopefully, the birthfather, voluntarily agree that their child may be adopted. **Surrender** and **relinquishment** are sometimes used instead of consent, but use of these words is discouraged by adoption experts.

Direct placement adoptions are adoptions in which a birthmother chooses the adoptive family.

Disruption of an adoption generally refers to an adoption that fails before finalization, although many people also use the term for any failed adoption. (See **dissolution**.)

Dissolution is sometimes used to refer to adoptions that fail after finalization.

Dossier is the collection of legal documents that must be compiled to adopt a child from another country.

Entitlement refers to a feeling that the adopter has the right to parent the child and that the adopter is worthy and ready to take on all the responsibilities and obligations of parenthood.

Finalization is the procedure in which the adopter goes to court to receive legal permission and recognition for the adoption.

Foster child is a child in the primary custody of a state, county, or private adoption agency. Foster children often live with foster families for varying periods. A foster child cannot be adopted unless a judge terminates the parental rights of the biological parents or they willingly sign consent to the adoption.

Genetic predisposition refers to a probability that a child will inherit some genetic feature that occurred in the biological family.

Gray market adoption connotes an adoption that is not quite "on the level" and is often used in association with non-agency adoptions. In reality, an adoption is either legal or not legal.

Home study refers to the process that includes interviewing prospective parents, talking to them in their homes, checking their references, and reviewing medical, financial, and other relevant information. They are then either approved or disapproved for adoption.

Immigration and Naturalization Service (INS) is a federal agency that oversees international adoption.

Independent adoption refers to non-agency adoption. Sometimes it is also called "private adoption," but that term confuses people who don't understand the difference between the involvement of a private adoption agency and their non-involvement.

Independent contractors are social workers who are hired by adoption agencies to handle the home study process.

International adoption refers to adopting a child from another country. Also called "intercountry adoption." The term "foreign adoption" is considered negative and passe.

Irrevocable consent means that consent may not be taken back.

Legal guardian is a person who can make legal and often parental decisions for a minor child. But the legal guardian can't adopt the child unless the biological parents (or whoever has custody) agrees.

Legal risk refers to a program in which parents may become foster parents to children who may become available for adoption.

Multiracial refers to a child with a heritage of more than two races in his or her background.

Namesake refers to naming a child after someone in the family.

Nonrelative adoption refers to an adoption in which the adoptive parent is a "biological stranger" to the child.

Non-sectarian agencies are adoption agencies that serve families for whom religion is not a pivotal matter.

Open adoption is an adoption in which there is an exchange of identities, first and last names, between the adopting parents and the birthparents. They may or may not decide to have a continuing relationship.

Open records refers to a system wherein an adult adoptee can merely request his original sealed birth certificate and it will be provided. No court order is required.

Orphan is a child in another country who has no parents or who has only one parent who cannot care for him or her.

Orphan visa is permission granted to a specific child by the U.S. State Department so that the adopted child may be admitted to the U.S. and reside with adopting parents.

Positive adoption mindset (PAM) is an attitude that an adopter will succeed with the adoption and become a parent.

Positive adoption language refers to words or phrases that depict adoption in a favorable, or at least neutral, manner. For example, the word "birthmother" or "biological mother" is preferred over "natural mother" or "real mother."

Postplacement home study is a background investigation and interview of the adopting parents after the child has already been placed with the family.

Preplacement home study is a background investigation and interview of the adopting parents, accomplished before a child is placed with the family. Followup interviews occur after placement as well.

Private agencies are nongovernmental agencies licensed by the state to arrange adoptions and usually are run by someone with an advanced degree in social work or psychology.

Public agencies are state social services agencies that are run by state or county governments. These agencies usually deal with foster children.

Putative father is the alleged birthfather. He may or may not verify that he is in fact the father.

Putative father registry, also called "birthfather registry," provides an opportunity whereby unmarried men who believe they have fathered children may register their alleged paternity. Registered birthfathers may then register their protest to a birthmother's adoption plans. About one-half of all states in the U.S. operate putative father registries.

Rapture of the adoption refers to when adopters suspend all normal judgment and common sense, often because they have little information or time to make a decision—a kind of sensory overload.

Readoption refers to a process in which international adopters adopt their children a second time, in front of a U.S. judge. (The first time was in the country of the child's birth.)

Relative adoption refers to an adoption in which the adopter is biologically related to the adopted child.

Reunion refers to a face-to-face meeting of an adopted person and a birth relative.

Revoke means to take back consent to an adoption. Some states allow birthparents to revoke consent for varying time periods, while others do not.

Sealing of the birth certificate happens after finalization, when most states *seal* the adopted child's original birth certificate. The original birth certificate will not be available except through a court order. A new birth certificate will be issued, listing the adoptive parents' names as the parents to the child.

Search refers to seeking out a biological relative, usually a birthmother.

Search group is an organization that assists adoptees and/or birthparents with the search process.

Second-parent adoption is used in gay and lesbian adoptions to refer to the adoption of the biological child of one person by a homosexual parent. This is a new phenomenon and not legal in every state.

Sectarian agencies are adoption agencies that specialize in assisting families with particular religious interests.

Semi-open adoption refers to an adoption in which the adopters and birthparents may meet once or twice and on a first-name-only basis. It's always important to ask the agency for their definition of this term because agencies vary greatly on how they define the phrase.

Social worker or **caseworker** is a person who will perform your home study. A social worker also interviews the birthparents who are considering adoption and gathers social and medical information.

Special needs refers to problems faced by children whom agencies consider hard to place. Children with illnesses or impediments are often referred to as children with special needs. Children who are older children or in sibling groups and also some minority children are considered to have special needs.

State Department is the federal agency that issues orphan visas enabling Americans to adopt children from other countries.

Transracial adoption refers to a situation in which a family adopts a child who is of another race. Generally, transracial adoption refers to whites adopting African-American children.

Voluntary mutual consent registry, also called simply mutual consent registry, refers to a system that matches names when both a birthparent and an adopted adult seek identifying information. It is "mutual" because both parties must seek the information.

Waiting children is a term sometimes used to describe children in foster care and for whom adoption is sought.

Wrongful adoption refers to an adoption that would not have taken place had the adopters been given information that was known to the adoption arranger. The information was purposely withheld or misrepresented.

Bibliography

Adamec, Christine and Pierce, William L., Ph.D., *The Encyclopedia of Adoption*. New York: Facts on File, Inc., 1991.

Adamec, Christine, *Explaining Adoption to Your Child*. Rockville, Md.: National Adoption Information Clearinghouse, 1993.

Adamec, Christine, "The Fear Factor," *Adoptive Families*. January/February 1995, pp. 29–31.

Adamec, Christine, *How to Live with a Mentally Ill Person: A Handbook of Day-to-Day Strategies*. New York: John Wiley & Sons, 1996.

Adamec, Christine, "What's In a Name?," *National Adoption Reports*. Vol. XVIII, Issue No. 4, April 1997, p. 7.

Adamec, Christine, *There ARE Babies to Adopt: A Resource Guide for Prospective Parents*. New York: Kensington, 1996.

Alexander Roberts, Colleen and Snyder, Mark T., M.D., *Does My Child Need a Therapist?* Dallas: Taylor Publishing, 1997.

Altstein, Howard, et al., "Clinical Observations of Adult Intercountry Adoptees and Their Adoptive Parents," *Child Welfare*. May–June 1994, Vol. 73, No. 3, pp. 261–269.

Andersen, Robert S., "The Nature of Adoptee Search: Adventure, Cure, or Growth?" *Child Welfare*. Nov–Dec 1989, Vol. 68, No. 6, pp. 623–632.

Askin, Jayne, *Search: A Handbook for Adoptees and Birthparents*. New York: Harper & Row, Publishers, 1982.

Auth, Patricia J. and Zaret, Shirley, "The Search in Adoption: A Service and a Process," *Social Casework: The Journal of Contemporary Social Work*. Nov. 1986, Vol. 67, No. 9, pp. 560–568.

Baker, Robert H., "Gibbs v. Ernst: Pennsylvania Recognizes Negligent Nondisclosure in Wrongful Adoption Cases," *Tort & Insurance Law Journal*. Vol. 321, No. 1, Fall 1995, pp. 103–119.

Benson, Peter L., Ph.D., Sharma, Anu R., Ph.D., L.P., and Roehlkepartain, Eugene C., *Growing Up Adopted: A Portrait of Adolescents and Their Families*. Minneapolis: The Search Institute, 1994.

Blum, Louis H., M.M.H., "When Adoptive Families Ask for Help," *Primary Care*. Vol. 3, No. 2, June 1976, pp. 241–249.

Bonker, Dawn, "Partners in Parenting: Increasingly, Gay Men and Lesbians Are Becoming Parents," *Los Angeles Times*. December 22, 1996, p. E-2.

Boult, Brenda Ernestine, "The Complexity of Adult Adoptee Need to Search for Their Origins: A Research Finding," *Maatskaplike Werk/Social Work*. March 1992, Vol. 28, No. 1, pp. 13–18.

Bothun, Linda, *Dialogues About Adoption: Conversations Between Parents and Their Children*. Chevy Chase, Md.: Swan Publications, 1994.

Brodzinsky, David M. and Schechter, Marshall D., *The Psychology of Adoption*. New York: Oxford University Press, 1990.

Brown University Child and Adolescent Behavior Letter, "Being Adopted May Not Pose a Problem Until Adolescence." Jan. 1994, Vol. 10, No. 1, p. S1.

Chesey, Gordon, "Adoption. Adoption for the Disabled," *Accent on Living*. Fall 1995, Vol. 40, No. 2, pp. 86–91.

Child Welfare League of America, *Issues in Gay and Lesbian Adoption: Proceedings of the Fourth Annual Peirce–Warwick Adoption Symposium*. Washington, DC: 1995.

Cohen, Nancy J., Coyne, James and Duvall, James, "Adopted and Biological Children in the Clinic: Family, Parental and Child Characteristics," *Journal of Child Psychology and Psychiatry and Allied Disciplines*." Vol. 34, No. 4, pp. 545–562.

De Simone, Michael, Ph. D., BCD, "Birth Mother Loss: Contributing Factors to Unresolved Grief," *Clinical Social Work Journal*. Vol. 24, No. 1, Spring 1996.

DeWoody, Madelyn, *Adoption and Disclosure: A Review of the Law*. Washington, DC: Child Welfare League of America, 1993.

Donovan, Denis M. and McIntyre, Deborah, *Healing the Hurt* Child. New York: W. W. Norton Co., 1990.

Dubucs, R., "Food and the Adopted Child," *Adoption Advocates NEWSletter*. January 1996, Vol. 4, No. 1, pp. 3–6.

Duggan, Paul, "A Baby Arrives Amid Joy, Departs Amid Heartache," *Washington Post*. April 2, 1997, p. A1.

Dunn, Linda, Ed., *Adopting Children with Special Needs: A Sequel*. Washington, DC: North American Council on Adoptable Children, 1983.

Ebert, Alan, "'Adopting 14 Children Saved Our Marriage.'," *Good Housekeeping*. May 1994, Vol. 218, No. 5, p. 172(4).

Fioto, Lou, "Domestic Adoption Is Their Choice," *Accent on Living*. Winter 1996, Vol. 41, No. 3, p. 62(5).

Forman, Deborah L., "Unwed Fathers and Adoption: A Theoretical Analysis in Context," *Texas Law Review*. April 1994, Vol. 72, No. 5m, pp. 967–1045.

Fukofsky, Ward M., and Sherr, Eileen Reichenberg, "1996 Tax Legislation Offers Planning Opportunities," *The Tax Adviser*. March 1997, Vol. 28, No. 3, p. 156(7).

Gaber, Ivor and Aldridge, Jane, Eds., *In the Best Interests of the Child: Culture, Identity and Transracial Adoption*. London: Free Association Books, 1994.

Garn, Stanley M., et al., "Similarities Between Parents and Their Adopted Children," *American Journal of Physical Anthropology*. Nov. 1976, Vol. 45, No. 3, Part 2, pp. 539–543.

Greer, Joyce, "The Fears of Knowing," My Turn, *Newsweek*. Jan. 14, 1997, Vol. XXV, No. 2.

Groze, Victor, *Successful Adoptive Families: A Longitudinal Study of Special Needs Adoption*. Westport, Conn.: Praeger, 1996.

Gunderson, Ted L., *How to Locate Anyone, Anywhere*. New York: Plume Book, 1996.

Helwig, Andrew A. and Ruthven, Dorothy H., "Psychological Ramifications of Adoption and Implications for Counseling," *Journal of Mental Health Counseling*. January 1990, Vol. 12, No. 1, pp. 24–37.

Hibbs, Euthymia D., Ph.D., *Adoption: International Perspectives*. Madison, Conn.: International Universities Press, 1991.

Holden, Constance, "Small Refugees Suffer the Effects of Early Neglect," *Science*. Nov. 15, 1996, Vol. 274, No. 5290, p. 1076–78.

Hopkins–Best, Mary, *Toddler Adoption: The Weaver's Craft*. Indianapolis, Ind.: Perspectives Press, 1997.

Humphrey, Heather and Humphrey, Michael, "Damaged Identity and the Search for Kinship in Adult Adoptees," *British Journal of Medical Psychology*. 1989, Vol. 62, pp. 301–309.

Jackson, Maggie, "Aspiring Adoptive Parents Face Greed, Competition, Exploitation," *Los Angeles Times*. April 23, 1995, p.1.

Jenista, Jerri Ann, M.D., "Creating a Support Network," *Adoptive Families*. Sept./Oct. 1994, pp. 34–35.

Jenista, Jerri Ann, M.D., "Medical Primer for the Adoptive Parents," in *Handbook for Single Adoptive Parents*. Chevy Chase, Md.: National Council of Single Adoptive Parents, 1996.

Johnson, Jill, et al., "Sociobiology and the Naming of Adopted and Natural Children, *Ethnology and Sociobiology*. Vol. 12, 1991, pp. 365–375.

Johnston, Patricia Irwin, *Launching a Baby's Adoption: Practical Strategies for Parents and Professionals*. Indianapolis, Ind.: Perspectives Press, 1997.

Keen-Payne, Rhonda, and Bond, Mary Lou, "Voices of Clients and Caregivers in a Maternity Home," *Western Journal of Nursing Research*. April 1997, Vol. 19, No. 2, pp. 190–205.

Kermani, Ebrahim J., M.D. and Weiss, Bonnie, MA, Eds., "Biological Parents Regaining Their Rights: A Psycholegal Analysis of a New Era in Custody Disputes," *Bulletin American Academy Psychiatry Law*. Vol. 23, No. 2, 1995, pp. 261–267.

Kleiman, Erika Lynn, "Caring for Our Own: Why American Adoption Law and Policy Must Change," *Columbia Journal of Law and Social Problems*. Winter 1997, Vol. 30, No. 2, pp. 327–368.

Koepke, Jean E., et al., "Becoming Parents: Feelings of Adoptive Mothers," *Pediatric Nursing*. Vol. 17, No. 4, July–August 1991, pp. 333–336.

Kowal, Katherine, A., Ph.D. and Schilling, Karen Maitland, Ph.D., "Adoption Through the Eyes of Adoptees," *American Journal of Orthopsychiatry*. July 1985, Vol. 55, No. 3, pp. 354–362.

Lazare, Aaron, M.D., "A Family's Adoption of Eight children of Three Races," unpublished paper, University of Massachusetts Medical School. University of Massachusetts Medical Center, 1996.

Levine, Elaine S., Ph.D, and Sallee, Alvin L, M.S.W, "Critical Phases Among Adoptees and Their Families: Implications for Therapy," *Child and Adolescent Social Work*. June 1990, Vol. 7, No. 3, pp. 217–232.

Lichtenstein, Tovah, "To Tell or Not to Tell: Factors Affecting Adoptees' Telling Their Adoptive Parents About Their Search," *Child Welfare,* January–February 1996, pp. 61–72.

Marindin, Hope, *Handbook for Single Adoptive Parents*. National Council for Single Adoptive Parents, P.O. Box 15084, Chevy Chase, MD 20825, 1997.

Mason, Mary Martin, *Designing Rituals of Adoption for the Religious and Secular Community*. Minneapolis: Resources for Adoptive Parents, 1995.

McGue, Matt, et al., "Parent and Sibling Influences on Adolescent Alcohol Use and Misuse: Evidence from a U.S. Adoption Cohort," *Journal of Studies on Alcohol*. January 1996, Vol. 57, No. 1, pp. 8–19.

Melina, Lois Ruskai and Roszia, Sharon Kaplan, *The Open Adoption Experience*. New York: HarperPerennial, 1993.

Mishra, Debjani, "The Road to Concord: Resolving the Conflict of Law Over Adoption by Gays and Lesbians," *Columbia Journal of Law and Social Problems*. Fall 1996, Vol. 30, No. 1, pp. 91–136.

Moran, Ruth, "Stages of Emotion: An Adult Adoptee's Postreunion Perspective," *Child Welfare*. May 1994, Vol. 73, No. 3, pp. 249–260.

Nadelson, Carol C., "The Emotional Aftermath of Adoption," *American Family Physician*. September 1986. Vol. 14, No. 3, pp. 124–127.

National Council For Adoption, *The Adoption Factbook*, Washington, DC, 1989.

Nelson–Erichsen, Jean and Erichsen, Heino R., *How to Adopt Internationally: A Guide for Agency-Directed and Independent Adoptions*. Fort Worth, Tex.: Mesa House Publishing, 1997.

Nickman, Steven L., Challenges of Adoption," *Harvard Mental Health Letter*. Jan. 1, 1996, Vol. 12, No. 7.

Nickman, Steven L., M.D. and Ewis, Robert G., M.Ed., MSW, "Adoptive Families and Professionals: When the Experts Make Things Worse," *Journal of the American Academy of Child and Adolescent Psychiatry*. June 1994, Vol. 33, No. 5, pp. 753–755.

Nordgren, Sarah, "Baby Richard's Dad Moves Out on Him, Fierce Court Battle Apparently for Naught," *Detroit Free Press*. January 21, 1997, p. 5A.

Norment, Lynn, "Am I Black, White or In Between?" *Ebony*. August 1995, Vol. 50, No. 10, p. 108–11.

Oppenheim, Elizabeth, "Adoption Assistance," *Public Welfare*. Winter 1996, Vol. 54, No. 1, pp. 8–9.

Ostrom, Brian J., Director, et al., *Examining the Work of State Courts, 1995: A National Perspective From the Court Statistics Project*. Williamsburg, Va.: National Center for State Courts, 1996.

Parco, Vincent, *Researching Public Records: How to Get Anything on Anybody*. New York: Citadel Press, 1995.

Patterson, Charlotte J. and Redding, Richard E., "Lesbian and Gay Families with Children: Implications of Social Science Research for Policy, *Journal of Social Issues*. Vol. 52, No. 3, 1996, pp. 29–50.

Pressley, Sue Anne, "Texas Interracial Adoption Case Reflects National Debate," *Washington Post*. Jan. 2, 1997, pp. A1–A3.

365

Proch, Kathleen, "Differences Between Foster and Adoption: Perceptions of Adopted Foster Children and Adoptive Foster Parents," *Child Welfare*. May 1982, Vol. LXI, No. 5, pp. 259–268.

Raynor, Lois, *The Adopted Child Comes of Age*. London: George Allen & Unwin, 1980.

Reilly, Thom, "Gay and Lesbian Adoptions: A Theoretical Examination of Policy-Making and Organization Decision Making," *Journal of Sociology and Social Welfare*. December 1996, Vol. 23, No. 4, pp. 99–115.

Reitz, Miriam, Ph.D, LCSW and Watson, Kenneth, W. MSW, LCSW, *Adoption and the Family System: Strategies for Treatment*. New York: The Guildford Press, 1992.

Rhone, Marcia, *Adoption Love Stories*. P.O. Box 179, New London, WI 54961: Clear Pond Press, 1995.

Report on Intercountry Adoption, 1997. Boulder, Colo.: International Concerns for Children, 1997.

Sanford, Donna, "Since You Asked . . . ," *EXPO*. May 1997, Vol. 9, No. 5, p. 6.

Scarr, Sandra, Scarf, Elizabeth and Weinberg, Richard A., "Perceived and Actual Similarities in Biological and Adoptive Families: Does Perceived Similarity Bias Genetic Inferences," *Behavior Genetics*. 1980, G. 10, No. 5, pp. 445–458.

Schneider, Pat, "Innocents From Abroad: International Adoptions Soaring in Popularity," *Wisconsin State Journal*. Aug. 22, 1996, p. 1A.

Schooler, Jayne, *Searching for a Past: The Adopted Adult's Unique Process of Finding Identity*. Colorado Springs, Colo.: Pinon, 1995.

Science News, "Homosexual Parents: All in the Family." Jan. 21, 1995, Vol. 147, No. 3, p. 42.

Schwartz, Edward M., Ph.D., "Problems After Adoption: Some Guidelines for Pediatrician Involvement," *The Journal of Pediatrics*. Dec. 1975, Vol. 87, No. 6, pp. 991–994.

Serwah, Joseph J., "Inaction by Eaken Criticized: Adoptee Claimed Privacy Violation, *Harrisburg Pennsylvania Patriot*. Dec. 30, 1995.

Sharma, Anu R., McGue, Matthew K. and Benson, Peter L, "The Emotional and Behavioral Adjustment of United States Adopted Adolescents: Part II. Age at Adoption," *Children and Youth Services Review*. 1996, Vol. 18, No. 1/2, pp. 101–114.

Silber, Kathleen and Speedlin, Phylis, *Dear Birthmother: Thank You for Our Baby*. San Antonio, Tex.: Corona, 1982.

Sills Mitchell, Marie A., BSN, RN, CPNP, and Jenista, Jerri Ann, M.D., "Health Care of the Internationally Adopted Child: Part 1: Before and At Arrival into the Adoptive Home," *Journal of Pediatric Health Care*. March/April 1997, Vol. 11, No. 2, pp. 512–60.

Sills Mitchell, Marie A., BSN, RN, CPNP and Jenista, Jerri Ann, M.D., "Health Care of the Internationally Adopted Child: Part 2: Chronic Care and Long-term Medical Issues," *Journal of Pediatric Health Care*. May/June 1997, Vol. 11, No. 3, pp. 117–126.

Silverman, Phyllis R., et al., "Reunions Between Adoptees and Birth Parents: The Adoptive Parents' View," *Social Work*. Sept. 1994, Vol. 39, No. 5, pp. 542–549.

Simon, Rita J., Altstein, Howard and Melli, Marygold S., *The Case for Transracial Adoption*. Washington, DC: The American University Press, 1994.

Simon, Rita in *In the Best Interests of the Child: Culture, Identity and Transracial Adoption*. (Gaber, Ivor and Aldridge, Jane, Eds.) London: Free Association Press, 1995.

Smart, Jennifer, ed., "How Are Our Orphanage Children Doing?," Post-adoption Helper, June 1997. Handout at 1997 National Reunion of Adoptive Families of Romanian Children, San Antonio, Texas, July 31–August 2, 1997.

Smith, Jerome and Miroff, Franklin, *You're Our Child: The Adoption Experience*. Lanham, Md.: Madison Books, 1987.

Sokoloff, Burton, M.D., "Adoptive Families Needs for Counseling," *Clinical Pediatrics*. March 1979, Vol. 18, No. 3, pp. 184–190.

Townsel, Lisa Jones, "'Neither Black Nor White,'" *Ebony*. November 1996, Vol. 52, No. 1, pp. 44–48.

"Memorandum on Adoption and Alternate Permanent Placement of Children in the Public Child Welfare System," *Weekly Compilation of Presidential Documents*. Dec. 23, 1996.

U.S. Department of Health and Human Services, National Center for Health Statistics, *Fertility, Family Planning, and Women's Health: New Data From the 1995 National Survey of Family Growth*." May 1997, Series 23, No. 19.

Ward, Margaret, M.A. and Lewko, John H., Ph.D., "Support Sources of Adolescents in Families Adopting Older Children," *American Journal of Orthopsychiatry*. Oct. 1987, Vol. 57, No. 4, pp. 610–612.

Watkins, Mary and Fisher, Susan, *Talking with Young Children About Adoption*. New Haven, Conn.: Yale University Press, 1993.

Wegar, K., "In Search of Bad Mothers: Social Constructions of Birth and Adoptive Motherhood," *Women's Studies International Forum*. Jan.–Feb. 1997, Vol. 20, No. 1.

Westhues, Anne, "A Comparison of the Adjustment of Adolescent and Young Adult Inter-country Adoptees and Their Siblings," *International Journal of Behavioral Development*. 1997, Vol. 20, No. 1, pp. 47–65.

Winkler, Robin C., et al., *Clinical Practice in Adoption*. New York: Pergamon Press, 1988.

Index

B

C

J - K - L

M

T

U - V

When You're Smart Enough to Know
That You Don't Know It All

For all the ups and downs you're sure to encounter in life, The Complete Idiot's Guides give you down-to-earth answers and practical solutions.

Personal **B**usiness

The Complete Idiot's Guide to Terrific Business Writing
ISBN: 0-02-861097-0 ▪ $16.95

The Complete Idiot's Guide to Winning Through Negotiation
ISBN: 0-02-861037-7 ▪ $16.95

The Complete Idiot's Guide to Managing People
ISBN: 0-02-861036-9 ▪ $18.95

The Complete Idiot's Guide to a Great Retirement
ISBN: 1-56761-601-1 ▪ $16.95

The Complete Idiot's Guide to Protecting Yourself From Everyday Legal Hassles
ISBN: 1-56761-602-X ▪ $16.99

The Complete Idiot's Guide to Surviving Divorce
ISBN: 0-02-861101-2 ▪ $16.95

The Complete Idiot's Guide to Getting the Job You Want
ISBN: 1-56761-608-9 ▪ $24.95

The Complete Idiot's Guide to Managing Your Time
ISBN: 0-02-861039-3 ▪ $14.95

The Complete Idiot's Guide to Speaking in Public with Confidence
ISBN: 0-02-861038-5 ▪ $16.95

The Complete Idiot's Guide to Starting Your Own Business
ISBN: 1-56761-529-5 ▪ $16.99

You can handle it!

Personal Finance

The Complete Idiot's Guide to Buying Insurance and Annuities
ISBN: 0-02-861113-6 ▪ $16.95

The Complete Idiot's Guide to Managing Your Money
ISBN: 1-56761-530-9 ▪ $16.95

Complete Idiot's Guide to Buying and Selling a Home
ISBN: 1-56761-510-4 ▪ $16.95

The Complete Idiot's Guide to Doing Your Extra Income Taxes 1996
ISBN: 1-56761-586-4 ▪ $14.99

The Complete Idiot's Guide to Making Money with Mutual Funds
ISBN: 1-56761-637-2 ▪ $16.95

The Complete Idiot's Guide to Getting Rich
ISBN: 1-56761-509-0 ▪ $16.95

You can handle it!

Look for The Complete Idiot's Guides at your favorite bookstore, or call 1-800-428-5331 for more information.

The Complete Idiot's Guide to Learning French on Your Own
ISBN: 0-02-861043-1 ▪ $16.95

The Complete Idiot's Guide to Dating
ISBN: 0-02-861052-0 ▪ $14.95

The Complete Idiot's Guide to Hiking and Camping
ISBN: 0-02-861100-4 ▪ $16.95

The Complete Idiot's Guide to Cooking Basics
ISBN: 1-56761-523-6 ▪ $16.99

The Complete Idiot's Guide to Learning Spanish on Your Own
ISBN: 0-02-861040-7 ▪ $16.95

The Complete Idiot's Guide to Gambling Like a Pro
ISBN: 0-02-861102-0 ▪ $16.95

The Complete Idiot's Guide to Choosing, Training, and Raising a Dog
ISBN: 0-02-861098-9 ▪ $16.95

You can handle it!

The Complete Idiot's Guide to Trouble-Free Car Care
ISBN: 0-02-861041-5 ▪ $16.95

The Complete Idiot's Guide to the Perfect Wedding
ISBN: 1-56761-532-5 ▪ $16.99

The Complete Idiot's Guide to Getting and Keeping Your Perfect Body
ISBN: 0-286105122 ▪ $16.99

The Complete Idiot's Guide to the Perfect Vacation
ISBN: 1-56761-531-7 ▪ $14.99

The Complete Idiot's Guide to First Aid Basics
ISBN: 0-02-861099-7 ▪ $16.95

The Complete Idiot's Guide to Trouble-Free Home Repair
ISBN: 0-02-861042-3 ▪ $16.95

The Complete Idiot's Guide to Getting into College
ISBN: 1-56761-508-2 ▪ $14.95

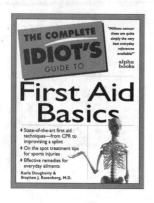